Australasian Language Technology Association Workshop 2011

(ALTA 2011)

AA005893

Canberra, Australia
1 – 2 December 2011

Editors:

Diego Molla
David Martinez

ISBN: 978-1-62276-510-2
ISSN: 1834-7037

Printed from e-media with permission by:

Curran Associates, Inc.
57 Morehouse Lane
Red Hook, NY 12571

Some format issues inherent in the e-media version may also appear in this print version.

Printed by Curran Associates, Inc. (2012)

Association for Computational Linguistics
209 N. Eighth Street
Stroudsburg, Pennsylvania 18360

Phone: 1-570-476-8006
Fax: 1-570-476-0860

acl@aclweb.org

Additional copies of this publication are available from:

Curran Associates, Inc.
57 Morehouse Lane
Red Hook, NY 12571 USA
Phone: 845-758-0400
Fax: 845-758-2634
Email: curran@proceedings.com
Web: www.proceedings.com

Australasian Language Technology Association Workshop 2011

Proceedings of the Workshop

Editors:
Diego Mollá
David Martinez

1-2 December 2011
Australian National University
Canberra, Australia

Australalasian Language Technology Association Workshop 2011
(ALTA 2011)

URL: http://www.alta.asn.au/events/alta2011

Sponsors:

Australian National University

NICTA

Appen ButlerHill

ALTA 2011 Workshop Committees

Workshop Co-Chairs

- Diego Mollá (Macquarie University)
- David Martinez (NICTA Victoria Research Lab and University of Melbourne)

Workshop Local Organisers

- Hanna Suominen (NICTA Canberra Research Lab and ANU)
- Wray Buntine (NICTA Canberra Research Lab and ANU)

Program Committee

- Timothy Baldwin (University of Melbourne)
- Francis Bond (Nanyang Technological University, Singapore)
- Wray Buntine (NICTA Canberra Research Lab and ANU)
- Lawrence Cavedon (NICTA Victoria Research Lab and University of Melbourne)
- Eric Choi (NICTA)
- Jean-Yves Delort (Google, Zurich)
- Mark Dras (Macquarie University)
- Rebecca Dridan (University of Melbourne)
- Dominique Estival (University of Western Sydney)
- Tanja Gaustad (Tilburg University, The Netherlands)
- Ben Hachey (Macquarie University and CMCRC)
- Nitin Indurkya (University of New South Wales and eBay Research Labs)
- Alistair Knott (University of Otago, New Zealand)
- Kazunori Komatani (Nagoya University, Japan)
- Meladel Mistica (ANU)
- Scott Nowson (Appen Butler Hill)
- Cécile Paris (CSIRO)
- Son Bao Pham (Vietnam National University, Vietnam)
- Luiz Augusto Pizzato (University of Sydney)
- David Powers (Flinders University)
- Adam Saulwick (DSTO)
- Andrea Schalley (Griffith University)
- Rolf Schwitter (Macquarie University)
- Hanna Suominen (NICTA Canberra Research Lab and ANU)
- Menno Van Zaanen (Tilburg University, The Netherlands)
- Jette Viethen (Tilburg University, The Netherlands)
- Wayne Wobcke (University of New South Wales)
- Simon Zwarts (Google, Sydney)

Preface

This volume contains the papers accepted for presentation at the Australasian Language Technology Workshop (ALTA) 2011, held at the Australian National University (ANU), Canberra, Australia on December 1-2, 2011. This is the ninth annual instalment of the ALTA workshop in its most-recent incarnation, and the continuation of an annual workshop series that has existed in various forms Down Under since the early 1990s.

The goals of the workshop are:

- to bring together the growing Language Technology (LT) community in Australia and New Zealand and encourage interactions;
- to encourage collaboration within the community and with the wider international LT community;
- to foster interaction between academic and industrial researchers, to encourage dissemination of research results;
- to provide a forum for the discussion of new and ongoing research and projects;
- to provide an opportunity for the broader artificial intelligence community to become aware of local LT research;
- and finally, to increase visibility of LT research in Australia, New Zealand and overseas.

This year's ALTA Workshop includes 18 peer-reviewed papers, of which 12 have been presented orally, and 6 have been presented as posters. We received a total of 29 submissions. Each paper in the 'peer-reviewed papers' and the 'peer-reviewed posters' section was independently peer-reviewed by at least two members of an international program committee, in accordance with the DEST requirements for E1 conference publications. The review process was double-blind: Great care was exercised to avoid all conflicts of interest whenever an author also served as program committee/co-chair or the reviewer worked at the same institution as an author. Such conflicts of interest were resolved by transferring the reviewing task to other members of the program committee.

The proceedings also include the abstracts of the keynote presentation by Wray Buntine (National ICT Australia Ltd – NICTA) and of the special presentation by Dominique Estival (MARCS Auditory Laboratories) about the Australian Computational Linguistics Olympiad (OzCLO). There is also description of the second ALTA shared task by Diego Mollá and Abeed Sarker (Macquarie University).

We would like to thank all the authors who submitted papers to ALTA, the members of the program committee for the time and effort they put into the review process, the local organisers for their commitment and work organising this conference, and our invited speaker: Wray Buntine.

Finally, we would like to thank our sponsors, NICTA, ANU and Appen Butler Hill for supporting the workshop.

Diego Mollá and David Martinez
Program Co-Chairs

ALTA 2011 Program

Thursday, 1st December 2011

9:00-10:00	Keynote: *Discovery in Text: Visualisation, Topics and Statistics* by Wray Buntine (NICTA, Canberra)
10:00-10:30	Coffee break
10:30-10:40	ALTA Opening remarks
Session 1 - 10:40 - 12:20	
	Paper Presentations
10:40-11:05	Benjamin Börschinger and Mark Johnson *A Particle Filter algorithm for Bayesian Wordsegmentation*
11:05-11:30	Bevan Jones, Mark Johnson and Sharon Goldwater *Formalizing Semantic Parsing with Tree Transducers*
11:30-11:55	Mark Johnson *Parsing in Parallel on Multiple Cores and GPUs*
11:55-12:20	Mehdi Parviz, Mark Johnson, Blake Johnson and Jon Brock *Using Language Models and Latent Semantic Analysis to Characterise the N400m Neural Response*
12:45-14:00	Lunch break
Session 2 - 14:00 - 15:15	
	Paper Presentations
14:00-14:25	Shunichi Ishihara *A Forensic Authorship Classification in SMS Messages: A Likelihood Ratio Based Approach Using N-gram*
14:25-14:50	Su Nam Kim and Lawrence Cavedon *Classifying Domain-Specific Terms Using a Dictionary*
14:50-15:15	Stephen Merity and James R. Curran *Frontier Pruning for Shift-Reduce CCG Parsing*
15:15-15:45	Coffee break
Session 3 - 15:45 - 16:15	
	Poster presentations (5 mins per poster)
	John Cocks and Te Taka Keegan *A word-based approach for diacritic restoration in Māori*
	Nobuagi Akagi and Francesco-Alessio Ursini *The Interpretation of Complement Anaphorae: the case of The Others*
	Francesco-Alessio Ursini and Nobuagi Akagi *The Interpretation of Plural Pronouns in Discourse: The Case of They*
	Jenny Mcdonald, Alistair Knott, Richard Zeng and Ayelet Cohen *Learning from student responses: A domain-independent natural language tutor*
	Md. Waliur Rahman Miah, John Yearwood and Sid Kulkarni *Detection of child exploiting chats from a mixed chat dataset as a text classification task*
	Marcin Nowina-Krowicki, Andrew Zschorn, Michael Pilling and Steven Wark *ENGAGE: Automated Gestures for Animated Characters*
16:15-17:25	**Presenters put up their posters**
17:25-18:45	**Poster session with ALS (drinks and nibbles provided)**
19:30	**Dinner with ADCS**

Friday, 2nd December 2011

Session 4 - 9:00 - 10:40	
	Joint Session with ADCS
	Li Wang, Diana Mccarthy and Timothy Baldwin
	Predicting Thread Linking Structure by Lexical Chaining
	Diego Mollá and Maria Elena Santiago-Martinez
	Development of a Corpus for Evidence Based Medicine Summarisation
	Mike Symonds, Peter Bruza, Laurianne Sitbon and Ian Turner
	Tensor Query Expansion: A cognitively motivated relevance model
	Yan Shen, Yuefeng Li, Yue Xu, Renato Lannella, Abdulmohsen Algarni and Xiaohui Tao
	An Ontology-based Mining Approach for User Search Intent Discovery
10:40-11:10	Coffee break
Session 5 - 11:10-12:25	
	Paper Presentations
11:10-11:35	**(best paper award)** François Lareau, Mark Dras, Benjamin Börschinger and Robert Dale
	Collocations in multilingual text generation: Lexical Functions meet Lexical Functional Grammar
11:35-12:00	Abeed Sarker, Diego Mollá and Cécile Paris
	Outcome Polarity Identification of Medical Papers
12:00-12:25	Sze-Meng Jojo Wong, Mark Dras and Mark Johnson
	Topic Modeling for Native Language Identification
12:25-14:00	Lunch break
14:00-15:00	**Prizes and ALTA AGM Meeting**
Special presentation - 15:00-15:30	
	Dominique Estival
	OzCLO: The Australian Computational Linguistic Olympiad
15:30-16:00	Coffee break
Special presentation - 16:00-16:45	
	Diego Mollá and Abeed Sarker
	Automatic Grading of Evidence: The 2011 ALTA Shared Task
16:45-17:00	**Wrap-up**
17:25-18:45	**Poster session with ALS (drinks and nibbles provided)**

Contents

Non-reviewed papers

Discovery in Text: Visualisation, Topics and Statistics

Wray Buntine
NICTA
Canberra, Australia
wray.buntine@nicta.com.au

Abstract

Discovery in or understanding of a text collection can be viewed from many angles: the text aspect of the data mining paradigm, the discover aspect of the information seeking paradigm, or the text content aspect of visualisation. This talk will view topic models as a technique within these paradigms. Some visualisations will be reviewed, as well as a variety of different topic models, and some of the natural language processing issues involved in working with the models. Finally, some of the non-parametric statistical methods underlying the analysis will be reviewed because they are fascinating as well.

Short Biography

Dr. Wray Buntine joined NICTA in Canberra Australia in April 2007 and is a Principal Researcher working on applying machine learning and probabilistic methods to tasks such as information access and text analysis. In 2009 he was co-chair of ECMLPKDD in Bled, Slovenia and in 2011 he co-organised a PASCAL2 Summer School on Machine Learning in Singapore. He reviews for conferences such as ECIR, CIKM, ECMLPKDD, ICML, KDD, SIGIR, UAI and WWW and is on the editorial board of Data Mining and Knowledge Discovery. He was previously at University of Helsinki, Helsinki Institute for Information Technology, NASA Ames Research Center, UC Berkeley, and Google.

OzCLO: The Australian Computational Linguistic Olympiad

Dominique Estival
MARCS Auditory Laboratories
University of Western Sydney
d.estival@uws.edu.au

Abstract

Since 2008 when we organised the First Australian Computation and Linguistic Olympiad (OzCLO), this high-school competition has become an annual event, with almost 800 participants across Australia in 2011. For the third time, we sent an Australian team to the International Linguistics Olympiad (ILO) and the team came back with one silver medal. In this talk, I will give an overview of OzCLO, first presenting the background and history of the competition internationally and in Australia, then explaining how it is organised and run in Australia, and finally discussing the impact and importance of reaching out to high-school students in our discipline.

Short Biography

Dominique Estival received a PhD in Linguistics from the University of Pennsylvania in 1986. Her research experience in Natural Language Processing has been at the frontier between industry and academia, with positions at ISSCO, The University of Melbourne, the Defence Science and Technology Organisation and private language technology companies in the US and Australia. In 2010, she joined the University of Western Sydney to manage AusTalk, the largest Australian audio-visual speech data collection. Her research interests have included the computational modelling of language change, machine translation, grammar formalisms for linguistic engineering, spoken dialogue systems and aviation communication. She co-founded OzCLO in 2008 and has been the main driving force behind it since then.

Automatic Grading of Evidence: the 2011 ALTA Shared Task

Diego Molla and **Abeed Sarker**
Centre for Language Technology
Macquarie Univeristy
Sydney, NSW 2109
{diego.molla-aliod, abeed.sarker}@mq.edu.au

Abstract

The ALTA shared tasks are programming competitions where all participants attempt to solve the same problem, and the winner is the system with the best results. The 2011 ALTA shared task is the second in the series and it focuses on trying to automatically grade the level of clinical evidence in medical research papers. In this paper we describe the task, present the results of several baselines, and the results of our method. We apply a sequence of high precision machine learning classifiers with varying feature sets for each. In addition to using n-grams, we incorporate domain knowledge by representing specific medical concepts using their semantic categories. We also apply a specialised rule-based approach for automatically identifying the publication types of articles, which is then used as a feature set. Our approach obtains an accuracy of 62.84% which is a significant improvement over the baselines.

1 Introduction

An important step for physicians who practise Evidence Based Medicine (EBM) is the grading of the quality of the clinical evidence present in the medical literature. Evidence grading is a manual process, and the time required to perform it adds to the already time-consuming nature of EBM practice. It has been shown that EBM practitioners often do not pursue evidence based answers to clinical questions because of the time required (Ely et al., 1999; Ely et al., 2005). Therefore, there is a strong motivation for systems that can automatically appraise the evidence present in medical publications and generate evidence grades on a specialised scale.

The 2011 ALTA shared task addressed the problem of automatic evidence grading. The goal of the task was to build a system that can predict the grade of evidence given a set of medical publications from which the evidence has been extracted. This is a difficult task, and as we show below, machine learning methods that use simple bag-of-word features do not perform significantly better than a trivial baseline. We attempt to solve the problem using supervised machine learning using features such as abstract and title n-grams and publication types. We employ a set of classifiers that utilise the different feature sets and apply them sequentially to obtain an accuracy value of 62.84%, which is a significant improvement over the baseline and also the best result obtained among all the submissions for the shared task.

In the following sections, we provide a brief background of EBM, evidence grading, and related work in this area, followed by a description of our methods and the final results.

2 Evidence Based Medicine and Evidence Grading

EBM is the '*conscientious, explicit, and judicious use of current best evidence in making decisions about the care of individual patients*' (Sackett et al., 1996). Current clinical guidelines urge physicians to practise EBM when providing care for their patients. Good practice of EBM requires practitioners to search for the best quality evidence, synthesise collected information and grade the quality of the evidence.

2.1 The Strength of Recommendation Taxonomy

There are over 100 grading scales to specify grades of evidence in use today. The Strength of Recommendation Taxonomy (SORT) (Ebell et al., 2004) is one such grading scale. It is a simple, straightforward and comprehensive grading system that can be applied throughout the medical literature. Consequently, it is used by various family medicine and primary care journals, such as the Journal of Family Practice (JFP)[1]. SORT uses three ratings — **A** (strong), **B** (moderate) and **C** (weak) — to specify the Strength of Recommendation (SOR) of a body of evidence. In SORT, grade **A** reflects a recommendation based on *consistent* and *good-quality, patient-oriented* evidence; grade **B** reflects a recommendation based on *inconsistent* or *limited-quality patient-oriented* evidence; and grade **C** reflects a recommendation based on consensus, usual practice, opinion or *disease-oriented* evidence. This is the chosen grading scale for the ALTA shared task.

3 Related Work

Related research has focused mostly on automatic quality assessment of medical publications for purposes such as retrieval and post-retrieval re-ranking, where approaches based on word co-occurrences (Goetz and von der Lieth, 2005) and bibliometrics (Plikus et al., 2006) have been proposed for improving the retrieval of medical documents. Tang et al. (2009) propose a post-retrieval re-ranking approach that attempts to re-rank results returned by a search engine, which may or may not be published research work. However, their approach is only tested in a specific sub-domain (i.e., Depression) of the medical domain. Kilicoglu et al. (2009) focus on identifying high-quality medical articles and build on the work by Aphinyanaphongs et al. (2005). They use machine learning and obtain 73.7% precision and 61.5% recall. These approaches rely heavily on meta-data associated with the articles, making them dependent on the database from which the articles are retrieved. Hence, these approaches would not work on publications that do not have associated meta-data.

The definitions of 'good-quality evidence' (Ebell et al., 2004) suggest that the publication types of medical articles are good indicators of their qualities. Literature in the medical domain consists of a large number of publication types of varying qualities[2]. For example, a randomised controlled trial is of much higher quality than a case study of a single patient. Evidence obtained from the former is thus more reliable. Greenhalgh (2006) mentions some other factors that influence the grade of an evidence, such as the number of subjects included in a study and the mechanism by which subjects are allocated (e.g., randomisation/ no randomisation), but the latter is generally specified by the publication type (e.g., randomised controlled trial) of the article. Recently, Sarker and Mollá (2010) emphasised on the importance of publication types for SOR determination and showed that automatic identification of high-quality publication types (e.g., Systematic Review and Randomised Controlled Trial) is relatively simple.

Factors influencing the automatic detection of evidence grades have been explored by Sarker et al. (2011). In this research work, information such publication types, publication years, journal titles, and article titles were obtained from a specialised corpus and used as features. Publication types were shown to be the most useful features giving accuracy values of approximately 68%. This research work is almost identical to the shared task. The only difference is that for the shared task, all features are required to be generated automatically since information from a specialised corpus is not available.

4 Methods

4.1 Shared Task Data

The data for the shared task consisted of a set of 'evidences' with the SOR grade for each. Each evidence was represented as a list of publications from which the evidence had been generated. Information for each publication was provided in the form of an

[1] http://www.jfponline.com

[2] A list of publication types used by the US National Library of Medicine can be found at http://www.nlm.nih.gov/mesh/pubtypes2006.html. This list is not exhaustive.

```
41711 B 10553790 15265350
53581 C 12804123 16026213 14627885
53583 B 15213586
52401 A 15329425 9058342 11279767
```

Figure 1: Sample data for the shared task

XML file per publication obtained from PubMed[3] and named according to the publication PubMed ID. This XML file contained bibliographic data (title, author, etc), the text of the abstract, and additional annotations provided by PubMed such as the medical semantic concepts found in the publication. Two sets of such data were provided initially for training (677 evidences) and development time testing (178 evidences), and an additional set was used for testing the final system (183 evidences).

An additional file contains the information related to the evidences, their SOR grades, and their publications (Figure 1). Each line represents an evidence. The first item in the line is the evidence ID. This is followed by the SOR grade (A, B, or C), and then the PubMed IDs of the abstracts that form the evidence. Thus, the first evidence listed in Figure 1 contains the abstracts with PubMed IDs 10553790 and 15265350, and is graded with SOR B.

The evidences were obtained from the corpus described by Mollá and Santiago-Martínez (2011) , which in turn uses the references and SOR judgements present in the 'Clinical Inquiries' section of the website from the Journal of Family Practice.[4]

4.2 Baselines

The most trivial baseline is to classify all of the elements with majority according to the training set, which is SOR B. With such a baseline, the accuracy is 48.63% (CI: 41.50-55.83).

A more complex baseline uses a machine learning classifier based on bag-of-word features. We tried with several variants. The best-performing system uses all non-stop n-grams ($n = 1, 2, 3$) from the abstract after stemming and lowercasing as the features, and Naïve Bayes as the classifier, and achieves an accuracy of 45.90%. These results appear worse than the simpler baseline, though the difference is not statistically significant.

4.3 Preliminary Analysis

In our approach, we built on the work by Sarker et al. (2011). Our preliminary analysis involved using simple features such as n-grams and various other information (including publication types) from the training set data. As noted above, obtaining significant improvements over the 'majority class' baseline was extremely difficult using any classifier. Furthermore, the *'PublicationType'* tags in the PubMed articles did not cover important publication types such as cohort study and systematic review. As a result, even the use of these tags did not produce accuracies greater than 60%. We therefore applied a rule-based approach for identifying publication types of articles and used them as features.

4.4 Feature Selection

Our final system utilises three feature sets — n-grams (semantic types replaced), titles, and publication types[5].

4.4.1 N-grams

We generated n-grams ($n = 1, 2, 3$ and 4) for each of the abstracts in the training set and replaced specific medical concepts in the texts with generic *'sem_type'* tags. We used MetaMap[6] to identify domain specific concepts as defined in the UMLS[7] (Unified Medical Language System). The UMLS provides a vast vocabulary of medical concepts and also broad semantic groups into which the concepts can be classified. For example, all disease names fall under the semantic category *Disease or Syndrome (dsyn)*. Replacing each occurrence of a disease or syndrome name with the generic tag ensures that the name does not have an influence on the classifiers used and reduces over-fitting. We used the same semantic groups as Uzuner et al. (2009): pathological function, disease or syndrome, mental or behavioural dysfunction, cell or molecular dysfunction, virus, neoplastic process, anatomic abnormality, acquired abnormality, congenital abnormality and injury or poisoning. We also preprocessed

[3]http://www.ncbi.nlm.nih.gov/pubmed/

[4]Data obtained with kind permission from the publishers.

[5]We have experimented with other features but this combination produced the best results.

[6]http://metamap.nlm.nih.gov/

[7]http://www.nlm.nih.gov/research/umls/

the n-grams by stemming, lowercasing and removing stop words.

4.4.2 Publication Types

We employed a rule-based approach for automatically identifying publication types of the articles from their abstracts. It has been shown that such an approach obtains very accurate results for high quality publication types (Sarker and Mollá-Aliod, 2010). We extended this approach by creating regular expressions for identifying publication types such as cohort studies that are not tagged in the PubMed XML files. We combined the publication types identified by our rule-based approach with the publication types given in the articles. For articles with multiple publication types, we only kept the tag that represents the highest quality. For example, if an article was tagged as a Randomised Controlled Trial, a Clinical Trial, and a Journal Article, we only kept the Randomised Controlled Trial tag since it has the highest quality among the three types. In this way, we identified the publication types of all articles (total of 23 publication types) and used them as features.

4.4.3 Titles

Since titles have been shown to be informative and to produce better results than baseline in the past (Sarker et al., 2011), we used them as features as well. We generated uni- and bi-grams from the titles, preprocessed them (in the same manner as the n-grams) and used them as features.

4.5 Classification

We modelled the problem of evidence grading as a three-way classification problem using the above-mentioned features. Our preliminary analysis revealed that combining a set of features for a single classifier does not produce significant improvements over the baseline. Furthermore, beating the majority class baseline is difficult itself. We, therefore, attempted to develop a sequential approach that would achieve small improvements in accuracy over the baseline at each step. Thus, we use a sequence of classifiers that attempt to separate A and C grade instances from B with high precision. At each step, instances classified as A or C are removed and the rest are passed on to the next step. The sequence in which the classifiers were applied and specific details about each of them are as follows:

Step 1: Classify all evidences as grade B (majority class).

Step 2: SVMs with n-grams ($n = 1, 2, 3, 4$ and semantic types replaced) as features. Parameters: $cost = 2.0$ and $\gamma = 0.0$. Attribute selection: Using the information gain measure to select the top 400 n-grams.

Step 3: SVMs with publication types as features. For each instance, the frequency of each publication type is used. Parameters: $cost = 1.0$ and $\gamma = 0.0$.

Step 4: SVMs with titles as features. Parameters: $cost = 32.0$ and $\gamma = 0.002$.

The parameters for each of the SVMs were tuned using the training set for training and the development time test set for evaluation. All experiments were carried out using the software package Weka[8]. Each of the above classifiers and their parameters were chosen based on their precision in classifying A and C grade evidences. Using this approach, the classification accuracy increases with each step of the algorithm as more instances are correctly classified as A and C.

5 Results and Discussion

For the final evaluation, we trained all our classifiers using the training set and the development test set, and evaluated the performance using test set instances. Among the 183 instances of the test set, our classifiers classify 42 as grade A, 124 as grade B, and 17 as grade C. This achieves an overall accuracy of 62.84%, meaning that 115 instances out of the 183 were correctly classified. This is significantly better than the baseline of classifying all instances as grade B, which has an accuracy of 48.63% (CI: 41.50 – 55.83).

Our results show that extracting specific information such as the publication types from text can significantly improve accuracy of grading. As Sarker et

[8]http://www.cs.waikato.ac.nz/ml/weka/

al. (2011) point out, features such as sizes of studies and consistency among studies play an important role in influencing evidence grades. However, identifying these factors automatically pose difficult problems themselves.

6 Conclusion

The 2011 ALTA Shared Task turned out to be a difficult one. A simple bag-of-word baseline does not significantly improve the results of a trivial majority-based baseline, and in fact none of the participants to the shared task managed to achieve results significantly better than this trivial baseline except us.

We have approached the problem of evidence grading as a three-way classification problem. We use three feature sets — n-grams, publication types, and titles. For the n-grams, we apply generic tags for specific medical concepts and we obtain publication type information using a rule-based approach. By employing a sequence of classifiers that attempt to identify A and C grade classes with high precision, our approach obtains an accuracy of 62.84%, which is a significant improvement over the baseline.

References

Yindalon Aphinyanaphongs, Ioannis Tsamardinos, Alexander Statnikov, Douglas Hardin, and Constantin F Aliferis. 2005. Text categorization models for high-quality article retrieval in internal medicine. *Journal of the American Medical Informatics Association : JAMIA*, 12(2):207–216.

Mark H Ebell, Jay Siwek, Barry D Weiss, Steven H Woolf, Jeffrey Susman, Bernard Ewigman, and Marjorie Bowman. 2004. Strength of recommendation taxonomy (SORT): a patient-centered approach to grading evidence in the medical literature. *Am Fam Physician*, 69(3):548–556, February.

John W. Ely, Jerome A. Osheroff, Mark H. Ebell, George R. Bergus, Barcey T. Levy, M. Lee Chambliss, and Eric R. Evans. 1999. Analysis of questions asked by family doctors regarding patient care. *BMJ*, 319(7206):358–361, August.

John Ely, Jerome A. Osheroff, M. Lee Chambliss, Mark H Ebell, and Marcy E. Rosenbaum. 2005. Answering physicians' clinical questions: Obstacles and potential solutions. *J Am Med Inform Assoc.*, 12(2):217–224.

Thomas Goetz and Claus-Wilhelm von der Lieth. 2005. PubFinder: a tool for improving retrieval rate of relevant PubMed abstracts. *Nucleic Acids Research*, 33:W774–W778.

Trisha Greenhalgh. 2006. *How to read a paper: The Basics of Evidence-based Medicine*. Blackwell Publishing, 3 edition.

Halil Kilicoglu, Dina Demner-Fushman, Thomas C. Rindflesch, Nancy L. Wilczynski, and Brian R. Haynes. 2009. Towards automatic recognition of scientifically rigorous clinical research evidence. *JAMIA*, 16(1):25–31, January.

Diego Mollá and María Elena Santiago-Martínez. 2011. Development of a corpus for evidence based medicine summarisation. In *Proceedings ALTA 2011*.

Maksim V Plikus, Zina Zhang, and Cheng-Ming Chuong. 2006. PubFocus: semantic MEDLINE/PubMed citations analytics through integration of controlled biomedical dictionaries and ranking algorithm. *BMC Bioinformatics*, 7(1):424–439.

David L Sackett, William M C Rosenberg, J A Muir Gray, R Brian Haynes, and W Scott Richardson. 1996. Evidence based medicine: what it is and what it isn't. *BMJ*, 312(7023):71–72.

Abeed Sarker and Diego Mollá-Aliod. 2010. A Rule-based Approach for Automatic Identification of Publication Types of Medical Papers. In *Proceedings of the ADCS Annual Symposium*, pages 84–88, Melbourne, Australia, December.

Abeed Sarker, Diego Mollá-Aliod, and Cecile Paris. 2011. Towards automatic grading of evidence. In *Proceedings of LOUHI 2011 Third International Workshop on Health Document Text Mining and Information Analysis*, pages 51–58.

Thanh Tang, David Hawking, Ramesh Sankaranarayana, Kathleen Griffiths, and Nick Craswell. 2009. Quality-Oriented Search for Depression Portals. In Mohand Boughanem, Catherine Berrut, Josiane Mothe, and Chantal Soule-Dupuy, editors, *Advances in Information Retrieval*, volume 5478 of *Lecture Notes in Computer Science*, chapter 60, pages 637–644. Springer Berlin / Heidelberg, Berlin, Heidelberg.

Ozlem Uzuner, Xiaoran Zhang, and Tawanda Sibanda. 2009. Machine Learning and Rule-based Approaches to Assertion Classification. *JAMIA*, 16:109–115.

Peer-reviewed papers: Oral presentations

A Particle Filter algorithm for Bayesian Wordsegmentation

Benjamin Börschinger
Department of Computing
Macquarie University
Sydney
benjamin.borschinger@mq.edu.au

Mark Johnson
Department of Computing
Macquarie University
Sydney
mark.johnson@mq.edu.au

Abstract

Bayesian models are usually learned using batch algorithms that have to iterate multiple times over the full dataset. This is both computationally expensive and, from a cognitive point of view, highly implausible. We present a novel online algorithm for the word segmentation models of Goldwater et al. (2009) which is, to our knowledge, the first published version of a Particle Filter for this kind of model. Also, in contrast to other proposed algorithms, it comes with a theoretical guarantee of optimality if the number of particles goes to infinity. While this is, of course, a theoretical point, a first experimental evaluation of our algorithm shows that, as predicted, its performance improves with the use of more particles, and that it performs competitively with other online learners proposed in Pearl et al. (2011).[1]

1 Introduction

Bayesian models have recently become quite popular in Computational Linguistics. One undesirable property of many such models is, however, that the inference algorithms usually applied to them, in particular popular Markov Chain Monte Carlo Methods such as Gibbs Sampling, require multiple iterations over the data — this is both computationally expensive and, from a cognitive point of view, implausible. Online learning algorithms directly address this problem by requiring only a single pass over the data, thus providing a first step from 'ideal learner' analyses towards more realistic learning scenarios (Pearl et al., 2011). In this paper, we present a Particle Filter algorithm for the word segmentation models of Goldwater et al. (2009), to our knowledge showing for the first time how a Particle Filter can be applied to models of this kind. Notably, Particle Filters are mathematically well-motivated algorithms to produce a finite approximation to the true posterior of a model, the quality of which increases with larger numbers of particles and recovering the true posterior if the number of particles goes to infinity. This sets them qualitatively apart from most previously proposed online learners that usually are based on heuristic ideas.

The structure of the rest of the paper is as follows. First, we give a high-level description of the Bayesian word segmentation model our algorithm applies to and make explicit our notion of an online learner. Then, we give a quick overview of previous work and go on to describe the word segmentation model in more detail, introducing the relevant notation and formulae. Finally, we give a description of the algorithm and present experimental results, comparing the algorithm with other proposed learning algorithms for the model and its performance across different numbers of particles.

2 The Goldwater model for word segmentation

The model[2] assumes that a segmented text is created by a random process that generates a sequence

[1] The source code for our implementation is available for download from http://web.science.mq.edu.au/~bborschi/

[2] We only provide a high-level idea of the Bayesian Unigram model for word segmentation of Goldwater et al. (2009). For more details and a description of the Bigram model, we refer the reader to the original paper.

of words $\sigma = w_{1:n}$ which can be interpreted as a segmentation of the unsegmented text T that is the result of concatenating these words.[3]

The first word is generated by a distribution over possible words, the so-called base distribution P_0 that, in principle, can generate words of unbounded length. We'll come back to the details of the base distribution in section 4.1. Each further word is either generated by 'reusing' one of the previously generated words, or by making a new draw from the base distribution. This generative process, also known as the (labelled) Chinese Restaurant Process, is formally described as:

$$P(W_1{=}w \mid \alpha) = P_0(w) \tag{1}$$

$$P(W_{i+1}{=}w \mid W_{1:i}, \alpha) = \frac{c_w(W_{1:i}) + \alpha P_0(w)}{i + \alpha} \tag{2}$$

where P_0 is the base distribution over words and $c_w(W_{1:i})$ is the number of times the word w has been observed in the sequence $W_{1:i}$. α is the hyperparameter for the process, also known as the concentration parameter, and controls the probability of generating previously unseen words by making a new draw from P_0.

This process can be understood in terms of a restaurant metaphor: each generated word corresponds to the order of a customer in a restaurant, and each customer who enters the restaurant either sits at an already occupied table with probability proportional to the number of people already sitting there, ordering the exact same dish they are already eating (the label of the table), or sits at a new table with probability proportional to α and orders a new dish which corresponds to making a draw from the base distribution.[4] In principle, there is an infinite number of tables in the restaurant but we only are interested in those that are actually occupied, allowing us to actually represent the state of this process with finite means. We will be using the metaphor of customers and tables in the following, for ease of presentation and lack of a better terminology.

[3]We take an expression of the form $x_{1:n}$ to refer to the sequence $x_1, \ldots, x_n$.

[4]Note that the same word may label several different tables, as the base distribution may generate the same word multiple times.

The conditional distributions defined by eq. 1 and eq. 2 is exchangeable, i.e. every permutation of the same sequence of words is assigned the same probability. This allows us to completely capture the state of the generative process after having generated i words by a description of the seating for the i customers.

2.1 Inference for the model

While this description has focused on the generative side of the model, probabilistic models like this are usually not used to *generate* random sequences of words but to do *inference*. In this case, we are interested in the posterior distribution over segmentations σ for a specific text T, $P(\sigma \mid T)$.

While it is easy to calculate the probability of any given segmentation using eq. 1 and eq. 2, determining the posterior distribution or even just finding the most probable segmentation is computationally intractable. Instead, an approximation to the posterior can be calculated using, for example, Markov Chain Monte Carlo algorithms such as Gibbs Sampling. Going into the details of Gibbs Sampling is beyond the scope of the paper, and in fact we propose an alternative algorithm here. We refer the reader to the original Goldwater et al. (2009) paper for a detailed description of their Gibbs Sampling algorithm and to Bishop (2006) for a general introduction.

2.2 Motivation for Online Algorithms

Gibbs Sampling is a batch method that requires multiple iterations over the whole data — in practice, it is not uncommon to have 20,000 iterations on the amount of data we are working with here. This is both computationally expensive and, from a cognitive point of view, highly implausible. Having online learning algorithms is therefore a desirable goal, and their failure to obtain an optimal solution can be seen as telling us how a constrained learner might make use of certain models; in this sense, they provide a first step from ideal learner analyses to more realistic settings (Pearl et al., 2011).

Constraints on Online Algorithms In our opinion, a plausible constraint on an online learner is that it (a) sees each example only once[5] and (b) has to

[5]Note that this applies to example tokens. There may well be multiple tokens of the same example type.

make a learning decision on the basis of one example at a time immediately after having seen it, using a finite amount of computation. While this is certainly a very strict view, we think it is a plausible first approximation to the constraints human learners are subject to, and it is certainly interesting in and of itself to see how well a learner constrained in this manner can perform. It will be an interesting question for future research to see how relaxing these constraints to a certain extent effects the performance of the learner.

Note that our constraints on online learners exclude certain algorithms that have been labelled 'online' in the literature. For example, the Online EM algorithms in Liang and Klein (2009) make local updates but iterate over the whole data multiple times, thus violating (a). Pearl et al.'s (2011) DMCMC algorithm, discussed in the next section, is able to revisit earlier examples in the light of new evidence, violating thus both (a) and (b).

3 Previous work

Online learning algorithms for Bayesian models are discussed within both Statistics and Computational Linguistics but have, to our knowledge, not yet been widely applied to the specific problem of word segmentation. Both Brent (1999) and Venkataraman (2001) propose heuristic online learning algorithms employing Dynamic Programming that have, however, been shown to not actually maximize the objective defined by the model (Goldwater, 2007). Brent's algorithm has recently been reconsidered as an online learning algorithm in Pearl et al. (2011).

It is an instance of the familiar Viterbi algorithm that efficiently finds the optimal solution to many problems; not, however, for the word segmentation models under discussion. The algorithm is "greedy" in that it determines the locally optimal segmentation for an utterance given its current knowledge using Dynamic Programming, adding the words of this segmentation to its knowledge and proceeding to the next utterance. Both this Dynamic Programming Maximization (DPM) algorithm and a slight variant called Dynamic Programming Sampling (DPS) are described in detail in Pearl et al., the main difference between the two algorithms being that the latter does not pick the most probable segmentation but rather samples a segmentation according to its probability. Note that DPS is, in effect, a Particle Filter with just one particle.

Pearl et al. also present a Decayed Markov Chain Monte Carlo algorithm (Marthi et al., 2002) that is basically an 'online' version of Gibbs Sampling. For each observed utterance, the learner is allowed to reconsider any possible boundary position it has encountered so far in light of its current knowledge, but the probability of reconsidering any specific boundary position decreases with its distance from the current utterance. In effect, boundaries in recent utterances are more likely to be reconsidered than boundaries in earlier ones. While this property is nice in that it can be interpreted as some kind of memory decay, the algorithm breaks our constraints on online learners, as has already been mentioned above: the DMCMC learner explicitly remembers each training example, effectively giving it the ability to learn from and see each example multiple times. It has, in a sense, "knowledge of 'future' utterances when it samples boundaries further back in the corpus than the current utterance", as Pearl et al. point out themselves.

As for non-online algorithms, the state of the art for this word segmentation problem is the adaptor grammar MCMC sampler of Johnson and Goldwater (2009), which achieves 87% word token f-score on the same test corpus as used here. The adaptor grammar model learns both syllable structure and inter-word dependencies, and performs Bayesian inference for the optimal hyperparameters and word segmentation.

4 Model Details

Our models are basically the unigram and bigram models described in Goldwater et al. (2009) and quickly introduced above. There is, however, an important difference with respect to the choice of the base distribution that we describe in what follows. Also, our assumption about what constitutes a hypothesis is different from Goldwater et al., which is why we describe it in some detail.[6] The mathematical details are given in figure 1 while in the text, we focus on a high-level explanation of the ideas.

[6] Again, we focus on the Unigram model.

$$P_c(C = k \mid s, \phi) = \frac{cc_{s,k} + \phi}{\sum_j cc_{s,j} + |\text{chars}|\phi} \quad (j \in \text{chars}) \tag{3}$$

$$P_0(W = k_{1:n} \mid s, \phi) = \left(\prod_{i=1}^{n} P_c(k_i \mid s, \phi)\right) \times P_c(\# \mid s, \phi) \tag{4}$$

$$P_{\text{add}}(\langle wo, t\rangle \mid s, \alpha) = \begin{cases} \frac{ct_{s,t}}{ct_{s,\cdot}+\alpha} & \text{if } t \in s \text{ and } wo \text{ is the label of } t \\ \frac{\alpha P_0(wo|\text{labels}(s),\phi)}{ct_{s,\cdot}+\alpha} & \text{if } t \text{ is a new table.} \end{cases} \tag{5}$$

$$P_\sigma(\boldsymbol{\sigma} \mid s, \alpha) = P_{\text{add}}(\sigma_1 \mid s, \alpha) \times \cdots \times P_{\text{add}}(\sigma_n \mid s \cup \sigma_1 \cup \cdots \cup \sigma_{n-1}) \tag{6}$$

$$Q_\sigma(\boldsymbol{\sigma} \mid s, \alpha) = \prod_{i=1}^{n} P_{\text{add}}(\sigma_i \mid s, \alpha) \tag{7}$$

$$\boldsymbol{\sigma}_{i+1}^{(l)} \sim Q_\sigma(\cdot \mid s_i^{(l)}, o_{i+1}, \alpha) \tag{8}$$

$$s_{i+1}^{(l)} = s_i^{(l)} \bigcup \boldsymbol{\sigma}_{i+1}^{(l)} \tag{9}$$

$$\begin{aligned} w_{i+1}^{*(l)} &= w_i^{(l)} \frac{P(o_{i+1} \mid s_{i+1}^{(l)}, \alpha) P(s_{i+1}^{(l)} \mid s_i^{(l)}, \alpha)}{Q(s_{i+1}^{(l)} \mid s_i^{(l)}, o_{i+1}, \alpha)} = w_i^{(l)} \frac{P(o_{i+1}, s_{i+1}^{(l)} \mid s_i^{(l)}, \alpha)}{Q_\sigma(\boldsymbol{\sigma}_{i+1}^{(l)} \mid s_i^{(l)}, o_{i+1}, \alpha)} \\ &= w_i^{(l)} \frac{P_\sigma(\boldsymbol{\sigma}_{i+1}^{(l)} \mid s_i^{(l)}, \alpha)}{Q_\sigma(\boldsymbol{\sigma}_{i+1}^{(l)} \mid s_i^{(l)}, o_{i+1}, \alpha)} \end{aligned} \tag{10}$$

$$w_{i+1}^{(l)} = \frac{w_{i+1}^{*(l)}}{\sum_{j=1}^{N} w_{i+1}^{*(j)}} \tag{11}$$

$$\widehat{ESS}_i = \frac{1}{\sum_j^N (w_i^{(j)})^2)} \tag{12}$$

Figure 1: The mathematical details needed for implementing the algorithm. $cc_{s,k}$ is the number of times character k has been observed in the words in $\text{labels}(s)$ which, in turn, refers to the words labeling (unigram) tables in model state s. chars is the set of different characters in the language, including the word-boundary symbol $\#$. $ct_{s,t}$ refers to the number of customers at table t in model state s, and $ct_{s,\cdot}$ refers to the total number of customers in s. A segmentation $\boldsymbol{\sigma}$ is a sequence of word-table pairs $\langle wo, t\rangle$ that indicates both which words make up the segmentation and at which table each word customer is seated. $s \cup \sigma_i$ refers to the model state that results from adding the ith word-table pair of $\boldsymbol{\sigma}$ to hypothesis s, and the probability of adding this pair is given by P_{add} in eq. 5. $s \bigcup \boldsymbol{\sigma}$ refers to adding all word-table pairs in $\boldsymbol{\sigma}$ to s. Q_σ is the proposal distribution from which we can efficiently sample segmentations, given an observation o, i.e. an unsegmented utterance, and a model state s. P_σ is the true distribution over segmentations according to which we can efficiently score proposals to calculate (the unnormalized) weights w^* using eq. 10. Eq. 8 and eq. 10 can be calculated because $Q_\sigma(\boldsymbol{\sigma} \mid s, \alpha, o) = \frac{Q(\boldsymbol{\sigma}, o|s,\alpha)}{Q(o|s,\alpha)} = \frac{Q_\sigma(\boldsymbol{\sigma}|s,\alpha)}{Q(o|s,\alpha)}$, the denominator of which can be efficiently calculated using the forward-algorithm.

4.1 The Lexical-Model

Even though Goldwater et al. found the choice of the lexical model to make virtually no difference for the performance of an unconstrained learner, this does not hold for online learners, an observation already made by Venkataraman (2001). In the original model, each character is assumed to have the same probability $\theta_0 = \frac{1}{|characters|}$ of being generated, and words are generated by a zero-order (Unigram) markov process with a fixed stopping probability. In contrast, we assume that there is a symmetric Dirichlet prior with parameter ϕ on the probability distribution over characters:

$\boldsymbol{\theta} \sim Dir(\phi)$

$P_c(k) = \theta_k$

By integrating out θ, we get a 'learned' conditional distribution over characters, and consequently words, given the learner's lexicon up to that point (eq. 3 and eq. 4).

In addition, we do not fix the probability for the word-boundary symbol, treating it as a further special character $\#$ that may only occur at the end of a word.[7]

[7]While this makes possible in principle the generation of empty words, we are confident that this does not pose a prac-

4.2 Probability of a segmentation

Since we are interested in the posterior distribution over hypotheses given unsegmented utterances, it is important to be clear about what constitues a hypothesis. At a high level, a hypothesis s can be thought of as a lexicon that arises from the segmentation decisions made for the observations up to this point. For example, if the learner previously assumed the segmentations "a dog" and "a woman", its lexicon contains two occurences of "a" and one occurence of "dog" and "woman", respectively.

More precisely, a hypothesis is a model state and a model state is an assignment of observed (or rather, previously predicted) word 'customers' to tables (see section 2).[8] At time k, the model state s_k is the seating arrangement after having segmented the current observation o_k given the previous model state s_{k-1}, where each observation is an unsegmented string. As our incremental learner can only make additive changes to the 'restaurant' — no customers ever leave the table they are assigned to — the hypothesis at time $k+1$ is uniquely determined by the seating arrangement at time k and the proposed segmentation for observation o_{k+1}, as a segmentation not only indicates the actual words, e.g. "a" and "dog", but also the table at which each word should be seated (which may be a new table). Thus, going from one model state to the next corresponds to sampling a segmentation for the new observation (eq. 8) and adding this segmentation to the current model state (eq. 9). The formulae that assign probabilities to segmentations are given in eq. 5 to eq. 7.

5 The Particle Filter algorithm

Our algorithm is an instance of a Particle Filter, or more precisely, of the Sequential Importance Resampling (SIR) algorithm (Doucet et al., 2000). The idea is to sequentially approximate a target posterior distribution P by N weighted point samples or particles, updating each particle and its weight in light of each succeeding observation. Hypotheses that do conform to the data gain weight, mimicking a kind of a "survival of the fittest" dynamic. Notably, the accuracy of the approximation increases with the number of particles, a result borne out by our experiments.

At a very high-level, a Particle Filter is very similar to a stochastic beam-search in that a number of possibilities is explored in parallel, and the choice of possibilities that are further explored is biased towards locally good, i.e. high-probable ones.

At any given stage, the weighted particles give a finite approximation to the target posterior distribution up to that point, the weight of each particle representing its probability under the approximation. Therefore, we can use it to approximate any expectation of the posterior, e.g. some measure of its word segmentation accuracy, as a weighted sum.

5.1 Description of the Algorithm

A formal description of the algorithm is given in Figure 2 which we explain in more detail here. The algorithm starts at time $i = 0$ with N identical model states (particles) $s_0^{(n)}$, in our case empty lexicons, or rather empty restaurants.[9] At each time step $i+1$, it propagates each particle by sampling a segmentation $\sigma_{i+1}^{(l)}$ for the next observation o_{i+1} according to the the current model state $s_i^{(l)}$ (eq. 8) and adding this segmentation to it, yielding the updated particle $s_{i+1}^{(l)}$ (eq. 9). Intuitively, at each step the learner predicts a segmentation for the current observation in light of what it has learned so far. Adding a segmentation to a model state corresponds to adding the word customers in the segmentation to the corresponding tables. As there are multiple particles, in principle the algorithm can explore alternative hypotheses, reminiscent of a beam-search.

Not all hypotheses, however, fit the observations equally well, and as new data becomes available at each time step, the relative merit of different hypotheses may change. This is captured in a particle filter by assigning weights $w_i^{(l)}$ to each particle that are iteratively updated, using eq. 10 and eq. 11. This update takes both into account how well the particle fit previously seen data in the form of the old weight, and how well it fits the last observation in the form

tical problem as we only use the model for inference, not for generation.

[8]The reason our description involves an explicit record of table assignments is that this is needed for the Bigram model. While actually not needed for the Unigram case, our formulation can be extended to the Bigram model in a straight-forward way, given the description in Goldwater et al. (2009).

[9]The superscript indexes the individual particles, the subscript indicates the time.

of the probability of the proposed segmentation under the current model.

Also, the formula we use for calculating the particle weights, taken from Doucet et al. (2000), overcomes a fundamental problem in applying Particle Filters to this kind of model: we are usually not able to efficiently sample directly from P, because P does not decompose in the way required for Dynamic Programming (Johnson et al., 2007; Mochihashi et al., 2009). The SIR algorithm, however, allows us to use an arbitrary proposal distribution Q for the samples. All that is needed is that we can calculate the true probability of each sample according to P, which is easily done using eq. 6. Our proposal distribution Q ignores the dependencies between the words within an utterance, as in eq. 7. This can be thought of as 'freezing' the model in order to determine a segmentation, just as in the PCFG proposal distribution of Johnson et al. (2007). Thus, the proposal segmentations and other quantities required to calculate the weights and propagate the particles are efficiently computable using the formulae in Figure 1 and the efficient algorithms described in detail in Johnson et al. (2007) and Mochihashi et al. (2009). Interestingly, even though the proposal distribution is only an approximation to the true posterior, Doucet et. al point out that as the number of particles goes to infinity, the approximation still converges to the target (Doucet et al., 2000).

Resampling A well known problem with Particle Filters is that after a number of observations most particles will be assigned very low weights which means that they contribute virtually nothing to the approximation of the target distribution. This is directly addressed by resampling steps in the SIR algorithm: whenever a quantity known as Effective Sample Size (ESS), approximated by eq. 12, falls below a certain threshold, say, $\frac{N}{2}$, the current set of particles is resampled by sampling with replacement from the current distribution over particles defined by the current weights. This results in high weight particles having multiple 'descendants', and in low weight particles being 'weeded out'. We experiment with two thresholds, N and $\frac{N}{2}$.

6 Experiments

We evaluate our algorithm along the lines of experiments discussed in Pearl et al. (2011), using Brent's

```
create N empty models s_0^(1) to s_0^(N)
set initial weights w_0^(l) to 1/N
for example i = 1 → K do
    for particle l = 1 → N do
        sample σ_i^(l) ~ Q_σ(· | s_{i-1}^(l), o_i, α)
        s_i^(l) = s_{i-1}^(l) ∪ σ_i^(l)
        calculate the unnormalized particle weight w_i^{*(l)}
    end for
    calculate the normalized particle weights w_i^(l) and
    calculate \widehat{ESS}
    if \widehat{ESS} ≤ THRESHOLD then
        resample all particles according to w_i^(l)
        set all weights to 1/N
    end if
end for
```

Figure 2: Our Particle Filter algorithm. N is the number of particles, K is the number of examples. The formulae needed are given in Figure 1.

version of the Bernstein corpus (Brent, 1999). Unlike them, however, we see no reason for actually splitting the data into training and test sets, following in this respect previous work such as Goldwater et al. (2009) by training and evaluating on the full corpus.

6.1 Evaluation

Evaluation is done for each learner by 'freezing' the model state after the learner has processed all examples and then sampling a proposed segmentation for each example o from $Q_\sigma(\cdot \mid s, o, \alpha)$, where s is the final model state. As we have multiple weighted final model states, the scores are calculated by evaluating each model state and then taking a weighted sum of the individual scores. This corresponds to taking an expectation over the posterior. Note that under the assumption that at the end of learning the 'lexicon' no longer changes, sampling from Q no longer constitutes an approximation as the intra-utterance dependencies Q ignores correspond to making changes to the lexicon.

As is common, we calculate precision, recall and the harmonic mean of the two, f-measure, for tokens, boundaries and elements in the lexicon. To illustrate these scores, assume the learner segmented the two utterances "the old woman" and "the old man" into "theold wo man" and "theold man". It has correctly identified 1 of the 6 tokens and predicted a total of 5 tokens, yielding a token recall of 1/6 and a token precision of 1/5. It has also identified 2 of the 4 boundaries, and has predicted a total of 3 boundaries, yielding a precision of 2/3 and a recall of 1/2. Lastly, it has correctly found only 1 of the 4 word types and predicted a total of 3 word types, giving a precision and a recall of of 1/3 and 1/4, respectively. So as to not clutter the table, we only report f-measure.

6.2 Experimental Results

There are two questions of interest with respect to the performance of the algorithm. First, we would like to know how faithful the algorithm is to the original model, i.e. whether the 'optimal' solution it finds is close to the 'optimal' solution according to the true model. For this, we compare the log-probability of the *training* data each algorithm assigns to it after learning. Second, we would like to know how well each algorithm performs in terms of the segmentation objectives.

For comparison to our Particle Filter algorithm, we used Pearl et al.'s (2011) implementation of their proposed online learners, the DPM and the DMCMC algorithm, and their implementation of a batch MCMC algorithm, a Metropolis Hastings sampler.[10] We set the threshold for resampling to N and $\frac{N}{2}$, ϕ to 0.02 and the remaining model parameters to the values reported in Goldwater et al. (2009): $\alpha = 20.0, \rho = 2.0$ for the unigram model, and $\alpha_0 = 100.0, \alpha_1 = 3000.0, p_\$ = 0.5$ for the bigram model.[11] In addition, we decided to not use annealing for either of the algorithms to get an idea of the 'raw' performance of their performance and simply run the unconstrained sampler for 20,000 iterations. While this does not reflect a 'true' ideal learner performance, it seems to us to be a reasonable method for an initial comparision, in particular since we have not yet applied ideas such as annealing or hyper-parameter sampling to the Particle Filter.

The particle filter results vary considerably, especially with small numbers of particles, which is why we report an average over multiple runs and report the standard deviation in brackets.[12] The results are given in Table 1.

6.3 Discussion

As could be expected, faithfulness to the original model increases with larger numbers of particles — the log-probability of the training-data seems to be positively related to N, though obviously non-linearly, and we expect that using even larger numbers of particles will bring the log-probability even closer to that assigned by the unconstrained learner. Also, the Particle Filters seem to work generally better for the Unigram model which is not very surprising, considering that "when tracking bigrams instead of just individual words, the learner's hypothesis space is much larger" (Pearl et al., 2011), and that Particle Filters are known to perform rather poorly in high dimensional state spaces.

In the Unigram setting, the Particle Filter is able to outperform the DPM algorithm in the 1000 particle / $\frac{N}{2}$ threshold setting, both in terms of log-probability and segmentation scores. With respect to the latter, it also outperforms the unconstrained learner in all but lexical f-measure. This is not very surprising, however, as Goldwater (2007) already found that sub-optimal solutions with respect to the actual model may be better with respect to segmentation, simply because the strong unigram assumption is so blatantly wrong.

For both the models, using a resampling threshold of $\frac{N}{2}$ instead of N seems to lead to better performance with respect to both measures, in particular in the Bigram setting. We are not sure how to interpret this result but have the suspicion that this difference may disappear as a larger number of particles is used and that what may be going on is that for 'small' numbers of particles, the diversity of samples drops too fast if resampling is applied after each observa-

[10]The scores reported in their paper apply only to their training-test split. We weren't able to run the DMCMC algorithm for the Unigram setting which is why we omit these scores — the scores reported for the Unigram learner on a five-fold training-test split in Pearl et al. are slightly better than for our best performing particle filter but not directly comparable, and no log-probability is given.

[11]$p_\$$ is the fixed utterance-boundary base-probability, ρ is the beta-prior on the utterance-boundary probability in the unigram model.

[12]For 1, 50 and 100 particles, we run 10 trials, for 500 and 1000 particles 2 trials. In principle, the unconstrained learners are also subject to some variance (Goldwater, 2007; Goldwater et al., 2009) but not to the extent of the particle filters.

	Learner		TF	BF	LF	log-prob$\times 10^3$
Unigram	MH-MCMC		63.11	80.29	**59.68**	**-209.57**
	DPM		65.65	80.05	44.96	-234.11
	PF	1	56.84 (4.36)	74.94 (2.92)	35.34 (3.21)	-244.28 (5.56)
		50	60.33/59.84 (5.82)/(6.00)	77.08/76.98 (3.68)/(3.75)	41.61/41.62 (3.40)/(3.15)	-240.38/-240.58 (6.43)/(5.18)
		100	62.97/61.02 (3.21)/(4.94)	79.05/77.87 (2.09)/(3.14)	43.04/43.61 (2.29)/(2.90)	-238.73/-238.92 (4.64)/(5.69)
		500	60.81/68.46 (7.05)/(1.87)	77.50/**82.27** (4.36)/(1.11)	45.25/47.52 (3.67)/(0.23)	-236.55/-231.85 (6.13)/(2.25)
		1000	64.11/**66.54** (4.84)/(5.31)	79.70/80.99 (2.74)/(3.24)	45.82/47.08 (1.36)/(2.90)	-234.87/**-231.93** (3.10)/(3.55)
Bigram	MH-MCMC		63.71	79.52	47.45	**-240.79**
	DMCMC		**70.78**	**83.97**	47.85	**-244.85**
	DPM		66.92	81.07	**52.54**	-250.52
	PF	1	48.55 (3.04)	71.22 (1.82)	35.02 (2.14)	-266.90 (2.40)
		50	55.98/57.85 (2.29)/(3.85)	75.21/76.49 (1.42)/(1.93)	43.34/45.21 (1.76)/(1.79)	-258.42/-256.16 (2.22)/(4.24)
		100	57.77/61.55 (2.77)/(2.06)	76.40/78.47 (1.45)/(1.30)	43.77/45.79 (1.46)/(1.50)	-257.93/-254.66 (2.03)/(1.47)
		500	57.99/63.58 (0.59)/(1.73)	76.33/80.05 (0.33)/(0.94)	44.70/47.82 (0.16)/(0.82)	-256.44/-252.14 (1.01)/(0.46)
		1000	57.88/61.76 (0.48)/(1.11)	76.55/78.30 (0.05)/(1.31)	46.93/49.33 (0.41)/(0.88)	-254.17/-251.33 (0.92)/(0.03)

Table 1: F-measure and log-probabilities on the Bernstein corpus for Pearl et al.'s (2011) batch MCMC algorithm (MH-MCMC), the online algorithms Dynamic Programming Maximization (DPM) and Delayed Markov Chain Monte Carlo (DMCMC), and our online Particle Filter (PF) with different numbers of particles (1, 50, 100, 500, 1000). TF, BF and LF stand for token, boundary and lexical f-measure, respectively. For the Particle Filter, numbers left of a '/' report scores for a resampling threshold of N, those on the right for $\frac{N}{2}$. Numbers in brackets are standard-deviations across multiple runs. Numbers in bold indicate the best overall performance, and the best performance of an online learner (if different from the best overall performance).

tion.

In the Bigram setting, even 1000 particles and a threshold of $\frac{N}{2}$ cannot outperform the conceptually much simpler DPM algorithm, let alone the DMCMC algorithm that comes pretty close to the unconstrained learner. The increased dimensionality of the state-space may require the use of even more particles, a point we plan to address in the future by optimizing our implementation so as to handle very large numbers of particles.

Also, there is no clear relation between the number of particles that are used and the variance in the results, in particular in the Unigram setting. While we are not sure about how to interpret this result, again it may have to do with the increased dimensionality: a possible explanation is that in the Unigram setting, 500 and 1000 particles already allow the model to explore very different hypotheses, leading to a larger variance in results, whereas in the Bigram setting, this number of particles only suffices to find solutions very close to each other.

All in all, however, the results suggest that using more particles gradually increases the learner's performance. This is unconditionally true for both settings in our experiments with respect to the log-probability; while this trend is not consistent for all segmentation scores, this simply reflects that the relation between log-probability and segmentation performance is not transparent, even for the Bigram model, as is clearly seen by the difference between the DMCMC and the Unconstrained learner.

Finally, we'd like to point out again that the DMCMC learner is, strictly speaking, not an online learner. Its ability to 'resample the past' corresponds closely to he idea of rejuvenation (Canini et al., 2009) in which each individual particle reconsiders past examples for a fixed amount of time at certain intervals and can, in principle, be added to our algorithm, something we plan to do in the future. Also, while the performance of the DPM algorithm for the Bigram model is rather impressive, it should be noted that the DPM algorithm embodies a heuristic greedy strategy that may or may not work in certain cases. While it obviously works rather well in this case, there is no mathematical or conceptual motivation for it and we can't be sure that its performance does not depend on accidental properties of the data.

7 Conclusion and Outlook

We have presented a Particle Filter algorithm for the Bayesian word segmentation models presented in Goldwater et al. (2009). The algorithm performs competitively with other proposed online algorithms for this kind of model, and as predicted, its performance increases with larger numbers of particles.

To our knowledge, it constitutes the first Particle Filter for this kind of model. Our formulation of the Particle Filter should extend to similarly complex Bayesian models in Computational Linguistics, e.g. the grammar models proposed in Johnson et al. (2007) and Liang et al. (2010), and may serve as a starting point for applying other Particle Filter algorithms to these models, a point we want to address in future research.

Also, while the strict online nature is desirable from a cognitive point of view, for practical purposes variants of Particle Filters that violate these strong assumptions, e.g. using the idea of rejuvenation that has previously been applied to Particle Filters for Latent Dirichlet Allocation in Canini et al. (2009), might offer considerable performance gains for practical NLP tasks, and we plan to extend our algorithm in this direction as well.

8 Acknowledgments

We would like to thank the reviewers for their helpful comments, and Lisa Pearl and Sharon Goldwater for sharing the source code for their learners and their data with us. This work was supported under the Australian Research Councils Discovery Projects funding scheme (project number DP110102506).

References

Christopher M. Bishop. 2006. *Pattern Recognition and Machine Learning*. Springer.

Michael R. Brent. 1999. An efficient, probabilistically sound algorithm for segmentation andword discovery. *Machine Learning - Special issue on natural language learning*, 34:71 – 105.

Kevin Canini, Lei Shi, and Thomas Griffiths. 2009. Online inference of topics with latent dirichlet allocation. In *Proceedings of the Twelfth International Conference on Artificial Intelligence and Statistics*.

Arnaud Doucet, Simon Godsill, and Christophe Andrieu. 2000. On sequential monte carlo sampling methods for bayesian filtering. *Statistics and Computing*, 10:197–208.

Sharon Goldwater, Thomas Griffiths, and Mark Johnson. 2009. A bayesian framework for word segmentation: Exploring the effects of context. *Cognition*, 112:21–54.

Sharon Goldwater. 2007. *Nonparametric Bayesian Models of Lexical Acquisition*. Ph.D. thesis, Brown University.

Mark Johnson and Sharon Goldwater. 2009. Improving nonparameteric bayesian inference: experiments on unsupervised word segmentation with adaptor grammars. In *Proceedings of Human Language Technologies: The 2009 Annual Conference of the North American Chapter of the Association for Computational Linguistics*, pages 317–325.

Mark Johnson, Thomas Griffiths, and Sharon Goldwater. 2007. Bayesian inference for pcfgs via markov chain monte carlo. In *Proceedings of NAACL HLT 2007*, pages 139–146.

Percy Liang and Dan Klein. 2009. Online em for unsupervised models. In *Proceedings of NAACL 2009*.

P. Liang, M. I. Jordan, and D. Klein. 2010. Probabilistic grammars and hierarchical dirichlet processes. In T. O'Hagan and M. West, editors, *The Handbook of Applied Bayesian Analysis*. Oxford University Press.

Bhaskara Marthi, Hanna Pasula, Stuart Russell, and Yuval Peres. 2002. Decayed mcmc filtering. In *Proceedings of the Conference on Uncertainty in Artificial Intelligence, 2002 (UAI-02)*.

Daichi Mochihashi, Takeshi Yamada, and Naonori Ueda. 2009. Bayesian unsupervised word segmentation with nested pitman-yor language modeling. In *Proceedings of the 47th Annual Meeting of the ACL and the 4th IJCNLP of the AFNLP*, page 100108.

Lisa Pearl, Sharon Goldwater, and Mark Steyvers. 2011. Online learning mechanisms for bayesian models of word segmentation. *Research on Language and Computation*, Special issue on computational models of language acquisition.

Anand Venkataraman. 2001. A statistical model for word discovery in transcribed speech. *Computational Linguistics*, 27:351–372.

Formalizing Semantic Parsing with Tree Transducers

Bevan Keeley Jones & Mark Johnson
Department of Computing
Macquarie University
Sydney, NSW 2109, Australia
Bevan.Jones@students.mq.edu.au
Mark.Johnson@mq.edu.au

Sharon Goldwater
School of Informatics
University of Edinburgh
Edinburgh, EH8 9AB, UK
sgwater@inf.ed.ac.uk

Abstract

This paper introduces tree transducers as a unifying theory for semantic parsing models based on tree transformations. Many existing models use tree transformations, but implement specialized training and smoothing methods, which makes it difficult to modify or extend the models. By connecting to the rich literature on tree automata, we show how semantic parsing models can be developed using completely general estimation methods. We demonstrate the approach by reframing and extending one state-of-the-art model as a tree automaton. Using a variant of the inside-outside algorithm with variational Bayesian estimation, our generative model achieves higher raw accuracy than existing generative and discriminative approaches on a standard data set.

1 Introduction

Automatically interpreting language is an important challenge for computational linguistics. *Semantic parsing* addresses the specific task of learning to map natural language sentences to formal representations of their meaning, a problem that arises in developing natural language interfaces, for example. Given a set of (sentence, meaning representation) pairs like the example below, we want to to learn a map that generalizes to previously unseen sentences.

1. Sentence: what is the capital of texas ?
   Meaning: answer(capital_1(stateid(texas)))

Researchers have formalized the learning problem in various ways, with approaches including string classifiers (Kate and Mooney, 2006), synchronous grammar (Wong and Mooney, 2006), combinatory categorial grammar (Zettlemoyer and Collins, 2005; Kwiatkowski et al., 2010), and PCFG-based approaches (Lu et al., 2008; Borschinger et al., 2011). Each approach has required its own custom algorithms, which has made model development and innovation slow. Nevertheless, there are many similarities between the approaches, which all exploit parallels between the structure of the meaning representation and that of the natural language. The meaning representation, as a context-free formal language, has an obvious tree structure. Trees are also widely used to describe natural language structure. Consequently, the semantic parsing problem can be generally defined as learning a mapping between trees, one of which may be latent. This mapping can be expressed as a *tree transducer*, a formalism from automata theory that maps input trees to output trees or strings. Tree transducers have well understood properties and algorithms, and a rich literature, making them a particularly appealing model class.

Although some previous approaches strongly resemble tree transducers, to our knowledge, we are the first to explicitly formulate the problem in this way. We argue that connecting semantic parsing to the tree automata literature will free researchers from devising custom solutions and allow them to focus on studying and improving their models and developing more general learning algorithms.

To demonstrate the effectiveness of the approach, we choose one state-of-the-art model, the hybrid tree (Lu et al., 2008), translate it into the tree transducer

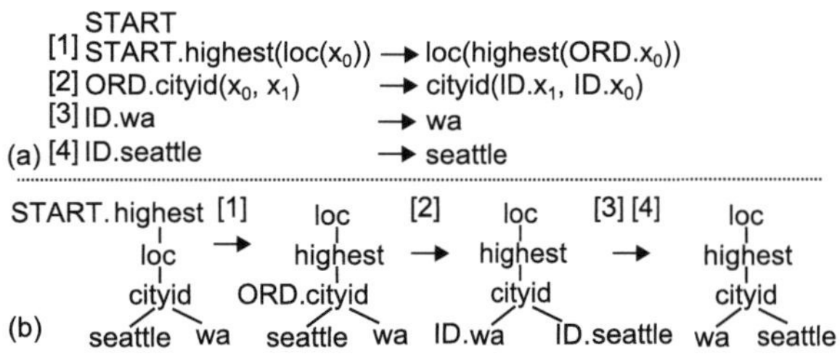

Figure 1: An extended left hand side, root-to-frontier, linear, non-deleting, tree-to-tree transducer (a) and an example derivation (b). Numbered arrows in the derivation indicate which rules apply during that step. Rule [1] is the only rule with an extended left hand side.

framework, and add a small extension, made easy by the framework. We also update a standard tree transducer training algorithm to incorporate a Variational Bayes approximation. The result is the first purely generative model to achieve state-of-the-art results on a standard data set.

2 Extended, root-to-frontier, linear, non-deleting tree transducers

Tree transducers (Rounds, 1970; Thatcher, 1970) are generalizations of finite state machines that take trees as inputs and either output a string or another tree. Mirroring the branching nature of its input, the tree transducer may simultaneously transition to any number of successor states, assigning a separate state to process each sub-tree. Although they were originally conceived of by Rounds (1970) as a way to formalize tree transformations in linguistic theory, they have since received far more interest in theoretical computer science. Recently, however, they have also been used for syntax-based statistical machine translation (Graehl et al., 2008; Knight and Greahl, 2005).

Figure 1 presents an example of a tree-to-tree transducer. It is defined using tree transformation rules, where the left hand side identifies a state of the transducer and a fragment of the input tree, and the right hand side describes a fragment of the output tree. Variables x_i stand for entire sub-trees. There are many classes of transducer, each with its own selection of algorithms (Knight and Greahl, 2005). In this paper we restrict consideration primarily to the extended left hand side, root-to-frontier, linear, non-deleting tree transducers (Maletti et al., 2009), and we particularly make use of tree-to-string transducers.

Formally, an extended left hand side, root-to-frontier, tree-to-tree transducer is a 5-tuple $(Q, \Sigma, \Delta, q_{start}, \mathcal{R})$. Q is a finite set of states, Σ and Δ are the input and output tree alphabets, q_{start} is the start state, and $\mathcal{R}$ is the set of rules. We denote a pair of symbols, a and b by $a.b$, and the cross product of two sets A and B by $A.B$. Let X be the set of variables $\{x_0, x_1, ...\}$. Finally, let $T_\Sigma(A)$ be the set of trees with non-terminals from alphabet Σ and leaf symbols from alphabet A. Then, each rule $r \in \mathcal{R}$ is of the form $[q.t \rightarrow u].v$, where $q \in Q$, $t \in T_\Sigma(X)$, $u \in T_\Delta(Q.X)$ such that every $x \in X$ in u also occurs in t, and $v \in \Re^{\geq 0}$ is the weight of the rule.

We say $q.t$ is the left hand side of the rule and u is the right hand side. The transducer is *linear* iff no variable appears more than once on the right hand side. It is *non-deleting* iff all variables on the left hand side also occur on the right hand side. Iff every tree t on the left hand side is of the form $\sigma(x_0, ...x_n)$, where $\sigma \in \Sigma$ (i.e., it is a tree of depth ≤ 1), then the transducer is simply root-to-frontier, otherwise we say it has an *extended left hand side* with the added power to look a bounded depth into the tree at each step. Finally, for a *tree-to-string* transducer, Δ is an alphabet, and the right hand sides of the rules consist of finite tuples of elements taken from $\Delta \cup Q.X$.

A weighted tree transducer may define a probability distribution, either a joint distribution over input and output pairs or a conditional distribution of the output given the input. Here, we will use joint distributions, which can be defined by ensuring that the weights of all rules with the same state on the left-hand side sum to one. In this case, it can be helpful to view the transducer as simultaneously generating both the input and output, rather than the usual view of reading inputs and writing outputs.

3 Semantic parsing and meaning representation languages

The goal of semantic parsing is to assign formal meanings to natural language (NL) sentences, requiring a formal meaning language. Some systems use lambda expressions; others use variable free logical languages or functional languages (such as that of example 1 in the introduction). Here we deal with meaning representations (MRs) of the latter form where the bracketing makes the tree structure obvious [1] We refer to functions and predicates in the MR as either symbols or entities. Since MRs are trees, the language can be defined by a Regular Tree Grammar (a kind of CFG that generates trees). We refer to this grammar as the *meaning representation grammar* or MR grammar. Figure 3 shows a fragment of such a grammar and an MR parse. The parse is just the MR with each symbol labeled with its grammar rule. Like most systems, the MR grammar is one of our inputs.

4 The hybrid tree model

The idea of the hybrid tree model (Lu et al., 2008) is to start with the MR and apply a series of transformations to create a kind of parse tree for the NL. There are two types of transformation. The first determines word order by simultaneously choosing where to attach words (but not the particular words) and whether or not to swap the order of siblings (Figure 2a). Once the order is determined, word generating transformations are then applied to insert specific words in the determined locations (Figure 2b).

The hybrid tree includes parameters for the MR as well as the transformations in Figure 2 that relate words to meaning representations. The probability of each symbol in the MR is conditioned on the MR grammar rules that derive its parent symbol. Defining symbol probabilities in terms of their parents' grammar rules (as opposed to parent symbols as in a standard PCFG) distinguishes between functions and predicates with the same name but different semantics (Wong and Mooney, 2006).

To formally define the probability of the MR, let $paths$ be the set of paths from the root to every node in the MR where paths are represented using a variety of Gorn's notation (Gorn, 1962)[2]. Let $args_i$ be the set of indices of the children of the node at path i; and R_i be the grammar rule that derives the symbol at i according to the MR parse. Then, the following equation defines $P(MR)$.

$$P(MR) = P(R_\epsilon) \prod_{i \in paths} \prod_{j \in args_i} P(R_{i \cdot j} | j, R_i) \quad (1)$$

In other words, each node in the tree is generated according to the probability of the MR rule that derives it conditioned on (1) the MR rule R_i that derives its parent symbol and (2) its position j beneath that parent.

The hybrid tree model then re-orders and extends this basic skeleton to include the NL. The probability of this hybrid tree can be formally defined as follows if we let pat_i be the word order pattern used to generate the children of the node at path i, and $words_i$ be the indices of the words attached under the node at i.

$$P(\textit{NL-MR hybrid}) = P(R_\epsilon) \prod_{i \in paths} P(pat_i | R_i) \cdot \prod_{j \in args_i} P(R_{i \cdot j} | j, R_i) \prod_{k \in words_i} P(w_{i \cdot k} | R_i) \quad (2)$$

Note that $P(pat|R)$ and $P(w|R)$ correspond respectively to the weights on the word order and word generation transformations. In fact, equation 2 is a joint probability over not only the NL and MR pair but also the actual set of transformations chosen to produce the particular hybrid tree relating them.

5 Reframing the hybrid tree as a tree transducer

We now define a tree transducer that simultaneously generates an MR tree and NL string according to the joint probability defined by equation 2. We create separate states for each of the two transformation types (*order* states for word order selection and *word* states for word generation). In order to model the properties of the MR grammar (necessary for modeling equation 1), we create one additional state type for selecting MR children (*arg* states) and embed the MR grammar rules into the states so that each state is identified with exactly one grammar rule. Transitions between transducer states then simulate the action of the MR grammar as it generates a new MR tree. Notationally, we employ subscripts to indicate each state's basic type (*arg*, *order*, or *word*) and superscripts to indicate the associated MR grammar

[1] With a pre-parsing step, it may also be possible to represent lambda expressions with trees (see Liang et al. (2011)).

[2] I.e., paths are represented by strings where the empty string ϵ is the path to the root, and if i is a path and j is the index of a child of the node at i, $i \cdot j$ is the path to that child.

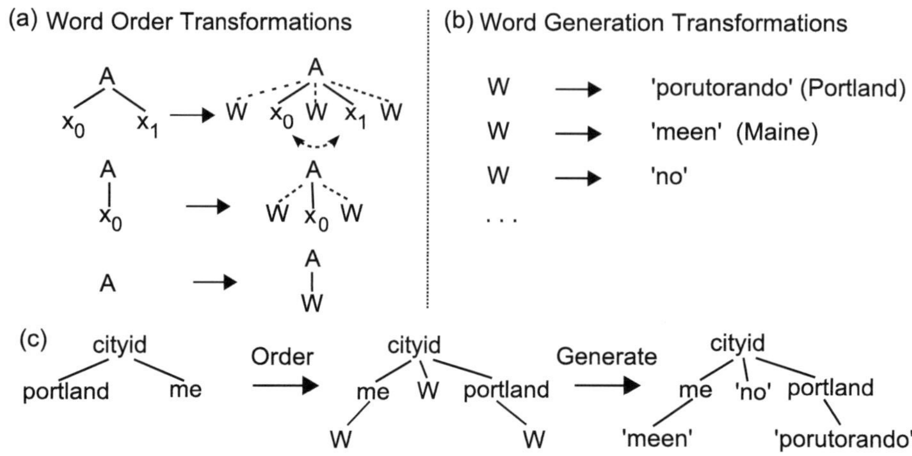

Figure 2: The two transformation types of the hybrid tree model and an example of their application. (a) Word order transformations simultaneously permute arguments and add W symbols where words should be attached. The dotted lines indicate that W symbols may or may not be attached in each of the possible locations, and siblings may or may not be swapped. Each possible configuration of sibling orderings and W attachments corresponds to a single transformation. Thus there are 4 different transformations for the case where A has one child, and 16 for when it has 2. In the case where A has no children, word attachment is not optional. (b) Word generation replaces each W symbol with actual words. (c) The series of transformations from example MR *cityid(portland,me)* to produce a parse for the Japanese equivalent of 'portland, maine'.

rule, so that, for instance, state $q^R_{\textbf{order}}$ is an *order* state associated with MRL grammar rule R.

Figure 3 presents a graphical representation of the basic state transitions of the transducer, where the states for each grammar rule are clustered inside dotted lines beneath its associated grammar rule label. The transducer begins in an *arg* state and proceeds as follows. First, the *arg* state selects the next child by transitioning to an *order* state corresponding to the MR rule that generates the appropriate child. The *order* state then chooses the appropriate word order pattern and transitions to the *word* and *arg* states associated with that same grammar rule[3]. The *word* states proceed to generate words one at a time in a loop and finally terminate the string. Then the *arg* state begins the cycle over again by transitioning to the *order* of the next child in the MR tree.

Table 1 lists the actual transducer rule types. Rule probabilities are conditioned on the state on the left hand side. Thus, since states identify both their function and the grammar rule of the current MR node, rule weights correspond directly to the terms in equation 2: $P(R_{i\cdot j}|j, R_i)$, $P(pat|R)$, and $P(w|R)$.

[3]Note that only *arg* states are permitted to transition to states for different grammar rules.

5.1 Source tree language model: $P(R_{i\cdot j}|j, R_i)$

Rule type 1 in Table 1 begins the process by transitioning from start state $q_{\textbf{start}}$ to $q^R_{\textbf{order}}$, where the grammar rule R ranges over those rules with the start symbol S on the left hand side. Choosing exactly which $q^R_{\textbf{order}}$ to transition to corresponds to the decision of choosing the root symbol of the MR tree (the symbol generated by R), and these transducer rules define the $P(R_\epsilon)$ term in equation 1, i.e., the probability of the grammar rule corresponding to the root symbol of the MR tree.

For each pair of MR grammar rules R^p and R^c, we add a transducer rule of the form of rule type 2 that transitions from the states associated with R^p to those for R^c if R^c generates a valid child of the symbol generated by R^p. Thus, the choice of state transition here corresponds to choosing the child of the last generated symbol of the input tree. State $q^{R^p}_{\textbf{arg},i}$ selects the ith argument of the current function in the MR without generating anything in the input tree. With rules described in the next section, state $q^{R^c}_{\textbf{order}}$ then writes the symbol to the input tree specified by MR grammar rule R^c.

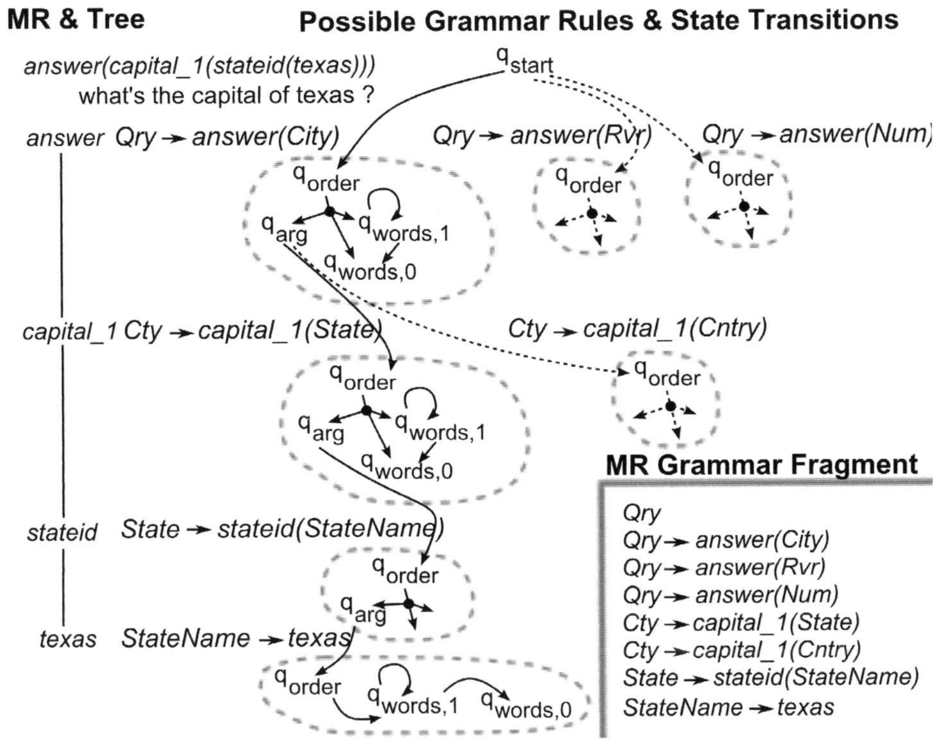

Figure 3: State transitions selecting appropriate grammar rules for generating an MR. Solid arcs indicate a state transition was taken; dotted lines are alternatives. States are divided up into disjoint sets and associated with a specific MR rule. Transitioning between state sets implicitly chooses an MR rule. The rules lined up with the MR tree to the left constitute an MR parse. The bottom right shows the grammar fragment corresponding to this portion of the transducer.

Since the state on the left encodes the rule of the parent and the argument number, and the state on the right the child rule, the weights for transducer rules of type 2 define $P(R_{i \cdot j}|j, R_i)$ in equation 1.

5.2 Order decisions: $P(pat|R)$

Word ordering decisions are made with the aid of preprocessing step that adds W symbols to the input tree wherever words can be attached. These symbols are just a convenience: it is easier to design rules where every output structure has a counterpart in the input. The symbols are removed later in a postprocessing step (also using a tree transducer). Attachment decisions are then made by deciding which of these W symbols to replace with the empty string (no attachment) or a string of words.

We add transducer rules of the form of rule type 3 in Table 1 for each MR grammar rule R^f, to define the selection of one of the word order patterns of the hybrid tree. These rules simply enumerate the conjunction of all the possible word attachment patterns and argument order decisions. Binary sequence i indicates the word attachment portion of the hybrid tree pattern, where each bit is either 1 indicating an attachment, or 0 for a decision not to attach. For an n argument function, there are $n+1$ such choices, requiring an $n+1$ bit sequence, where i_k is the decision for the kth position. Argument order is indicated by j, a permutation of the numbers $0, 1, ...n-1$, and j_k is the kth number in the permutation, indicating which argument appears at position k. State $q^{Rf}_{\mathbf{words},1}$ generates the words for f, state $q^{Rf}_{\mathbf{words},0}$ replaces the symbol W with the empty string, and the states $q^{Rf}_{\mathbf{arg},k}$ select the grammar rule with which to generate the kth child. When there is only a single child W, no decisions about argument order or child attachment are needed; rule type 4 always generates words for these constants.

$$q_{\textbf{start}}.x_0 \rightarrow q^{R}_{\textbf{order}}.x_0 \quad (1)$$

$$q^{R^p}_{\textbf{arg},i}.x_0 \rightarrow q^{R^c}_{\textbf{order}}.x_0 \quad (2)$$

$$q^{R^f}_{\textbf{order}}.f(w_0, x_0, w_1, x_1, w_2, ...x_{n-1}, w_n) \rightarrow q^{R^f}_{\textbf{words},i_0}.w_0 \; q^{R^f}_{\textbf{arg},j_0}.x_{j_0} \; q^{R^f}_{\textbf{words},i_1}.w_1 \; q^{R^f}_{\textbf{arg},j_1}.x_{j_1} \; q^{R^f}_{\textbf{words},i_2}.w_2 \; ... \; q^{R^f}_{\textbf{arg},j_{n-1}}.x_{j_{n-1}} \; q^{R^f}_{\textbf{words},i_n}.w_n \quad (3)$$

$$q^{R^f}_{\textbf{order}}.f(w_0) \rightarrow q^{R^f}_{\textbf{words},1}.w_0 \quad (4)$$

$$q^{R}_{\textbf{words},1}.x_0 \rightarrow word_k \; q^{R}_{\textbf{words},1}.x_0 \quad (5)$$

$$q^{R}_{\textbf{words},1}.x_0 \rightarrow word_k \; q^{R}_{\textbf{words},0}.x_0 \quad (6)$$

$$q^{R}_{\textbf{words},0}.W \rightarrow \epsilon \quad (7)$$

Table 1: Seven transducer rule types for three classes of transformation. (1)-(2) define $P(R_{i\cdot j}|j, R_i)$, (3)-(4) define $P(pat|R_i)$, and (5)-(7) define $P(w|R_i)$.

The following input tree and output string pair is illustrates an intermediate computation produced by interleaving these two kinds of ordering rules with the argument selection rules of the previous section, and applying them to the example in Figure 2:

$$q^{R^{cityid}}_{\textbf{order}}.cityid(W, portland(W), W, me(W), W) \stackrel{*}{\Rightarrow} q^{R^{cityid}}_{\textbf{words},0}.W \; q^{R^{me}}_{\textbf{words},1}.W \; q^{R^{cityid}}_{\textbf{words},1}.W \; q^{R^{portland}}_{\textbf{words},1}.W \; q^{R^{cityid}}_{\textbf{words},0}.W$$

The weights on these rules define the conditional probability $P(pat|R)$, where pat is one of the patterns of the word transformations illustrated in Figure 2.

5.3 Word generation: $P(w|R)$

Rule types 5 and 6 in Table 1 define the conditional probability of a word $word_k$ given an MR grammar rule, and rule type 7 terminates generation by generating W in the input and ϵ in the output. Using the same example as in the previous section, this yields 5 W symbols in the input tree and the string 'meen no porutorando' in the output.

$$q^{R^{cityid}}_{\textbf{words},0}.W \stackrel{*}{\Rightarrow} \epsilon$$

$$q^{R^{me}}_{\textbf{words},1}.W \stackrel{*}{\Rightarrow} \text{`meen'} \; \epsilon$$

$$q^{R^{cityid}}_{\textbf{words},1}.W \stackrel{*}{\Rightarrow} \text{`no'} \; \epsilon$$

$$q^{R^{portland}}_{\textbf{words},1}.W \stackrel{*}{\Rightarrow} \text{`porutorando'} \; \epsilon$$

$$q^{R^{cityid}}_{\textbf{words},0}.W \stackrel{*}{\Rightarrow} \epsilon$$

5.4 Derivation weights and the joint probability distribution

The transducer applies the rules from the three classes of transformation in Table 1 to ultimately produce an MR-NL pair. The probability of this derivation is essentially the same quantity as that of the hybrid tree of the original model (shown in equation 2).

6 An extension: head-switching

Reordering siblings allows the hybrid tree to capture a large number of word orders, but it is still constrained by the hierarchy of the tree. This constraint reduces the search space but also prevents the model from learning some word orders. Figure 4 illustrates with trees from the following Japanese sentence meaning *what's the highest point in the USA?* (the third line gives the correct alignment of words to components of the gold MR, which cannot be learned by the hybrid tree):

beikoku no	*mottomo takai*	*chiten*	*wa nan desu ka*
america's	most high	point	what is
loc(america)	*highest()*	*place()*	*answer()*

To address this problem, we modify the transducer to allow it to rotate parents with their children in addition to re-ordering siblings. This change is easy within the transducer framework but would be difficult in the original implementation, requiring a complete reworking of the training and decoding algorithms. In the original transducer, rules oper-

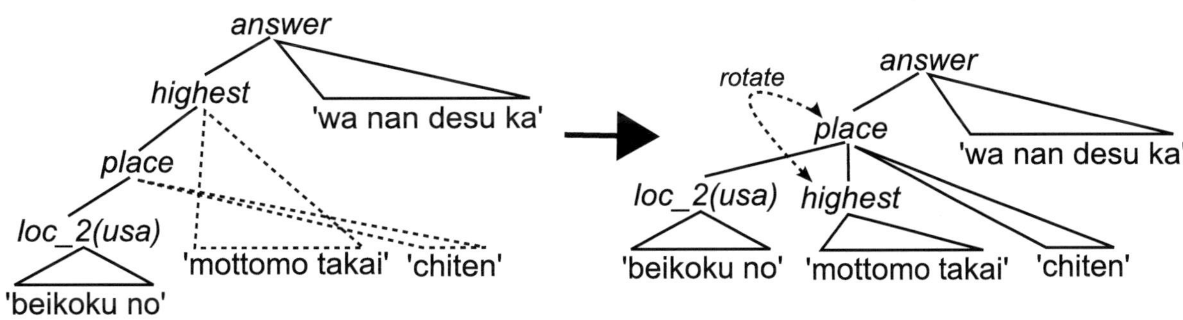

Figure 4: An example from Japanese illustrating head-switching. The tree on the left attempts (and fails) to generate the target sentence from the gold meaning representation. Switching *highest* and *place* allows the correct MR-NL map.

ate on tree fragments of depth ≤ 1. We implement the change using extended left-hand-side transducers, which can operate on larger fragments as long as the depth is bounded (Maletti et al., 2009). In particular, we introduce rules like the following:

$$q^{R^p}_{\mathbf{order}}.p(w^p_0, c(w^c_0, x^c_0, w^c_1), w^p_1) \rightarrow q^{R^c}_{\mathbf{words},i_0}.w^c_0$$
$$q^{R^p}_{\mathbf{words},i_1}.w^p_0\ q^{R^c}_{\mathbf{arg},0}.x^c_0\ q^{R^p}_{\mathbf{words},i_2}.w^p_1\ q^{R^c}_{\mathbf{words},i_3}.w^c_1$$

This rule begins the word generation process simultaneously for both the parent and child, reordering the words to simulate the new nesting structure, and then proceeds to choose the child function's argument. We add similar rules for the various cases where the child and parent have multiple arguments.

7 Varitional Bayes parameter estimation

Tree transducer derivations are themselves trees, allowing for the computation of inside and outside probabilities much as for the derivation trees of PCFGs. EM can then be applied in much the same way as for PCFGs, substituting the tree-to-string derivation algorithm for standard PCFG parsing (Graehl et al., 2008). Note that while EM maximizes the likelihood of the training data, items not observed during training receive zero probability, limiting the ability of models to generalize to new data sets. Furthermore, many items that are actually present in the training data are only seen a very few times, which can lead to a poor estimate of their distribution in the target data set. Bayesian estimation techniques such as Variational Bayes (VB) address these problems by allowing us to place a prior probability over the parameters, which particularly influence parameter estimates for sparse items and, depending on the choice of prior, may also assign some non-zero probability to unseen items.

We give a high-level outline of how a Dirichlet prior can be incorporated into tree transducer training using Variational Bayes, drawing heavily on the essential similarity of inside-outside for PCFGs and training for tree transducers. We direct the reader to Kurihara and Sato (2006) for the details of PCFG training using VB, and to Graehl et al. (2008) for the full treatment of the basic EM algorithm for tree transducers, on which our VB training algorithm is closely based. See Bishop (2006) for a general introduction to VB and Beal (2003) for a derivation of VB as applied to Dirichlet-multinomials.

The objective of training is to find an estimate for the weights θ of the transducer rules given some symmetric Dirichlet prior with hyperparameter α and observed pairs of natural language sentences W and meaning representation trees Y.

$$p(\theta|\alpha, W, Y) = \frac{p(W, Y, \theta|\alpha)}{p(W, Y|\alpha)} \quad (8)$$

The tree transducer defines the probability $p(W, X, Y|\theta)$, where X is a vector of derivations such that $x_i \in X$ is the derivation from MRL tree $y_i \in Y$ to NL string $w_i \in W$. We put a symmetric Dirichlet prior over θ so that the probability $p(\theta|\alpha)$ follows directly from the definition of the Dirichlet distribution. Thus, computing the denominator of equation 8 involves integrating out θ and X.

$$p(W, Y|\alpha) = \int p(W, X, Y|\theta)p(\theta|\alpha)dXd\theta$$

However, this integral is intractable, so instead, following from Variational Bayes, we make an approximation $q(X, \theta)$ for the posterior probability $p(X, \theta|W, Y, \alpha)$.

$$\begin{aligned}\log p(W, Y|\alpha) &= \log \int p(W, X, Y, \theta|\alpha) dX d\theta \\ &= \log \int q(X, \theta) \frac{p(W, X, Y, \theta|\alpha)}{q(X, \theta)} dX d\theta \\ &\geq \int q(X, \theta) \log \frac{p(W, X, Y, \theta|\alpha)}{q(X, \theta)} dX d\theta \\ &= \mathcal{F}\end{aligned}$$

We can minimize the KL divergence between $q(X, \theta)$ and $p(W, Y|\alpha)$ by maximizing the lower bound $\mathcal{F}$, called the variational free energy. Since $\mathcal{F}$ is a function of q, this amounts to maximizing q.

Following from Kurihara and Sato (2006)'s treatment of PCFGs, we employ the mean field approximation that assumes the posterior is well approximated by a factorized function $q(X, \theta) = q_1(X)q_2(\theta)$, which treats the derivations X and the rule weights θ as independent. This allows us to maximizing q by alternately updating parameters for q_1 with q_2 fixed, and then updating parameters for q_2 with q_1 fixed, essentially in the same manner that E and M steps alternate in EM. The mathematical derivation of the modified inside-outside algorithm then follow directly from Kurihara and Sato (2006).

In practice, VB requires only a slight modification to the basic EM algorithm, and we refer the reader to Graehl et al. (2008) for the details of EM for tree transducers. As in inside-outside for PCFGs, the E-step involves computing estimated rule counts, weighted using inside and outside probabilities. The M-step resolves to calculating the vector parameters of the multinomial distributions over transducer rules using these count estimates. That is, if θ_s is a multinomial parameter vector for transducer rules with state s on the left hand side, $\theta_{s,k}$ is its kth component (i.e., the weight of the kth rule with s on the left hand side), and $c_{s,k}$ is the corresponding expected count, we have the following equation for straight EM.

$$\theta_{s,k} = \frac{c_{s,k}}{\sum_{k'} c_{s,k'}}$$

Incorporating a Dirichlet prior with parameter α using our VB approximation simply requires replacing this ratio with the following alternative quantity τ, where Ψ is the digamma function.

$$\tau_{s,k} = \exp\left(\Psi(c_{s,k} + \alpha) - \Psi\left(\sum_{k'} c_{s,k'} + \alpha\right)\right)$$

For each step of EM, the updated τ vectors from the previous M-step are then used to compute the expected counts c during the current E-step.

8 Experimental setup

We use Tiburon (May and Knight, 2006), a tree transducer toolkit, to train our transducer using 40 iterations of its inside-outside-like EM training procedure, and modify it slightly to include the mean field VB approximation for a symmetric Dirichlet prior over the multinomial parameters as just described.

Decoding is handled the same by Tiburon for both training procedures, producing the MR input tree with the tree transducer derivation that maximizes the probability over derivations of equation 2.

In keeping with the original hybrid tree, we run 100 iterations of IBM alignment model 1 (Brown et al., 1993) to initialize the word distribution parameters. Also in keeping with Lu et al. (2008), we use the standard noun phrase list from the given language to help initialize the word distributions for their counterparts in the meaning representation language.

9 Results

To evaluate our models, we use the the GeoQuery corpus, a standard benchmark data set. The corpus contains English sentences (questions about U.S. geography) paired with an MR in a database query language, 250 of which were translated into Japanese (among other languages) yielding two training sets using the same MRs. For testing we run 10-fold cross validation, using the standard train and test splits of Wong and Mooney (2006), and micro-average our performance metrics across folds.

We measure performance using precision, recall, and f-score (the harmonic mean of precision and recall) as standardly defined in the semantic parsing literature. Recall is simply the raw accuracy: the percentage of correct parses found out of all test sentences (where a parse is considered correct if it retrieves the same results from the GeoQuery database

System	English			Japanese		
	Pre.	Rec.	F1	Pre.	Rec.	F1
UBL-s	80.8	80.4	80.6	80.6	80.5	80.6
WASP	**95.4**	70.0	80.8	**92.0**	74.4	**82.9**
Lu-uni	80.2	71.2	75.4	79.7	73.6	76.5
Lu-dis	91.5	72.8	81.1	87.6	76.0	81.4
trs	88.3	69.6	77.9	82.4	67.2	74.0
trsVB	82.0	82.0	82.0	78.0	78.0	78.0
hs	89.5	71.6	79.6	84.3	68.8	75.8
hsVB	82.8	**82.8**	**82.8**	80.8	**80.8**	80.8

Table 2: Performance of the various models on the multilingual section of GeoQuery.

as the gold MR). Precision is the percentage of correct parses out of all sentences for which we find any parse at all.

Table 2 compares our models' performance to previously published results. We list two versions of our model: the direct adaptation of the hybrid tree and the transducer with parent-child swapping rules. We train each version with both standard EM and the VB approximation (hyperparameter 0.1). The other state-of-the-art systems shown are: 1) two versions of the original hybrid tree (Lu et al., 2008): *Lu-uni*, which uses a unigram distribution over words, and is therefore the most similar to our transducer implementation, and *Lu-dis*, the best-performing version, which uses a mixture of unigram and bigram model with discriminative re-ranking; 2) WASP (Wong and Mooney, 2006), which uses a synchronous grammar approach; and 3) UBL-s (Kwiatkowski et al., 2010), the model with the highest published raw accuracy (recall).

The transducers are competitive with the state-of-the-art, especially when using VB. VB smooths the parameter estimates, so there are no parse failures in the test set due to unseen words or functions; precision, recall, and f-score all reduce to raw accuracy. The basic transducer with VB has higher accuracy (recall) than all other models except for UBL-s, which does better on Japanese. The head-switch transducer is better still, with the highest recall on both languages. Although the improvement over the basic transducer is small, we anticipate that using the transducer framework will allow us to easily explore many other possible extensions that could increase performance further.

As expected, the basic EM-trained transducer gets numbers that are similar, though not identical, to Lu-uni. The main reason for the discrepancy is that Lu et al. (2008) use custom smoothing methods for the source tree language model and word probabilities. While these could be emulated in a transducer, we instead use a more general approach, VB, with better pay-off. Lu-uni was the simplest model presented by Lu et al. (2008), yet applying VB to our transducer implementation yields a fully generative model whose performance rivals their best-performing system that uses discriminative reranking.

10 Conclusion

In this paper, we have shown how to formulate semantic parsing as tree transduction. This formulation is more general than previous approaches and allows us to exploit the rich literature on transducers, including theoretical results as well as standard algorithms and toolkits. We focused here on extended left hand side, root-to-frontier, linear, non-deleting, tree-to-string transducers (Maletti et al., 2009), using them to reformulate and extend an existing model (Lu et al., 2008). Although we tried only one simple extension, our purely generative model already outperforms all previous models on raw accuracy, with comparable f-score. Since the transducer framework makes modifications easy, we anticipate further gains in future, especially if we add a discriminative reranking step as in Lu et al. (2008). We also hope to investigate other transducer classes. Finally, we note that working with a general framework encourages the development of algorithms that are widely applicable, even if developed for a particular application. The VB training algorithm presented here is just one example of such a contribution.

Acknowledgments

We would like to thank Wei Lu and Jon May for generously providing source code and support for the hybrid tree parser and Tiburon, respectively. Also, this work was supported under the Australian Research Council's Discovery Projects funding scheme (project number DP110102506).

References

Matthew J. Beal. *Variational Algorithms for Approximate Bayesian Inference*. PhD thesis, Gatsby Computational Neuroscience unit, University College London, 2003.

Christopher M. Bishop. *Pattern Recognition and Machine Learning*. Springer, 2006.

Benjamin Borschinger, Bevan K. Jones, and Mark Johnson. Reducing grounded learning tasks to grammatical inference. In *Proc. of the Conference on Empirical Methods in Natural Language Processing*, 2011.

Peter F. Brown, Stephen A. Della Pietra, Vincent J. Della Pietra, and Robert L. Mercer. The mathematics of statistical machine translation: Parameter estimation. *Computational Linguistics*, 19:263–311, 1993.

Saul Gorn. Processors for infinite codes of shannon-fano type. In *Symp. Math. Theory of Automata*, 1962.

Jonathon Graehl, Kevin Knight, and Jon May. Training tree transducers. *Computational Linguistics*, 34, 2008.

Rohit J. Kate and Raymond J. Mooney. Using string-kernels for learning semantic parsers. In *Proc. of the 21st International Conference on Computational Linguistics and the 44th annual meeting of the ACL*, pages 913–920, 2006.

Kevin Knight and Jonathon Greahl. An overview of probabilistic tree transducers for natural language processing. In *Proc. of the 6th International Conference on Intelligent Text Processing and Computational Linguistics*, 2005.

Kenichi Kurihara and Taisuke Sato. Variational bayesian grammar induction for natural language. In *Proc. of the 8th International Colloquium on Grammatical Inference*, 2006.

Tom Kwiatkowski, Luke Zettlemoyer, Sharon Goldwater, and Mark Steedman. Inducing probabilistic ccg grammars from logical form with higher-order unification. In *Proc. of the Conference on Empirical Methods in Natural Language Processing*, 2010.

Percy Liang, Michael I. Jordan, and Dan Klein. Learning dependency-based compositional semantics. In *Association for Computational Linguistics (ACL)*, 2011.

Wei Lu, Hwee Tou Ng, Wee Sun Lee, and Luke S. Zettlemoyer. A generative model for parsing natural language to meaning representations. In *Proc. of the Conference on Empirical Methods in Natural Language Processing*, 2008.

Andreas Maletti, Jonathan Graehl, Mark Hopkins, and Kevin Knight. The power of extended top-down tree transducers. *SIAM J. Comput.*, 39:410–430, June 2009.

Jon May and Kevin Knight. Tiburon: A weighted tree automata toolkit. In *Proc. of International Conference on Implementation and Application of Automata*, 2006.

W.C. Rounds. Mappings and grammars on trees. *Mathematical Systems Theory 4*, pages 257–287, 1970.

J.W. Thatcher. Generalized sequential machine maps. *J. Comput. System Sci. 4*, pages 339–367, 1970.

Yuk Wah Wong and Raymond J. Mooney. Learning for semantic parsing with statistical machine translation. In *Proc. of Human Language Technology Conference / North American Chapter of the Association for Computational Linguistics Annual Meeting*, pages 439–446, New York City, NY, 2006.

Luke. S. Zettlemoyer and Michael Collins. Learning to map sentences to logical form: Structured classification with probabilistic categorial grammars. In *Proc. of the 21st Conference on Uncertainty in Artificial Intelligence*, 2005.

Parsing in Parallel on Multiple Cores and GPUs

Mark Johnson
Centre for Language Sciences and Department of Computing
Macquarie University
Sydney, Australia
Mark.Johnson@MQ.edu.au

Abstract

This paper examines the ways in which parallelism can be used to speed the parsing of dense PCFGs. We focus on two kinds of parallelism here: Symmetric Multi-Processing (SMP) parallelism on shared-memory multicore CPUs, and Single-Instruction Multiple-Thread (SIMT) parallelism on GPUs. We describe how to achieve speed-ups over an already very efficient baseline parser using both kinds of technology. For our dense PCFG parsing task we obtained a 60×speed-up using SMP and SSE parallelism coupled with a cache-sensitive algorithm design, parsing section 24 of the Penn WSJ treebank in a little over 2 secs.

1 Introduction

Performance improvements in computing come increasingly through greater parallelism. This paper studies ways in which this parallelism can be used to improve the speed of PCFG parsing in computational linguistics. Although we focus on a particular task here (constructing the inside chart for dense PCFGs), we expect the insights to be generally applicable.

There are three major ways in which computers are becoming more parallel. At the broadest level, it is now common to network large numbers of computers together into clusters, which are controlled by software such as the Message-Passing Interface (MPI) (Gropp et al., 1999) or Map-Reduce (Lin and Dyer, 2010).

At a lower level, even commodity computers typically have multiple processors or cores, which are connected by a high-speed bus to a shared memory, enabling Symmetric Multi-Processor (SMP) parallelism. SMP parallelism is typically controlled by software such as OpenMP (Chapman et al., 2007) or pThreads. Commodity computers also possess on-chip parallel floating point vectorised arithmetic units. The CPUs we used here have SSE (Streaming SIMD Extensions) vectorised arithmetic, where SIMD abbreviates "Single-Instruction Multiple-Data". SSE is enabled by appropriate compiler flags.

Finally, Graphics Processor Units (GPUs) are increasingly becoming both less specialised and more powerful (on many commodity machines they can perform more floating-point operations per second than the CPU); as we will see here, a GPU can yield quite respectable parsing performance. GPUs are designed for massively parallel Single-Instruction Multiple-Thread (SIMT) programs; each GPU thread is comparatively slow, but the GPU can execute hundreds or thousands of threads in parallel. GPUs are typically programmed using tools such as OpenCL or CUDA (Sanders and Kandrot, 2011).

We concentrate on SMP multi-core and GPU parallelism in this paper because we expect that communication latencies with conventional networking hardware make parallel parsing with networked clusters impractically inefficient. Communication latency is much less of a problem with shared memory SMP and GPU parallelism as communication takes place over the machine's high-speed bus.

A base-line approach for exploiting parallelism in parsing is simply to parse different sentences in parallel on separate instances of the parser. This is likely to be the best way to exploit parallelism with networked clusters and SMP multi-core machines when parsing a large corpus of sentences off-line. However, there are situations where parsing must be on-line; e.g., when parsing is a component of a system that interacts with users, or with machine-learning algorithms such as Metropolis-Hastings Sampling that update after each sentence is parsed (Johnson et al., 2007).

2 Previous work

Parsing in parallel has been studied for several decades, and space constraints prevent anything but a cursory summary here. Hill and Wayne (1991) identified the basic data dependencies between the entries in chart cells, and discussed their implications for parallel parsing. Nijholt (1994) also studied the order in which chart cells can be filled, and discusses its implications for a variety of shift-reduce and chart-based parsing algorithms. Thompson (1994) pointed out that the close relationship between CKY parsing and matrix multiplication can be exploited for parsing in parallel; we rely on similiar observations below. Ninomiya et al. (1997) described an agenda-based approach for parallelising CKY parsing on large SMP machines, while Bordim et al. (2002) describes the implementation of a CKY parser on Field-Programmable Gate Arrays (FPGAs). Sandstrom (2004) describes a parallel implementation of Earley's parsing algorithm. Dunlop et al. (2010) stresses importance of minimising cache misses in the design of efficient parsing algorithms and described how to restructure the CKY algorithm to reduce grammar constant,[1] which as we show below has a dramatic impact on parallel SMP parsing.

3 The CKY algorithm for dense PCFGs

This section introduces the basic CKY parsing algorithm used below. Here we're assuming that the grammar is in Chomsky-Normal Form (CNF), i.e., all rules in the grammar are of the form $A \rightarrow B\,C$

```
for i in 0, . . ., n−1:
  for a in 0, . . ., m−1:
    C[i,i+1,a] = T[W[i],a]

for gap in 2, . . ., n:
  for i in 0, . . ., n−gap:
    k = i+gap
    for a in 0, . . ., m−1:
      C[i,k,a] = 0
      for j in i+1, . . ., k−1:
        for b in 0, . . ., m−1:
          for c in 0, . . ., m−1:
            C[i,k,a] += R[a,b,c]∗C[i,j,b]∗C[j,k,c]
```

where:

m	number of nonterminals in grammar
n	length of input string
$W[i]$	word in input string at position i
$T[w, A]$	probability of $A \rightarrow w$
$R[A, B, C]$	probability of $A \rightarrow B\,C$
$C[i, k, A]$	inside probability of A spanning (i, k)

Figure 1: Pseudo-code for baseline CKY algorithm for dense PCFG parsing and an explanation of the variables used in the algorithm. All arrays are in row-major order, except that the inside chart C uses specialised indexing to take advantage of the fact that the first string position index is always less than the second.

[1]The "grammar constant" refers to the variation in parsing time as a function of grammar size. Standard analyses study how parsing time varies as a function of sentence length while the grammar is held constant; the choice of grammar affects parsing time in such analyses via a "grammar constant".

```
for i in 0, . . ., n−1:
  for a in 0, . . ., m−1:
    C[i,i+1,a] = T[W[i],a]

for gap in 2, . . ., n:
  for i in 0,..,n−gap:
    k = i+gap
    BC = Zero
    for j in i+1, . . ., k−1:
      for b in 0, . . ., m−1:
        for c in 0, . . ., m−1:
          BC[b,c] += C[i,j,b]∗C[j,k,c]
    for a in 0, . . ., m−1:
      C[i,k,a] = 0
      for b in 0, . . ., m−1:
        for c in 0, . . ., m−1:
          C[i,k,a] += R[a,b,c]∗BC[b,c]
```

where:

m	number of nonterminals in grammar
n	length of input string
$W[i]$	word in input string at position i
$T[w, A]$	probability of $A \rightarrow w$
$R[A, B, C]$	probability of $A \rightarrow B\,C$
$C[i, k, A]$	inside probability of A spanning (i, k)
BC	an $m \times m$ scratch array
Zero	an $m \times m$ array of zeros.

Figure 2: Pseudo-code for the factored CKY algorithm for dense PCFG parsing.

or $A \rightarrow w$, where A, B and C are nonterminals and w is a terminal (Aho and Ullman, 1972). In this paper we focus on *dense* PCFGs, i.e., where most of the possible rules have positive probability. Dense grammars with these properties occur in applications such as unsupervised grammar induction. While sparse grammars have many important applications, there are many different possible patterns of sparsity, and the optimal parsing algorithm may depend on the particular sparsity pattern the grammar instantiates. Moreover, it is extremely difficult to develop effective search procedures (such as heuristic $A^\star$ search) for dense grammars in which most rules have approximately equal probabilities, so this is a situation where a brute-force exhaustive calculation of the kind that the algorithms discussed below may well be the preferred approach.

We focus on CKY-style pure bottom-up parsing algorithms here because of their simplicity, and with dense grammars their performance often equals or exceeds that of more complex parsing algorithms: if every possible chart cell will be filled with a non-trivial probability, a predictive parsing algorithm (such as the Earley algorithm) will have to instantiate every cell anyway.

We also focus on the construction of the "inside chart" here, i.e., $\mathrm{P}(A \Rightarrow^+ w_i, \ldots, w_{j-1})$ for each nonterminal A and $0 \leq i < j < n$, where n is the number of words in the input string. Constructing the inside chart is the crucial $O(n^3)$ step of the Inside-Outside algorithm for estimating PCFGs (Charniak, 1993), and this computation is typically the rate-limiting computation in PCFG sampling algorithms (Johnson et al., 2007) as well. By replacing a sum with a max, the same algorithms can be used to constuct the Viterbi chart, from which a most probable parse tree can be extracted in $O(n^2)$ time, so again the Inside computation is the rate-limiting step. Because our grammar is dense we used pre-allocated fixed-sized arrays to hold the grammar rules and the inside chart, thus minimising expensive memory management and pointer arithmetic (in our experience unless great care is taken while coding, these costs can dominate parsing time).

Figure 1 presents pseudo-code for the baseline CKY parsing algorithm. The main part of the algorithm consists of six nested loops. All these loops except the outermost (over the *gap* variable) can be freely reordered without affecting correctness. We experimented with a large number of reorderings of these variables; in preliminary experiments we found that the order presented here resulted in fastest parsing.[2]

Dunlop et al. (2010) point out that the algorithm in Figure 1 requires a grammar rule retrieval for each mid-point *j* of each (i, k) span (as well as each combination of nonterminals *a*, *b* and *c*), and show how to reduce this by factoring the algorithm as shown in Figure 2. This changes the "grammar constant" as mentioned above. They point out that this also improves the cache efficiency on modern CPUs. As we experimentally confirm below, the improvement that factoring brings can be dramatic.

4 Multi-core SMP parallelism using OpenMP

It is straight-forward to parallelise both the baseline and factored algorithms for multi-core SMP machines using OpenMP (Chapman et al., 2007). OpenMP programs are C++ programs with pragmas that indicate which loops should be parallelised. We experimented with several alternative reorderings of the loops and using an optimised matrix-algebra package (Guennebaud et al., 2010), but these did not improve parsing speed.

Developing OpenMP versions of the baseline and factored CKY algorithms is relatively straightforward. The main technical challenges in parallelising the CKY algorithm are synchronising the parallel threads and ensuring that different parallel threads do not interfere with each other. This is achieved by using synchronisation constructs with implicit barriers, *thread-private* temporary variables and constructs that ensure that updates to shared variables occur as *atomic* operations.

For the baseline CKY algorithm we constructed three parallel variants by parallelising (i) the outermost two for loops (over the *i* and *a* variables) using the OpenMP *parallel for* construct, (ii) the inner three loops (over *j*, *b* and *c*) using a *parallel for reduction* into a temporary variable, and (iii) a variant in which all loops (except the one involving the *gap* variable) are parallelised.

For the factored CKY algorithm we constructed three parallel variants by parallelising (i) the outermost for loop (involving the *i* variable), (ii) the innermost variables (involving the *j*, *b*, *c* and *a* variables), and (iii) a variant in which all loops (except the one involving the *gap* variable) are parallelised. Multiple *thread-private* instances of the *BC* variable are required when the outermost loops are parallelised, and we used the OpenMP *atomic* construct to synchronise updates to *BC* when the innermost loops were parallelised.

5 A CUDA GPU kernel for PCFG parsing

We experimented with several approaches to GPU parsing based on standard GPU matrix algebra packages (NVIDIA Corporation, 2010) but results were extremely disappointing; the resulting code ran orders of magnitude slower than the baseline CPU-based parser above. In order to obtain results competitive with the multi-core SMP algorithms described above we developed custom GPU programs. Our GPU subroutines or *kernels* were written in CUDA, which is a C++ dialect for specifying programs consisting of CPU code and GPU kernels (Sanders and Kandrot, 2011).

We focused on developing a CUDA implementation of the factored CKY algorithm here. CUDA programming is considerably more complicated than OpenMP programming, and we don't claim to have produced an optimal program here; additional experimentation could yield further speed improvements.[3]

A straight-forward translation into CUDA kernels of the baseline and factored algorithms above produced disappointing results: it ran approximately *200 times slower* than the factored CKY parser described above. A quick survey of the CUDA devel-

[2] These reorderings do not affect the theoretical complexity of the CFG parsing algorithm; it is still $O(n^3)$, where n is the length of the sentence being parsed. However, the loop ordering may affect the opportunities for SIMD optimisation and memory cache efficiency, since reordering the loops affects locality of memory access.

[3] We also experimented with CUBLAS, a CUDA implementation of BLAS (Basic Linear Algebra Subprograms), which we found yielded performance one to two orders of magnitude slower than our custom CUDA kernels. However, a new version of CUBLAS was released after this paper was submitted; this new version has several technical improvements that may enable it to be effective for PCFG parsing.

oper message boards showed that direct translations of CPU-based programs often perform poorly, and for good performance one needs to redesign the algorithms to take advantage of the specialised GPU hardware.

Computation on NVIDIA GPUs is organised into *blocks* of up to 1,024 parallel threads. A single CUDA *launch* starts up to hundreds of thousands of blocks; modern GPUs can execute several hundred thread blocks in parallel (the remainder are queued). Just as with SMP programming, the chief technical challenges in CUDA programming are synchronising the parallel threads and ensuring that different parallel threads do not interfer with each other. CUDA programming is more difficult than SMP programming because each individual GPU processor is much less capable than a CPU (CUDA programming is done using a restricted subset of C++), and data access must follow a very tightly prescribed set of rules if it is to perform reasonably efficiently.

Unlike on a regular CPU, the memory on a GPU has a complex organisation which the CUDA programmer must be aware of; the following sketch omits many details. *Global memory* is comparatively slow but accessible to all threads of all blocks; it is used to store persistent information and communicate between threads in different blocks; we store the inside chart C in global memory. *Texture memory* is a kind of global memory that permits more efficient cached read-only access; we stored the grammar rules R and the terminal probabilities T in texture memory. *Shared memory* is local to and accessible to all threads in the same block and is much faster than global memory; we stored (a local copy of) the *BC* array in shared memory. In addition, we also use *thread-local variables* to maintain local state and accumulate intermediate results within a single thread.

Our CUDA kernels consist of over 500 lines of code, so we only sketch them here. Our central data structures are the chart C, the rule probabilities R and the lexical probabilities T. Our CUDA implementation starts by launching a kernel that copies the terminal probabilities T for each of the words W into the chart C; this is easily and completely parallelised, and takes very little time.

Then it computes the chart one diagonal at a time in parallel. It launches one or more kernels for each value of *gap* in $2, \ldots, n$. If $n - gap$ is small enough then all of the chart entries $C[i, k, \cdot]$ (where $k = i + gap$) can be computed by a single thread block, and only one kernel launch is required. But for larger values of *gap* we decompose the computation into multiple thread blocks based on the mid string position j and store intermediate results in global memory; a second kernel launch is used to reduce these into the chart entries $C[i, k, \cdot]$.

A major goal in designing the CUDA kernel was to perform the sum

$$BC[b,c] \mathrel{+}= C[i,j,b] * C[j,k,c]$$

in the factored CKY algorithm as efficiently as possible. In order to achieve this we first copy all of the relevant chart entries $C[i, j, \cdot]$ and $C[j, k, \cdot]$ from global memory into the faster shared memory (this can be done in parallel), and then accumulate the results into BC, which is also stored in shared memory. This step can also be done completely in parallel.

Finally, we compute the chart entries $C[i, k, a]$ for all $k = i + gap$ and all a in parallel. If $n - gap$ is small enough that the computation can be done in one thread group then this is done only using shared memory, otherwise temporary results are stored in global memory so they are visible to other thread blocks. The reduction

$$C[i,k,a] \mathrel{+}= R[a,b,c] * BC[b,c]$$

in the factored CKY algorithm is also tricky, as it requires a double sum over b and c. In order to do this we generalised the parallel tree-based reduction algorithm presented in Harris (2010) to compute all of the chart entries $C[i, k, \cdot]$ as a parallel reduction.

6 Evaluation on a dense PCFG

We experimented with a number of different grammars, but because the results were generally similiar, we only describe one experiment here. The strings we parsed consist of the yields of the 1,345 trees in section 24 of the Penn WSJ treebank. Any word that did not appear 5 or more times in sections 2–21 was replaced with ⋆UNC⋆. We constructed a dense PCFG with 32 non-terminals (i.e., 32,768 binary rules) and random rule probabilities, which might be typical of the initial grammar in an unsupervised

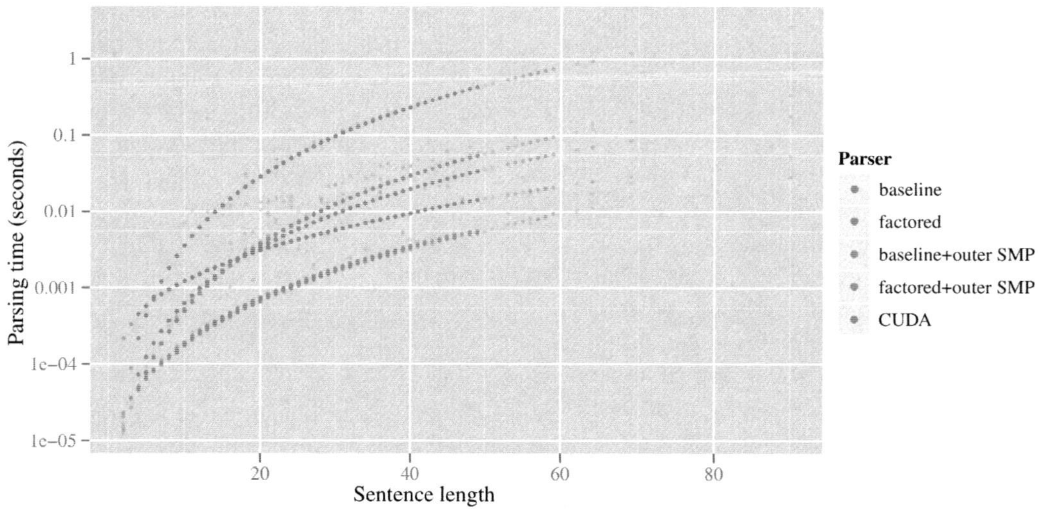

Figure 3: Parsing times as a function of sentence length on 1,345 sentences from section 24 of the Penn WSJ treebank for the baseline CYK parser, the baseline parser with SMP parallelism (outer loops parallelised), the factored CKY parser, the factored CKY parser (outer loops parallelised), and the CUDA implementation of the factored CKY parser.

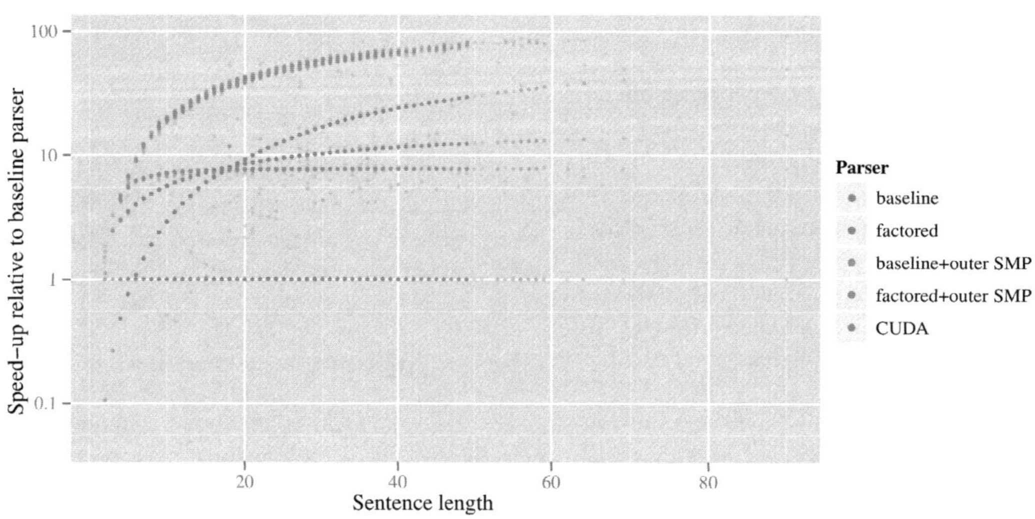

Figure 4: Speed-up relative to the baseline CKY parser as a function of sentence length on 1,345 sentences from section 24 of the Penn WSJ treebank for the baseline parser with SMP parallelism (outer loops parallelised), the factored CKY parser, the factored CKY parser (outer loops parallelised), and the CUDA implementation of the factored CKY parser.

Parser	Sentences/sec	Speed-up
Baseline	11	1.0
(i) outer parallel	84	7.5
(ii) inner parallel	11	1.0
(iii) both parallel	29	2.6
Factored	122	11.0
(i) outer parallel	**649**	**60.0**
(ii) inner parallel	27	2.4
(iii) both parallel	64	5.7
CUDA	206	18.4

Table 1: Parsing speeds of the various algorithms on 1,345 sentences from section 24 of the Penn WSJ treebank. Speed-up is relative to the baseline parser.

PCFG induction system using the Inside-Outside algorithm or a Metropolis-Hastings sampler. We used single-precision floating-point arithmetic in all experiments, and multiplied the terminal rule probabilities $A \to w$ by 10^4 to avoid underflow.

We ran our experiments on a single node of an SGI Altix XE 320 cluster with two quad-core 3.0GHz Intel Harpertown CPUs, a 1600MHz front side bus, 16GB DDR2-800 memory and two NVIDIA Fermi s2050 GPUs, each with 448 CUDA cores running at 1.15GHz (we only used one GPU here). We used the CUDA 3.2 toolkit and gcc 4.4.4. We selected compiler flags that enabled full optimisation, including enabling SSE3 SIMD floating-point vector subsystem, as prior experiments showed that this significantly speeds all calculations.

Table 1 presents the results of our experiments. We repeated all of our experiments twice in succession and report the time of the second run here; however, run-times varied by less than 1% between the two runs. Figures 3 and 4 depict parsing time and speed-up as a function of sentence length respectively (in order to avoid overloading the graphs, they only show a subset of the results). It's important to recognise that even our baseline parser is very fast (averaging 11 sentences/second), and both our SMP and GPU implementations were significantly faster.

7 Conclusions

We obtained large speedups over an already very fast baseline parser using both multi-core SMP and CUDA parallelism. Parallelising the outer loops in the multi-core SMP algorithms seems to be extremely effective; we see speed-ups close to the theoretical maximum of 8 times for both the baseline and factored algorithms. Parallelising the inner loops is devastating to performance, perhaps because it interfers with cache optimisation and SSE3 SIMD vectorisation (turning off the SSE SIMD vectorisation in these cases did not improve performace). The factored algorithm with parallelised outer loops performed fastest in our experiments, but the CUDA implementation was next best, parsing faster than all of the parallelised baseline algorithms.

As Figure 4 makes clear, the speed-up obtained by both the CUDA and factored algorithm with parallelised outer loops relative to the baseline increases with sentence length (with the CUDA speed-up increasining fastest), which suggests that parallelisation helps most where it is most needed, i.e., on longer sentences.

It is surprising that the CUDA implementation did not outperform the best SMP implementation. Perhaps this is because our SMP implementation uses highly-optimised, OpenMP/SSE3-parallelised code and can exploit the powerful Xeon CPUs. It is also possible that our dense PCFG parsing task is "too easy" to take full advantage of the power of the GPU; the entire corpus of 1,345 sentences took just a few seconds to parse, and it's possible that initialisation and data-transfer from the host machine to the GPU imposed a significant overhead. It would be interesting to repeat the experiments described here with a grammar that is one or two orders of magnitude larger.

In fact, as Figures 3 and 4 make clear, the CUDA implementation is comparatively slow on short sentences; for sentences of length 5 or less, the CUDA implementation is slower than even the baseline parser, which is consistent with the hypothesis that initialisation and data-transfer are imposing significant performance costs. It would be interesting to repeat these experiments on a larger corpus with larger and perhaps sparser grammars. It also might be more efficient to parse more than one sentence in parallel on a single GPU, which might keep more of the CUDA cores busy more of the time, although we did not try this here.

There are several lessons to draw from these results. First, parallelisation does not always produce speed-ups; indeed parallelising the inner loops did not improve performance on either the baseline or factored algorithms. Second, parsing algorithms that perform well on conventional CPUs may need considerable redesign in order to produce good results on GPUs. Third, as the impressive performance of the factored algorithm shows, good algorithm design is of crucial importance.

Finally, this is an area where both the hardware and software are still rapidly improving. The number of cores in a single multi-core processor is likely to increase rapidly; already it is possible to obtain commodity machines with 24 cores. The improvement in GPU technology is if anything even more dramatic: as well as increasing the number of processors, new GPUs are equipped with more flexible buses that permit more complex kinds of data parallelism and ease programming. On the software side, up-coming versions of OpenMP will permit a greater range of efficient reduction constructs, which may permit us to avoid using the relatively expensive *atomic* synchronisation primitive. For GPUs, upcoming versions of CUDA will provide a variety of parallel programming libraries (including for sparse matrix algebra), which may make it easier to write considerably more efficient parallel parsing algorithms. Thus it is reasonable to expect a dramatic improvement in parallel parsing in the near future.

Acknowledgments

I'd like to thank the reviewers for their thoughtful comments and suggestions. This work was supported was supported under the Australian Research Councils Discovery Projects funding scheme (project number DP110102593).

References

Alfred V. Aho and Jeffery D. Ullman. 1972. *The Theory of Parsing, Translation and Compiling; Volume 1: Parsing*. Prentice-Hall, Englewood Cliffs, New Jersey.

Jacir Bordim, Yasuaki Ito, and Koji Nakano. 2002. Accelerating the CKY parsing algorithm using FPGAs. In Sartaj Sahni, Viktor Prasanna, and Uday Shukla, editors, *High Performance Computing HiPC 2002*, volume 2552 of *Lecture Notes in Computer Science*, pages 41–51. Springer Berlin / Heidelberg.

Barbara Chapman, Gabriele Jost, and Ruud van der Pas. 2007. *Using OpenMP: Portable Shared Memory Parallel Programming*. The MIT Press, Cambridge, Massachusetts.

Eugene Charniak. 1993. *Statistical Language Learning*. The MIT Press, Cambridge, Massachusetts.

Aaron Dunlop, Nathan Bodenstab, and Brian Roark. 2010. Reducing the grammar constant: an analysis of CKY parsing efficiency. Technical Report CSLU-2010-02, Oregon Health and Science University.

William Gropp, Ewing Lusk, and Anthony Skjellum. 1999. *Using MPI: Portable Parallel Programming with the Message Passing Interface*. The MIT Press, Cambridge, Massachusetts.

Gaël Guennebaud, Benoît Jacob, et al. 2010. Eigen v3.0beta2. http://eigen.tuxfamily.org.

Mark Harris. 2010. Optimizing parallel reduction in CUDA. Technical report, NVIDIA Corporation.

Jane C. Hill and Andrew Wayne. 1991. A CYK approach to parsing in parallel: a case study. In *Proceedings of the twenty-second SIGCSE technical symposium on Computer science education*, SIGCSE '91, pages 240–245, New York, NY, USA. ACM.

Mark Johnson, Thomas Griffiths, and Sharon Goldwater. 2007. Bayesian inference for PCFGs via Markov chain Monte Carlo. In *Human Language Technologies 2007: The Conference of the North American Chapter of the Association for Computational Linguistics; Proceedings of the Main Conference*, pages 139–146, Rochester, New York, April. Association for Computational Linguistics.

Jimmy Lin and Chris Dyer. 2010. *Data-Intensive Text Processing with MapReduce*. Morgan and Claypool.

Anton Nijholt. 1994. Parallel approaches to context-free language parsing. In Geert Adriaens and Udo Hahn, editors, *Parallel Natural Language Processing*, pages 135–167. Ablex Publishing Corporation.

Takashi Ninomiya, Kentaro Torisawa, Kenjiro Taura, and Jun'ichi Tsujii. 1997. A parallel CKY parsing algorithm on large-scale distributed-memory parallel machines. In *The Proceedings of the Pacific Association for Computational Linguistics (PACLING 97)*, pages

223–231, Tokyo. Department of Informatics, Meisei University.

NVIDIA Corporation, 2010. *CUDA CUBLAS Library*, PG-05326-032 v02 edition.

Jason Sanders and Edward Kandrot. 2011. *CUDA by Example: An Introduction to General-Purpose GPU Programming*. Addison-Wesley, Upper Saddle River, New Jersey.

Greg Sandstrom. 2004. A parallel extension of Earleys parsing algorithm. Technical report, Earlham College.

Henry Thompson. 1994. Parallel parsers for context-free grammars: Two actual implementations compared. In Geert Adriaens and Udo Hahn, editors, *Parallel Natural Language Processing*, pages 168–187. Ablex Publishing Corporation.

Using Language Models and Latent Semantic Analysis to Characterise the N400m Neural Response

Mehdi Parviz, Mark Johnson
Department of Computing
Macquarie University
Sydney, Australia
{mehdi.parviz,mark.johnson}
@mq.edu.au

Blake Johnson, Jon Brock
Macquarie Centre for Cognitive Science
Macquarie University
Sydney, Australia
{blake.johnson,jon.brock}
@mq.edu.au

Abstract

The N400 is a human neuroelectric response to semantic incongruity in on-line sentence processing, and implausibility in context has been identified as one of the factors that influence the size of the N400. In this paper we investigate whether predictors derived from Latent Semantic Analysis, language models, and Roark's parser are significant in modeling of the N400m (the neuromagnetic version of the N400). We also investigate significance of a novel pairwise-priming language model based on the IBM Model 1 translation model. Our experiments show that all the predictors are significant. Moreover, we show that predictors based on the 4-gram language model and the pairwise-priming language model are highly correlated with the manual annotation of contextual plausibility, suggesting that these predictors are capable of playing the same role as the manual annotations in prediction of the N400m response. We also show that the proposed predictors can be grouped into two clusters of significant predictors, suggesting that each cluster is capturing a different characteristic of the N400m response.

1 Introduction

There is increasing interest in using computational models to help understand on-line sentence processing in humans. New experimental techniques in psycholinguistics and neurolinguistics are producing rich data sets that are difficult to interpret using standard techniques, and it is reasonable to ask if the statistical models developed in computational linguistics can be helpful here (Keller, 2010).

The N400 is a human brain response to semantic incongruity or implausibility that has been widely studied in psycholinguistics and neurolinguistics. A large set of factors has been shown to influence the strength of the N400, including intra- and extra-sentential context (Kutas and Federmeier, 2000; Van Petten and Kutas, 1990). Here we study the strength of the N400 as measured by magnetoencephalography (MEG) (so the signal we study is sometimes called the N400m) on sentence-final words in a variety of "constraining" and "non-constraining" sentential contexts (Kalikow et al., 1977). For example, *Her entry should win first prize* is an example of a constraining-context sentence, while *We are speaking about the prize* is a non-constraining context sentence (target words are underlined in this paper).

This paper shows that language models of the kind developed in computational linguistics can be used to help identify the factors that determine the strength of the N400. We investigate a number of different kinds of predictors constructed from a variety of language models and Latent Semantic Analysis (LSA) to determine how well they describe the N400. The first set of predictors is derived from LSA, which is a method for analysing relationships between a set of documents and the terms they contain (Mitchell et al., 2010). LSA has been successfully applied in similar research areas such as eye-movements and word-by-word reading times. Our experiments show that these predictors are significant in modeling the N400m response. The second set of predictors is that proposed by Roark et al. (2009), which is derived from the Roark (2001) parser and designed to be useful in psycholinguistic modeling. While one of these predictors is statistically significant (lexical entropy), we observe that many of the prime-target word pairs appearing in our experimental sentences do not appear in the 1-million word Wall Street Journal - Penn Treebank (WSJ-PTB) corpus that this parser is trained on, so this model cannot capture the association between these words. This leads us to experiment with language models trained on larger corpora.

Using the SRI-LM toolkit (Stolcke, 2002) we construct a 4-gram language model based on the Gigaword corpus (Graff et al., 2005), and show that predictors based on it are also statistically significant predictors of the N400m. However, we go on to observe that many of the prime-target word pairs in our experimental sentences are separated by more than 3 words, so there is no way that a 4-gram language can capture the relationship between these words.

This leads us to develop a "pairwise-priming" language model that captures longer-range dependencies between pairs of words. This pairwise priming model is based on the IBM Model 1 machine translation model (Brown et al., 1993), and trained using a similar EM-procedure. We train this model on Gigaword, and show that predictors based on this model are also statistically significant.

Finally, we compare the predictors from the various language models with the original manual classification of the experimental sentences into "constraining" or "non-constraining" contexts given by Kalikow et al. (1977). We show that the predictor based on LSA is statistically significant even when the human "constraining" annotations are present as a factor. We also find out that the 4-gram model and the pairwise-priming model are highly correlated with this manually-annotated context predictor. These findings suggest that the predictors can be grouped into two clusters i.e., one that contains the LSA predictor, and another one that contains the manually-annotated context predictor, the pairwise-priming predictor, the 4-gram language model predictor, and the lexical entropy predictor.

2 Related work

One recent strand of work uses machine-learning to perform "mind reading", i.e., predicting what a subject is seeing or thinking based on information about their neural state. Mitchell et al. (2008) have trained a classifier that identifies the word a subject is thinking about from input derived from fMRI images of the subject's brain, and Murphy et al. (2009) have constructed a similar classifier that takes EEG signals as its input. Abstractly then, this work uses classifiers that take as input information about a subject's brain state to predict the (linguistic or visual) stimulus the subject is exposed to.

A more traditional line of research tries to identify factors that cause particular psycholinguistic or neurolinguistic responses. For example, Hale (2001), Bicknell and Levy (2009) and many others show that predictors derived from on-line parsing models can help explain eye-movements and word-by-word reading times. Abstractly, this work involves building statistical models which take as input properties of the stimuli presented to the subject (i.e., the sentence they are hearing or reading) to predict their psychological or neural responses. The goal of this line of research is to establish which properties of the input sentence or the parsing model's state determine the psychological or neural responses, rather than just predicting these responses as accurately as possible.

The work that is perhaps most closely related to this paper is by Bachrach (2008), who tries to identify which factors are responsible for specific activation patterns in fMRI brain images of subjects reading natural texts. He found that predictors derived from the Roark (2001) parser were most explanatory. Roark et al. (2009) have subsequently identified a number of such predictors; we investigate these in our analysis below.

3 Experimental data

The N400 is a component of time-locked EEG signals known as *event-related potentials* (ERP) that occurs in sentences containing semantically unexpected or anomalous words (Kutas and Hillyard, 1980). It is so-called because it is a negative-going deflection that peaks around 400 milliseconds post-stimulus onset. There has been considerable research into the factors that influence the strength of the N400. Inverse word frequency and contextual unpredictability (e.g., as quantified by Cloze probability) are both significant predictors of the N400 (Van Petten and Kutas, 1990). The strength of the N400 is sometimes taken to be a measure of the "effort" required for "semantic integration" in on-line sentence processing.

For example, there is a much stronger N400 at the target word *building* in the sentence *a sparrow is a kind of building* than there is at the word *bird* in *A sparrow is a kind of bird*. Interestingly, while the N400 is sensitive to the global context in which the target word is located, the N400 does not seem to be directly sensitive to the truth conditions of the sentence (Kutas and Federmeier, 2000). Thus sentential negation does not seem to directly affect the strength of the N400. For example, a strong N400 occurs in *A sparrow is not a kind of building*, as compared to *A sparrow is not a kind of bird*.[1] This observation inspired the pairwise-priming model discussed below.

As previously mentioned, N400s are usually studied using EEG. In this work we use magnetoencephalography (MEG) to study the N400; the signal we analyse here is sometimes called the N400m to indicate its provenance. We used MEG because this study is the first step in a project to use statistical models to study the neural mechanisms involved in language processing, and MEG seems ideally suited to this work.

MEG is a non-invasive technique for imaging electrical activity in the brain by measuring the magnetic fields it produces using arrays of SQUIDs (superconducting quantum interference devices). It has a number of potential advantages over competing technologies such as fMRI and EEG. For example, MEG has a much faster response latency than fMRI because MEG directly measures electrical activity while fMRI measures the hemodynamic response caused by that activity. Because magnetic fields are less distorted than electric fields by the scalp and the skull, MEG has a better spatial resolution than EEG, which should help us localise neural processes more accurately.

However in this first study we do not exploit these advantages of MEG, but just average the signals collected by 12 MEG sensors over a time window containing the target word. This produces a single numeric value for each trial which we call the N400m, which we model below.

Stimuli consisted of 180 sentences drawn from the list published by Kalikow et al. (1977) and synthesized using TextAlound (NextUp, Clemmons, NC). They were presented to 22 listeners via insert earphones (Etymotic Research Inc. Model ER-30, Elk Grove Village, IL). There were 90 examples of "constraining context" sentences, i.e., with predictable endings (e.g. *He got drunk in the local bar*) and 90 examples of "non-constraining context" sentences, i.e., with unpredictable endings (e.g. *He hopes Tom asked about the bar*). Each target word appears both in a constraining context sentence and in a non-constraining context sentence. To maintain vigilance during the experiment, there were 10 catch trials consisting of sentences containing the word *mouse*, where subjects were required to press a button. The three types of sentences were presented in randomized order.

MEG amplitudes were extracted from a cluster of 12 sensors over the left hemisphere where the largest N400m responses were obtained over subjects. Amplitudes in femto-Tesla were averaged over these sensors and over a time window of 400-600 ms. MEG data was digitized with a sample rate of 1000 Hz and were filtered offline with a bandpass of 0.1 to 40 Hz. Data was epoched relative to the onset of the terminal word of each sentence using a 1200 ms window (-200 to 1000 ms).

4 Hypothesis-testing

Our goal in this paper is to identify the factors that significantly influence the N400m, rather than predicting the N400m responses as accurately as possible. We use statistical methods for hypothesis testing (e.g., likelihood ratio tests) to do this. The next two paragraphs explain why we use these methods rather than the held-out test set methodology usually used in computational linguistics.

The goal of most statistical modeling in computational linguistics is prediction, which in turn involves generalisation to previously-unseen contexts, and the held-out test set methodology measures the ability of a model to generalise correctly. One might attempt to identify significant predictors by build-

[1] The fact that the conditional probability of a word in a sentence does not depend on that sentence's veracity may be relevant here.

ing the best machine learning model of the N400m one can, and see which features that model incorporates. However, many state-of-the-art machine learning methods are capable of exploiting very large sets of possibly redundant features and control over-learning via regularisation. The fact that such a method includes a particular predictor as a feature does not mean that this predictor is significant; e.g., the method may assign the feature a very small (but non-zero) weight. Intuitively, the goal of a machine-learning method is to make the most accurate prediction possible, not to identify the significant predictors.

Instead, we formulate the problem as one of *hypothesis testing*. The statistical techniques used to do this involve the construction of linear models similar to those used in some machine-learning methods, but they also permit us to perform hypothesis testing and posterior inference. For example, by computing confidence intervals on a predictor's weight in such a model we can see whether that confidence interval contains zero, and hence whether the predictor is significant. We also use likelihood-ratio tests below to assess the significance of predictors.

We used a quantile plot to identify outliers in the N400m data; four responses were removed, and one response value was unavailable, producing five missing values for the N400m in total. The N400m data range from -1,054 to 1,362 with a mean of 14, a variance of 172 and an interquartile range of (-68,100). We normalised the N400m responses by subtracting the per-subject mean and then dividing by the per-subject standard deviation. The N400m responses are the values of the `Response` variable in the models below.

4.1 Parser-based predictors

The Roark (2001) parser is an incremental syntactic parser based language model that uses rich lexical and syntactic contexts as features to predict its next moves. It uses a beam search to explore the space of partial parse trees. Bachrach (2008) found that predictors derived from the incremental state of the Roark parser were highly significant in models of their fMRI data; this work motivated us to explore predictors like lexical entropy and lexical surprisal based on the Roark parser here. Roark et al. (2009) describes in detail how a variety of predictors can be extracted from the Roark parser. We used Roark's parser to compute these predictors for the target words in all 180 of the experimental sentences used here.

4.2 4-gram language model predictors

We used the Gigaword corpus which contains 1.5 billion words in 82 million sentences (Graff et al., 2005). We trained a 4-gram language model with Kneser-Ney smoothing and unigram caching using the SRI-LM toolkit (Stolcke, 2002). We used this language model to estimate the conditional probabilities of the target words given the words in their preceding context in all of the experimental sentences. These probabilities are often very close to zero, can vary by many orders of magnitude, and may be highly skewed. In order to mitigate the effect of these properties we used log ratio of these probabilities to the unigram probabilities of the target words as predictors. This is called the `P4` predictor below.

4.3 Pairwise-priming predictors

By definition, a 4-gram language model only captures dependencies between words within a 4 word window. However, many of the experimental sentences contain dependencies between words that are more than 3 words apart. For example, in "constraining context" sentences such as *The steamship left on a <u>cruise</u>* or *We camped out in our <u>tent</u>*, the priming words *steamship* and *camped* do not appear in the 4 word window containing the target words *cruise* and *tent*, but these priming words are intuitively responsible for making the corresponding target words more likely.

It is plausible that "trigger" language models can capture these kinds of longer-range dependencies (Goodman, 2001). There are a wide variety of such models, and it would be interesting to see which of them are most useful for constructing N400 predictors. Rather than using an existing trigger language model, we develop our own "pairwise-priming" language model here. This model is especially designed to identify longer-range interactions between pairs of words, which we believe is consistent with the description given by Kutas and Federmeier (2000) of the factors influencing the strength of the N400. This model is also especially simple to estimate using a variant of the EM training procedure for IBM Model 1.

The model is a simple additive mixture model. Each word w_i in a sentence is associated with a *context* C_i which is used to predict w_i. The context C_i is a bag containing the words that precede w_i in the sentence and that also belong to a 60,000 word vocabulary W, plus 5 instances of a special *null word* token.[2] The vocabulary consists of the most frequent words in the Gigaword corpus, from which 60 open-class stop words have been removed. Our model is parameterised by a matrix $\boldsymbol{\theta}$, where $\theta_{w_i|w_j}$ is the probability of generating w_i given that w_j is in the context C_i. The probability $\mathrm{P}(w_i \mid C_i)$ of generating w_i in the context C_i is approximated by an additive mixture:

$$\mathrm{P}(w_i \mid C_i) \quad = \quad \frac{1}{|C_i|} \sum_{w_j \in C_i} \theta_{w_i|w_j}.$$

This is a conventional generative model in which each word w_i is generated from the words in its context C_i, and it is straightforward to estimate the pairwise-priming parameters $\boldsymbol{\theta}$ using a variant of the IBM Model 1 EM training procedure. This EM procedure computes a sequence of estimates $\boldsymbol{\theta}^{(1)}, \boldsymbol{\theta}^{(2)}, \ldots$ that approximate the maximum likelihood estimate $\widehat{\boldsymbol{\theta}}$ for $\boldsymbol{\theta}$. The M-step computes $\boldsymbol{\theta}^{(t+1)}$ from the expected pairwise counts obtained using $\boldsymbol{\theta}^{(t)}$:

$$\theta^{(t+1)}_{w'|w} \quad = \quad \frac{\mathrm{E}_{\boldsymbol{\theta}^{(t)}}[n_{w',w}]}{\sum_{w'' \in \mathcal{W}} \mathrm{E}_{\boldsymbol{\theta}^{(t)}}[n_{w'',w}]}.$$

The E-step calculates the expected counts $\mathrm{E}_{\boldsymbol{\theta}^{(t)}}[n_{w',w}]$ given the current parameters $\boldsymbol{\theta}^{(t)}$:

$$\mathrm{E}_{\boldsymbol{\theta}^{(t)}}[n_{w',w}] \quad = \quad \sum_{\substack{i:\, w_i = w' \\ j:\, w_j = w, w_j \in C_i}} \frac{\theta^{(t)}_{w'|w}}{\sum_{w'' \in C_i} \theta^{(t)}_{w'|w''}}$$

In the E-step we skip the first four w_i words of every sentence because we think their contexts C_i are likely to be too small to be useful, but we did no experiments to test this. We initialised with the uniform distribution (by using an argument analogous to the one for IBM model 1 it is easy to show the log-likelihood surface is convex), and ran 10 EM iterations on the Gigaword corpus to estimate $\widehat{\boldsymbol{\theta}}$.

[2]The null word token plays the same role here as it does in the IBM Model 1 machine translation model (Brown et al., 1993). Moore (2004) points out that including multiple null word tokens reduces the tendency of the IBM Model 1 to find spurious low-frequency associations; we found here that while including multiple null word tokens in the C_i is important, the results do not depend strongly on the number of null word tokens used.

Just as for the 4-gram models, we used the pairwise priming model to compute the conditional probability of the target words in the experimental sentences. Like the 4-gram models, we used log ratio of these probabilities to the probabilities of the target words as predictors. This is called the `Pq` predictor below.

4.4 Latent semantic analysis predictors

Another predictor used in applications such as modeling eye-movements and word-by-word reading times, is Latent Semantic Analysis (LSA). The basic idea of the LSA model is to create a "meaning representation" for words from a term-document co-occurrence matrix. Here we construct the model based on the co-occurrence of vocabulary and content-bearing words in a fixed-sized window of the Gigaword corpus (Graff et al., 2005). We used the 2,000 most-frequent words in the corpus as the content words and the 50,000 most-frequent words as the vocabulary. Each row in the matrix represents a vocabulary word, each column represents a content word, and each entry is the co-occurrence count $n_{i,j}$ of the ith vocabulary word and the jth content word within a window with 15 words length. The co-occurrence counts are normalised by dividing each $n_{i,j}$ by the sum of all the counts in the corresponding column:

$$w_{i,j} = \frac{n_{i,j}}{\sum_k n_{k,j}}$$

LSA performs dimensionality reduction using Singular Value Decomposition (SVD). In order to retain 99% of the total variance, we used 795 right eigenvectors of the normalised co-occurrence matrix. Following Mitchell et al. (2010), we used the LSA model to generate a numerical value indicating the "similarity" of the target word to the words in its preceding context as follows: Let W_1, W_2, $\cdots$, W_n denote vectors representing the context words and let W_t denote a vector representing the target in a given sentence.

$$\begin{matrix} W_1 & W_2 & \cdots & W_n & W_t \\ \begin{bmatrix} w_{1,1} \\ w_{1,2} \\ \vdots \\ w_{1,m} \end{bmatrix} & \begin{bmatrix} w_{2,1} \\ w_{2,2} \\ \vdots \\ w_{2,m} \end{bmatrix} & \cdots & \begin{bmatrix} w_{n,1} \\ w_{n,2} \\ \vdots \\ w_{n,m} \end{bmatrix} & \begin{bmatrix} w_{t,1} \\ w_{t,2} \\ \vdots \\ w_{t,m} \end{bmatrix} \end{matrix}$$

We multiply the context-word vectors element-wise to produce a single vector H representing the context as follows:

$$h_i = \prod_{j=1}^{n} w_{j,i}$$

Then the similarity of a target word to the context words is given by the cosine of the angle between H and W_t, i.e.:

$$\text{sim}(H, W_t) = \frac{H^T W_t}{\|H\| \| W_t\|}$$

We call $\text{sim}(H, W_t)$ the `LSA` predictor below.

5 Experimental Results

We normalised the N400m responses by subtracting the per-subject mean and then dividing by the per-subject standard deviation. Similarly, we normalised the values of predictors. We used the non-linear regression package mgcv v1.7-6 (Wood, 2006; Wood, 2011) distributed with the *R* statistical environment to predict the N400m response. We used the manually-annotated context predictor (`Context`) as a linear parametric predictor, and all the other types of predictors i.e., the 4-gram language model predictor (`P4`), the pairwise priming predictor (`Pq`), the LSA predictor, and the predictors based on Roark's parser, as penalized cubic spline functions (up to 20 degrees of freedom).

5.1 Models with one predictor

We first start with models with one predictor to find out which predictors are significant. Table 1 lists the significant predictors, where significance is determined by a likelihood ratio test. Of all the predictors described by Roark et al. (2009) only the `LexH` predictor (lexical entropy) is a significant predictor according to a likelihood-ratio test. Perhaps it should not be surprising that lexical entropy strongly predicts the N400m response; the lexical entropy is a measure of the predictive uncertainty of the target word, and the N400 is strongest in less predictive contexts.

Predictor	Df	p-value
Context	1	1.53e-11 ***
Pq	2.3479	4.84e-10 ***
P4	2.067	5.30e-10 ***
LexH	3.2197	1.75e-04 ***
LSA	1.6707	5.28e-04 ***

Table 1: P-values and degrees of freedom as determined by likelihood ratio test for non-linear regression models with only one predictor

	Context	Pq	P4	LexH
Pq	-0.76***			
P4	-0.76***	0.96***		
LexH	0.41***	-0.38***	-0.38***	
LSA	-0.15*	0.09	0.10	-0.06

Table 2: Correlation matrix of different types of predictor

5.2 Combining predictors

In this section, we combine all the predictors to create a single model. From the correlation matrix of the predictors (Table 2), we can see that some of these predictors are highly correlated. Not surprisingly, when we combined all the predictors we discovered that some of predictors are redundant. We performed backwards selection using p-values to drop insignificant predictors (Wood, 2011). In backwards selection, first we construct a model with all the predictors, then we drop the single predictor with the highest non-significant p-value from the model. We repeat re-fitting, dropping insignificant predictors until all remaining predictors are significant. The results of performing backwards selection show that only the manually-annotated context predictor and the LSA predictor are significant (Table 3):

```
Response ~ Context + LSA
```

In order to construct a model without the manually-annotated context predictor, we removed the manually-annotated context predictor from the model and re-performed backwards selection. The

Predictor	Df	p-value
Context	1	2.34e-10 ***
LSA	2.779	0.0186 *

Table 3: P-values and degrees of freedom of the predictors in the combined model after performing backwards selection

Predictor	Df	p-value
LSA	3.165	0.00405 **
Pq	1.987	0.01817 *
P4	2.158	0.04340 *

Table 4: P-values and degrees of freedom of the predictors in the combined model without the manually-annotated context predictor after performing backwards selection

results show that the combination of the pairwise priming predictor, the 4-gram language model predictor, and the LSA predictor are significant (Table 4):

`Response ~ LSA + Pq + P4`

In order to minimise the effect of collinearity of predictors, we applied PCA to find principal components of the predictors' space. In Table 5, the matrix of eigenvectors is shown. Treating the principal components as predictors, we performed backwards selection to find a set of significant principal components. In Table 6 the p-values of all the principal components are presented. After performing backwards selection, only the first two principal components are significant (Table 7):

`Response ~ PC1 + PC2`

As can be seen, in the first principal component (PC1) `Context`, `Pq` and `P4` are dominant, while in the second principal component `LSA` is dominant. We can conclude that proposed predictors can be grouped into two clusters; one that contains the LSA predictor, and another that contains the manually-annotated context predictor, the pairwise-priming predictor, the 4-gram language model predictor, and the lexical entropy predictor.

Hierarchical clustering also suggests that the set of predictors cluster into two groups. Figure 1 depicts a hierarchical clustering of the predictors based on Spearman's rank correlation (Myers and Well, 2003). As this figure shows, the similarity between

	PC1	PC2	PC3	PC4	PC5
Context	0.52	-0.01	0.10	0.85	0.01
Pq	-0.55	-0.09	-0.24	0.36	0.71
P4	-0.55	-0.07	-0.24	0.37	-0.71
LexH	0.33	0.05	-0.94	-0.10	-0.00
LSA	-0.10	0.99	0.01	0.07	0.01
Eigenvalue	2.92	0.98	0.76	0.29	0.04

Table 5: The principal components of the predictors' correlation matrix

	Df	p-value
PC1	1.000	2.23e-10 ***
PC2	5.230	0.00627 **
PC3	1.445	0.85781
PC4	1.000	0.59922
PC5	2.412	0.21918

Table 6: P-values and degrees of freedom for the principal components in the combined model before performing backwards selection

the LSA predictor and other predictors is close to zero.

6 Conclusions and future work

This paper has studied a variety of predictors of the N400m response derived from an incremental parsing model (Roark et al., 2009), from Latent Semantic Analysis, and from two language models trained on the Gigaword corpus (Graff et al., 2005). We found that many of the predictors derived from these models were significant, suggesting that these kinds of models may be useful for understanding the N400m response. We also examined combining predictors to build a single model.

We can summarize our results as follows:

- A wide range of predictors are significant predictors of the N400m response on their own:
  -the manually-annotated context predictor, `Context`
  -the LSA predictor, `LSA`
  -the lexical entropy predictor, `LexH`, based on Roark's parsing model
  -the 4-gram language model predictor, `P4`, and
  -the pairwise-priming predictor, `Pq`
- These predictors can be grouped into two clusters:

	Df	p-value
PC1	1.188	5.78e-14 ***
PC2	4.848	0.0052 **

Table 7: P-values and degrees of freedom for the principal components in the combined model after performing backwards selection

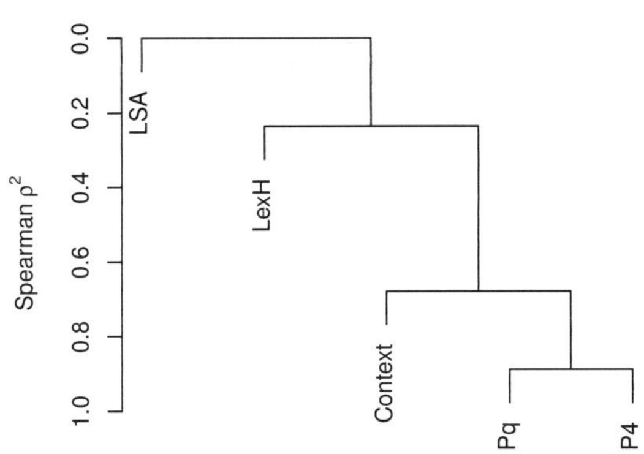

Figure 1: Hierarchical clustering of predictors, using square of Spearman's rank correlation as similarity measure

-1: The manually-annotated context predictor (`Context`), the 4-gram language model predictor (`P4`), the pairwise-priming predictor (`Pq`), and the lexical entropy (`LexH`), and
-2: The Latent Semantic Analysis predictor (`LSA`)

This latter result suggests that these two groups of predictors are capturing separate factors of the N400m response. Of course this work just scratches the surface in terms of possible applications of statistical language models to neurolinguistics. Clearly it would be interesting to apply a much wider variety of statistical models to the N400 data. Perhaps parsing models would do better if they could be trained on Gigaword-sized corpora. As we noted above, MEG is capable of producing rich temporal and spatial information about neural processes, presenting new opportunities for using statistical language models to help understand how language is instantiated in the human brain.

References

Asaf Bachrach. 2008. *Imaging Neural Correlates of Syntactic Complexity in a Naturalistic Context*. Ph.D. thesis, Massachusetts Institute of Technology, Cambridge, Massachusetts.

Klinton Bicknell and Roger Levy. 2009. A model of local coherence effects in human sentence processing as consequences of updates from bottom-up prior to posterior beliefs. In *Proceedings of Human Language Technologies: The 2009 Annual Conference of the North American Chapter of the Association for Computational Linguistics*, pages 665–673, Boulder, Colorado, June. Association for Computational Linguistics.

P. Brown, S. Della Pietra, V. Della Pietra, and R. Mercer. 1993. The mathematics of statistical machine translation: Parameter estimation. *Computational Linguistics*, 19(2).

Joshua Goodman. 2001. A bit of progress in language modeling. *Computer Speech and Language*, 14:403–434.

David Graff, Junbo Kong, Ke Chen, and Kazuaki Maeda. 2005. *English Gigaword Second Edition*. Linguistic Data Consortium, Philadelphia.

John Hale. 2001. A probabilistic Earley parser as a psycholinguistic model. In *Proceedings of the Second Meeting of the North American Chapter of the Association for Computational Linguistics*, volume 2, pages 159–166. Association for Computational Linguistics.

D. N. Kalikow, K. N. Stevens, and L. L. Elliott. 1977. Development of a test of speech intelligibility in noise using sentence materials with controlled word predictability. *The Journal ofthe Acoustical Society of America*, 61(5):1337–1351.

Frank Keller. 2010. Cognitively plausible models of human language processing. In *Proceedings of the ACL 2010 Conference Short Papers*, pages 60–67, Uppsala, Sweden, July. Association for Computational Linguistics.

Marta Kutas and Kara D. Federmeier. 2000. Electrophysiology reveals semantic memory use in language comprehension. *Trends in Cognitive Science*, 4(12):463–470.

Marta Kutas and Steven A. Hillyard. 1980. Reading senseless sentences: Brain potentials reflect semantic incongruity. *Science*, 207:203–208.

Tom M. Mitchell, Svetlana V. Shinkareva, Andrew Carlson, Kai-Min Chang, Vicente L. Malave, Robert A.

Mason, and Marcel Adam Just. 2008. Predicting human brain activity associated with the meanings of nouns. *Science*, 320:1191–1195.

Jeff Mitchell, Mirella Lapata, Vera Demberg, and Frank Keller. 2010. Syntactic and semantic factors in processing difficulty: An integrated measure. In *ACL*, pages 196–206.

Robert C. Moore. 2004. Improving IBM word-alignment Model 1. In *Proceedings of the 42nd Annual Meeting on Association for Computational Linguistics*, Stroudsburg, PA, USA. Association for Computational Linguistics.

Brian Murphy, Marco Baroni, and Massimo Poesio. 2009. EEG responds to conceptual stimuli and corpus semantics. In *Proceedings of the 2009 Conference on Empirical Methods in Natural Language Processing*, pages 619–627, Singapore, August. Association for Computational Linguistics.

Jerome L. Myers and Arnold D. Well. 2003. *Research Design and Statistical Analysis (second edition ed.)*. Lawrence Erlbaum.

Brian Roark, Asaf Bachrach, Carlos Cardenas, and Christophe Pallier. 2009. Deriving lexical and syntactic expectation-based measures for psycholinguistic modeling via incremental top-down parsing. In *Proceedings of the 2009 Conference on Empirical Methods in Natural Language Processing*, pages 324–333, Singapore, August. Association for Computational Linguistics.

Brian Roark. 2001. Probabilistic top-down parsing and language modeling. *Computational Linguistics*, 27(2):249–276.

Andreas Stolcke. 2002. SRILM - an extensible language modeling toolkit. In *Proceedings of the International Conference on Spoken Language Processing*, pages 901–904.

Cyma Van Petten and Marta Kutas. 1990. Interactions between sentence context and word frequency in event-related brain potentials. *Memory and Cognition*, 18(4):380–393.

S.N Wood. 2006. *Generalized Additive Models: An Introduction with R.* Chapman and Hall/CRC.

S. N. Wood. 2011. Fast stable restricted maximum likelihood and marginal likelihood estimation of semiparametric generalized linear models. *Journal of the Royal Statistical Society (B)*, 73(1):3–36.

A Forensic Authorship Classification in SMS Messages: A Likelihood Ratio Based Approach Using N-gram

Shunichi Ishihara
The Australian National University
School of Culture, History and Language
Department of Linguistics, Canberra ACT 0200 Australia
shunichi.ishihara@anu.edu.au

Abstract

Due to its convenience and low–cost, short message service (SMS) has been a very popular medium for communication for quite some time. Unfortunately, however, SMS messages are sometimes used in illicit acts, such as communication between drug dealers and buyers, extortion, fraud, scam, hoax, false reports of terrorist threats, and many more. This study is a forensic study on the authorship classification of SMS messages in the Likelihood Ratio (LR) framework with the N–gram modelling technique. The aims of this study are to investigate 1) how accurately it is possible to classify the authors of SMS messages; 2) what degree of strength of evidence (LR) can be obtained from SMS messages and 3) how the classification performance and the LRs are affected by the sample size for modelling. The resultant LRs are calibrated by means of the logistic regress calibration technique. The results of the classification tests will be rigorously assessed from different angles, using the techniques proposed for automatic speaker recognition and forensic voice comparison.

1 Introduction

We often come across news stories on so–called cyber crimes which take advantage of the high visual anonymity of, for example, email and SMS messages. In order to combat these cyber crimes, the Australian Government is currently trying to pass the Cybercrime Legislation Amendment Bill 2011 (hereafter, Cyber Law). This Cyber Law was introduced and read for the first time at the House of Representatives in June, 2011.[1] This legislation will enable police and intelligence agencies to instruct phone companies and internet carriers not to destroy sensitive information, such as text messages or emails from terrorists or criminals, that is important for investigations and prosecutions. This legislation also set the framework for Australia to join the Council of Europe Convention on Cybercrime, which more than 40 nations have joined or plan to join.

Needless to say, SMS messages, which are the focus point of the current study, hold a very important position in the above–mentioned legislation. As Grant (2007, p2) states "[o]ver recent years there has been considerable and growing interest in forensic authorship analysis", it is predicted that SMS messages will be increasingly used as evidence in Australian courts and in national and international security contexts (Coulthard and Johnson, 2007).[2] The fact that the use of mobile phones has been increasing exponentially and that the SMS is becoming a more and more common medium of communication, is apparently a strong driving force and motivation for the above–mentioned legislation and the conduct of fundamental research on SMS messages as scientific evidence.

Having said that, there is a large amount of research on authorship attribution in general (Thisted and Efron, 1987; Pennebaker and King, 1999; Doddington, 2001; Woolls, 2003; Slatcher et al., 2004)

[1] http://www.aph.gov.au/house/committee/jscc/cybercrime_bill/

[2] Some actual cases where authorship attribution was performed on SMS and email messages are given in Grant (2007) and Mohan et al. (2010).

and on individual linguistic idiosyncrasies (Webber et al., 2002; Shriberg and Stolcke, 2008; Ishihara, 2010) whereas studies specifically focusing on the authorship of SMS messages in forensic contexts are conspicuously sparse (cf. Mohan et al. 2010).

A possible scenario in which SMS messages can be used as evidence of an incriminating act is as follows: the police authority obtained a set of incriminating messages written by a criminal while another set of messages were obtained from a suspect. The relevant parties would like to know whether these two sets of messages were actually written by the same author or different authors. We simulate this scenario in our study.

This study adopts the approach used in other forensic fields, such as DNA and speaker recognition, the Likelihood Ratio (LR)–based evidence evaluation (Aitken and Stoney, 1991; Aitken, 1995; Robertson and Vignaux, 1995; Aitken and Taroni, 2004). As we know, SMS messages are usually (very) short while the ways people write their messages are unique (e.g. the use of acronyms, shorthand, etc) (Tagg, 2009). However, to the best of our knowledge, there have not been any empirical studies on the authorship classification of SMS messages in the framework of the LR (cf. Grant, 2007; Mohan et al., 2010) . Thus, we cannot answer even some fundamental questions, such as "How well can we correctly identify two groups of messages that were written by the same author as being written by the same author, and *mutatis mutandis*, by different authors?" and "What is the degree of strength of evidence (= LR) that we are likely to obtain from SMS messages?". We attempt to provide some answers to these questions by conducting a series of simple authorship classification tests in the LR framework.

Thus, more precisely, the aims of this study are to investigate 1) how accurately it is possible to classify the authors of SMS messages; 2) what degree of strength of evidence (LR) can be obtained from SMS messages; and 3) how the performance of the authorship classification and the strength of evidence are influenced by the sample size for modelling. The resultant LRs are calibrated by means of the logistic regress calibration technique (Brümmer and du Preez, 2006). The results of the classification tests are evaluated by means of the techniques originally proposed for automatic speaker recognition and forensic voice comparison (Gonzalez–Rodriguez et al., 2007). The effect of the calibration on the LRs obtained from the SMS messages will also be discussed.

2 Likelihood Ratio–based Approach

2.1 Likelihood Ratio

In the Bayesian analysis of evidence, opinions about the hypotheses are expressed in the form of posterior probabilities (or the posterior odd which is the ratio of the two conditional probabilities) as shown in (1), where H_p = prosecution hypothesis; H_d = alternative or defence hypothesis; E = forensic evidence. In the context of the forensic authorship classification of SMS messages, E will be the similarities/differences between the offender and defendant SMS messages. Thus, the posterior odd is the ratio between the probability that the same author hypothesis (or the prosecution hypothesis) is true ($p(H_p|E)$) and the probability that the different author hypothesis (or the defence hypothesis) is true ($p(H_d|E)$), given the evidence (E).

$$\underbrace{\frac{p(H_p|E)}{p(H_d|E)}}_{\textit{posterior odds}} \tag{1}$$

The solution to (1) is Bayes' theorem as the posterior odds is the product of the prior odds (province of the court) and the likelihood ratio (province of the forensic scientist) as shown in (2).

$$\underbrace{\frac{p(H_p|E)}{p(H_d|E)}}_{\textit{posterior odds}} = \underbrace{\frac{p(H_p)}{p(H_d)}}_{\textit{prior odds}} * \underbrace{\frac{p(E|H_p)}{p(E|H_d)}}_{\textit{likelihood ratio}} \tag{2}$$

It has been stressed that the task of the forensic expert is to provide the court with a strength–of–evidence statement by estimating the LR, and that they should NOT be asked their opinion about the probabilities given the evidence (= posterior odds) (Aitken and Stoney, 1991; Aitken, 1995; Robertson and Vignaux, 1995; Aitken and Taroni, 2004).

The likelihood ratio (LR) is the probability that the evidence would occur if an assertion is true, relative to the probability that the evidence would occur if the assertion is not true (Robertson and Vignaux, 1995, p17). For forensic authorship classification, it will be the probability of observing the difference between the group of messages written by the offender and that written by the suspect if they have come from the same author (i.e. if the prosecution hypothesis is true) relative to the probability of observing the same evidence if they have been produced by different authors (i.e. if the defence hypothesis is true). Thus, LR can be expressed in (3).

$$LR = \frac{p(E|H_p)}{p(E|H_d)} \quad (3)$$

The relative strength of the given evidence supporting the hypothesis is reflected in the magnitude of the LR. The more the LR deviates from unity (LR = 1; logLR = 0), the greater support for either the prosecution hypothesis (LR $>$ 1; logLR $>$ 0) or the defence hypothesis (LR $<$ 1; logLR $<$ 0). It is also common practice to express the LR logarithmically, in which case the neutral value is 0. Unless specifically expressed, $\log_{10}$LR values are used in this study.

Although the value of LR quantifies the strength of evidence, the value is not readily interpretable to the court. Thus, in order to aid the court to interpret LR values, some verbal interpretations of the ranges of LR values have been proposed. The one proposed by Champod and Evett (2000) is given in Table 1. In this study, whenever appropriate, we verbally express the strength of evidence based on Table 1.

2.2 Likelihood Ratios in Forensic Science

LRs show many advantages for evidence evaluation and presentation (Robertson and Vignaux, 1995, p21). Firstly, the majority of evidence submitted to the court is by nature only indicative, not determinative. For the indicative nature of evidence, which means, in other words, forensic evidence has an uncertain nature, probability is ideal to use in the inference process in a scientific way.

Another reason is that the role of forensic experts is clearly defined in the legal system, with the decision on whether or not the defendant is guilty not being left to the forensics experts: this is the job of juries (or judges in some judicial systems). Thus, as expressed in §2.1, the task of the forensic expert is NOT to provide their opinion about the source of evidence, but to estimate and give the court the strength of the evidence in the form of an LR.

Besides the appropriateness for the legal system as explained above, LRs have another advantage in evidence presentation: they allow evidence from different sources (e.g. voice, blood-stain) to be combined to give an overall LR in support of a hypothesis.

According to *Daubert*,[3] any scientific and technical evidence needs to satisfy certain criteria to be admitted in court. These criteria can be summarised as the issues of *transparency* and *testability*. It has been well discussed that the use of LR for evidence evaluation and presentation is appropriate from the view points of *transparency* and *testability* (Gonzalez–Rodriguez et al., 2007).

3 Authorship Classification Tests: Methodology

3.1 Database

In this study, we use the SMS corpus compiled by the National University of Singapore (the NUS SMS corpus).[4] A new version of the NUS SMS corpus has been released almost monthly, and we use *version 2011.05.11* which contains 38193 messages collected from 228 authors. The top three countries that contributed the most to the NUS SMS corpus by the number of messages are Singapore, India and the USA. 69% of the total messages were written by native speakers of English; 30% by non–native; 1% unknown. Male authors account for 71%; female for 16%; unknown for 13%. The average length of a message is 13.8 words with punctuations (sd = 13.5; max = 231; min = 1).

3.2 Selection of Messages

In authorship classification tests, two types of author pairs—same author pairs and different author pairs—are compared and evaluated using an LR as discriminant function. The former same author pairs are used for so–called *Same Author Comparison* (SA comparison) where two groups of messages produced by the same author need to be correctly identified as the same author whereas the latter different author pairs are for *mutatis mutandis*, *Different Author Comparison* (DA comparison). Thus, we

[3] *Daubert v. Merrel Dow Pharmaceuticals Inc., 509 US 593 (1993).*

[4] http://wing.comp.nus.edu.sg:8080/SMSCorpus/

LR	Log_{10} equivalent	Possible verbal equivalent	
> 10000	> 4	Very strong ...	support for the prosecution hypothesis
1000 to 10000	3 to 4	Strong ...	
100 to 1000	2 to 3	Moderately strong ...	
10 to 100	1 to 2	Moderate ...	
1 to 10	0 to 1	Limited ...	
1 to 0.1	0 to -1	Limited ...	support for the defence hypothesis
0.1 to 0.01	-1 to -2	Moderate ...	
0.01 to 0.001	-2 to -3	Moderately strong ...	
0.001 to 0.0001	-3 to -4	Strong ...	
< 0.0001	< -4	Very strong ...	

Table 1: Verbal equivalents of LRs and Log_{10}LRs (Champod and Evett, 2000).

need two groups of messages from each of the authors in authorship classification tests.

As explained in §1, one of the aims of this study is to investigate how the performance of the authorship classification and the strength of evidence are influenced by the sample size, i.e. the number of message words used for modelling. It can be safely predicted that the more messages we can use, the better the performance will be. However, each SMS message is essentially short, and it is forensically unrealistic to conduct experiments using thousands of messages to model an author's attribution. Thus, as shown in Table 2, we created 15 different datasets (DS) in which the number of words appearing in each message group is different (N = 200, 400, ... 2800, 3000 words).

For DS200, each message group contains a total of approximately 200 words. Since we cannot control the number of the words appearing in one message, it needs to be *approximately* 200 words. In order to compile a message group of about 200 words, we added one message by one message from the chronologically sorted messages to the group until the word number reached more than 200 words. As explained earlier, we need two groups of messages from the same author. For one message group, we started from the top of the chronologically sorted messages while for the other of the same author, from the bottom so that the two groups of messages from the same author are non–contemporaneous. Thus, the topics of the messages belonging to one group are likely to be different from those belonging to the other.

It should be noted that the number of messages

DS+N	auths.	SA	DA
DS200	85	85x2	14280x2
DS400	68	68x2	9112x2
DS600	56	56x2	6160x2
DS800	49	49x2	4704x2
DS1000	43	43x2	3612x2
DS1200	41	41x2	3280x2
DS1400	38	38x2	2812x2
DS1600	37	37x2	2664x2
DS1800	35	35x2	2380x2
DS2000	34	34x2	2244x2
DS2200	31	31x2	1848x2
DS2400	28	28x2	1512x2
DS2600	25	25x2	1200x2
DS2800	24	24x2	1104x2
DS3000	24	24x2	1104x2

Table 2: Dataset (DS) configurations: sample size (N) = the number of words included in each message group; auths. = the number of authors appearing in the DS; SA = number of SA comparisons; DA = number of DA comparisons.

which were contributed by each author to the NUS SMS Corpus is not the same: some contributed hundreds of messages, but some just one. Thus, some authors may not have enough messages to create two groups of messages as specified by the sample size. The second column of Table 2 shows the number of authors included in each DS. According to the second column, the number of authors included in the DSs decreases as the sample size increases. For example, as for DS3000, two sets of 3000 word messages can be created only from 24 authors. For DS3000, 24x2 same author (SA) comparisons and

1104x2 different author (DA) comparisons are possible.

3.3 Tokenisation and N-grams

The SMS messages were tokenised using the *SimpleTokenizer* function of the *opennlp-tools version 1.5.0*[5] without any stemming algorithms. The *SimpleTokenizer* provides simple tokenisation based on space and punctuations.

In some cases, it is difficult to automatically locate a sentence boundary in SMS messages as the use of upper/lower cases, punctuation, space, etc do not always conform to the standard orthographic rules. Therefore, the words appearing in the same message were treated as a sequence of words, without parsing them into sentences in this study.

We use the *ngram-count* and *ngram* functions of the *Speech Technology and Research Laboratory Language Modelling Toolkit (SRLM)*[6] in this study. As explained in §3.2, we need to compare two groups of messages many times. The *ngram–count* function is used to build an N–gram language model for a group of messages (model group). The resultant N–gram language model should represent the characteristics of this particular group of messages. The *ngram* function is used to calculate log probabilities between the N–gram language model of a given group of messages (model group) and another given group of messages (test group). The log probabilities calculated by the *ngram* function show the degree of similarities/differences between the former group of messages which were modelled in the form of the N–grams (model group) and the latter group of messages (test group). The backoff technique was used for the calculation of log probabilities (Jurafsky and Martin, 2000).

An 'open–vocabulary' N–gram language model (N = 1,2,3) was built for each group of messages. The minimal count of N–grams was set as > 9, which is the default setting of the *SRLM toolkit.* Thus, all N–grams with frequency of < 9 was discounted to 0. This is based on the results of some test experiments, in which the classification performance did not significantly improve with the threshold being set as ≥ 5. The default Good–Turing discounting was used for smoothing.

3.4 Likelihood Ratio Calculation

There are some different formulae proposed for calculating LRs (Lindley, 1977; Doddington, 2001; Aitken and Lucy, 2004). In this study, a conventional $\log_{10}$LR was estimated using the formula given in (4) (Doddington, 2001).

$$LR_{i,j} = \frac{log_{10} \frac{\Lambda^{i}_{author}(j)}{\Lambda_{background}(j)}}{N_j} \qquad (4)$$

Thus, the $LR_{i,j}$ of the test message group (j) against the model message group (i) is defined to be the log ratio of the similarity between the test message group (j) and the author model (Λ^{i}_{author}) of the model message group (i) to the typicality of the test message against the background author model $(\Lambda_{background})$, normalised by the number of words appearing in the test message group (N_j). The background author model was built in the cross–validated manner, using all messages appearing in the NUS SMS corpus, except those in comparison. The configurations of the N–grams for the background author model are the same as those used for the model message group.

The calculated raw LRs were calibrated using linear logistic regression using the *FoCal toolkit*[7]. Calibration is an affine transformation to a set of scores (e.g. LRs) which involves a linear monotonic shifting and scaling to the scores relative to a decision boundary in order to minimise the magnitude and incidence of scores which are known to misleadingly support the incorrect hypothesis (Morrison et al., 2011).

3.5 Evaluation

In this study, the results of the authorship classification tests are rigorously assessed using the equal error rate (*EER*), the Tippett plot, and the *log–likelihood–ratio cost* or C_{llr} matrices (Brümmer and du Preez, 2006). Using LR values as discriminant scores, we can measure the accuracy of the authorship classification systems in terms of *EER*. *EER* is a good indicator of the overall accuracy of a system, but does not refer to how *good* the LR values are. An LR is an estimate of the *degree* of support for a

[5]http://incubator.apache.org/opennlp/

[6]http://www.speech.sri.com/projects/srilm/

[7]http://www.dsp.sun.ac.za/ nbrummer/focal/

hypothesis against its alternative. Thus, the value of an LR itself is very important.

The Tippett plots show the distributions of the LRs given the prosecution hypothesis and the defence hypothesis, respectively together. Useful information that the Tippett plots can graphically provide is not only how strongly the LRs support the correct hypotheses but also how strongly the LRs support the incorrect hypotheses. More detailed explanations will be given about the Tippett plots when the results of the classification tests are presented in §4.

In short, the Tippett plots are graphical representations of the 'goodness of LRs' (Brümmer and du Preez, 2006). However, they do not give a scalar value of this goodness. The solution for this problem is the *log–likelihood–ratio cost function* or C_{llr} (5), which is a measure proposed in the area of automatic speaker recognition (Brümmer and du Preez, 2006),

$$C_{llr} = \frac{1}{2}\left(\frac{1}{N_{H_p}} \sum_{i for H_p = true}^{N_{H_p}} \log_2\left(1 + \frac{1}{LR_i}\right) + \frac{1}{N_{H_d}} \sum_{j for H_d = true}^{N_{H_d}} \log_2\left(1 + LR_j\right)\right) \tag{5}$$

where N_{H_p} and N_{H_d} are the number of LR values in the evaluation set for the prosecution hypothesis H_p being true or the defence hypothesis H_d being true. As can be seen from (5), incorrect LR values (i.e. same author comparisons with LR $<$ 1; logLR $<$ 0 and different author comparisons with LR $>$ 1; logLR$<$ 0) will have a strong penalty (high C_{llr}) and *vice versa*. The lower the C_{llr} value is, the better the performance of the system is. C_{llr} can be split into a discrimination loss (C_{llr}^{min})—which is the value achievable after the application of a calibration procedure—and a calibration loss (C_{llr}^{cal}) ($C_{llr} = C_{llr}^{min} + C_{llr}^{cal}$). Thus, the C_{llr} can provide an overall evaluation of a system while the C_{llr}^{min} and C_{llr}^{cal} can specifically show how the discrimination loss and the calibration loss contributed to the overall performance of the system. The *FoCal toolkit* is used to calculate C_{llr} in this study.

4 Authorship Classification Tests: Results and Discussions

The results of the authorship classification tests with different sample sizes are given in Table 3 in terms of *EER*, C_{llr}, C_{llr}^{min} and C_{llr}^{cal}.

DS+N	*EER*	C_{llr}	C_{llr}^{min}	C_{llr}^{cal}
DS200	0.40	1.29	0.96	0.33
DS400	0.39	1.14	0.93	0.21
DS600	0.37	1.08	0.90	0.18
DS800	0.36	1.04	0.87	0.16
DS1000	0.32	0.99	0.84	0.14
DS1200	0.30	0.97	0.82	0.15
DS1400	0.30	0.94	0.78	0.15
DS1600	0.30	0.93	0.77	0.15
DS1800	0.28	0.90	0.78	0.12
DS2000	0.23	0.87	0.72	0.14
DS2200	0.20	0.86	0.68	0.17
DS2400	0.21	0.84	0.65	0.18
DS2600	0.20	0.81	0.67	0.14
DS2800	0.20	0.82	0.67	0.15
DS3000	0.20	0.80	0.62	0.17

Table 3: The results of the authorship classification tests are given in terms of *EER*, C_{llr}, C_{llr}^{min}, C_{llr}^{cal} with 15 different sample sizes (N).

With respect to *EER*, C_{llr} and C_{llr}^{min}, the results of the authorship classification tests improve as the sample size increases. However, the C_{llr}^{cal} values do not show much improvement after a sample size of 400. When the sample size is greater than 400, the C_{llr}^{cal} values fluctuate between 0.12 and 0.18. That is, the degree of calibration is more or less stable with a sample size of 600 or greater, and the C_{llr} values improve as the sample size increases because the discrimination (not calibration) performance improves. The C_{llr}^{cal} values given in Table 3 are fairly small, even with a sample size of 200. That means that the LRs obtained from SMS messages are well calibrated.

The accuracy of the authorship classification increases from c.a. 60% with a sample size of 200 words to c.a. 80% with a sample size between 2200$\sim$3000 words. As can be judged from these accuracies, SMS messages carry some idiosyncratic information about the authors. The best result was achieved with a sample size of 3000 in terms of C_{llr}

(0.80).

To the best of our knowledge, Mohan et al. (2010) is the only study on authorship attributions of SMS messages, having an application to forensics in mind. They reported in their study, in which the NUS SMS corpus and an N–gram technique were also used, that the author of an SMS message could be correctly predicted with an accuracy of 65%∼70%. Their reported accuracy is comparable with that of the current study. However, what their study lacks is the reference to the strength of evidence (or LRs) as they did not employ the likelihood ratio based approach.

Figure 1 contains the Tippets plots of the LRs obtained with a sample size of 200 (panel 1), 1000 (2), 2000 (3) and 3000 (4). Figure 1 graphically shows how the 'goodness of the LRs' changes with the increase in sample size. The LRs, which are equal to or greater than the value indicated on the x-axis, are cumulatively plotted separately for the SA comparisons (black) and the DA comparisons (grey). In Figure 1, both uncalibrated (dotted curves) and calibrated (solid curves) LRs are included. The calibrated LRs were obtained by the logistic–regression calibration procedure which is a linear monotonic transformation, using the *FoCal toolkit*. Calibration aims to present the relevant information in such a way that the fact finder makes appropriate decisions (Ramos–Castro, 2007).

It can be observed from Figure 1 that before calibration, the crossing points of the SA and DA LRs (dotted curves) are slightly off from $\log_{10}LR = 0$, whereas, after calibration, the crossing points (solid curves) are right on $\mathrm{Log}_{10}LR = 0$. Theoretically speaking, the crossing point of the SA and DA LRs should align with $\log_{10}LR = 0$ even before calibration.

The logistic–regression calibration brought different effects on the LR values. When the sample size is small (i.e. 200 and 1000), the calibration has resulted in a major reduction in LR values (both correct and incorrect LRs). This major reduction of the LRs resulted in the calibrated LRs being not very meaningful as evidence. The ranges of the calibrated LRs are from -0.220 to 0.439 for the SA comparisons and from -0.281 to 0.443 for the DA comparisons with a sample size of 200 (Figure 1–1). According to Table 1 in which the verbal interpretations of LR values are given, the LRs between 0 and 1 for the SA comparisons and those between -1 and 0 for the DA comparisons provide only "limited" support for the prosecution and defence hypothesis, respectively.

Even with a sample size of 1000 (Figure 1–2), almost all of the calibrated LRs fall in the range of between -1 and 1. That is, again, the calibrated LR values give only "limited" support for either hypothesis.

With a sample size of 3000 (Figure 1–4), the calibration leads to the enhancement of the LRs: the ranges of the calibrated LRs are 2.868 (from -0.657 to 2.211) and 4.711 (from -2.735 to 1.976) for the SA and DA comparisons, respectively, which are much larger than the ranges of the uncalibrated LRs: 1.606 (from -0.184 to 1.422) and 2.640 (-1.349 to 1.291) for the SA and DA comparisons, respectively. The strongest calibrated LR values are 2.211 and -2.735 for the SA and DA comparisons, respectively. These values can be quoted as showing "moderately strong" support for the same and different author hypothesis, respectively.

Approximately 10% of the same author LRs "moderately" or "moderately strongly" support the same author hypothesis and approximately 65% have only "limited" support for the same author hypothesis. Likewise, approximately 15% of the different author LRs have "moderate" or "moderately strong" support for the different author hypothesis and approximately 60% have only "limited" support for the different author hypothesis.

The downside of this enhancement in LR values with a large sample size (i.e. 3000 words) is that the misleading LRs also increased their values after calibration. For example, the most misleading uncalibrated LR value for the DA comparisons is LR 1.291, which is incorrectly in favour of the same author hypothesis. After calibration, this misleading LR was intensified to LR 1.976. This value could be presented in court by a forensic expert as "moderately" supporting the same author hypothesis. This is a grave concern.

Considering the fact that SMS messages are usually (very) short, it may not be forensically realistic to be able to use as many as 3000 words for SMS authorship classification. Please note that the average length of a message is 13.8 words in the NUS

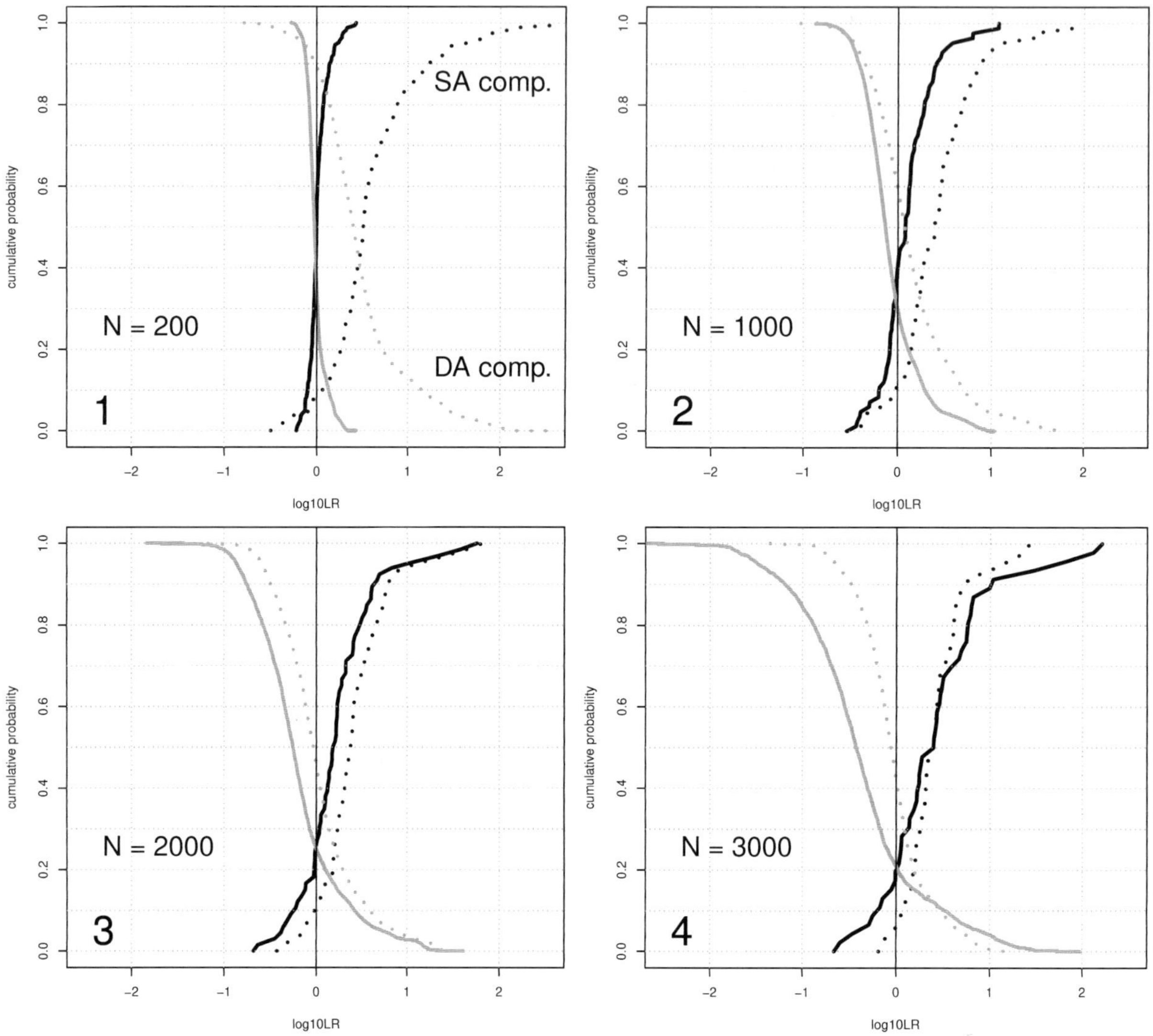

Figure 1: Tippet plots showing uncalibrated (solid curves and calibrated (dotted curves) LRs for the sample size (N) of 200 (panel 1); 1000 (2); 2000 (3) and 3000 (4). Grey = same author (SA) comparisons; black = different author (DA) comparisons.

SMS corpus, and therefore about 218 messages are required to be equivalent to 3000 words. However, our results demonstrated that if the sample size is small ($\leq$ 1000), having real cases in mind, the obtained LRs only give "limited" support for either hypothesis.

5 Conclusions

We found out that 1) the classification accuracy reaches c.a. 80% when we use a sample size of 2200 words or more; 2) the calibrated LR values are very weak, in particular when the sample size is small ($\leq$ 1000), in that the LR values provide only "limited" support for either hypothesis; 3) when we use a large sample size (i.e. 3000), the approximately 10$\sim$15% of the calibrated LR values provide "moderately strong" support for either of the correct hypotheses whereas the calibration undesirably increases the values of the misleading LRs as well.

6 Future Studies

The techniques we employed are rather simple and standard. Therefore, there is some room whereby the classification accuracy and the magnitude of the

LRs can improve even with a small set of messages if we apply different techniques. For this purpose, we should try different techniques at all different stages of the authorship classification (i.e. focus on specific words/expressions which are high in idiosyncrasy, pre–process of messages prior to modelling, different modelling techniques, different LR calculation techniques) to see how much we can improve the results of the authorship classification.

In order to estimate the strength of evidence as an LR, a background sample from the relevant population—in other words, the potential population of offenders—is essential. The SMS messages included in the NUS SMS Corpus are largely from Singaporeans. If we know that the offender is Singaporean, the SMS messages which were contributed by Singaporeans are appropriate as a background population data and desirable to estimate the accurate strength of evidence in LRs. However, if we know that the criminal is an Australian person, the use of this corpus is not suited in order to estimate the strength of evidence. Thus, in order to operate a forensic SMS authorship classification analysis in real cases, and calculate an LR as accurately as possible, the choice of appropriate population data is important. However, it goes without saying that this is difficult in many cases due to the lack of appropriate corpora. In the context of Australia, we lack a corpus of SMS messages written by Australians, which prevents forensic scientists from using SMS messages as evidence and limits the fundamental forensic studies on authorship classification in SMS messages. Thus, a compilation of a relevant corpus is an urgent task in Australia.

Acknowledgments

This study was financially supported by the Research School of Asia and the Pacifc, ANU. The author thanks anonymous reviewers for their valuable comments.

References

C. G. G. Aitken. 1995. *Statistics and the Evaluation of Evidence for Forensic Science*. UK, Chichester: Wiley.

C. G. G. Aitken and D. Lucy. 2004. Evaluation of trace evidence in the form of multivariate data, *Applied Statistics*. 53(4):109–122.

C. G. G. Aitken and D. A. Stoney. 1991. *The Use of Statistics in Forensic Science*. UK, Chichester: Ellis Horwood.

C. G. G. Aitken and F. Taroni. 2004. *Statistics and the Evaluation of Forensic Evidence for Forensic Scientist*. UK, Chichester: Wiley.

N. Brümmer and J. du Preez. 2006. Application-independent evaluation of speaker detection. *Computer Speech & Language*, 20(2–3):230–275.

C. Champod and I. W. Evett. 2000. Commentary on A. P. A. Broeders (1999) 'Some observations on the use of probability scales in forensic identification, Forensic Linguistics 6(2):228–41', *Forensic Linguistics*. 7:238–243.

M. Coulthard and A. Johnson. 2007. *An Introduction to Forensic Linguistics: Language in Evidence*. London, New York: Routledge.

G. Doddington. 2001. Speaker recognition based on idiolectal differences between speakers, *Proceedings of the Eurospeech 2001*, 2521–2524.

J. Gonzalez-Rodriguez, P. Rose, D. Ramos, D. T. Toledano, J. Ortega-Garcia. 2007. Emulating DNA: Rigorous quantification of evidential weight in transparent and testable forensic speaker recognition, *IEEE Transactions on Audio, Speech, and Language Processing*, 15:2104–2115.

T. Grant. 2007. Quantifying evidence in forensic authorship analysis. *The International Journal of Speech, Language and the Law*, 14(1):1–25.

S. Ishihara. 2010. Variability and consistency in the idiosyncratic selection of fillers in Japanese monologues: Gender differences, *Proceedings of the ALTA Workshop 2010*, 9–17.

D. Jurafsky and J. H. Martin. 2000. *Speech and Language Processing: An Introduction to Natural Language Processing, Computational Linguistics, and Speech Recognition*. Prince–Hall, Inc.

D. V. Lindley 1977. A problem in forensic science. *Biometrika*, 64:207–213.

A. Mohan, I. M. Baggili, M. K. Rogers. 2010. Authorship attribution of SMS messages using an N-grams approach. *CERIAS Tech Report 2011–11*.

G. S. Morrison, C. Zhang, P. Rose. 2011. An empirical estimate of the precision of likelihood ratios from a forensic-voice-comparison system. *Forensic Science International*. 208:59–65.

J. W. Pennebaker and L. A. King. 1999. Linguistics styles: Language use as an individual difference. *Journal of Personality and Social Psychology*, 77(6):1296–1312.

D. Ramos–Castro. 2007. *Forensic Evaluation of the Evidence Using Automatic Speaker Recognition Systems*. A PhD thesis, Universidad Politécnica de Madrid.

B. Robertson and G. A. Vignaux. 1995. *Interpreting Evidence*. UK, Chichester: Wiley.

E. Shriberg and A. Stolcke. 2008. The case for automatic higher–level features in forensic speaker recognition, *Proceedings of Interspeech 2008*, 1509–1512.

R. Slatcher, C. Chunga, J. Pennebaker and L. Stone. 2004. Winning words: Individual differences in linguistic style among U.S. presidential and vice presidential candidates. *Journal of Research in Personality*, 41(1):63–75.

C. Tagg. 2009. *A Corpus Linguistic Study of SMS Text Messaging*. A PhD thesis, the University of Birmingham.

R. Thisted and B. Efron. 1987. Did Shakespeare write a newly–discovered poem? *Biometrika*, 74(3):445–455.

F. Weber, L. Manganaro, B. Peskin and E. Shriberg. 2002. Using Prosodic and lexical information for speaker identification, *Proceedings of the ICASSP 2002*, 141–144.

D. Woolls. 2003. Better tools for the trade and how to use them. *Forensic Linguistics. The International Journal of Speech, Language and the Law*, 10(1):102–112.

Classifying Domain-Specific Terms Using a Dictionary

Su Nam Kim
Dept. of CSSE
University of Melbourne
Melbourne, Australia
snkim@csse.unimelb.edu.au

Lawrence Cavedon
School of CS
IT
RMIT University
Melbourne, Australia
lawrence.cavedon@rmit.edu.au

Abstract

Automatically building domain-specific ontologies is a highly challenging task as it requires extracting domain-specific terms from a corpus and assigning them relevant domain concept labels. In this paper, we focus on the second task: i.e., assigning domain concepts to domain-specific terms. Motivated by previous approaches in related research (such as word sense disambiguation (WSD) and named entity recognition (NER)) that use semantic similarity among domain concepts, we explore three types of features — contextual, domain concepts, topics — to measure the semantic similarity of terms; we then assign the domain concepts from the best matching terms. As evaluation, we collected domain-specific terms from FOLDOC, a freely available on-line dictionary for the the *Computing* domain, and defined 9 domain concepts for this domain. Our results show that beyond contextual features, using domain concepts and topics derived from domain-specific terms helps to improve assigning domain concepts to the terms.

1 Introduction

Domain-specific terms are terms that have significant meaning(s) in a specific domain. For example, terms such as *Gulf* and *Kuwait* are associated with the domain of oil due to their frequent appearances in contexts related to oil although they indicate geographical areas. In some resources, domain-specific terms are further categorized in terms of their domain concepts (i.e., semantic labels/classes). For example, *Firefox* belongs to the domain concept Software, while *Prolog* is associated with the domain concept Programming. In this paper, we use the term **domain concept** for consistency. Note that in previous work, the meaning of the domain-specificity is associated with either word senses (e.g. (Magnini et al., 2002; Rigutini et al., 2005)) or the statistical use of terms in context (e.g. (Drouin, 2004; Milne et al., 2006; Kida et al., 2007; Park et al., 2008; Kim et al., 2009; Vivaldi and Rodrguez, 2010)). In WordNet, the domain concept is assigned based on the word senses. Similarly, WordNet Domain has terms with domain concepts per sense. However, most work previously conducted work used domain-specificity is based on statistical use. In this paper, we follow the latter definition, i.e., domain-specificity associated with the statistical use of the term.

Domain-specificity of terms has been leveraged in various natural language processing (NLP) and related tasks, such as word sense disambiguation (WSD) (Magnini et al., 2002), named entity recognition (NER) (Kazama and Torisawa, 2007), and query expansion (Rigutini et al., 2005). Resources containing domain information fall into two groups: the list of domain-specific terms without domain concepts (e.g. Agrivoc, EUROVOC, ASFA Thesaurus); and with domain concepts (e.g. WordNet, WordNet Domain, Unified Medical Language System (UMLS)). Although there have been efforts developing such knowledge resources, the task has been generally carried out by hand, requiring high cost and time. Further, even hand-crafted resources are often limited in terms of quality and quantity.

Moreover, the content needs to be constantly updated/maintained as new words are added. As a result, there has been recent work on automatic ontology builders (e.g. `OntoLearn`, `Text2Onto`) that work by extracting domain-specific terms and tagging domain-concepts to build such resources.

Building a domain-specific ontology requires two main tasks — extracting domain-specific terms and assigning the domain concept(s). There have been several methods proposed for each task and also as a complete ontology builder—we describe such work in Section 2. In this paper, our interest lies on assigning domain concepts to the existing domain-specific resources. In one sense our task can be viewed as building a taxonomy from dictionaries (Rigau et al., 1998) and/or a semantic class labelling task (Punuru and Chen, 2007). Since some resources are already publicly available (despite shortcomings), utilizing these resources reduces the time for manually developing training data, and should lead to robust systems due to consistent labeling. In addition, such resources are reusable for enlarging the existing resources or creating new semantic resources.

Our basic approach is to use semantic similarity between domain-specific terms. Contextual features have often been employed for semantic similarity in various tasks, such as text categorization (Joachims, 1998) and dialogue act classification (Ivanovic, 2005). Thus, we also explore using context as base features. Furthermore, we explore the use of rich semantic features. That is, we employ the domain concepts and topics derived from known domain-specific terms over the same resource as additional features. We detail our rich semantic features in Section 4.2 and 4.3. In evaluation, we applied our approaches to the domain Computing, as the interest in this domain is growing due to the large volume of web corpora, including social media such as web forums and blogs.

In the following sections, we describe related work and the existing resources in Section 2 and 3. We then describe our features in Section 4, and evaluate our methods in Section 5. We summarize our work in Section 6.

2 Related Work

There are two individual sub-tasks that deal with domain-specific terms — extraction/identification and labeling domains/concepts. Further, extracting domain-specific terms is combined with technical term extraction in order to extract candidates, while identification of domain-specific terms is a binary decision (i.e., with a given term, determining whether it is domain-specific to the target domain).

A number of extraction methods have been proposed (Drouin, 2004; Rigutini et al., 2005; Milne et al., 2006; Kida et al., 2007; Park et al., 2008; Kim et al., 2009; Vivaldi and Rodrguez, 2010). Most used supervised approaches while (Park et al., 2008; Kim et al., 2009; Vivaldi and Rodrguez, 2010) undertook the task in an unsupervised manner. In addition, (Rigutini et al., 2005) used sense-based domain-specificity, while others used statistical use-based measures to determine domain-specificity of the candidate terms. (Rigutini et al., 2005) is motivated by the intuition that, similar to word sense disambiguation, domain-specificity can be identified using contextual semantic similarity in which those terms occur, since domain-specificity is associated with the word senses. (Milne et al., 2006) studied Wikipedia entries as domain-specific terms and crosschecked the terms in `Agrivoc` with Wikipedia entries to verify the domain-specificity of Wikipedia entries. The basic idea in (Kida et al., 2007) is that a domain can be identified via a list of known technical domain terms. As unsupervised approaches, (Park et al., 2008) introduced a probability based weighting in order to measure the domain-specificity of the term over a large corpus. Similarly, (Kim et al., 2009) used term frequencies across the documents using modified TF·IDF, which replace a document with a domain. (Vivaldi and Rodrguez, 2010) made use of Wikipedia categories and page structures. The intuition is that the Wikipedia categories are domain-specific, thus, by retrieving the Wikipedia entries through the category trees starting with a target domain, the domain-specific terms under the target domain can be automatically retrieved.

The task of domain assignment has some relationship to the word sense disambiguation (WSD) and named entity recognition (NER) tasks. While WSD attempts to assign the correct sense of terms from some given repository of senses (typically, WordNet), assigning domains to domain-specific terms in our work first requires that we construct the repository. NER is a subtask of information extraction that involves finding named entities and assigning each a tag from a predefined set of categories, such as LOCATION or PERSON. The difference with our task in this paper is that in both WSD and NER, the target terms are generally in some use context (i.e., the correct word sense of target term depends on that context), while our targets are isolated, i.e., appear out of context. In this paper, our approach is closer to corpus-based WSD which normally uses co-occurrence of terms between two corpora.

In recent years, there have been systems proposed to extract terms and to assign semantic labels to them (Navigli and Velard, 2004; Cimiano and Vlker, 2005; Nicola et al., 2009). OntoLearn (Navigli and Velard, 2004) has three components. First, it extracts a domain terminology from Web sites. It then assigns the domain concepts in order to build a hierarchical structure of ontologies. The system uses semantic similarity between WordNet concepts for component words in a candidate and conceptual relations among the concept components based on word senses. Finally, ontologies in WordNet are trimmed and enriched with the extracted domain concepts. Text2Onto (Cimiano and Vlker, 2005) is another ontology builder and includes three components. First, the system represents the knowledge as metadata in the form of instantiated modeling primitives called Probabilistic Ontology Model, which is language-independent. Second, the system uses the user interaction in order to measure the domain-specificity for candidates. Finally, it accumulates the ontologies based on previously added ontologies to overcome computational redundancy over time when corpus/documents are changed. More recently, (Nicola et al., 2009) developed an automatic ontology builder by combining Unified Software Development Processing (UP) and UML. It bases its characteristics on UP and uses UML to support the preparation of the blueprints of the ontology development.

3 Data

Multiple taxonomy resources such as WordNet and Wikipedia are available for identifying terms in the Computing domain. However, not all of these systematically assign semantic labels to terms. To determine suitability of popularly used resources for our task, we first investigated their utility.

WordNet3.0 (Fellbaum, 1998) includes domain information but the number of terms with domain information is very limited. Moreover, it does not include many terms related to the Computing domain, and those terms it does include are often proper nouns (e.g. *Firefox*) or compound nouns (e.g. *wireless connection*). For WordNet Domain, (Magnini et al., 2002) developed a domain system and semi-manually assigned domains to WordNet terms in terms of their word senses. Although the size of the resource with domain information is larger than WordNet3.0 (i.e., 6,050 nouns with one sense), it is still a relatively small resource. Moreover, the domain called *factotum* (i.e., "undecided") is used for many terms, which makes it less usable.

Wikipedia[1] is the largest folksonomy taxonomy. It contains terms (hereafter, *entries*) and categories per entry. It also provides hyperlinks between entries and entry pages. Despite its vast size, Wikipedia is not designed to be a dictionary, thus it does not contain definitions entries. Moreover, the categories are not systematically organized and often contain noise (which are not relevant to the target domains).

Wiktionary[2], on the other hand, is a growing online dictionary for all domains. It has characteristics similar to WordNet, such as definitions and relations (e.g. hypernym, synonym). It also partially contains domain information per word sense. In addition, it is linked to Wikipedia. However, since one term could have multiple senses and not all senses are tagged with a specific domain, it requires a preprocessing step to discover terms related to the specific domain (for this paper, Computing domain only). The number of unique terms in Wiktionary is 10,586 without counting individual word senses.

[1]http://en.wikipedia.org/wiki/Main_Page
[2]http://en.wiktionary.org/wiki/dictionary

The final resource we consider is FOLDOC[3]. FOLDOC is the (so far) largest handcrafted on-line dictionary for the Computing domain. It also contains definitions and sub-domains such as *hardware* and *operating system*, and provides hyperlinks to other dictionary terms in the definition and links to Wikipedia and OneLook dictionary search[4]. Unlike Wiktionary, only word senses of terms related to Computing are listed, thus, all terms in the dictionary are relevant to the Computing domain. For these reasons, as well as the size of the resource being sufficient to evaluate our method, we decided to use FOLDOC for our purposes. To understand FOLDOC better, we checked the overlaps between it and other resources in Table 1. Note that all resources were retrieved in March 2011.

Source	WikiDic	Wikipedia	WordNet
Instance	10,586	10,863,326	117,798
Overlap	1,682	9,917	2,756

Table 1: Overlap between the FOLDOC dictionary and other resources.

FOLDOC contains 14,826 unique terms with multiple senses, resulting in 16,450 terms in total. 13,072 and 3,378 terms are *direct* and *redirect*, respectively (the concept of *direct* and *redirect* is the same as that in Wikipedia). Among direct terms, 8,621 terms have manually assigned domain concept(s). The total number of domain concepts in the dictionary is 188. Finally, we manually mapped 188 onto 9 domain concepts which are super-labels. For example, labels in FOLDOC, security, specification, Unix are mapped on to Networking, Documentation, OS, respectively. Note that, based on our observations, we found many of the labels defined in FOLDOC are too fine-grained, and some are used only for 1 or 2 terms. Furthermore, the labels are not hierarchically structured. In addition, similar to the trade-off between fine-grained vs. coarse-grained word senses, we believe coarse-grained labels would be more usable (e.g. document classification using coarse-grained labels of terms), thus, we used 9 super-labels in this work.

Table 2 shows the final domain concepts we used and the number of instances in each domain concept. Note that since one term can have multiple semantic labels, the total number of instances with one label is 10,147. Table 3 shows the number of terms with multiple senses and multiple domain concepts.

Domain (Terms)	Domain (Terms)
CS (755)	Documentation (1,906)
HW (1,490)	Jargon (298)
Networking (1,220)	OS (363)
Programming (3,042)	SW (144)
Other (929)	
Total	10,147(8,621)

Table 2: Data Size per Domain Concept. *8,621* is the number of word types, where *CS, HW, OS, SW* indicate *computer science*, *hardware*, *operating system*, and *software*, respectively.

Info.	1	2	3	4	5	6	7
Label	7172	1353	79	8	–	–	–
Sense	7957	475	124	41	11	2	2

Table 3: Terms with multiple labels and senses.

4 Methodology

4.1 Feature Set I: Bag-of-Words

n-gram-based bag-of-words (BoW) features are one of the most broadly applied features to measure the semantic similarity between two terms/texts. This has been used in various tasks such as document classification (Joachims, 1998), dialogue act classification (Ivanovic, 2005) and term classification (Lesk, 1986; Baldwin et al., 2008).

As shown in (Hulth and Megyesi, 2006), keywords along the contextual features (i.e., simple 1-grams) are useful in identifying semantic similarity. However, keywords are often multi-grams such as 2-grams (e.g. *Fast Ethernet, optical mouse*) and 3-grams (e.g. *0/1 knapsack problem, Accelerated Graphics Port*). Sharing the same intuition, some previous work (Ivanovic, 2005) employed not only 1-grams but also 2-grams for the classification task. Similarly, we also observed that terms are often multi-grams. Thus, in this work, we also explored various n-grams. In evaluation, we tested 1- and 2-grams individually as well as the combination of 1-

[3]http://foldoc.org/

[4]http://www.onelook.com/

and 2-grams together (i.e., 1+2-grams). Note that since previous work has shown that the use of lemmas performed better than raw words, we chose to use lemmas as features. We also tested BoWs from nouns and verbs only. As feature weights, we tested simple Boolean and TF·IDF. In evaluation, the features are filtered with respect to the frequency of indexing words. That is, we tested three different term frequencies (i.e., frequency $\geq$ 1, 2, and 3) in order to select the indexing terms as BoW features.

4.2 Feature (II): Domain Concepts of Domain-Specific Terms

BoW features are useful for measuring the semantic similarity between two targets. However, we observed that since the number of terms in the dictionary definition is small, there will be a lack of context (similar to shortcomings reported in (Lesk, 1986) for WSD using dictionary definition). On the other hand, we noticed that a term's definition often contains terms which belong to the same domain concepts. For example, the target term *Ethernet* belongs to the domain concept Networking, and its definition is "A local area network first described by ...". *Local area network* in the definition also belongs to the same domain concept Networking. Hence, we use the domain concept(s) of dictionary terms found in the definition of the target term as a feature.

We also extend the target's definition with its dictionary terms. To overcome the pitfall of the algorithm in (Lesk, 1986) due to lack of terms in the definition, (Baldwin et al., 2008) utilized the extended definition from the dictionary terms found in the target's definition. Similarly, instead of the definition of dictionary terms in the target's definition (i.e., extended definition), we used the domain concept(s) of dictionary terms in the extended definition. We hypothesised that using these domain concepts would provide more direct information about domain concepts of the target term.

In Table 4, we demonstrate how and what to extract as domain concepts for the target *database*. The definition of the target *database* contains dictionary terms *database, table, flat file, comma-separated values*. Since *database* is the target term itself and *comma-separated values* is not found in the dictionary, we use the domain concepts from *table* and *flat file* only, which include CS, and OS, HW. Note that some terms have multiple labels as described in Section 3. We also extend *table* and *flat file* to obtain the extended domain concepts from the extended definition. Finally, we accumulated domain concepts, CS, Programming, Documentation from *records*, CS from *relational database* and Documentation from *flat ASCII* from the extended definitions.

4.3 Feature (III): Topics of Domain-Specific Terms

Topic modeling (Blei et al., 2003) is an unsupervised method to cluster documents based on context information. As it is not a classification method, the topics produced by the topic modeling algorithm are abstract, thus not directly associated with predefined semantic labels. However, we observed that topic terms for each topic are generally associated with the domain concepts. From our observation, we hypothesized that (ideally) one topic is associated with one domain concept (although some may contain multiple domain concepts same as multi-sensed words). As such, we assigned topic ID(s) per dictionary terms using topic modeling software[5], then used this as an additional feature with BoWs. Likewise, we also obtained topic ID(s) for dictionary terms found in the definition of the target term. Note that depending on the features used to obtain topics, the association between topic IDs and our 9 domain concepts would change. Table 5 demonstrates the topics and how we extract the *Topic* and *extended Topic* features using the same example use above. *database* is tagged with topic ID = 1,2,4 while *table* has topic ID = 4. We represented features by accumulating the topic IDs over 9 topic IDs which are the same number of our domain concepts.

5 Experiments

For our evaluation, we first replaced the email addresses, numbers, urls with their category *EMAIL, NUMBER, URL*, respectively. We then performed POS tagging and lemmatization using `Lingua::EN::Tagger` and `morph` tools (Minnen et al., 2001), respectively. For learning, we

[5]The topic modeling tool we used can be downloaded from http://www.ics.uci.edu/ newman/code/

Term	Label	Definition
Target Term, "database" and its Domain Concept and Definition		
database	CS	A ~~database~~ containing a single *table*$_{\text{CS}}$, stored in a single *flat file*$_{\text{OS,HW}}$, often in a human-readable format such as ~~comma-separated values~~ or fixed-width columns.
Extending Definitions of Dictionary Terms found in Target's Definition		
table	CS	A collection of *records*$_{\text{CS,Programming,Documentation}}$ in a *relational database*$_{\text{CS}}$.
flat file	OS, HW	A single file containing *flat ASCII*$_{\text{Documentation}}$ representing or encoding some structure, e.g. a ~~database~~, tree or network.

Table 4: Extracting domain concepts of dictionary terms in definitions.

Type	Value	Topics								
		T1	T2	T3	T4	T5	T6	T7	T8	T9
Target Term	*database*	1	1	0	1	0	0	0	0	0
Dictionary Term	*table*	0	0	0	1	0	0	0	0	0
in Target Definition	*flat file*	0	1	0	0	1	0	0	0	1
Feature	Direct	1	1	0	1	0	0	0	0	0
representation	Extended	1	2	0	2	1	0	0	0	1

Table 5: Extracting topics for target terms and dictionary terms.

simulated our method by both supervised and semi-supervised approaches. We used `SVM` (Joachims, 1998)[6] for supervised learning and `SVMlin` (Sindhwani and Keerthi, 2006)[7] for semi-supervised learning. For supervised learning, we performed 10-fold cross-validation over 8,621 terms which have manually assigned labels in `FOLDOC`. For semi-supervised learning, we used the same data for test and training and 4,451 unlabeled terms in `FOLDOC` as unlabeled data. As the baseline system, we used the feature TF·IDF valued *1-gram* from all terms with frequency ≥ 1. The performances are compared using micro-averaged F-score $\mathcal{F}_{\mu}$.

5.1 Supervised Learning

Table 6 shows performance by supervised learners with various BoWs. Note that we only report performance using TF·IDF since those using Boolean weights performed poorly. We also ran the experiments over different frequency which leads to various numbers of indexing terms. Finally, we tested noun- and verb-only features.

Overall, the best performance is produced by using both 1- and 2-grams with frequency ≥ 1, as this configuration contains the largest amount of features. However, the improvement by adding 2-grams is not significant (i.e., *52.01%* vs. *52.47%* in $\mathcal{F}_{\mu}$). Between using all terms vs. nouns and verbs only, using all terms performed slightly better. Despite dominant information derived from nouns and verbs, other POS tagged words also contributed to distinguishing the domain concepts. Likewise, the performances using nouns and verbs only are generally better when using features with frequency ≥ 1.

Table 7 shows performance using both n-grams and semantic features. At first, adding rich semantic features (i.e., *Domain Concept, Topic*) significantly improved performance (*52.01%* vs. *60.62%*). In particular, *Topic* features helped to improve performance. As we hypothesised, topics are likely associated with domain concepts which resulted in performance improvements. *Domain concept* features also helped to gain higher performance, as they provide more direct semantic information than n-gram features. Between direct and extended (i.e., indirect) semantic features, we noticed that *extended*

[6] http://www.cs.cornell.edu/People/tj/svm_light/svm_hmm.html
[7] http://vikas.sindhwani.org/svmlin.html

Feature	Indexing	Frequency≥1 (F1)			Frequency≥2 (F2)			Frequency≥3 (F3)		
		$\mathcal{P}_\mu$	$\mathcal{R}_\mu$	$\mathcal{F}_\mu$	$\mathcal{P}_\mu$	$\mathcal{R}_\mu$	$\mathcal{F}_\mu$	$\mathcal{P}_\mu$	$\mathcal{R}_\mu$	$\mathcal{F}_\mu$
All	1	56.64	48.07	*52.01*†	56.64	48.07	52.01	56.56	48.00	51.93
Terms	2	54.42	46.19	49.97	54.42	46.19	49.97	51.68	43.87	47.45
	1+2	57.14	48.50	**52.47**	57.14	48.50	52.47	57.05	48.42	52.38
Noun	1	55.56	47.16	51.02	55.56	47.16	51.02	55.49	47.10	50.95
+	2	52.39	44.47	48.10	52.39	44.47	48.10	49.30	41.84	45.27
Verb	1+2	56.37	47.85	51.76	56.37	47.85	51.76	56.19	47.69	51.59

Table 6: Performances with BoW Features: Performance of the baseline system is marked with †. The best performance is bold-faced. *Indexing* means n-grams. Indexing value is TF·IDF.

Feature	Index	All Words			Noun+Verb		
		F1	F2	F3	F1	F2	F3
Domain	1	57.30	57.02	57.20	56.90	56.96	**57.51**
Concept	2	55.61	55.78	55.22	55.70	55.77	55.54
	1+2	56.84	57.16	57.07	56.09	56.57	56.41
Extended	1	**55.97**	55.86	55.74	55.63	55.13	55.88
Domain	2	53.44	53.98	53.31	53.79	53.82	53.43
Concept	1+2	55.91	55.82	55.50	55.54	55.49	55.30
Topic	1	60.58	**60.62**	60.50	59.65	59.99	59.75
	2	50.94	54.27	53.30	50.99	54.03	52.88
	1+2	59.75	60.11	59.82	58.37	59.48	59.20
Extended	1	59.18	59.09	59.10	59.47	**59.60**	59.40
Topic	2	52.77	53.54	52.11	50.44	51.51	50.03
	1+2	58.73	58.98	58.56	56.52	56.85	56.58

Table 7: Performances with Rich Semantic Features in $\mathcal{F}_\mu$: The best performances in each group are bold-faced.

features decreased performance as they tend to introduce more erroneous instances. Likewise, using all words as well as 1-grams performed better among all various n-grams with few exceptions.

Table 8 and Figure 1 show performance over individual classes and detail of predicted labels. This is the system using TF·IDF valued *1-grams* from all terms with frequency ≥ 2, as this was our best-performing system. Overall, we found that many domain concepts are mislabeled with Programming and Documentation since they are most often used concepts and could be a border concept for terms labeled with other domain concepts. For example, CS and Documentation are often labeled as Programming, while Networking is mislabeled as Documentation.

Finally, we used randomized estimation to calculate whether any performance differences between methods are statistically significant (Yeh, 2000) and found all systems exceeding the baseline system had p-value ≤ 0.05, which indicates significant improvement.

5.2 Semi-supervised Learning

For semi-supervised learning, we evaluated the impact of the size of training data. We observed that despite increasing training data, performance does not significantly improve. However, to compare the performance between supervised and semi-supervised systems, we simulated semi-supervised system with unused training data from FOLDOC. Table 9 shows the performance of semi-supervised learning using two groups of features: *1-gram with frequency* $\geq$ *1*, and *1-gram with frequency* $\geq$ *1 + Domain Concept*. Note that we did not test with *Topic* as topic IDs change according to the data.

G/P	CS	Document	HW	Jargon	Network	OS	Program	SW	Other
CS	435(40.6)	95(8.9)	140(13.1)	9(0.8)	29(2.7)	23(2.1)	297(27.7)	12(1.1)	31(2.9)
Document	74(3.8)	1101(56.3)	151(7.7)	43(2.2)	174(8.9)	33(1.7)	252(12.9)	17(0.9)	111(5.7)
HW	35(3.0)	86(7.4)	850(72.7)	10(0.9)	41(3.5)	18(1.5)	93(8.0)	2(0.2)	34(2.9)
Jargon	23(4.8)	77(16.1)	62(13.0)	145(30.4)	29(6.1)	16(3.4)	74(15.5)	7(1.5)	44(9.2)
Network	19(1.7)	205(18.0)	22(1.9)	12(1.1)	766(67.4)	12(1.1)	58(5.1)	4(0.4)	39(3.4)
OS	14(2.7)	42(8.2)	60(11.7)	11(2.2)	31(6.1)	198(38.7)	130(25.4)	6(1.2)	19(3.7)
Program	51(2.7)	86(4.5)	48(2.5)	24(1.3)	38(2.0)	21(1.1)	1576(83.3)	7(0.4)	42(2.2)
SW	32(4.6)	94(13.4)	48(6.8)	7(1.0)	52(7.4)	27(3.8)	302(43.0)	73(10.4)	67(9.5)
Other	72(5.8)	120(9.7)	109(8.9)	37(3.0)	60(4.9)	15(1.2)	260(21.1)	16(1.3)	542(44.0)

Table 8: Confusion Matrix with *Noun+Verb:1-gram+F2+Topic* where the proportion is presented in ()

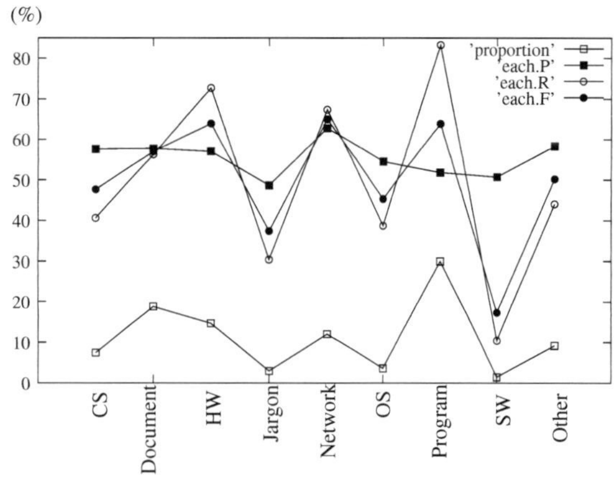

Figure 1: Performances over individual classes with *Noun+Verb:1-gram+F2+Topic*: *Proportion* means the amount of instances per domain concept in %.

	S	Semi-S (Unlabeled Term #)			
Fea.	0	1000	2000	3000	4415
1	52.01	56.94	58.05	57.97	58.86
1+D	57.30	**59.33**	58.02	57.83	57.17

Table 9: Performances by semi-supervised learning in %. *1* is unigram and *D* means domain concept.

The results show that the use of simple BoWs improves performance but does not exceed the best performance produced using *BoW+Domain Concept/Topic*. On the other hand, adding *Domain Concept* actually decreases performance when adding more unlabeled data, except when adding a small amount (i.e., 1000). We found that *Domain Concept* is sensitive, thus this decreased the overall performance when it includes more noise by semi-supervised learning. Previously, the outcomes of semi-supervised learning have shown that its effectiveness is somewhat dependent on the nature of the task and aspects of features. There have been mixed reports on improvement by semi-supervised learning; some work reported significant improvement while other showed little or no impact on the task. In this paper, we observed that semi-supervised learning would not help improve the performance on classifying domain concepts. We expect that since the best performance by the supervised system is not high enough, adding automatically assigned data as training data introduces further error.

6 Conclusion

We have proposed an automatic method to assign domain concepts to terms in `FOLDOC` using various contextual features as well as semantic features — *Domain Concept* and *Topic*. We demonstrated that the system performed best when using rich semantic features directly derived from dictionary terms. We also showed that for the target task, semi-supervised learning did not significantly improve performance, unlike for other tasks. As future work, we are interested in applying the proposed method to other existing resources in order to build a larger domain-specific ontology resource.

References

Timothy Baldwin, Su Nam Kim, Francis Bond, Sanae Fujita, David Martinez, and Takaaki Tanaka. 2008. Mrd-based word sense disambiguation: Further extending lesk. In *Proceedings of 3rd International Joint Conference on Natual Language Processing*, pages 775–780, Hyderabad, India.

David Blei, Andrew Ng, and Michael Jordan. 2003. Latent dirichlet allocation. *Journal of Machine Learning Research*, 3:993–1022.

Philipp Cimiano and Johanna Vlker. 2005. Text2onto - a framework for ontology learning and data-driven change discovery. In *10th International Conference on Applications of Natural Language to Information Systems (NLDB)*, pages 227–238.

Patrick Drouin. 2004. Detection of domain specific terminology using corpora comparison. In *Proceedings of the fourth international Conference on Language Resources and Evaluation*, pages 79–82, Lisbon, Portugal.

Christiane Fellbaum, editor. 1998. *WordNet, An Electronic Lexical Database*. MIT Press, Cambridge, Massachusetts, USA.

Annette Hulth and Beata B. Megyesi. 2006. A study on automatically extracted keywords in text categorization. In *Proceedings of 21st International Conference on Computational Linguistics and 44th Annual Meeting of the Association for Computational Linguistics*, pages 537–544, Sydney, Australia.

Edward Ivanovic. 2005. Dialogue act tagging for instant messaging chat sessions. In *Proceedings of the ACL Student Research Workshop*, pages 79–84, Ann Arbor, USA.

Thorsten Joachims. 1998. Text categorization with support vector machines: Learning with many relevant features. In *Proceedings of European Conference on Machine Learning*, pages 137–142.

Jun'ichi Kazama and Kentaro Torisawa. 2007. Exploiting Wikipedia as external knowledge for named entity recognition. In *Proceedings of the 2007 Joint Conference on Empirical Methods in Natural Language Processing and Computational Natural Language Learning*, pages 698–707.

Mitsuhiro Kida, Masatsugu Tonoike, Takehito Utsuro, and Satoshi Sato. 2007. Domain classification of technical terms using the web. *Systems and Computers*, 38(14):2470–2482.

Su Nam Kim, Timothy Baldwin, and Min-Yen Kan. 2009. An unsupervised approach to domain-specific term extraction. In *Australasian Language Technology Association Workshop*, pages 94–98.

Michael Lesk. 1986. Automatic sense disambiguation using machine readable dictionaries: How to tell a pine cone from an ice cream cone. In *Proceedings of the 1986 SIGDOC Conference*, pages 24–26, Ontario, Canada.

Bernardo Magnini, Carlo Strapparava, Giovanni Pezzulo, and Alfio Gliozzo. 2002. Using domain information for word sense disambiguation. *Natural Langauge Engineering*, 8(4):359–373.

David Milne, Olena Medelyan, and Ian H. Witten. 2006. Mining domain-specific thesauri from wikipedia : A case study. In *Proceedings of the 2006 IEEE/WIC/ACM International Conference on Web Intelligence*, pages 442–448, Washington, USA.

Guido Minnen, John Carroll, and Darren Pearce. 2001. Applied morphological processing of English. *Natural Language Engineering*, 7(3):207–223.

Robert Navigli and Paola Velard. 2004. Learning domain ontologies from document warehouses and dedicated web sites. *Computational Linguistics*, 30(2):151–179.

Antonio De Nicola, Michele Missikoff, and Roberto Navigli. 2009. A software engineering approach to ontology building. *Information Systems*, 34(2):258–275.

Youngja Park, Siddharth Patwardhan, Karhik Visweswariah, and Stephen C. Gates. 2008. An empirical analysis of word error rate and keyword error rate. In *Proceedings of International Conference on Spoken Language Processing*, Brisbane, Australia.

Janardhana Punuru and Jianhua Chen. 2007. Learning for semantic classification of conceptual terms. *Granular Computing, IEEE International Conference on*, 0:253.

German Rigau, Horacio Rodriguez, and Eneko Agirre. 1998. Building accurate semantic taxonomies from monolingual mrds. In *Proceedings of the 36th Annual Meeting of the Association for Computational Linguistics and 17th International Conference on Computational Linguistics, Volume 2*, pages 1103–1109.

Leonardo Rigutini, B. Liu, and Marco Magnini. 2005. An em based training algorithm for cross-language text categorization. In *Proceedings of the Web Intelligence Conference (WI)*, pages 529–535, Compiegne, France.

Vikas Sindhwani and S. Sathiya Keerthi. 2006. Large scale semi-supervised linear svms. In *Annual ACM SIGIR Conference on Research and Development in Information Retrieval(SIGIR)*.

Jorge Vivaldi and Horacio Rodrguez. 2010. Finding domain terms using wikipedia. In *Proceedings of the Seventh conference on International Language Resources and Evaluation (LREC2010)*.

Alexander Yeh. 2000. More accurate tests for the statistical significance of result differences. In *International Conference on Computational Linguistics (COLING)*, pages 947–953.

Frontier Pruning for Shift-Reduce CCG Parsing

Stephen Merity and **James R. Curran**
School of Information Technologies
University of Sydney
NSW 2006, Australia
{smerity, james}@it.usyd.edu.au

Abstract

We apply the graph-structured stack (GSS) to shift-reduce parsing in a Combinatory Categorial Grammar (CCG) parser. This allows the shift-reduce parser to explore all possible parses in polynomial time without resorting to heuristics, such as beam search. The GSS-based shift-reduce parser is 34% slower than CKY in the finely-tuned C&C parser. We perform *frontier pruning* on the GSS, increasing the parsing speed to be competitive with the C&C parser with a small accuracy penalty.

1 Introduction

Parsing is a vital component of sophisticated natural language processing (NLP) systems that require deep and accurate semantic interpretation, including question answering and summarisation. Unfortunately, the complexity of natural languages results in substantial ambiguity. For even a typical sentence, thousands of potential analyses may be considered by a wide-coverage parser, making parsing impractical for large-scale applications.

Several methods have been proposed to improve parsing speed, including supertagging (Bangalore and Joshi, 1999; Clark and Curran, 2004; Kummerfeld et al., 2010), coarse-to-fine parsing (Charniak and Johnson, 2005; Pauls and Klein, 2009), chart repair (Djordjevic, 2006), chart constraints (Roark and Hollingshead, 2009), structure caching (Dawborn and Curran, 2009) and chart pruning (Zhang et al., 2010). These heuristic methods offer a trade-off between accuracy and speed. A* parsing (Klein and Manning, 2003) offers speed increases with no reduction in accuracy. For parsers optimised for speed, the overhead required by additional efficiency techniques can exceed the speed gains they provide (Dawborn and Curran, 2009). As mistakes made in the parsing phase propagate to later stages, high speed but low accuracy parsers may not be useful in NLP systems (Chang et al., 2006).

In this paper, we modify the C&C (Clark and Curran, 2007) Combinatory Categorial Grammar (CCG) parser to enable shift-reduce (SR) parsing. The Cocke-Kasami-Younger (CKY) algorithm (Kasami, 1965; Younger, 1967) is replaced with the shift-reduce algorithm (Aho and Ullman, 1972). However, back-tracking in shift-reduce parsers make them exponential in the worst case.

To eliminate this duplication of work, a graph-structured stack (GSS; Tomita, 1988) is employed. This is the equivalent, for shift-reduce parsing, of the chart in CKY parsing, which stores all possible parse states compactly and enables polynomial time worst-case complexity. Due to the incremental nature of shift-reduce parsing, we can perform pruning of the parse state in the process of considering the next word (the frontier). Our *frontier pruning* model is an averaged perceptron trained to recognise the highest-scoring derivation that the C&C parser would have selected. By eliminating unlikely derivations , we substantially decrease the amount of ambiguity that the parser is required to handle.

The GSS SR parser considers all the derivations that the C&C parser would consider, but is 34% slower. When frontier pruning is applied, incremental parsing speed is improved by 39% relative to the GSS parser with a negligible impact on accuracy.

2 CCG Parsing

Combinatory Categorial Grammar (CCG; Steedman, 2000) is a lexicalised grammar formalism that incorporates both constituent structure and dependency information into its analyses.

In CCG, each word is assigned a category which encodes sub-categorisation information. Categories may be *atomic*, such as N and S; or *complex*, such as NP/N for a word that requires an N to the right to produce an NP. Similarly, $S\backslash NP$ is an intransitive verb and produces a sentence when an NP is found to the left. Finally, a transitive verb receives $(S\backslash NP)/NP$ as it consumes an NP on the right, producing a verb phrase. Figure 1 shows two examples of CCG derivations with lexical categories assigned to each word. Both examples also provide the word saw with the $(S\backslash NP)/NP$ category.

Lexicalised grammars typically have a small set of rules (the *combinatory rules* in CCG) and instead rely on categories that describe a word's syntactic role in a sentence. In Figure 1, the word with contains two separate categories indicating whether it modifies saw (first example) or John (second example). In a highly lexicalised grammar, a parser may need to explore a large search space of categories in order to select the correct category for each word.

Bangalore and Joshi (1999) proposed *supertagging*, where each word is assigned a reduced set of categories by a sequence tagger, rather than all of the categories previously seen with that word. Our supertags are CCG categories, and so are much more detailed than POS tags. By limiting the number of supertags for each word, there is a massive reduction in the number of derivations. The effectiveness of supertagging (Clark and Curran, 2004) demonstrates the influence of lexical ambiguity on parsing complexity for lexicalised grammars.

Hockenmaier and Steedman (2007) developed CCGbank, a semi-automated conversion of the Penn Treebank (Marcus et al., 1993) to the CCG formalism. A number of statistical parsers (Hockenmaier and Steedman, 2002; Clark et al., 2002) have been created for CCG parsing using CCGbank.

2.1 The C&C Parser

Clark and Curran (2007) describe the three stages of the high-performance C&C CCG parser. First, the supertagger provides each word with a set of likely categories, reducing the search space considerably. Second, the parser combines the categories, using the CKY chart-parsing algorithm and CCG's combinatory rules, to produce all derivations that can be constructed with the given categories. Finally, the decoder finds the best derivation from amongst the spanning analyses in the chart.

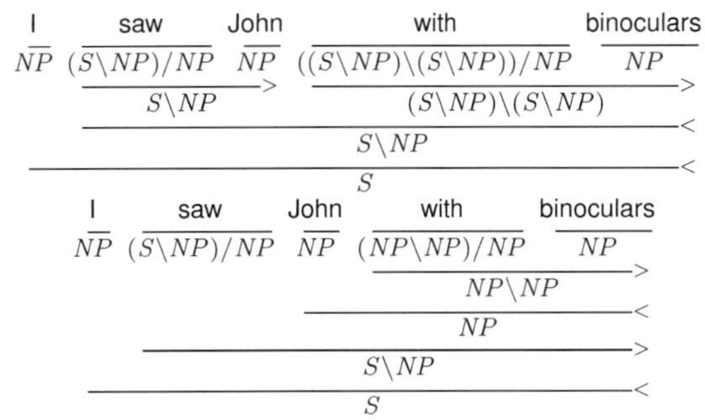

Figure 1: Two CCG derivations with PP ambiguity.

The C&C parser uses a maximum-entropy model to score each derivation, using a wide range of features defined over local sub-trees in the derivation, including the head words and their POS tags, the local categories, and word-word dependencies. We use the default normal-form mode with the derivations decoder (Clark and Curran, 2007) and a maximum of 1,000,000 categories in the chart.

Clark and Curran (2004) describe the role of supertagging in the C&C parser and its impact on parser speed. The supertagger initially assigns as few supertags as possible per word. If the parser is unable to provide a spanning analysis, the parser requests more supertags for each word. By restricting the number of supertags considered, this provides substantial pruning at the lexical level. Recent work by Kummerfeld et al. (2010) has shown that by training the supertagger on parser output, the parser's speed can be substantially increased whilst achieving the same accuracy as the baseline system. This exploits the idea that the only supertags the parser needs are those used by the highest-scoring derivation, reducing the search space even more than traditional supertagging.

Whilst the approach we present here focuses on CCG parsing, the techniques apply equally to any other binary branching or binarised grammars.

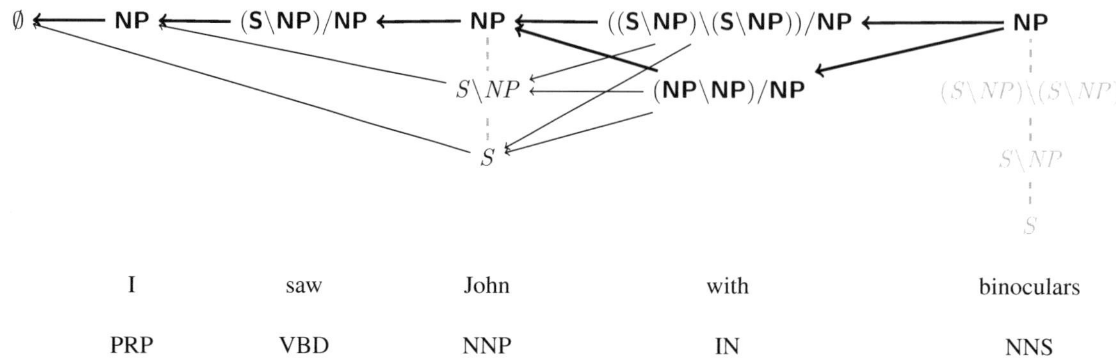

Figure 2: A graph-structured stack (GSS) representing an incomplete parse of the sentences found in Figure 1. The nodes and lines in bold were provided by the supertagger, whilst the non-bold nodes and lines have been created during parsing. The light gray lines represent what reduce operation created that lexical category.

3 Shift-Reduce Parsing

In its deterministic form, a shift-reduce parser performs a single left-to-right scan of the input sentence, selecting one or more actions at each step. The current state of the parser is stored in a stack, where the partial derivation is stored and the parsing operations are performed. For the actions, either we *shift* the current word onto the stack or *reduce* the top two (or more) items at the top of the stack (Aho and Ullman, 1972). As the scoring model can be defined over actions, this can allow for highly efficient parsing through greedy search (Sagae and Lavie, 2005). This has made shift-reduce parsing popular for high-speed dependency parsers (Yamada and Matsumoto, 2003; Nivre and Scholz, 2004).

Unfortunately, a deterministic shift-reduce parser cannot handle ambiguity because it only considers a single derivation. A simple extension is to eliminate determinism and perform a best-first search, backtracking if the parser reaches a dead end. This backtracking leads to duplicate construction of substructures and complete exploration is exponential in the worst case. Beam search has been used to handle this exponential explosion by discarding a large portion of the search space.

In Zhang and Clark (2011), a direct comparison is made between their shift-reduce CCG parser and the chart-based C&C parser. As CCG allows for a limited number of unary rules, specifically type-changing and type-raising, Zhang and Clark extend the shift-reduce algorithm to consider unary actions. In order to handle the exponential search space, their parser performs beam search, only keeping the top 16 scoring states. Whilst this approximate search may potentially lose the best scoring parse, they achieve competitive accuracies compared to the C&C chart parser.

3.1 Advantages of Semi-Incremental Parsing

Shift-reduce parsing allows for fully incremental parsing that does not require the full sentence. Whilst the C&C parser could be modified to perform in this fashion, POS tagging and supertagging accuracy would likely decrease, leading to lower overall parsing accuracy as mistakes propagate up the parsing pipeline.

Semi-incremental parsing can still be advantageous compared to non-incremental parsing. By using features to provide a partial understanding of the sentence structure to components not traditionally integrated with the parser, such as the POS tagger and supertagger, improved accuracy is possible. This is because these components currently only use the orthographic properties of the input text as features, with no understanding of how each word may be potentially used during parsing. In Merity (2011), we have begun exploring tightly integrating parsing and tagging, specifically for POS tags and supertags, by using semi-incremental parsing and shown improved tagging accuracy is possible.

3.2 Graph-Structured Stack

Back-tracking shift-reduce parsers are worst case exponential, preventing a full exploration of the search space. A graph-structured stack (GSS) is a general structure that allows for the efficient handling of non-determinism in shift-reduce parsing (Tomita, 1988). The GSS allows for polynomial time non-deterministic shift-reduce parsing and has been shown to be highly effective for dependency parsing (Huang and Sagae, 2010). The use of GSS allows for the incremental construction of the parse tree without being forced to discard large segments of the search space.

Here we will show an example of using a GSS to augment shift-reduce parsing and then show how it can be applied to CCG parsing. In the example grammar below, all three reduction rules are possible on the given stack. By performing backtracking and pursuing all possible reductions, shift-reduce parsing becomes worst-case exponential as previous results must be re-computed.

$$\emptyset \longleftarrow A \longleftarrow B \longleftarrow C \longleftarrow D \longleftarrow E$$

Reduction Rules				
F	$\leftarrow$	D	E	
G	$\leftarrow$	D	E	
H	$\leftarrow$	C	D	E

The GSS solves this by storing multiple possible derivations in a single structure. Note that all possible rules have been applied and are now stored in the GSS. These reduce operations are also non-destructive, leaving the original structure from the above figure in place. Thus, the GSS can store multiple possible derivations. Note that there is only a single bottom node, $\emptyset$, representing an empty stack.

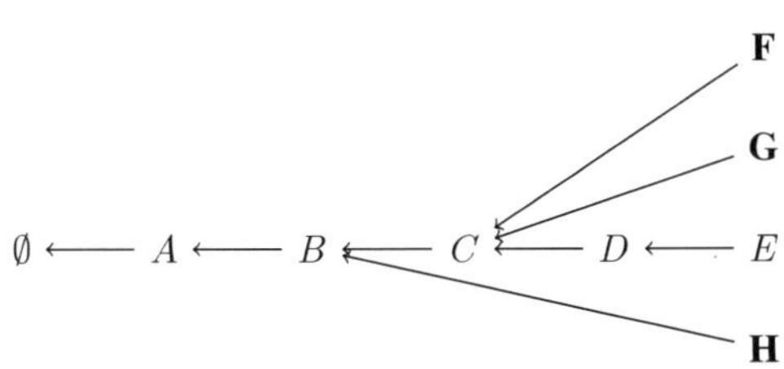

When a new node is pushed onto the stack, we combine it with the heads of all of the existing stacks stored in the GSS. This means that only a single shift action is necessary for the GSS instead of one for each possible derivation.

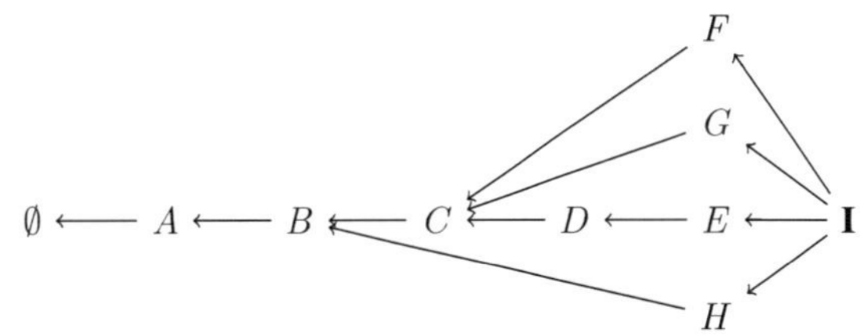

Finally, to prevent an exponential explosion due to local ambiguity, we check if a new partial derivation is equivalent to any existing partial derivations. If it is, we keep track of the ways the given node can be generated and then merge them into a single node. This is referred to as local ambiguity packing by Tomita (1988) and allows shift-reduce parsing to be performed in polynomial time. In the example below, the new reduction rules result in two new J nodes. These two nodes are merged to form a single node as they are equivalent.

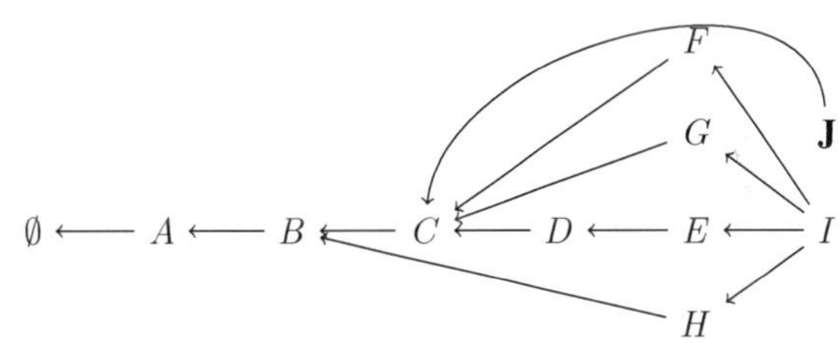

Reduction Rules			
J	$\leftarrow$	F	I
J	$\leftarrow$	G	I

When parsing an n word sentence, there are n possible stages in the GSS. We refer to these stages as *frontiers*, with the kth frontier containing all partial derivations that contain a total span of k. In CKY chart terms, a frontier can be considered as representing all cells on the diagonal from the top left to the bottom right, as seen in Figure 3.

Figure 2 represents an incomplete sentence processed using a GSS-based shift-reduce CCG parser. The frontier for the word with contains two heads, $((S\backslash NP)\backslash(S\backslash NP))/NP$ and $(NP\backslash NP)/NP$. When the CCG category for the

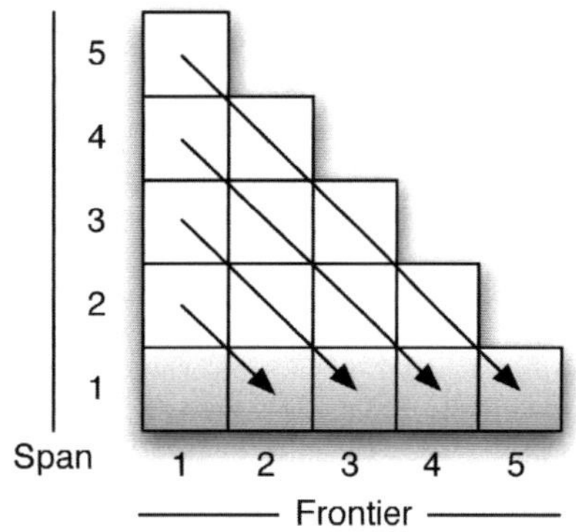

Figure 3: An illustration of the relation between the chart in CKY and the graph-structured stack in SR

word binoculars is shifted on to the GSS, it connects to both of the previous heads. As the category for the word binoculars is an NP, we can then reduce the stack by applying combinatory rules from CCG to both of the heads found in the previous frontier. In light gray, we show the full derivation for "John with binoculars".

During the parsing process, we start with an empty GSS. During the *shift* step, we add all the possible CCG categories provided by the supertagger for the kth word to the GSS and connect each category to all of the head categories on the GSS. Next, we attempt all possible *reduce* operations on the partial derivations in the current frontier. In CCG shift-reduce parsing, these reduce operations are the CCG combinatory rules. If a reduction is possible, we create a new top partial derivation from the result and place it in the kth frontier.

4 Frontier Pruning

The purpose of frontier pruning is to cut down the search space of the parser by only considering partial derivations that are likely to be in the highest-scoring derivation. Like adaptive supertagging, it exploits the idea that the only partial derivations the parser needs to generate are those used by the highest-scoring derivation. The model is trained using the parser's initial unpruned output and aims to distinguish between partial derivations that are necessary and those that are not. By eliminating a large number of those unnecessary partial derivations, parsing ambiguity is significantly decreased.

This approach is similar to beam search as frontier pruning removes partial derivations once it is likely they will not be used in the highest-scoring derivation. Beam search prunes nodes that are below a multiple (β) of the highest-scoring node in the frontier. For certain instances, such as n-best re-ranking, beam search would be preferred as derivations without the highest score are still useful in the parsing process. For one best parsing, however, the parser may waste time generating these additional derivations when it could be known in advanced that they will not be used. This could occur during attachment ambiguity where, although the parser is guaranteed to select one attachment, the other attachment may be constructed as it is valid and still competitive when considered by beam search's criteria.

5 Experiments

The only modifications are to the core parsing algorithm, which involves replacing CKY with SR, and to the parsing process via pruning. As the decoder and base models used for selecting the best-scoring derivation remain unchanged, any improvements seen are from an improved parsing process.

The C&C code base has been optimised for CKY parsing and we have made only limited attempts to optimise specifically for the shift-reduce approach. Due to this, the speed of the SR parser is 34% slower than the CKY parser. As the frontier pruning is implemented on the SR parser, all speeds will be relative to the SR baseline. For the frontier pruning SR parser to be competitive with the CKY parser, a speed improvement of 34% or more must be achieved.

5.1 Training and Processing

We train a binary averaged perceptron model (Collins, 2002) on parser output generated by the SR C&C parser using the standard parsing model. Once the base parser has successfully processed a sentence, all partial derivations that lead to the highest-scoring derivation are marked. For each partial derivation in the GSS, the perceptron model attempts to classify whether it was part of the marked set. If the classification is incorrect, the perceptron model updates the weights appropriately.

During processing, pruning occurs as each fron-

Feature Type	Example
Category	$S\backslash NP$
Binary Composition	$(S\backslash NP)/NP$ and NP
Forward Application	True
Head Word	*saw*
Head POS	VBD
Previous Frontier	NP
Next Frontier	$((S\backslash NP)\backslash(S\backslash NP))/NP$
Next Frontier	$(NP\backslash NP)/NP$

Table 1: Example features extracted from $S\backslash NP$ in the third frontier of Figure 2. For the frontier features, bold represents the highest-scoring feature selected for contribution to the classification decision.

tier is developed. For each partial derivation, the perceptron model classifies whether the partial derivation is likely to be used in the highest-scoring derivation. If not, the partial derivation is removed from the frontier, eliminating any paths that the partial derivation would have generated. Perfect frontier pruning would allow only a single derivation, specifically the highest-scoring one, to develop.

5.2 Model Features

For frontier pruning to be effective, the model must be able to accurately distinguish between partial derivations that will be used in the highest-scoring derivation and those that shall not. As the features of the C&C parser dictate the highest-scoring derivation, the features used for frontier pruning have been chosen to be similar. For a full description of the features used in the C&C parser, refer to Clark and Curran (2007).

Each partial derivation is given a base set of features derived from the current category. The initial features include a NULL which all categories receive, the CCG category itself and whether the category was assigned by the supertagger. There are also features that encode rule instantiation, including whether the category was created by type raising, a lexical rule, or any CCG combinatory rule. If the category was created by a CCG combinatory rule, the type of rule (such as forward/backward application and so on) is included as a feature.

Features representing the past decisions the parser has made are also included. Note that *current* represents the current category and *left/right* is the current category's left or right child respectively. For unary categories, a tuple of [current,current→left] is included as a feature. For binary categories, a tuple of [current→left, current, current→right] is included. If a category is a leaf, then two features [current, word] and [current, POS] are included. Features representing the root category of the partial derivation are also included, encoding the category head's word and POS tag.

Finally, additional features are added that represent the possible future parsing decisions. This is achieved by adding information about the remaining partial derivations on the stack (the past frontier) and the future incoming partial derivations (the next frontier). These do not exist in the C&C parser and are only possible due to the implementation of the GSS. For each category in the previous frontier, a feature is added of the type [previous, current]. For the next frontier, which is only composed of supertags at this point, the feature is [current, next]. These features allow the pruning classifier to determine whether the current category is likely to be active in any other reductions in future parsing work. As we only want to score the optimal path using the previous and next features, only the highest weighted of these features are selected. The rest of the previous and next features are discarded and do not contribute to the classification.

An example of this can be seen in Table 1, where the features for the partial derivation of $S\backslash NP$ are enumerated.

These features differ to the traditional features used by shift-reduce parsers due to the addition of the GSS. As traditional shift-reduce parsing only considers a single derivation at a time, it is trivial to include history further back than the current category's previous frontier. As GSS-based shift-reduce parsing encodes an exponential number of states, however, the overhead of unpacking these states into a feature representation is substantial. Our approximation of selecting the highest weighted previous and next frontier features approximates the non-deterministic shift-reduce solution.

5.3 Improving Marked Set Recall

Compared to the unmarked set, the marked set of partial derivations used to create the highest-scoring derivation is small. If a single CCG category from the marked set is pruned accidentally, the accuracy may be negatively impacted. The loss of a single category may even mean it is impossible to form a spanning analysis.

To prevent this loss of accuracy and coverage, the recall of the marked set needs to be improved. This can be achieved by biasing the binary perceptron algorithm towards a certain class, trading precision for recall. Traditionally, a binary perceptron classifier returns true if $w \cdot x > 0$, else false, with w being a vector of weights for each feature and x being a binary vector indicating whether a feature was active.

By providing a manual bias λ, $w \cdot x > \lambda$, we can bias the classifier towards a class. The value of λ modifies the perceptron threshold level, allowing us to improve the recall of the marked set by lowering the precision. The value for λ is obtained manually through the use of a development set.

Identifying the optimal threshold value is important. Too high a recall value would prevent pruning any parts of the parse tree whilst too low a threshold reverts back to traditional unpruned parsing. Due to the overheads involved in the frontier pruning process, ineffective frontier pruning may also be slower than traditional parsing, especially for an optimised parser such as the C&C parser. This value is determined experimentally using a development dataset.

5.4 Balancing Pruning Features and Speed

For frontier pruning to produce a speed gain, enough of the search space must be pruned in order to compensate for the additional computational overhead of the pruning step itself. This is a challenge as the C&C parser is written in *C++* with a focus on efficiency and already features substantial lexical pruning due to the use of supertagging.

For this reason, there were instances where expressive features needed to be traded for simpler features in the frontier pruning process. Whilst these simpler features may not prune as effectively, they take far less time to compute and result in higher speed gains than complex features with a further reduced search space. The complexity of the frontier pruning features may be dictated by the speed of the core parser itself, with more expressive features being possible if the core parser is slower.

The implementation of these features also had to focus on efficiency. To decrease the stress and improve memory locality of the hash table storing the feature weights, only a subset of features were stored. This feature subset was obtained from the gold standard training data as it contains far less ambiguity than the same training data which uses lexical categories supplied by the supertagger.

Hash tables were used for storing the relevant feature weights. Simple hash based feature representation were used for associating features with weights to reduce the complexity of equivalence checking. The hash values of features that were to be reused were also cached to prevent recalculation, substantially decreasing the computational overhead of feature calculation.

6 Evaluation

Our experiments are performed using CCGbank which was split into three subsets for training (Sections 02-21), development (Section 00), and the final evaluation (Section 23). The performance is measured in terms of sentence coverage, accuracy and parsing time. The accuracy is computed as F-score over the extracted labeled and unlabeled CCG dependencies found in CCGbank. All unmarked experiments use gold standard POS tags whilst experiments marked *Auto* use automatically assigned POS tags using the C&C POS tagger.

7 Results

7.1 Training the Frontier Pruning Algorithm

To establish bounds on the potential search space reduction, the size of the marked set compared to the total tree size was tracked over all sentences in the training data. This represents the size of the tree after optimal pruning occurs. Two figures are presented, one with gold supertags and the other with supertags supplied by the C&C supertagger. Gold represents the reduction in search space possible when only the correct CCG categories are used to parse the sentence. In contrast, the C&C supertagger may apply multiple CCG categories to improve supertagging accuracy, resulting in higher ambiguity and greater potential search space reductions.

As can be seen in Table 2, the size of the marked set is 10 times smaller for gold supertags and 15 times smaller for automatically supplied supertags.

Task	Acc.
Marked set recall (gold supertags)	84.4%
Marked set recall	72.9%
Average pruned size (gold supertags)	9.6%
Average pruned size	6.7%

Table 2: Recall of the marked set from the frontier pruning algorithm across all trees and the size of the pruned tree compared to the original tree.

This places an upper-bound on the potential speed improvement the parser may see due to aggressive frontier pruning.

The recall of the marked set was low for both gold supertags and automatically assigned supertags. This suggests the need for a modified perceptron threshold level in order to increase the recall of the marked set.

7.2 Tuning the Perceptron Threshold Level

Tuning the perceptron threshold level, as described in the previous section, has an important impact on frontier pruning. If the baseline parser cannot form a spanning analysis with the supertags initially supplied by the supertagger, it requests more supertags. Aggressive frontier pruning may counter-intuitively result in a slower parser as the parser spends more time attempting to unsuccessfully parse the sentence with an increasingly large number of supertags. By tuning the perceptron threshold level we can prevent potential slow-downs caused by aggressive pruning.

To optimise the threshold level, experiments were performed on the development portion of CCGbank, Section 00. The results are shown in Table 3. Decreasing the perceptron thresholds level (λ) is shown to decrease the speed of the parser substantially without increasing the accuracy. For extremely low values of λ, frontier pruning will keep partial derivations previously discarded as the perceptron classifier becomes biased towards recall. For a sufficiently low value, the accuracy would reach the same levels as the CKY and SR C&C parsers, but the speed would be far too slow due to the computational overhead of frontier pruning added to the small reduction in the search space. More work on fine-tuning the feature representation and allowing for more expressive features in a faster manner will be required.

Model	Coverage (%)	lf. (%)	uf. (%)	Speed (sents/sec)
CKY C&C	99.01	86.37	92.56	55.6
SR C&C	98.90	86.35	92.44	48.6
FP $\lambda = 0$	99.01	86.11	92.25	61.1
FP $\lambda = -1$	99.06	86.16	92.23	56.4
FP $\lambda = -2$	99.01	86.13	92.19	53.9
FP $\lambda = -3$	99.06	86.15	92.21	49.0
CKY C&C Auto	98.90	84.30	91.26	56.2
SR C&C Auto	98.85	84.27	91.10	47.5
FP $\lambda = 0$ Auto	98.80	84.09	90.97	60.0

Table 3: Comparison to baseline parsers and analysis of the impact of threshold levels on frontier pruning (FP). The perceptron threshold level is referred to as λ. All results are against the development dataset, Section 00 of CCGbank, which contains 1,913 sentences.

For $\lambda = 0$, however, frontier pruning increases the parser's speed by 25.7% compared to the baseline GSS-based SR parser on which the frontier pruning operates. There is also a small 9.8% speed increase compared to the CKY baseline parser. The F-score for both labeled and unlabeled dependencies is negatively impacted though.

7.3 Speed Improvements during Evaluation

Table 4 reports the impact frontier pruning has on speed compared to the baseline CKY and SR C&C parsers. Frontier pruning has improved the speed of the GSS-based SR C&C parser by 39%, an improvement over the speed increase seen during evaluation. Longer sentences seem to have a higher impact on the speed of the frontier pruning algorithm due to the increased computational complexity of feature generation. This indicates that implementing a form of beam search on top of this may be beneficial, keeping on the top k scoring states in a frontier. Currently all partial derivations that are greater than the perceptron threshold level λ are kept.

8 Discussion and future work

As the C&C parser is already highly tuned and thus extremely fast, the optimal balance between feature expressiveness and accurate pruning is difficult to achieve. However, there was still room for improvement. This suggests that on slower parsers than the C&C parser, frontier pruning may have a much more substantial impact on parsing speeds.

Model	Coverage (%)	lf. (%)	uf. (%)	Speed (sents/sec)
CKY C&C	99.34	86.79	92.50	96.3
SR C&C	99.58	86.78	92.41	71.3
FP $\lambda = 0$	99.38	86.51	92.25	95.4
CKY C&C Auto	99.25	84.59	91.20	82.0
SR C&C Auto	99.50	84.53	91.09	61.2
FP $\lambda = 0$ Auto	99.29	84.29	90.88	84.9

Table 4: Final evaluation on Section 23 of CCGbank for the top performing models from Table 3, containing 2,407 sentences.

More work needs to be done on reducing the number of computationally intensive feature look-ups and calculations. Even when using the gold-standard subset of the features, the feature look-up process accounts for the majority of the slow-down that the frontier pruning algorithm causes.

The C&C code has been highly optimised to suit CKY parsing. It should be possible to improve the GSS parser to be directly competitive with the CKY implementation. The frontier pruning provides speed increases for the GSS parser, allowing it to be competitive with the original CKY parser, but with an improved GSS parser, we could expect further improvements over the original CKY parser.

Finally, we are still using the separate maximum entropy model and decoder to find the best derivation. If we add more features to the perceptron model, it may be possible to use it for frontier pruning and finding the best derivation.

9 Conclusion

We present a shift-reduce CCG parser that can explore all possible analyses in polynomial time through the use of a graph-structured stack (GSS). Whilst this parser is 34% slower than the CKY parser on which it is based, it can parse 60 sentences per second whilst exploring the full search space. We show that by performing frontier pruning on the GSS and reducing this search space, the speed of the GSS parser can be improved by 39% whilst only incurring a small accuracy penalty. This allows for shift-reduce parsing to attain speeds directly competitive with the CKY parser, whilst allowing all the potential advantages of a semi-incremental parser.

We have also shown that whilst pruning is occurring at the lexical level due to supertagging, substantial speed-ups are still possible by performing pruning during the parsing process itself. This has also illustrated the difficulty in balancing expressive features and feature calculations overhead that frontier pruning needs to achieve.

Our approach uses the output of the original C&C parser as training data, and so we can use any amount of parser output to train the system. This self-training has been shown to be highly effective in adaptive supertagging for increasing parser speed (Kummerfeld et al., 2010). The final result will be a substantially faster wide-coverage CCG parser that can be used for large-scale NLP applications.

Acknowledgements

This work was supported by the Capital Markets Cooperative Research Centre, an Australian Research Council Discovery grant DP1097291 and a University of Sydney Honours Scholarship. We thank the anonymous reviewers for their insightful feedback.

References

Alred V. Aho and Jeffrey D. Ullman. 1972. *The Theory of Parsing, Translation, and Compiling. Volume I: Parsing*. Prentice-Hall.

Srinivas Bangalore and Aravind K. Joshi. 1999. Supertagging: An Approach to Almost Parsing. *Computational Linguistics*, 25(2):237–265.

Ming-Wei Chang, Quang Do, and Dan Roth. 2006. Multilingual Dependency Parsing: A Pipeline Approach. In Nicolas Nicolov, editor, *Recent Advances in Natural Language Processing*.

Eugene Charniak and Mark Johnson. 2005. Coarse-to-Fine n-Best Parsing and MaxEnt Discriminative Reranking. In *Proceedings of the 43rd Annual Meeting of the Association for Computational Linguistics (ACL-05)*, pages 173–180, Ann Arbor, Michigan, USA, June.

Stephen Clark and James R. Curran. 2004. The Importance of Supertagging for Wide-Coverage CCG Parsing. In *Proceedings of the 20th International Conference on Computational Linguistics (COLING-04)*, pages 282–288, Geneva, Switzerland, August.

Stephen Clark and James R. Curran. 2007. Wide-Coverage Efficient Statistical Parsing with CCG and Log-Linear Models. *Computational Linguistics*, 33(4):493–552.

Stephen Clark, Julia Hockenmaier, and Mark Steedman. 2002. Building Deep Dependency Structures using a Wide-Coverage CCG Parser. In *Proceedings of the 40th Annual Meeting of the Association for Computational Linguistics (ACL-02)*, pages 327–334, Philadelphia, Pennsylvania, USA, July.

Michael Collins. 2002. Discriminative Training Methods for Hidden Markov Models: Theory and Experiments with Perceptron Algorithms. In *Proceedings of the 2002 Conference on Empirical Methods in Natural Language Processing (EMNLP-03)*, pages 1–8.

Tim Dawborn and James R. Curran. 2009. CCG parsing with one syntactic structure per n-gram. In *Proceedings of the Australasian Language Technology Association Workshop 2009 (ALTA-09)*, pages 71–79, Sydney, Australia, December.

Bojan Djordjevic. 2006. Efficient Combinatory Categorial Grammar Parsing. In *Proceedings of the 2006 Australasian Language Technology Workshop (ALTW-06)*, pages 3–10, Sydney, Australia, December.

Julia Hockenmaier and Mark Steedman. 2002. Generative Models for Statistical Parsing with Combinatory Categorial Grammar. In *Proceedings of the 40th Annual Meeting of the Association for Computational Linguistics (ACL-02)*, pages 335–342, Philadelphia, PA.

Julia Hockenmaier and Mark Steedman. 2007. CCGbank: A Corpus of CCG Derivations and Dependency Structures Extracted from the Penn Treebank. *Computational Linguistics*, 33(3):355–396.

Liang Huang and Kenji Sagae. 2010. Dynamic programming for linear-time incremental parsing. In *Proceedings of the 48th Annual Meeting of the Association for Computational Linguistics (ACL-10)*, pages 1077–1086, Uppsala, Sweden, July.

Tadao Kasami. 1965. An efficient recognition and syntax analysis algorithm for context-free languages. Technical Report AFCRL-65-758, Air Force Cambridge Research Laboratory, Bedford, MA.

Dan Klein and Christopher D. Manning. 2003. A* Parsing: Fast Exact Viterbi Parse Selection. In *Proceedings of the Human Language Technology Conference and the North American Association for Computational Linguistics (HLT-NAACL-03)*, volume 3, pages 119–126.

Jonathan K. Kummerfeld, Jessika Roesner, Tim Dawborn, James Haggerty, James R. Curran, and Stephen Clark. 2010. Faster Parsing by Supertagger Adaptation. In *Proceedings of the 48th Annual Meeting of the Association for Computational Linguistics (ACL-10)*, pages 345–355, Uppsala, Sweden, July.

Mitchell P. Marcus, Beatrice Santorini, and Mary Ann Marcinkiewicz. 1993. Building a Large Annotated Corpus of English: The Penn Treebank. *Computational Linguistics*, 19(2):313–330.

Stephen Merity. 2011. *Integrated Tagging and Pruning via Shift-Reduce CCG Parsing*. Honours Thesis, The University of Sydney, Sydney, Australia.

Joakim Nivre and Mario Scholz. 2004. Deterministic Dependency Parsing of English Text. In *Proceedings of the 18nd International Conference on Computational Linguistics (COLING-04)*, pages 64–70, Geneva, Switzerland, August.

Adam Pauls and Dan Klein. 2009. K-Best A* Parsing. In *Proceedings of the Joint Conference of the 47th Annual Meeting of the ACL and the 4th International Joint Conference on Natural Language Processing of the AFNLP*, pages 958–966, Singapore, August.

Brian Roark and Kristy Hollingshead. 2009. Linear Complexity Context-Free Parsing Pipelines via Chart Constraints. In *Proceedings of 2009 Human Language Technology Conference of the North American Chapter of the Association for Computational Linguistics (HLT/NAACL-09)*, pages 647–655, Boulder, Colorado, June.

Kenji Sagae and Alon Lavie. 2005. A Classifier-Based Parser with Linear Run-Time Complexity. In *Proceedings of the Ninth International Workshop on Parsing Technology (IWPT-05)*, pages 125–132, Vancouver, British Columbia, Canada, October.

Mark Steedman. 2000. *The Syntactic Process*. MIT Press, Cambridge, Massachusetts, USA.

Masaru Tomita. 1988. Graph-structured Stack and Natural Language Parsing. In *Proceedings of the 26th Annual Meeting of the Association for Computational Linguistics*, pages 249–257, Buffalo, New York, USA, June.

Hiroyasu Yamada and Yuji Matsumoto. 2003. Statistical Dependency Analysis with Support Vector Machines. *Proceedings of International Conference on Parsing Technologies (IWPT-03)*, pages 195–206.

Daniel H. Younger. 1967. Recognition and Parsing of Context-Free Languages in Time n^3. *Information and Control*, 10(2):189–208, February.

Yue Zhang and Stephen Clark. 2011. Shift-Reduce CCG Parsing. In *Proceedings of the 49th Annual Meeting of the Association for Computational Linguistics: Human Language Technologies (ACL-11:HLT)*, pages 683–692, Portland, Oregon, USA, June.

Yue Zhang, Byung-Gyu Ahn, Stephen Clark, Curt Van Wyk, James R. Curran, and Laura Rimell. 2010. Chart Pruning for Fast Lexicalised-Grammar Parsing. In *Proceedings of the COLING 2010 Poster Sessions*, pages 1471–1479, Beijing, China, August.

Predicting Thread Linking Structure by Lexical Chaining

Li Wang,[♠♡] **Diana McCarthy**[◇] and **Timothy Baldwin**[♠♡]
♠ Dept. of Computer Science and Software Engineering, University of Melbourne
♡ NICTA Victoria Research Laboratory
◇ Lexical Computing Ltd
li.wang.d@gmail.com, diana@dianamccarthy.co.uk, tb@ldwin.net

Abstract

Web user forums are valuable means for users to resolve specific information needs, both interactively for participants and statically for users who search/browse over historical thread data. However, the complex structure of forum threads can make it difficult for users to extract relevant information. Thread linking structure has the potential to help tasks such as information retrieval (IR) and threading visualisation of forums, thereby improving information access. Unfortunately, thread linking structure is not always available in forums.

This paper proposes an unsupervised approach to predict forum thread linking structure using lexical chaining, a technique which identifies lists of related word tokens within a given discourse. Three lexical chaining algorithms, including one that only uses statistical associations between words, are experimented with. Preliminary experiments lead to results which surpass an informed baseline.

1 Introduction

Web user forums (or simply "forums") are online platforms for people to discuss and obtain information via a text-based threaded discourse, generally in a pre-determined domain (e.g. IT support or DSLR cameras). With the advent of Web 2.0, there has been rapid growth of web authorship in this area, and forums are now widely used in various areas such as customer support, community development, interactive reporting and online education. In addition to providing the means to interactively participate in discussions or obtain/provide answers to questions, the vast volumes of data contained in forums make them a valuable resource for "support sharing", i.e. looking over records of past user interactions to potentially find an immediately applicable solution to a current problem. On the one hand, more and more answers to questions over a wide range of domains are becoming available on forums; on the other hand, it is becoming harder and harder to extract and access relevant information due to the sheer scale and diversity of the data.

Previous research shows that the thread linking structure can be used to improve information retrieval (IR) in forums, at both the post level (Xi et al., 2004; Seo et al., 2009) and thread level (Seo et al., 2009; Elsas and Carbonell, 2009). These inter-post links also have the potential to enhance threading visualisation, thereby improving information access over complex threads. Unfortunately, linking information is not supported in many forums. While researchers have started to investigate the task of thread linking structure recovery (Kim et al., 2010; Wang et al., 2011b), most research efforts focus on supervised methods.

To illustrate the task of thread linking recovery, we use an example thread, made up of 5 posts from 4 distinct participants, from the CNET forum dataset of Kim et al. (2010), as shown in Figure 1. The linking structure of the thread is modelled as a rooted directed acyclic graph (DAG). In this example, UserA initiates the thread with a question in the first post, by asking how to create an interactive input box on a webpage. This post is linked to a virtual root with link label 0. In response, UserB and UserC pro-

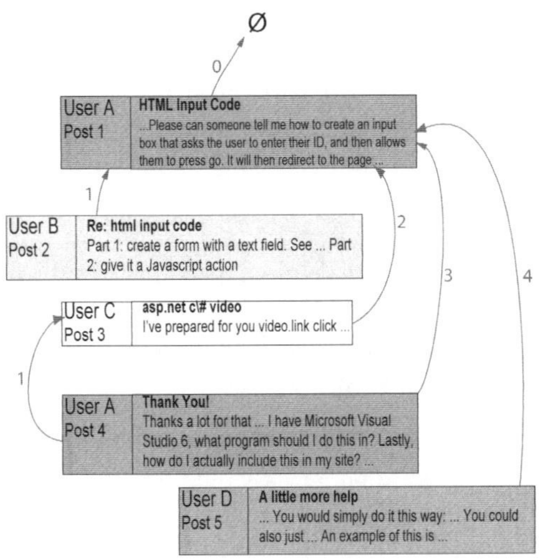

Figure 1: A snippeted CNET thread annotated with linking structure

vide independent answers. Therefore their posts are linked to the first post, with link labels 1 and 2 respectively. UserA responds to UserC (link = 1) to confirm the details of the solution, and at the same time, adds extra information to his/her original question (link = 3); i.e., this one post has two distinct links associated with it. Finally, UserD proposes a different solution again to the original question (link = 4).

Lexical chaining is a technique for identifying lists of related words (lexical chains) within a given discourse. The extracted lexical chains represent the discourse's lexical cohesion, or "cohesion indicated by relations between words in the two units, such as use of an identical word, a synonym, or a hypernym" (Jurafsky and Martin, 2008, pp. 685).

Lexical chaining has been investigated in many research tasks such as text segmentation (Stokes et al., 2004), word sense disambiguation (Galley and McKeown, 2003), and text summarisation (Barzilay and Elhadad, 1997). The lexical chaining algorithms used usually rely on domain-independent thesauri such as Roget's Thesaurus, the Macquarie Thesaurus (Bernard, 1986) and WordNet (Fellbaum, 1998), with some algorithms also utilising statistical associations between words (Stokes et al., 2004; Marathe and Hirst, 2010).

This paper explores unsupervised approaches for forum thread linking structure recovery, by using lexical chaining to analyse the inter-post lexical cohesion. We investigate three lexical chaining algorithms, including one that only uses statistical associations between words. The contributions of this research are:

- Proposal of an unsupervised approach using lexical chaining to recover the inter-post links in web user forum threads.
- Proposal of a lexical chaining approach that only uses statistical associations between words, which can be calculated from the raw text of the targeted domain.

The remainder of this paper is organised as follows. Firstly, we review related research on forum thread linking structure classification and lexical chaining. Then, the three lexical chaining algorithms used in this paper are described in detail. Next, the dataset and the experimental methodology are explained, followed by the experiments and analysis. Finally, the paper concludes with a brief summary and possible future work.

2 Related Work

The linking structure of web user forum threads can be used in tasks such as IR (Xi et al., 2004; Seo et al., 2009; Elsas and Carbonell, 2009) and threading visualisation. However, many user forums don't support the user input of linking information. Automatically recovering the linking structure of forum threads is therefore an interesting task, and has started to attract research efforts in recent years. All the methods investigated so far are supervised, such as ranking SVMs (Seo et al., 2009), SVM-HMMs (Kim et al., 2010), Maximum Entropy (Kim et al., 2010) and Conditional Random Fields (CRF) (Kim et al., 2010; Wang et al., 2011b; Wang et al., 2011a; Aumayr et al., 2011), with CRF models frequently being reported to deliver superior performance. While there is research that attempts to conduct cross-forum classification (Wang et al., 2011a) — where classifiers are trained over linking labels from one forum and tested over threads from other forums — the results have not been promising. This research explores unsupervised methods for thread linking structure recovery, by exploiting lexical cohesion between posts via lexical chaining.

The first computational model for lexical chain extraction was proposed by Morris and Hirst (1991), based on the use of the hierarchical structure of Roget's International Thesaurus, 4th Edition (1977). Because of the lack of a machine-readable copy of the thesaurus at the time, the lexical chains were built by hand. Research in lexical chaining has then been investigated by researchers from different research fields such as information retrieval, and natural language processing. It has been demonstrated that the textual knowledge provided by lexical chains can benefit many tasks, including text segmentation (Kozima, 1993; Stokes et al., 2004), word sense disambiguation (Galley and McKeown, 2003), text summarisation (Barzilay and Elhadad, 1997), topic detection and tracking (Stokes and Carthy, 2001), information retrieval (Stairmand, 1997), malapropism detection (Hirst and St-Onge, 1998), and question answering (Moldovan and Novischi, 2002).

Many types of lexical chaining algorithms rely on examining lexicographical relationships (i.e. semantic measures) between words using domain-independent thesauri such as the Longmans Dictionary of Contemporay English (Kozima, 1993), Roget's Thesaurus (Jarmasz and Szpakowicz, 2003), Macquarie Thesaurus (Marathe and Hirst, 2010) or WordNet (Barzilay and Elhadad, 1997; Hirst and St-Onge, 1998; Moldovan and Novischi, 2002; Galley and McKeown, 2003). These lexical chaining algorithms are limited by the linguistic resources they depend upon, and often only apply to nouns.

Some lexical chaining algorithms also make use of statistical associations (i.e. distributional measures) between words which can be automatically generated from domain-specific corpora. For example, Stokes et al. (2004)'s lexical chainer extracts significant noun bigrams based on the G^2 statistic (Pedersen, 1996), and uses these statistical word associations to find related words in the preceding context, building on the work of Hirst and St-Onge (1998). Marathe and Hirst (2010) use distributional measures of conceptual distance, based on the methodology of Mohammad and Hirst (2006) to compute the relation between two words. This framework uses a very coarse-grained sense (concept or category) inventory from the Macquarie Thesaurus (Bernard, 1986) to build a word-category co-occurrence matrix (WCCM), based on the British National Corpus (BNC). Lin (1998a)'s measure of distributional similarity based on point-wise mutual information (PMI) is then used to measure the association between words.

This research will explore two thesaurus-based lexical chaining algorithms, as well as a novel lexical chaining approach which relies solely on statistical word associations.

3 Lexical Chaining Algorithms

Three lexical chaining algorithms are experimented with in this research, as detailed in the following sections.

3.1 $Chainer_{Roget}$

$Chainer_{Roget}$ is a Roget's Thesaurus based lexical chaining algorithm (Jarmasz and Szpakowicz, 2003) based on an off-the-shelf package, namely the Electronic Lexical Knowledge Base (ELKB) (Jarmasz and Szpakowicz, 2001).

The underlying methodology of $Chainer_{Roget}$ is shown in Algorithm 1. Methods used to calculate the chain strength/weight are presented in Section 5. While the original Roget's Thesaurus-based algorithm by Morris and Hirst (1991) proposes five types of thesaural relations to add a candidate word in a chain, $Chainer_{Roget}$ only uses the first one, as is explained in Algorithm 1. Moreover, while Jarmasz and Szpakowicz (2003) use the 1987 Penguin's Roget's Thesaurus in their research, the ELKB package uses the Roget's Thesaurus from 1911 due to copyright restriction.

3.2 $Chainer_{WN}$

$Chainer_{WN}$ is a non-greedy WordNet-based chaining algorithm proposed by Galley and McKeown (2003). We reimplemented their method based on an incomplete implementation in NLTK.[1]

The algorithm of $Chainer_{WN}$ is based on the assumption of one sense per discourse, and can be decomposed into three steps. Firstly, a "disambiguation graph" is built by adding the candidate nouns of

[1] http://people.virginia.edu/~ma5ke/classes/files/cs65lexicalChain.pdf

Algorithm 1 $Chainer_{Roget}$

select a set of candidate nouns
for each candidate noun **do**
build all the possible chains, where each pair of nouns in each chain are either the same word or included in the same *Head* of *Roget's Thesaurus*, and select the strongest chain for each candidate noun.
end for
merge two chains if they contain at least one noun in common

the discourse one by one. Each node in the graph represents a noun instance with all its senses, and each weighted edge represents the semantic relation between two senses of two nouns. The weight of each edge is calculated based on the distances between nouns in the discourse. Secondly, word sense disambiguation (WSD) is performed. In this step, a score of every sense of each noun node is calculated by summing the weight of all edges leaving that sense. The sense of each noun node with the highest score is considered as the right sense of this noun in the discourse. Lastly, all the edges of the disambiguation graph connecting (assumed) wrong senses of every noun node are removed, and the remaining edges linking noun nodes form the lexical chains of the discourse. The semantic relations exploited in this algorithm include hypernyms/hyponyms and siblings (i.e. hyponyms of hypernyms).

3.3 $Chainer_{SV}$

$Chainer_{SV}$, as shown in Algorithm 2, is adapted from Marathe and Hirst (2010)'s lexical chaining algorithm. The main difference between $Chainer_{SV}$ and the original algorithm is the method used to calculate associations between words. Marathe and Hirst (2010) use two different measures, including Lin (1998b)'s WordNet-based measure, and Mohammad and Hirst (2006)'s distributional measures of concept distance framework. In $Chainer_{SV}$, we use word vectors from WORDSPACE (Schütze, 1998) models and apply cosine similarity to compute the associations between words. WORDSPACE is a multi-dimensional real-valued space, where words, contexts and senses are represented as vectors. A vector for word w is derived from words that co-occur with w. A dimensionality reduction technique is often used to reduce the dimension of the vector. We build the WORDSPACE model with SemanticVectors (Widdows and Ferraro, 2008), which is based on Random Projection dimensionality reduction (Bingham and Mannila, 2001).

The underlying methodology of $Chainer_{SV}$ is shown in Algorithm 2. This algorithm requires a method to calculate the similarity between two tokens (i.e. words): $sim_{tt}(x, y)$, which is done by computing the cosine similarity of the two tokens' semantic vectors. The similarity between a token t_i and a lexical chain c_j is then calculated by:

$$sim_{tc}(t_i, c_j) = \sum_{t_k \in c_j} \frac{1}{l_j} sim_{tt}(t_i, t_k)$$

where l_j represents the length of lexical chain c_j. The similarity between two chains c_i and c_j is then computed by:

$$sim_{cc}(c_i, c_j) = \sum_{t_m \in c_i, t_n \in c_j} \frac{1}{l_i \times l_j} sim_{tt}(t_m, t_n)$$

where l_i and l_j are the lengths of c_i and c_j respectively.

As is shown in Algorithm 2, $Chainer_{SV}$ has two parameters: the threshold for adding a token to a chain, $threshold_a$; and the threshold for merging two chains, $threshold_m$. A larger $threshold_a$ leads to conservative chains where tokens in a chain are strongly related, while a smaller $threshold_a$ results in longer chains where the relationship between tokens in a chain may not be clear. Similarly, a larger $threshold_m$ is conservative and leads to less chain merging, while a smaller $threshold_m$ may create longer but less meaningful chains. Our initial experiments show that the combination of $threshold_a = 0.1$ and $threshold_m = 0.05$ often results in lexical chains with reasonable lengths and interpretations. Therefore, this parameter setting will be used throughout all the experiments described in this paper.

4 Task Description and Dataset

The main task performed in this research is to recover inter-post links within forum threads, by

Algorithm 2 $Chainer_{SV}$

$chains = empty$
select a set of candidate tokens
for each candidate token t_i **do**
  $max\_score = \max_{c_j \in chains}(sim_{tc}(t_i, c_j))$
  $max\_chain = \arg\max_{c_j \in chains}(sim_{tc}(t_i, c_j))$
  if $chains = empty$ **or** $max\_score < threshold_a$ **then**
    create a new chain c_k containing t_i and add c_k to $chains$
  else if more than one max_chain **then**
    merge chains if the two chains' similarity is larger than $threshold_m$, and add t_i to the resultant chain or the first max_chain
  else
    add t_i to the max_chain
  end if
end for
return $chains$

analysing the lexical chains extracted from the posts. In this, we assume that a post can only link to an earlier post (or a virtual root node). Following Wang et al. (2011b), it is possible for there to be multiple links from a given post, e.g. if a post both confirms the validity of an answer and adds extra information to the original question (as happens in Post4 in Figure 1).

The dataset we use is the CNET forum dataset of Kim et al. (2010),[2] which contains 1332 annotated posts spanning 315 threads, collected from the Operating System, Software, Hardware and Web Development sub-forums of CNET.[3] Each post is labelled with one or more links (including the possibility of null-links, where the post doesn't link to any other post), and each link is labelled with a dialogue act. We only use the link part of the annotation in this research. For the details of the dialogue act tagset, see Kim et al. (2010).

We also obtain the original crawl of CNET forum collected by Kim et al. (2010), which contains 262,402 threads. To build a WORDSPACE model for $Chainer_{SV}$ as is explained in Section 3, only the threads from the four sub-forums mentioned above are chosen, which consist of 536,482 posts spanning 114,139 threads. The reason for choosing only a subset of the whole dataset is to maintain the same types of technical dialogues as the annotated posts. The texts (with stop words and punctuations removed) from the titles and bodies of the posts are then extracted and fed into the SemanticVectors package with default settings to obtain the semantic vector for each word token.

5 Methodology

To the best of our knowledge, no previous research has adopted lexical chaining to predict inter-post links. The basic idea of our approach is to use lexical chains to measure the inter-post lexical cohesion (i.e. lexical similarity), and use these similarity scores to reconstruct inter-post links. To measure the lexical cohesion between two posts, the texts (with stop words and punctuations removed) from the titles and bodies of the two posts are first combined. Then, lexical chainers are applied over the combined texts to extract lexical chains. Lastly, the following weighting methods are used to calculate the lexical similarity between the two posts:

LCNum: the number of the lexical chains which span the two posts.

LCLen: find the lexical chains which span the two posts, and use the sum of tokens contained in each as the similarity score.

LCStr: find the lexical chains which span the two posts, and use the sum of each chain's chain strength as the similarity score. The chain strength is calculated by using a formula suggested by Barzilay and Elhadad (1997):

$$Score(Chain) = Length \times Homogeneity$$

where $Length$ is the number of tokens in the chain, and $Homogeneity$ is $1-$ the number of distinct token occurrences divided by the $Length$.

LCBan: find the lexical chains which span the two posts, and use the sum of each chain's balance score as the similarity score. The balance score

[2]Available from http://www.csse.unimelb.edu.au/research/lt/resources/conll2010-thread/

[3]http://forums.cnet.com/

is calculated by using the following formula:

$$Score(Chain) = \begin{cases} n_1/n_2 & n_1 < n_2 \\ n_2/n_1 & else \end{cases}$$

where n_1 is the number of tokens from the chain belonging to the first post, and n_2 is the number of tokens from the chain belonging to the second post.

6 Assumptions, Experiments and Analysis

The experiment results are evaluated using micro-averaged Precision ($\mathcal{P}_\mu$), Recall ($\mathcal{R}_\mu$) and F-score ($\mathcal{F}_\mu$: $\beta = 1$), with $\mathcal{F}_\mu$ as the main evaluation metric. The statistical significance is tested using randomised estimation (Yeh, 2000) with $p < 0.05$.

As our baseline for the unsupervised task, an informed heuristic ($Heuristic$) is used, where all first posts are labelled with link 0 (i.e. link to a virtual root) and all other posts are labelled with link 1 (i.e. link to the immediately preceding post).

As is explained in Section 4, it is possible for there to be multiple links from a given post. Because these kinds of posts, which only account for less than 5% of the total posts, are sparse in the dataset, we only consider recovering one link per post in our experiments. However, our evaluation still considers all links (meaning that it is not possible for our methods to achieve an F-score of 1.0).

6.1 Initial Assumption and Experiments

We observe that in web user forum threads, if a post replies to a preceding post, the two posts are usually semantically related and lexically similar. Based on this observation, we make the following assumption:

Assumption 1. *A post should be similar to the preceding post it is linked to.*

This assumption leads to our first unsupervised model, which compares each post (except for the first and second) in a given thread with all its preceding posts one by one, by firstly identifying the lexical chains using the lexical chainers described in Section 3 and then calculating the inter-post lexical similarity using the methods explained in Section 5. The experimental results are shown in Table 1.

From Table 1 we can see that no results surpass the $Heuristic$ baseline. Further investigation reveals that while Assumption 1 is reasonable, it is not always correct —i.e. similar posts are not always linked together. For example, an answer post later in a thread might be linked back to the first question post but be more similar to preceding answer posts, to which it is not linked, simply because they are all answers to the same question. The initial experiments show that more careful analysis is needed to use inter-post lexical similarity to reconstruct inter-post linking.

Classifier	Weighting	$\mathcal{P}_\mu$	$\mathcal{R}_\mu$	$\mathcal{F}_\mu$
$Heuristic$	—	.810	.772	.791
$Chainer_{Roget}$	LCNum	.755	.720	.737
	LCLen	.737	.703	.720
	LCStr	.802	.764	.783
	LCBan	.723	.689	.706
$Chainer_{WN}$	LCNum	.685	.644	.660
	LCLen	.676	.651	.667
	LCStr	.718	.685	.701
	LCBan	.683	.651	.667
$Chainer_{SV}$	LCNum	.648	.618	.632
	LCLen	.630	.601	.615
	LCStr	.627	.598	.612
	LCBan	.645	.615	.630

Table 1: Results from the Assumption 1 based unsupervised approach, by using three lexical chaining algorithms with four different weighting schemes.

6.2 Post 3 Analysis

Because Post 1 and Post 2 are always labelled with link 0 and 1 respectively, our analysis starts from Post 3 of each thread. Based on the analysis, the second assumption is made:

Assumption 2. *If the Post 3 vs. Post 1 lexical similarity is larger than Post the 2 vs. Post 1 lexical similarity, then Post 3 is more likely to be linked back to Post 1.*

Assumption 2 leads to an unsupervised approach which combines the three lexical chaining algorithms introduced in Section 3 with the four weighting schemes explained in Section 5 to measure Post 3 vs. Post 1 similarity and Post 2 vs. Post 1 similarity. If the former is larger, Post 3 is linked back to Post 1, otherwise Post 3 is linked back to Post 2. As for the other posts, the link labels are the same as the ones from the $Heuristic$ baseline. The experimental results are shown in Table 2.

From the results in Table 2 we can see that $Chainer_{SV}$ is the only lexical chaining algorithm

Classifier	Weighting	$\mathcal{P}_\mu$	$\mathcal{R}_\mu$	$\mathcal{F}_\mu$
$Heuristic$	—	.810	.772	.791
$Chainer_{Roget}$	LCNum	.811	.773	.791
	LCLen	.811	.773	.791
	LCStr	.810	.772	.791
	LCBan	.813	.775	.794
$Chainer_{WN}$	LCNum	.806	.768	.786
	LCLen	.806	.769	.787
	LCStr	.806	.769	.787
	LCBan	.809	.771	.789
$Chainer_{SV}$	LCNum	.813	.775	.794
	LCLen	.813	.775	.794
	LCStr	.816	.778	.797
	LCBan	.818	.780	.799

Table 2: Results from the Assumption 2 based unsupervised approach, by using three lexical chaining algorithms with four different weighting schemes.

that leads to results which are better than the $Heuristic$ baseline. Analysis over the lexical chains generated by the three lexical chainers shows that both $Chainer_{Roget}$ and $Chainer_{WN}$ extract very few chains, most of which contain only repetitions of a same word. This is probably because these two lexical chainers only consider nouns, and therefore have limited input tokens. Especially for $Chainer_{Roget}$ which uses an old dictionary (1911 edition) that does not contain modern technical terms, such as *Windows*, *OSX* and *PC*. While $Chainer_{WN}$ uses WordNet which has a larger and more modern vocabulary, the chainer considers very limited semantic relations (i.e. hypernyms, hyponyms and hyponyms of hypernyms). Moreover, the texts in forum posts are usually relatively short and informal, and contain typos and non-standard acronyms. These factors make it very difficult for $Chainer_{Roget}$ and $Chainer_{WN}$ to extract lexical chains. As for $Chainer_{SV}$, because all the words (except for stop words) are considered as candidate words, and relations between words are flexible according to the thresholds (i.e. $threshold_a$ and $threshold_m$), relatively abundant lexical chains are generated. While some of the chains clearly capture lexical cohesion among words, some of the chains are hard to interpret. Nevertheless, the results from $Chainer_{SV}$ are encouraging for the unsupervised approach, and therefore further investigation is conducted using only $Chainer_{SV}$.

Because the experiments based on the Assumption 2 derive promising results, further analysis is conducted to enforce this assumption. We notice that the posts from the initiator of a thread are often outliers compared to other posts — i.e. these posts are similar to the first post because they are from the same author, but at the same time an initiator rarely replies to his/her own posts. This observation leads to a stricter assumption:

Classifier	Weighting	$\mathcal{P}_\mu$	$\mathcal{R}_\mu$	$\mathcal{F}_\mu$
$Heuristic$	—	.810	.772	.791
$Heuristic_{user}$	—	.839	.800	.819
$Chainer_{SV}$	LCNum	.832	.793	.812
	LCLen	.832	.793	.812
	LCStr	.831	.793	.812
	LCBan	.836	.797	.816

Table 3: Results from the Assumption 3 based unsupervised approach, by using $Chainer_{SV}$ with different weighting schemes

Assumption 3. *If Post 3 vs. Post 1 lexical similarity is larger than Post 2 vs. Post 1 lexical similarity and Post 3 is not posted by the initiator of the thread, then Post 3 is more likely to be linked back to Post 1.*

Based on Assumption 3, experiments are carried out using $Chainer_{SV}$ with different weighting schemes. We also introduce a stronger baseline ($Heuristic_{user}$) based on Assumption 3, where Post 3 is linked to Post 1 if these two posts are from different users and all the other posts are linked as $Heuristic$. The experimental results are shown in Table 3.

From Table 3 we can see that while all the results from $Chainer_{SV}$ are significantly better than the result from the $Heuristic$ baseline, with the LCBan weighting leading to the best $\mathcal{F}_\mu$ of 0.816, these results are not significantly different from the $Heuristic_{user}$ baseline. It is clear that the improvements attribute to the user constraint introduced in Assumption 3. This observation matches up with the results of supervised classification from Wang et al. (2011b), where the benefits brought by text similarity based features (i.e. TitSim and PostSim) are covered by more effective user information based features (i.e. UserProf).

Feature	Weighting	$\mathcal{P}_\mu$	$\mathcal{R}_\mu$	$\mathcal{F}_\mu$
$Heuristic$	—	.810	.772	.791
$Heuristic_{user}$	—	.839	.800	.819
NoLC	—	.898	.883	.891
WithLC	LCNum	.901	.886	.894
	LCLen	.902	.887	.894
	LCStr	.899	.884	.891
	LCBan	.905	.890	.897

Table 4: Supervised linking classification by applying $CRFSGD$ over features from Wang et al. (2011b) without (NoLC) and with (WithLC) features extracted from lexical chains, created by $Chainer_{SV}$ with different weighting schemes

6.3 Lexical Chaining for Supervised Learning

It is interesting to see whether our unsupervised approach can contribute to the supervised methods by providing additional features. To test this idea, we add a lexical chaining based feature to the classifier of Wang et al. (2011b) based on Assumption 3. The feature value for each post is calculated using the following formula:

$$feature = \begin{cases} \frac{sim(post3,post1)}{sim(post2,post1)} & Post3 \\ 0 & NonPost3 \end{cases}$$

where sim is calculated using $Chainer_{SV}$ with different weighting methods.

The experimental results are shown in Table 4. From the results we can see that, by adding the additional feature extracted from lexical chains, the results improve slightly. The feature from the $Chainer_{SV}$ with LCBan weighting leads to the best $\mathcal{F}_\mu$ of 0.897. These improvements are statistically insignificant, possibly because the information introduced by the lexical chaining feature is already captured by existing features. It is also possible that better feature representations are needed for the lexical chains.

These results are preliminary but nonetheless suggest the potential of utilising lexical chaining in the domain of web user forums.

6.4 Experiments over All the Posts

To date, all experiments have been based on just the first three posts in a thread, where the majority of our threads contain more than just three posts. We carried out preliminary experiments over full thread data, by generalising Assumption 3 to Post N for $N \geq 3$. However, no significant improvements were achieved over an informed baseline with our unsupervised approach. This is probably because the situation for later posts (after Post 3) is more complicated, as more linking options are possible. Relaxing the assumptions entirely also led to disappointing results. What appears to be needed is a more sophisticated set of constraints, to generalise the assumptions made for Post 3 to all the posts. We leave this for future work.

7 Conclusion

Web user forums are a valuable information source for users to resolve specific information needs. However, the complex structure of forum threads poses a challenge for users trying to extract relevant information. While the linking structure of forum threads has the potential to improve information access, these inter-post links are not always available.

In this research, we explore unsupervised approaches for thread linking structure recovery, by automatically analysing the lexical cohesion between posts. Lexical cohesion between posts is measured using lexical chaining, a technique to extract lists of related word tokens from a given discourse. Most lexical chaining algorithms use domain-independent thesauri and only consider nouns. In the domain of web user forums, where the texts of posts can be very short and contain various typos and special terms, these conventional lexical chaining algorithms often struggle to find proper lexical chains. To address this problem, we proposed the use of statistical associations between words, which are captured by the WORDSPACE model, to construct lexical chains. Our preliminary experiments derive results which are better than an informed baseline.

In future work, we want to explore methods which can be used to recover all the inter-post links. First, we plan to conduct more detailed analysis over inter-post lexical cohesion, and its relationship with inter-post links. Second, we want to investigate human linking behaviour in web user forums, hoping to find significant linking patterns. Furthermore, we want to investigate more methods and resources for constructing lexical chains, e.g. Cramer et al. (2012).

On top of exploring these potential approaches, it is worth considering stronger baseline methods such as using cosine similarity to measure inter-post similarity.

The $Chainer_{SV}$, as described in Section 4, is built on a WORDSPACE model learnt over a subset of four domains. It is also worth comparing with a more general WORDSPACE model learnt over the whole dataset.

As for supervised learning, it would be interesting to conduct experiments out of domain (i.e. train the model over threads from one forum, and classify threads from another forum), and compare with the unsupervised approaches. We also hope to investigate more effective ways of extracting features from the created lexical chains to improve supervised learning.

Acknowledgements

The authors wish to thank Malcolm Augat and Margaret Ladlow for providing access to their lexical chaining code, which was used to implement $Chainer_{WN}$. NICTA is funded by the Australian government as represented by Department of Broadband, Communication and Digital Economy, and the Australian Research Council through the ICT Centre of Excellence programme.

References

Erik Aumayr, Jeffrey Chan, and Conor Haye. 2011. Reconstruction of threaded conversations in online discussion forums. In *Proceedings of the Fifth International AAAI Conference on Weblogs and Social Media (ICWSM-11)*, pages 26–33, Barcelona, Spain.

Regina Barzilay and Michael Elhadad. 1997. Using lexical chains for text summarization. In *Proceedings of the Intelligent Scalable Text Summarization Workshop*, pages 10–17, Madrid, Spain.

J.R.L. Bernard, editor. 1986. *The Macquarie Thesaurus*. Macquarie Library,, Sydney, Australia.

Ella Bingham and Heikki Mannila. 2001. Random projection in dimensionality reduction: applications to image and text data. In *Proceedings of the Seventh ACM SIGKDD International Conference on Knowledge Discovery and Data Mining (KDD '01)*, pages 245–250, San Francisco, USA.

Léon Bottou. 2011. CRFSGD software. `http://leon.bottou.org/projects/sgd`.

Irene Cramer, Tonio Wandmacher, and Ulli Waltinger. 2012. Exploring resources for lexical chaining: A comparison of automated semantic relatedness measures and human judgments. In Alexander Mehler, Kai-Uwe Kühnberger, Henning Lobin, Harald Lüngen, Angelika Storrer, and Andreas Witt, editors, *Modeling, Learning, and Processing of Text Technological Data Structures*, volume 370 of *Studies in Computational Intelligence*, pages 377–396. Springer Berlin, Heidelberg.

Jonathan L. Elsas and Jaime G. Carbonell. 2009. It pays to be picky: An evaluation of thread retrieval in online forums. In *Proceedings of 32nd International ACM-SIGIR Conference on Research and Development in Information Retrieval (SIGIR'09)*, pages 714–715, Boston, USA.

Christiane Fellbaum, editor. 1998. *WordNet: An Electronic Lexical Database*. The MIT Press, Cambridge, USA.

Michel Galley and Kathleen McKeown. 2003. Improving word sense disambiguation in lexical chaining. In *Proceedings of the 18th International Joint Conference on Artificial Intelligence (IJCAI-03)*, pages 1486–1488, Acapulco, Mexico.

Graeme Hirst and David St-Onge. 1998. Lexical chains as representations of context for the detection and correction of malapropisms. In Christiane Fellbaum, editor, *WordNet: An electronic lexical database*, pages 305–332. The MIT Press, Cambridge, USA.

Mario Jarmasz and Stan Szpakowicz. 2001. The design and implementation of an electronic lexical knowledge base. *Advances in Artificial Intelligence*, 2056(2001):325–334.

Mario Jarmasz and Stan Szpakowicz. 2003. Not as easy as it seems: Automating the construction of lexical chains using rogets thesaurus. *Advances in Artificial Intelligence*, 2671(2003):994–999.

Daniel Jurafsky and James H. Martin. 2008. *SPEECH and LANGUAGE PROCESSING: An Introduction to Natural Language Processing, Computational Linguistics, and Speech Recognition*. Pearson Prentice Hall, 2nd edition.

Su Nam Kim, Li Wang, and Timothy Baldwin. 2010. Tagging and linking web forum posts. In *Proceedings of the 14th Conference on Computational Natural Language Learning (CoNLL-2010)*, pages 192–202, Uppsala, Sweden.

Hideki Kozima. 1993. Text segmentation based on similarity between words. In *Proceedings of the 31st Annual Meeting of the Association for Computational Linguistics*, pages 286–288, Columbus, USA.

Dekang Lin. 1998a. Automatic retrieval and clustering of similar words. In *Proceedings of the 36th An-*

nual Meeting of the ACL and 17th International Conference on Computational Linguistics (COLING/ACL-98), pages 768–774, Montreal, Canada.

Dekang Lin. 1998b. An information-theoretic definition of similarity. In *Proceedings of the 15th International Conference on Machine Learning (ICML'98)*, pages 296–304, Madison, USA.

Meghana Marathe and Graeme Hirst. 2010. Lexical chains using distributional measures of concept distance. In *Proceedings, 11th International Conference on Intelligent Text Processing and Computational Linguistics (CICLing-2010)*, pages 291–302, Iaşi, Romania.

Saif Mohammad and Graeme Hirst. 2006. Distributional measures of concept-distance: A task-oriented evaluation. In *Proceedings, 2006 Conference on Empirical Methods in Natural Language Processing (EMNLP 2006)*, pages 35–43, Sydney, Australia.

Dan Moldovan and Adrian Novischi. 2002. Lexical chains for question answering. In *Proceedings of the 19th International Conference on Computational Linguistics (COLING 2002)*, Taiwan.

Jane Morris and Graeme Hirst. 1991. Lexical cohesion computed by thesaural relations as an indicator of the structure of text. *Computational Linguistics*, 17(1):21–48.

Ted Pedersen. 1996. Fishing for exactness. In *Proceedings of the South-Central SAS Users Group Conference (SCSUG-96)*, Austin, USA.

Hinrich Schütze. 1998. Automatic word sense discrimination. *Computational Linguistics*, 24(1):97–123.

Jangwon Seo, W. Bruce Croft, and David A. Smith. 2009. Online community search using thread structure. In *Proceedings of the 18th ACM Conference on Information and Knowledge Management (CIKM 2009)*, pages 1907–1910, Hong Kong, China.

Mark A. Stairmand. 1997. Textual context analysis for information retrieval. In *Proceedings of the 20th annual international ACM SIGIR conference on Research and development in information retrieval (SIGIR '97)*, pages 140–147, Philadelphia, USA.

Nicola Stokes and Joe Carthy. 2001. Combining semantic and syntactic document classifiers to improve first story detection. In *Proceedings of the 24th annual international ACM SIGIR conference on Research and development in information retrieval (SIGIR 2001)*, pages 424–425, New Orleans, USA.

Nicola Stokes, Joe Carthy, and Alan F. Smeaton. 2004. SeLeCT: a lexical cohesion based news story segmentation system. *AI Communications*, 17(1):3–12.

Hongning Wang, Chi Wang, ChengXiang Zhai, and Jiawei Han. 2011a. Learning online discussion structures by conditional random fields. In *Proceedings of the 34th Annual International ACM SIGIR Conference (SIGIR 2011)*, pages 435–444, Beijing, China.

Li Wang, Marco Lui, Su Nam Kim, Joakim Nivre, and Timothy Baldwin. 2011b. Predicting thread discourse structure over technical web forums. In *Proceedings of the 2011 Conference on Empirical Methods in Natural Language Processing*, pages 13–25, Edinburgh, UK.

Dominic Widdows and Kathleen Ferraro. 2008. Semantic Vectors: a scalable open source package and online technology management application. In *Proceedings of the Sixth International Language Resources and Evaluation (LREC'08)*, pages 1183–1190, Marrakech, Morocco.

Wensi Xi, Jesper Lind, and Eric Brill. 2004. Learning effective ranking functions for newsgroup search. In *Proceedings of 27th International ACM-SIGIR Conference on Research and Development in Information Retrieval (SIGIR 2004)*, pages 394–401. Sheffield, UK.

Alexander Yeh. 2000. More accurate tests for the statistical significance of result differences. In *Proceedings of the 18th International Conference on Computational Linguistics (COLING 2000)*, pages 947–953, Saarbrücken, Germany.

Development of a Corpus for Evidence Based Medicine Summarisation

Diego Molla
Department of Computing
Macquarie University
Sydney, Australia
diego.molla-aliod@mq.edu.au

Maria Elena Santiago-Martinez
Department of Computing
Macquarie University
Sydney, Australia
maria.santiago-martinez@mq.edu.au

Abstract

In this paper we introduce some of the key NLP-related problems related to the practice of Evidence Based Medicine and propose the task of multi-document query-focused summarisation as a key approach to solve these problems. We have completed a corpus for the development of such multi-document query-focused summarisation task. The process to build the corpus combined the use of automated extraction of text, manual annotation, and crowdsourcing to find the reference IDs. We perform a statistical analysis of the corpus for the particular use of single-document summarisation and show that there is still a lot of room for improvement from the current baselines.

1 Introduction

An important form of medical practice is based on Evidence Based Medicine (EBM). (Sackett et al., 1996; Sackett et al., 2000). Within the EBM paradigm, the physician is urged to consider the best available evidence that is relevant to the patient at point of care. However, the physician is currently overwhelmed with the large volumes of published text available. For example, the US National Library of Medicine offers PubMed[1], a database of medical publications that comprises more than 19 million abstracts. The median time spent to conduct a clinical systematic review is 1,139 hours (Allen and Olkin, 1999). In contrast, the average time that a physician spends searching for a topic is two minutes (Ely et al., 1999). In practice, the physician would typically try to keep up to date by reading systematic reviews. However, systematic reviews are generic studies that may or may not be applicable to the particular case that the physician is concerned with. When there are no appropriate systematic reviews, the physician will need to search over the research literature, find the relevant information, and appraise it in terms of quality of the results and applicability to the patient (Sackett et al., 2000).

There is a range of NLP tasks that have been attempted on this area, but so far not much work has been done on multi-document query-based summarisation. We argue that this task would greatly help the physician but the lack of appropriate corpora has hindered the development and testing of such query-based summarisers for this domain. In this paper we present such a corpus, show some characteristics of the corpus, and advance some specific tasks that the corpus is suited for.

Section 2 introduces EBM and its connection with tasks related to multi-document query-based summarisation. Section 3 describes the corpus. Section 4 details how the corpus was built. Section 5 gives an indication of the use of the corpus for the specific task of single-document summarisation. Finally, Section 6 concludes the paper.

2 Evidence Based Medicine and Summarisation

In this section we introduce EBM and present work related to the use of NLP for EBM.

[1]http://www.ncbi.nlm.nih.gov/pubmed

2.1 Evidence Based Medicine

There are two key components in EBM: clinical expertise and external clinical evidence (Sackett et al., 1996). Clinical expertise is gained through clinical experience and clinical practice, whereas external clinical evidence needs to be obtained by consulting external sources. Systematic reviews enable physicians to quickly acquire the best evidence for a selection of topics. Such reviews are written by domain experts and are found at libraries such as the Cochrane Library[2] and UpToDate[3], to name two of the better known ones. However, EBM guides are quick to point out that there is not always a systematic review that addresses the specific topic at hand (Sackett et al., 2000) and then a search on the primary literature becomes necessary.

Ely *et al.* (Ely et al., 2002) highlight the following six obstacles for investigators and physicians to search and find the evidence: (1) the excessive time required to find information; (2) difficulty to modify the original question; (3) difficulty selecting an optimal strategy to search for information; (4) failure of a seemingly appropriate resource to cover the topic; (5) uncertainty about how to know when all the relevant evidence has been found; and (6) inadequate synthesis of multiple bits of evidence into a clinically useful statement. In this paper we will address the specific NLP technologies that can be used to overcome these obstacles, with special emphasis on summarisation technology.

The standard recommendation within EBM is to search the literature by determining specific information according to the PICO mnemonic (Armstrong, 1999). PICO highlights four components that reflect key aspects of patient care: primary **P**roblem or population, main **I**ntervention, main intervention **C**omparison, and **O**utcome of intervention.

PICO helps determining what terms are important in a query and therefore it helps building the query, which is sent to the search repositories. Once the documents are found, they need to be read by a person who eliminates irrelevant documents.

The retrieved documents need then to be appraised according to the strength of the evidence of the information reported in them. A number of guidelines for appraisal have been established. The Strength of Recommendation Taxonomy (SORT) (Ebell et al., 2004) is one of the better known ones and it specifies a scale of three grades based on the quality and type of evidence:

A Grade Consistent and good-quality patient-oriented evidence.

B Grade Inconsistent or limited-quality patient-oriented evidence.

C Grade Consensus, usual practice, opinion, disease-oriented evidence, or case series for studies of diagnosis, treatment, prevention, or screening.

Patient-oriented evidence relates to the impact in the patient (e.g. effect in mortality or in their quality of life), as opposed to disease-oriented evidence (e.g. lowering of blood pressure or blood sugar). Quality of evidence is assessed by the type of study (diagnosis, treatment, prevention, prognosis) and relevant variables for assessing the quality of evidence are the size and randomisation of the subjects and the consistency of the results.

As a final step, the physician still needs to locate the specific information presented in the documents. Current resources offer an array of presentation methods ranging from a list of bibliographic data (title, authors, publication details) sorted by date in PubMed to the clustering of information according to fields such as treatments, causes of condition, complications of condition, and pros & cons of treatment in HealthBase.[4]

2.2 Summarisation for Evidence Based Medicine

An important amount of research has been carried out on many aspects of medical support systems (Demner-Fushman et al., 2009; Zweigenbaum et al., 2007). In this section we present some of the NLP research that is relevant to EBM, with special emphasis on tasks that are related to multi-document query-based summarisation.

Much of the current work in NLP for EBM can be categorised as aiming to retrieve the evidence.

[2] http://www.thecochranelibrary.com/

[3] http://www.uptodateonline.com/

[4] http://healthbase.netbase.com

Recent studies aiming at increasing recall show that both Boolean and ranked retrieval have their limitations (Karimi et al., 2009). Using the Cochrane systematic reviews and their queries as sample data, Karimi *et al.* (Karimi et al., 2009) show that a combination of Boolean and ranked retrieval methods outperforms each of them individually but recall is still under 80% and precision is as low as 2.7% (Karimi et al., 2009).

The evidence found needs to be ranked by order of importance. A problem of PubMed is that the results are not presented in order of relevance or of importance. It is telling that, for example, generic search engines often find and present the correct information in a more prominent rank than specialised search engines like PubMed do, though the source of the information from where the answer is found is often questionable (Berkowitz, 2002; Tutos and Mollá, 2010). This has been addressed by PubFocus, which incorporates ranking functionality based on bibliometric data (Plikus et al., 2006).

Judging the quality of the evidence is one of the principal steps in EBM practice, and we advance that a good EBM summariser should provide information about the quality of the evidence summarised. Berkowitz (2002) mentioned that Google did "surprisingly well [in his study], but [it showed] low validity overall." If the information given is not from a reliable source it is not usable. PubMed abstracts contain meta-data information including the study type (e.g. "meta-analysis", "review") that can be used to filter the search results. This information is used by published search strategies (e.g. (Shojania and Bero, 2001; Haynes et al., 1994; Haynes et al., 2005)). Current implementations incorporating appraisal of the quality use information based on word co-occurrences (Goetz and von der Lieth, 2005) and bibliometrics (Plikus et al., 2006). More closely related to EBM are attempts to grade papers according to SORT or similar taxonomies (Tang et al., 2009; Sarker et al., 2011).

Question Answering (QA) technology is naturally suitable for the task of finding the required information, and in fact Zweigenbaum (2003) has argued for the use of the resources available in the medical domain to implement QA systems. However, the questions addressed by current QA technology seek simple answers. Whereas QA technology has traditionally focused on seeking names, lists, and definitions, EBM seeks more complex information that includes the type and quality of evidence.

Some QA systems for clinical answers are based on the PICO information. Those question-answering systems presume a preliminary processing stage that clearly identifies each component of PICO so that it can be processed by the computer, such as EPoCare's QA system (Niu et al., 2003) and CQA-1.0 (Demner-Fushman and Lin, 2007). Both EPoCare and CQA-1.0 follow specialised strategies to identify information addressing each field of the PICO query.

Some QA systems focus on specific kinds of questions. MedQA[5] (Yu et al., 2007) focuses on definitional questions. It accepts unstructured questions and integrates technology including question analysis, information retrieval, answer extraction and summarisation techniques (Lee et al., 2006). The work by Leonhard (2009), in contrast, focuses on comparison questions.

It has been shown that physicians want help to locate the information quickly by using lists, tables, bolded subheadings and by avoiding lengthy, uninterrupted prose (Ely et al., 2005). One of the findings by Ely et al. (2002) is the difficulty to synthesise the multiple bits of evidence into a clinically useful statement, which is the task of summarisation technology. The survey by Afantenos et al. (2005) presents various approaches to summarisation, including multi-document summarisation, from medical documents. Of particular interest are the context-based multi-document summarisation approaches such as CENTRIFUSER (Elhadad et al., 2005), which builds structured representations of the documents as source for the summaries.

SemRep (Fiszman et al., 2004) provides abstractive summarisation of biomedical research literature by producing a semantic representation based on the UMLS concepts and their relations as found in the text. The semantic representation is a set of predications (concept)-relation-(concept) that is presented graphically to the user.

Clustering methods can also help present the information. The Trip database,[6] for example, clus-

[5]This system is integrated in AskHERMES, http://www.askhermes.org/

[6]http://www.tripdatabase.com/

ters the search results by publication type and incorporates a sliding control to filter out publication types associated with lesser quality. The system by Demner-Fushman and Lin (2006) clusters the results by the intervention component of PICO. Using UMLS as a resource, interventions mentioned in the text are grouped into common categories and the clusters are presented labelled with the intervention type. The resulting system outperformed PubMed in their evaluations.

All of the techniques mentioned above are related to summarisation technology in one or another form, or are actual summarisation systems. By working on query-based multi-document summarisation for EBM we are contributing to some of the above research areas, and we are aiming at helping the physician practice EBM efficiently.

3 Source and Structure of the Corpus

Mollá (2010) argues that there is no corpus available for the development and testing of summarisation techniques in the EBM domain. We are providing such a corpus. The corpus is sourced from the Journal of Family Practice (JFP)[7] and uses the "Clinical Inquiries" section. A key advantage of using the "Clinical Inquiries" section of JFP instead of full systematic reviews such as the Cochrane Reviews[8] is that the text in each inquiry is much more compact but it still has the links to the references in case the physician needs more information. In other words, the text looks very much like what a summariser should deliver.

For each question, the corpus contains the following information:

1. The URL of the clinical inquiry from which the information has been sourced.

2. The question, e.g. *What is the most effective treatment for tinea pedis athlete's foot?*

3. The evidence-based answer. The answer may contain several parts, since a question may be answered according to distinct pieces of evidence. For each part, the corpus includes a short description of the answer, the Strength of Recommendation (SOR) grade of the evidence related to the answer, and a short description that explains the reasoning behind allocating such a SOR grade.

4. The answer justifications. For each of the parts of the evidence-based answer there is one or more justifications describing the actual findings reported in the research papers supporting the answer.

5. The references. Each answer justification includes one or more references to the source research paper. Each reference includes the PubMed ID and the full abstract information as encoded in PubMed, if available.

[7] http://jfponline.com/

[8] http://www.cochrane.org/cochrane-reviews

4 Creation of the Corpus

The conversion of the corpus from the original text in JFP to the machine-processable form followed several steps involving automatic extraction and conversion of text, manual annotation, and crowdsourcing annotation.

4.1 Extracting Questions and Answers

The process to extract the questions and answers was relatively straightforward. We obtained permission from the publishers to download all the freely available clinical inquiries. All of the inquiries were downloaded in their original HTML format, and a Python script was used to take advantage of the relatively uniform format that marks up the questions and answers in the source. We found that the markup had changed several times (the documents date from 2001 to 2010), so we had to accommodate all changes of format. The resulting information was stored in a local database.

The question corresponds with the title of the clinical inquiry, which is formulated as a question.

The answer parts are clearly marked in the original text. Each part (called "snip" in the corpus) contains the text, SOR grade, and criteria for the SOR grade.

4.2 Annotating Answer Justifications

The answer justifications were detected automatically. However, the source text did not match each

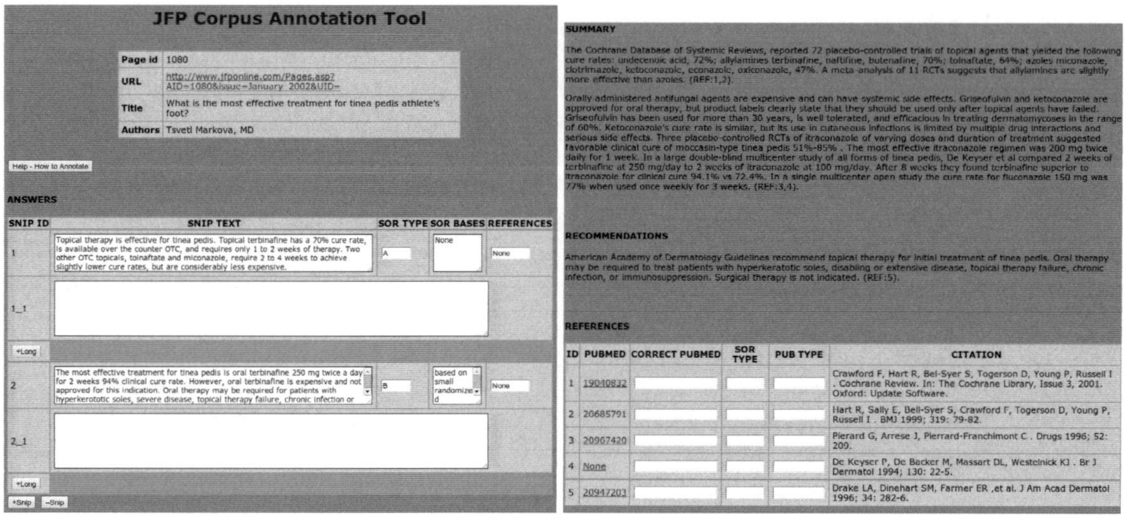

Figure 1: Screen shots of the annotation tool

justification to the specific answer snip. We therefore had to do the matching manually.

We created a web-based annotation tool that displays the question and each of the answer parts. Each answer part has associated empty slots where the annotator could copy and paste the answer justification. Figure 1 shows screen-shots of the annotation tool.

The total number of pages to annotate was distributed among three annotators. The annotators were members of the research team. A small percentage of the pages was annotated by all annotators (the annotators did not know beforehand which of the pages were annotated by all), to check for inconsistencies. The annotation process was done in several stages, with periodic checks on the common pages to detect and solve systematic inconsistencies in the annotation criteria. During those checks the annotators agreed on a set of criteria, an extract of which is:

1. Remove phrases connecting to text outside the answer justification and modify anaphora to make the text self-contained. For example, change *In another study* to *In a study* or *The second study* to *A study*.

2. Remove all general, introductory text.

3. If a justification has several references, split it into separate justifications whenever possible. In the process, some of the text may need to be copied so that each justification is self-contained.

4. If a paragraph does not have any references, check if it can be added to the previous or the next paragraph.

These criteria mostly addressed the need for each answer justification to be self-contained, and to match an answer justification to one reference only whenever possible. After inspection of a random sample of the common pages, the annotators agreed that the variations in the annotations are acceptable.

4.3 Crowdsourcing for Extracting Reference Information

Text formatting in the source text allowed the easy detection of references. To improve the usefulness of these references, we added the PubMed ID of those references found in PubMed.

We first tried to identify the PubMed ID automatically by searching on PubMed using information extracted from the reference text. The text was preprocessed by removing all the information about authors and pagination. We noted that if the authors or pagination items are present in the reference, they rarely appear in any other positions than first and last respectively. We also noted that authors and pagination are easy to find and ignore: authors contain initials and capital case surnames; while pagination always contains numbers and punctuation such as semi-colon, colon or hyphen.

Publication names such as the names of journals and books were more difficult to detect and to normalise. We decided, instead of trying to detect them, to run a list of searches containing all combinations of remaining sentences. For example, if after removing author and pagination information there are three sentences $S1, S2, S3$, the following searches were made: $S1$-$S2$-$S3$, $S1$-$S2$, $S1$-$S3$, $S2$-$S3$, $S1$, $S2$, $S3$. These individual searches were sent to PubMed via its "Entrez Utilities" interface. The ID of the search whose returned title had the largest substring overlap with the original string was selected. As a last resort, if no searches returned an ID, a final search was made with the complete reference text.

Manual inspection of a small random sample revealed, however, that this method often did not find the correct ID. We therefore created a crowdsourcing task using Amazon Mechanical Turk.

An initial pilot experiment was made with 30 references grouped in sets ("hits") of 10 references. Each hit was allocated to three Turkers. The Turkers were asked to check the ID using PubMed, and correct it if necessary. If no ID was available, the Turkers were asked to enter "nf". We later checked the Turkers' annotations by searching PubMed using the provided IDs and found an error rate of 18% (17 out of the total of 90 were incorrect). We examined the errors and concluded that:

1. Most workers got straight to work without reading the instructions provided. For example, they typically used the ID code "0" instead of "nf" when they could not find an ID.

2. We needed an automatic (or semi-automatic) way of judging whether the workers were cheating: manual checks were too time consuming.

3. There should be a threshold for approval of work. We decided to set the threshold to 2/10 wrong annotations per page to reject cheaters.

With these findings we performed the final Mechanical Turk task. Each hit had 10 references and was sent to five Turkers. The Turkers were asked to read the instructions and were asked to do an automated test with three references. After they passed the test they were given a passcode that was required to submit the work. Each hit included two "trick" questions with known answers. The following automated tests were done on each hit:

1. Did the user answer the known references correctly?

2. Is the ID valid? A script sent each ID to PubMed and checked whether it existed.

3. Is the ID correct? The automated test checked whether the percentage of matching between the reference title and the title returned by ID was beyond a threshold of 50%.

4. Did the Turker agree with the majority? Majority was 3 or more Turkers. This test was cancelled if the ID of majority was wrong or invalid (as determined by the other tests), or in the specific case that three Turkers agreed on one ID and two Turkers agreed on another ID (we just thought that this was too a close call).

The output of the automated test was visually inspected, and those Turker jobs with two or more errors were rejected. This was done by scrolling through the errors reported by the automatic tests, finding the disputed PubMed ids, manually checking the PubMed database to decide which one is "correct" and which one is "wrong" and then changing the tags if necessary.

The final accuracy of the annotation task was manually checked on a random sample of 100 references and double-checking them. No errors were detected.

Finally, once all IDs were found, the abstracts were automatically downloaded from PubMed and added to the corpus. We chose to download the XML format, which contains useful metadata that markups the bibliography details, the abstract text, and additional annotations such as classification tags and MeSH terms.

5 Utility of the Corpus

The final statistics of the corpus are: 456 questions (called "record" in the corpus), 1,396 answer parts (called "snip"), 3,036 answer justifications (called "long"), and 2,908 references. There is an average of 3.06 answer parts per question, 2.17 answer justifications per answer part, and 1.22 references per answer justification. There is an average of 6.57 references per question.

The distribution of SOR grades is: 345 for A, 535 for B, 330 for C, 15 for D,[9] and 171 without grade.

We envisage the use of this corpus for the following tasks:

Evidence-based summarisation. This is the main use of the corpus. It can be used to develop and test single-document summarisation by using the questions and original abstracts as the input source, and the answer justifications as the target summaries. Alternatively, it can be used to develop and test multiple-document summarisation by using the answer parts as the target summaries. Parts of the corpus have already been used for this purpose (Mollá, 2010).

Appraisal. The SOR grades can be used to test the ability to appraise the quality of the system. Appraisal can be done in the ranking component of a retrieval system, or as a separate classification task. Parts of the corpus have already been used for this purpose (Sarker et al., 2011).

Clustering. Given the natural grouping of references to form parts of the answer, the corpus can be used to develop query-focused clustering of the retrieved references.

Retrieval. The corpus references can be used as the target results of an information retrieval system. The usefulness of this corpus for assessing retrieval, however, is likely to be limited, given the findings by Dickersin et al. (1994) that between 20% and 30% of relevant literature present in MEDLINE is not present in systematic reviews.

In the remainder of this section we focus on the task of query-focused single-document summarisation, where the task is to summarise the abstract of a paper within the context of the question. The target summary is the answer justification, and the evaluation metric is ROUGE-L with stemming (Lin, 2004), a very popular metric used in the evaluation of summarisation systems.

For every answer justification/reference pair, we extracted all combinations of three sentences from the abstract and computed their ROUGE-L scores against their answer justification. With this information we computed the ROUGE-L boundary points of the document deciles. For example, the boundary points of the first decile of a document indicate the minimum and maximum values of the 10% proportion of combinations of 3-sentences with lowest ROUGE-L scores. Then we aggregated the decile boundaries of all documents to create the set of document decile boundaries according to the formula

$$Boundary[i] = \{boundary[i](x)|x \in D\}$$

where $boundary[0](x)$ is the minimum ROUGE-L score of the first decile of document x, $boundary[1](x)$ is the maximum ROUGE-L score of the first decile of document x, and so on. The resulting boxplot is shown in Figure 2. The means and standard deviations are listed in Table 1. This information shows that, in order to perform better than simple random choice of sentences, we need to obtain a ROUGE-L score of at least 0.188. For reference, a simple baseline that returns the last three sentences obtains a ROUGE-L score of 0.193, and the best system configuration that uses information of the abstract structure of those described by Mollá (2010)[10] achieves a ROUGE-L score of 0.196 when applied to our corpus. We can see that these baselines are in the range between 50% and 60% percentiles.

6 Conclusions

We have presented a corpus for the development of research in NLP in medical texts. The corpus was sourced from the Clinical Inquiries section of the Journal of Family Practice, and the process involved a set of manual and automatic methods for the extraction and annotation of information. We also describe a process of crowdsourcing that was used to find the PubMed IDs of the references.

[9]SORT has only grades A, B, and C, but apparently some authors used one more level D to indicate very poor evidence.

[10]This is the system configuration that uses abstract structure but does not use question information.

Boundary	0	1	2	3	4	5	6	7	8	9	10
Mean	0.094	0.136	0.153	0.164	0.176	0.188	0.200	0.213	0.229	0.249	0.299
Std Dev	0.060	0.062	0.065	0.067	0.070	0.073	0.076	0.081	0.087	0.094	0.112

Table 1: Statistics of the decile boundaries of ROUGE-L data

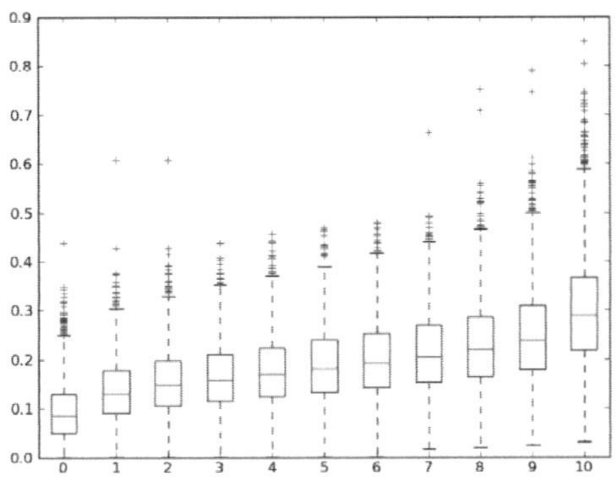

Figure 2: ROUGE-L boxplots for all decile boundaries

The emphasis of this corpus is the development and testing of query-focused multi-document summarisation systems for Evidence Based Medicine, but we envisage its use in other tasks such as text classification, and clustering.

We have shown a set of statistics of the ROUGE-L scores of the abstracts within the context of document summarisation. The data show that current baselines do not perform much better than simple random choice and there is still much room for improvement. The challenge is up for researchers to take.

Further work includes the use of this corpus for some of the tasks described above. We are also studying the possibility of including additional annotation of the specific abstract sentences that are found to be most relevant to the answer justifications. This information could be used to perform pyramidal-style evaluation such as the one described by Dang and Lin (2007).

References

Stergos Afantenos, Vangelis Karkaletsis, and Panagiotis Stamatopoulos. 2005. Summarization from medical documents: a survey. *Artificial Intelligence in Medicine*, 33(2):157–177, February. PMID: 15811783.

I. Elaine Allen and Ingram Olkin. 1999. Estimating time to conduct a meta-analysis from number of citations retrieved. *JAMA: The Journal of the American Medical Association*, 282(7):634–635, August. PMID: 10517715.

E. C. Armstrong. 1999. The well-built clinical question: the key to finding the best evidence efficiently. *WMJ*, 98(2):25–28.

Lyle Berkowitz. 2002. Review and evaluation of internet-based clinical reference tools for physicians. Technical report, UpToDate.

Hoa Dang and Jimmy Lin. 2007. Different structures for evaluating answers to complex questions: Pyramids won't topple, and neither will human assessors. In *Proceedings ACL*.

Dina Demner-Fushman and Jimmy Lin. 2006. Answer extraction, semantic clustering, and extractive summarization for clinical question answering. In *Proceedings ACL*. The Association for Computer Linguistics.

Dina Demner-Fushman and Jimmy J. Lin. 2007. Answering clinical questions with knowledge-based and statistical techniques. *Computational Linguistics*, 33(1):63–103.

Dina Demner-Fushman, Wendy W. Chapman, and Clement J. McDonald. 2009. What can natural language processing do for clinical decision support? *Journal of Biomedical Informatics*. Online uncorrected proof.

K. Dickersin, R. Scherer, and C. Lefebvre. 1994. Identifying relevant studies for systematic reviews. *BMJ (Clinical Research Ed.)*, 309(6964):1286–1291, November. PMID: 7718048.

Mark H. Ebell, Jay Siwek, Barry D. Weiss, Steven H. Woolf, Jeffrey Susman, Bernard Ewigman, and Marjorie Bowman. 2004. Strength of recommendation taxonomy (SORT): a patient-centered approach to grading evidence in the medical literature. *Am Fam Physician*, 69(3):548–556, Feb.

N. Elhadad, M.-Y. Kan, J. L. Klavans, and K. R. McKeown. 2005. Customization in a unified framework for summarizing medical literature. *Artificial Intelligence in Medicine*, 33(2):179–198, February. PMID: 15811784.

John W. Ely, Jerome A. Osheroff, Mark H. Ebell, George R. Bergus, Barcey T. Levy, M. Lee Chambliss, and Eric R. Evans. 1999. Analysis of questions asked by family doctors regarding patient care. *BMJ*, 319(7206):358–361, Aug.

John Ely, Jerome A Osheroff, Mark H Ebell, M. Lee Chambliss, DC Vinson, James J. Stevermer, and Eric A. Pifer. 2002. Obstacles to answering doctors' questions about patient care with evidence: Qualitative study. *BMJ*, 324(7339):710.

John W. Ely, Jerome A. Osheroff, M. Lee Chambliss, Mark H Ebell, and Marcy E. Rosenbaum. 2005. Answering physicians' clinical questions: Obstacles and potential solutions. *J Am Med Inform Assoc.*, 12(2):217–224.

Marcelo Fiszman, Thomas C. Rindflesch, and Halil Kilicoglu. 2004. Abstraction summarization for managing the biomedical research literature. In *Procs. HLT-NAACL Workshop on Computational Lexical Semantics*, pages 76–83.

T. Goetz and C.-W. von der Lieth. 2005. PubFinder: a tool for improving retrieval rate of relevant PubMed abstracts. *Nucleic Acids Research*, 33(Web Server):W774–W778.

R. Brian Haynes, Nancy L. Wilczynski, K. Ann McKibbon, Cynthia J. Walker, and John C. Sinclair. 1994. Developing optimal search strategies for detecting clinically sound studies in MEDLINE. *Journal of the American Medical Informatics Association: JAMIA*, 1(6):447–458, December. PMID: 7850570.

R. Brian Haynes, K. Ann McKibbon, Nancy L. Wilczynski, Stephen D. Walter, and Stephen R. Werre. 2005. Optimal search strategies for retrieving scientifically strong studies of treatment from medline: analytical survey. *BMJ (Clinical Research Ed.)*, 330(7501):1179, May. PMID: 15894554.

Sarvnaz Karimi, Justin Zobel, Stefan Pohl, and Falk Scholer. 2009. The challenge of high recall in biomedical systematic search. In *Proc. DTMBIO*, pages 89–92, Honk Kong.

Minsuk Lee, James Cimino, Hai Ran Zhu, Carl Sable, Vijay Shanker, John Ely, and Hong Yu. 2006. Beyond information retrieval — medical question answering. In *Proc. AMIA 2006*.

Annette Leonhard. 2009. Towards retrieving relevant information for answering clinical comparison questions. In *Proceddings BioNLP 2009*, pages 153–161.

Chin-Yew Lin. 2004. Rouge: A package for automatic evaluation of summaries. In *Proc. ACL workshop on Text Summarization Branches Out*, page 10.

Diego Mollá. 2010. A corpus for evidence based medicine summarisation. In *Proceedings of the Australasian Language Technology Workshop*, volume 8, pages 76–80.

Yun Niu, Graeme Hirst, Gregory McArthur, and Patricia Rodriguez-Gianolli. 2003. Answering clinical questions with role identification. In *Proc. ACL, Workshop on Natural Language Processing in Biomedicine*.

Maksim Plikus, Zina Zhang, and Cheng M. Chuong. 2006. PubFocus: Semantic MEDLINE/PubMed citations analysis through integration of controlled biomedical dictionaries and ranking algorithm. *BMC Bioinformatics*, 7(1):424.

David L. Sackett, William M. Rosenberg, Jamuir Gray, R. Brian Haynes, and W. Scott Richardson. 1996. Evidence based medicine: What it is and what it isn't. *BMJ*, 312(7023):71–72.

David L. Sackett, Sharon E. Straus, W. Scott Richardson, William Rosenberg, and R. Brian Haynes. 2000. *Evidence-Based Medicine: How to Practice and Teach EBM*. Churchill Livingstone, 2 edition.

Abeed Sarker, Diego Mollá, and Cécile Paris. 2011. Towards automatic grading of evidence. In *Proceedings of the Third International Workshop on Health Document Text Mining and Information Analysis (LOUHI 2011)*, pages 51–58, Bled, Slovenia.

Kaveh G. Shojania and Lisa A. Bero. 2001. Taking advantage of the explosion of systematic reviews: an efficient MEDLINE search strategy. *Effective Clinical Practice: ECP*, 4(4):157–162, August. PMID: 11525102.

Thanh Tang, David Hawking, Ramesh Sankaranarayana, Kathleen M. Griffiths, and Nick Craswell. 2009. Quality-oriented search for depression portals. In *ECIR '09 Proceedings of the 31th European Conference on IR Research on Advances in Information Retrieval*, Berlin, Heidelberg. Springer.

Andreea Tutos and Diego Mollá. 2010. A study on the use of search engines for answering clinical questions. In *Proceedings HIKM 2010*.

Hong Yu, Minsuk Lee, David Kaufman, John W. Ely, Jerome A. Osheroff, George Hripcsak, and James J. Cimino. 2007. Development, implementation, and a cognitive evaluation of a definitional question answering system for physicians. *Journal of Biomedical Informatics*, 40(3):236–251.

Pierre Zweigenbaum, Dina Demner-Fushman, Hong Yu, and Kevin B. Cohen. 2007. Frontiers of biomedical text mining: current progress. *Briefings in Bioinformatics*, 8(5):358–375.

Pierre Zweigenbaum. 2003. Question answering in biomedicine. In *Proc. EACL2003, workshop on NLP for Question Answering*, Budapest.

Collocations in Multilingual Natural Language Generation: Lexical Functions meet Lexical Functional Grammar

François Lareau **Mark Dras** **Benjamin Börschinger** **Robert Dale**
Centre for Language Technology
Macquarie University
Sydney, Australia
Francois.Lareau|Mark.Dras|Benjamin.Borschinger|Robert.Dale@mq.edu.au

Abstract

In a collocation, the choice of one lexical item depends on the choice made for another. This poses a problem for simple approaches to lexicalisation in natural language generation systems. In the Meaning-Text framework, recurrent patterns of collocations have been characterised by lexical functions, which offer an elegant way of describing these relationships. Previous work has shown that using lexical functions in the context of multilingual natural language generation allows for a more efficient development of linguistic resources. We propose a way to encode lexical functions in the Lexical Functional Grammar framework.

1 Introduction

Natural Language Generation (NLG) is the generation of natural language text from some underlying representation: numerical data, knowledge bases, predicate logic, and so on. Multilingual Natural Language Generation (MNLG) is NLG where the output is in more than one language. Most NLG systems are in some way modular (see Reiter and Dale (2000) for a discussion of typical architectures); one advantage to modularity is the scope for separating language-independent components from those which are language-dependent, making it possible to add multilinguality with much less work than would be involved in building a new system from scratch (Bateman et al., 1999). Such claims have been made since the very first MNLG systems; the FoG system generating weather forecasts in English and French (Bourbeau et al., 1990) is a case in point.

Consequently, MNLG has been applied for a large number of text types: government statistics reports (Iordanskaja et al., 1992), technical instruction manuals (Paris et al., 1995), fairy tales (Callaway and Lester, 2002), museum tours (Callaway et al., 2005), medical terminology (Rassinoux et al., 2007), codes of practice (Evans et al., 2008), and so on.

Marcu et al. (2000), in reviewing some of the earlier work, comment that MNLG systems need to abstract as much as possible away from the individual language generated:

> If an [MNLG] system needs to develop language dependent knowledge bases, and language dependent algorithms for content selection, text planning, and sentence planning, it is difficult to justify its economic viability. However, if most of these components are language independent and/or much of the code can be reused, an [MNLG] system becomes a viable option.

Bateman et al. (1999) similarly emphasise the importance of reducing language dependence.

One kind of abstraction generalises across language-specific collocations: for example, we might note that *heavy rain*, *strong wind* or *intense bombardment* all refer to the intensification of some phenomenon, as similarly does the French *pluie battante* ('beating rain'), but the particular intensifier used is determined by collocational appropriateness. These kinds of collocations are modeled within the Meaning-Text Theory (MTT) framework via lexical functions (LFs) (Mel'čuk, 1995); for some lexeme L, the above semantic notion of intensification or strength is represented by `Magn`(L). MTT-based MNLG systems, from the early works of Heid and Raab (1989) and Iordanskaja et al. (1992) onwards, have used LFs to abstract away from the specific collocational phenomena of individual languages.

In terms of resources developed and applications within the computational linguistics community, however, MTT has not been very prominent outside of NLG. In work that is more geared towards natural language understanding, other formalisms such as Lexical Functional Grammar (LFG) (Bresnan, 2001), Head-driven Phrase Structure Grammar (HPSG) (Pollard and Sag, 1994), Tree Adjoining Grammar (TAG) (Joshi and Schabes, 1997) and Combinatory Categorial Grammar (CCG) (Steedman, 2000) have received much more attention. Of course, all of these frameworks have also been applied in NLG. LFG, for example, has a sophisticated grammar development environment called Xerox Linguistic Environment (XLE) (Maxwell and Kaplan, 1993) for both parsing and generation, with wide-coverage grammars for a number of languages such as English and German (Butt et al., 2002), and advanced statistical models for tasks such as realisation ranking (Cahill et al., 2007).

The existence of a wide-coverage English LFG grammar for XLE convinced us to build our resources on this platform for the MNLG project described below. However, LFG comes from a tradition quite different from MTT, and has no concept that corresponds to MTT's LFs. In this paper, we demonstrate that LFs cannot be straightforwardly introduced into the LFG formalism via direct manipulation of f-structures, and then show how glue semantics (Dalrymple, 2001) can incorporate them in an elegant way.

We first describe our MNLG system to provide a contextual background for the problem (§2), along with some basic notions on LFG (§3). We then describe LFs in more detail, and discuss how they have been used in other MNLG systems (§4), along with how they would fit into our system. We then return to LFG and glue semantics (§5), and present our proposal for incorporating LFs into LFG, using a running example (§6).

2 Our System

The context for this work is a project involving an MNLG system for generating commentary-style textual descriptions of Australian Football League (AFL) games, in both English and the Australian Aboriginal language Arrernte. A typical sentence in a human-authored commentary for a game might look as follows:

> Led by Brownlow medallist Adam Goodes and veteran Jude Bolton, the Swans kicked seven goals from 16 entries inside their forward 50 to open a 30-point advantage at the final change—to that point the largest lead of the match.

For the games we want to describe, there is a corresponding database which contains quantitative and other data regarding the game: who scored which goal when, from where, and so on. The system will use handwritten grammars in the LFG formalism—for English, there is an already-existing wide-coverage one developed for XLE as part of the ParGram project (Butt et al., 2002)—and the research around the grammar development will have a number of foci. In particular, we are interested in exploring how to handle morphologically rich non-configurational languages such as Arrernte, which are not usually tackled in the field of language technology; these exhibit a number of interesting and complicated phenomena, as outlined by, for example, Austin and Bresnan (1996) or Nordlinger and Bresnan (2011). Given the radical language differences between such languages and those which are more typically the focus of NLG projects, we are particularly interested in investigating the possible extent of language independence (see §4 for a discussion). LFs are an important facet of the semantic abstractions we require. For example, in the short text cited above, the expression *kick a goal* would be rendered in Arrernte as *goal arrerneme*, where *arrerneme* literally means 'put'. We view *kick* and *arrerneme* as support verbs in these expressions.[1] These collocations exhibit the same syntactic structure, and express the same meaning; they are instances of the same pattern

[1]Note that in AFL one can only score goals by kicking the ball, so in this context, the semantic contribution of *kick* is weak; we believe that for practical purposes it can be viewed as empty.

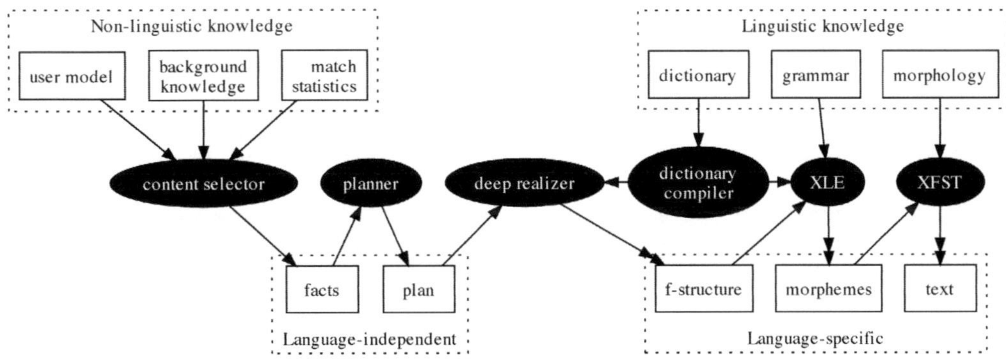

Figure 1: System architecture

of collocation, which is described in MTT by the LF $\texttt{Oper}_1(L)$. We will return to this example in §4.

Our system more or less follows the "consensus architecture" of Reiter and Dale (2000), as schematised in Figure 1. Data is selected using domain-specific knowledge and statistical methods, to produce a collection of facts to be expressed. These facts are organised into a document plan, which is then passed to a deep realiser that produces one or more f-structures for each sentence of the text (cf. §3). This is then passed to XLE, which uses linguistic knowledge to produce ordered lexical items with attached morphemes. This is finally passed to a two-level morphology model compiled with the Xerox Finite-State Tool (XFST) system, which produces fully inflected text. The double-headed arrows in Figure 1 indicate non-deterministic output; a stochastic reranking technique is used to select between alternative results.

The module which is the focus of the present discussion is the deep realiser, which maps a semantic representation to one or more f-structures, for which in turn XLE will produce textual realisations. It is not our purpose in this paper to discuss the technical details of the implementation of this component; rather, we focus on the mapping between semantic representations and f-structures from a theoretical point of view. To explain the approach, and to motivate the need for glue semantics, we now present an outline of LFG.

3 Lexical Functional Grammar

LFG is a formalism for a non-derivational theory of linguistic structure that posits at least two levels of representation: c(onstituent)-structure and f(unctional)-structure.[2] Mappings specify the relationship between the different levels of structure. C-structure is represented by phrase-structure trees, capturing hierarchical relationships between constituents and surface phenomena such as word order; while f-structure is represented by attribute–value matrices, describing more abstract functional relationships such as subject and object (indeed, syntactic dependencies). LFG assumes that these functional syntactic concepts are universally relevant across languages (Dalrymple, 2001, p. 3), and "so may be regarded as a major explanatory source of the relative invariance of f-structures across languages" (Bresnan, 2001, p 98). As an illustration, the c- and f-structures for the sentence (1) below are given in Figure 2.

(1) Bradshaw kicked a beautiful goal.

The mapping between f- and c-structures is given by annotations on phrase structure and lexical rules as in (2) and (3) below.

(2) S $\rightarrow$ NP VPall
$(\uparrow\text{SUBJ})=\downarrow$ $\uparrow=\downarrow$

(3) *kicked* V $(\uparrow\text{PRED})=\text{'kick}\langle(\uparrow\text{SUBJ}),(\uparrow\text{OBJ})\rangle\text{'}$
$(\uparrow\text{TENSE})=\text{past}$

Lexical entries such as (3) are in fact only a different notation used for terminal nodes in c-structures; this could be written instead as in (4).

(4) V $\rightarrow$ *kicked*
$(\uparrow\text{PRED})=\text{'kick}\langle(\uparrow\text{SUBJ}),(\uparrow\text{OBJ})\rangle\text{'}$
$(\uparrow\text{TENSE})=\text{past}$

[2] See Dalrymple (2001) or Bresnan (2001) for extensive discussions of LFG; here, we provide only the basic essentials required to understand our treatment.

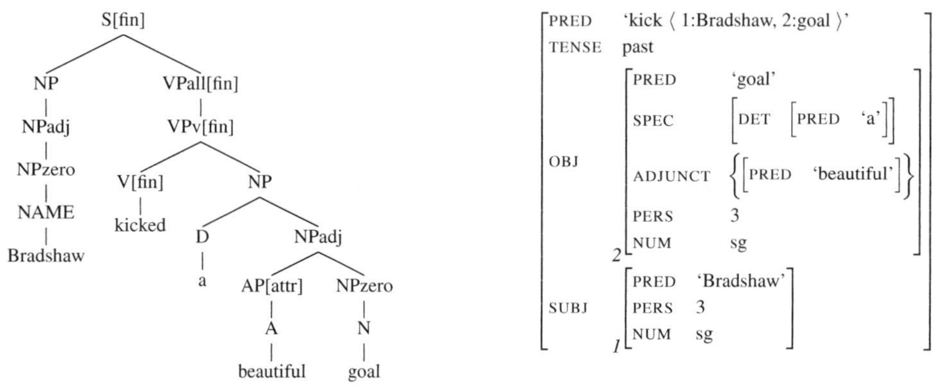

Figure 2: c-structure (left) and f-structure (right) for *Bradshaw kicked a beautiful goal*

The symbol ↑ is a metavariable representing the f-structure of the parent of a node in the c-structure, and ↓ the f-structure of that node itself. These can be followed by a sequence of attributes that specify a path to an element in the f-structure. For example, in rule (2), the annotation on the NP means that the SUBJ of the f-structure corresponding to the node above it in the c-structure (S) is the f-structure corresponding to this NP (in plain English: this NP is the subject of the sentence). The annotation on the VPall node means that it shares the same f-structure as its mother (i.e., it is the head of S). In the lexical rule for *kicked* (3), the annotation (↑OBJ) inside the PRED attribute refers to the f-structure numbered 2 in Figure 2, which represents *goal*. A less common way of referring to elements of an f-structure, albeit one that is necessary in a number of cases, is "inside-out" function application, where the ↑ or ↓ follows an attribute sequence. An annotation such as (OBJ↑) refers to the f-structure of which the current one is the OBJ.

First-order predicate logic is often used as the fundamental meaning representation in LFG, although other more expressive representations are also possible, such as intensional logic or Discourse Representation Theory. The issue then is how to relate the core LFG structures above to this meaning representation. Dalrymple (2001, p. 217) notes that early work in LFG took the f-structure element PRED to represent the locus of the semantics, with the PRED in fact originally being referred to as the *semantic form*. If our meaning representation for (1) were as in (5a) (ignoring here tense and number), the mapping to the f-structure in the right of Figure 2 would be

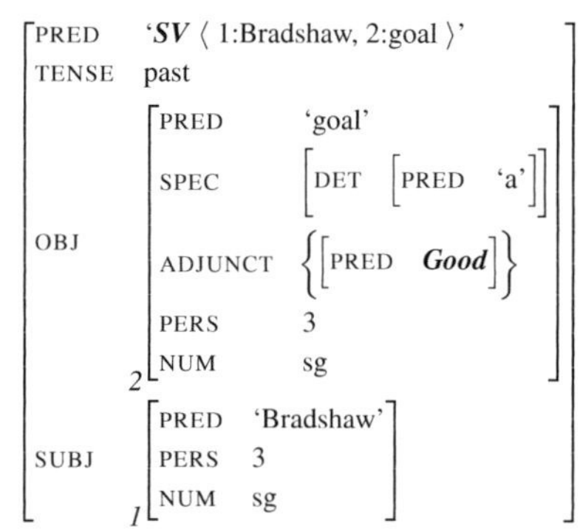

Figure 3: 'Quasi-'f-structure with variables

straightforward: the basic hierarchical structure of the f-structure is preserved, although predicativity is reversed in the case of the adjunct.

(5) a. *kick(bradshaw, beautiful(goal))*
 b. *good(goal(bradshaw))*

However, simple semantic forms like this cannot represent many aspects of semantics, such as scope of modifiers or quantification. More particularly for our purposes, if we start from a semantic representation that abstracts away from the collocationally determined use of *beautiful* to characterise the goal, or from the collocational use of *kick* to refer to the goal event,[3] a suitable starting meaning representation might be as in (5b); what the mapping should look like is then much less clear.

A (quasi-)f-structure corresponding to this might be as in Figure 3. The top-level PRED could be a variable (***SV***) that would have to be instantiated to

[3]We might think of this as the action of "goaling"; another possible supporting verb would then be *score*.

a collocationally appropriate support verb; alternatively, for some types of action, it could indicate that both the top-level PRED and its object could be realised as a single verb through some kind of structure merging.[4] The adjunct PRED could similarly be a variable (***Good***) whose value is a word that retains the desired semantics but is collocationally determined. However, it is not possible for f-structures to have variable predicates, or to be of indeterminate structure, because of their role in ensuring the LFG wellformedness conditions of Coherence and Completeness; in addition, the mapping between meaning representation and f-structure is less straightforward, with quite different hierarchical relations.

In §6, we show how the mapping of such abstract meaning representations to f-structures can be done in an elegant way using glue semantics. First, we present more formally the MTT notion of LFs that these quasi-f-structure "variables" of Figure 3 are trying to capture, and we then give a brief description of glue semantics.

4 Lexical Functions and MNLG

An important step in the NLG task of surface realisation is lexicalisation, where specific lexemes are chosen to express the content of a message. Most of the time, this can be achieved by mapping either concepts or language-specific meanings to lexemes in a straightforward way. For example, the concept RAIN can be mapped to the lexemes *rain* (English), *pluie* (French), *lluvia* (Spanish), and so on. Often, however, concepts are lexicalised in a different way depending on the lexemes they appear with, as with our example from §3 above. Consider for example the phrases *strong preference*, *intense flavour*, *heavy rain* and *great risk*. While the lexemes *preference*, *flavour*, *rain* and *risk* are chosen freely according to their meaning, the lexemes *strong*, *intense*, *heavy* and *great* are not. They have roughly the same meaning of intensification, but their choice is tied to the lexeme they modify. Such collocations pose a non-trivial problem for lexicalisation in NLG systems. Under the MTT framework these are modeled via LFs. Collocations are viewed as instances of recurrent patterns of semantico-syntactic mappings, described in terms of functions (in a mathematical sense) between lexemes. Hence, these four collocations can be described in terms of a function f such that f(*preference*)=*strong*, f(*flavour*)=*intense*, etc. Over the years, more than fifty basic recurrent functions of this type, and hundreds of complex ones, have been identified across languages and given names; the one discussed above has been called Magn. Detailed descriptions of these functions can be found elsewhere (Mel'čuk, 1995; Wanner, 1996; Kahane and Polguère, 2001; Apresjan et al., 2002).

[4]This kind of structure merging has not, to our knowledge, been implemented in LFG. In practice, it could be carried out by mapping from one f-structure to another, using the sort of mechanism found in XLE for use in machine translation. However, it would inelegantly add an unprincipled layer to the formalism.

ATTENTION [of X to Y]

Magn	close/whole/complete/undivided ~
Func_2	X's ~ is on Y
nonFunc_0	X's ~ wanders
Oper_{12}	X gives his/pays ~ to Y
Oper_2	Y attracts/receives/enjoys X's ~
$\text{Oper}_2\text{+Magn}_{\text{quant-}X}$	Y is the center of ~ (of many Xs)
IncepOper_{12}	X turns his ~ to Y
IncepOper_2	Y gets X's ~
ContOper_2	Y holds/keeps X's ~
CausFunc_2	Z draws/calls/brings X's ~ to Y
LiquFunc_2	Z diverts/distracts/draws X's ~ from Y

Figure 4: Dictionary entry for *attention*

The use of LFs allows the handling of lexicalisation in two steps. In the first step, unbound lexemes are chosen, and collocation patterns identified, while the actual value of the LF is only computed in the second step: INTENSE+RAIN → Magn(*rain*)+*rain* → *heavy*+*rain*.

The values for these functions are stored in the dictionary; for example, the entry for *attention* must contain the information in Figure 4. We will not discuss each of these functions here; the key point is that LFs offer a very efficient way of describing a wide range of collocations.

Each pattern must be defined in the grammar, but this is done only once for all languages and domains. We discuss in §6 how this can be done in LFG. The fact that the patterns must be defined only once for all languages makes this technique a cost-efficient way of developing MNLG resources by sharing parts of the grammar across languages, as advocated notably by Bateman et al. (1991), Bateman et al. (1999) and

Cahill et al. (2000). This was the approach taken by Lareau and Wanner (2007) for the system MARQUIS, which generated air quality reports in eight European languages (Catalan, English, Finnish, French, German, Polish, Portuguese and Spanish). Their use of LFs was an important factor that contributed to the low number of language-specific rules they reported for the deeper modules of their grammars, making the addition of new languages in their framework relatively cheap. It is LFs such as these that we wish to incorporate into LFG.

5 Glue Semantics

In the context of LFG, there have been several approaches to developing a compositional notion of semantics derived from the f-structure; one that is well developed, and is the basis of our work, is glue semantics (Dalrymple, 2001; Andrews, 2010). We give only a brief summary here; for a full treatment, see Dalrymple (2001).[5]

Glue semantics is based on linear logic. This differs from classical logic in its resource-sensitivity, in that premises are treated as resources that can be kept track of. For example, consider the statements *If you have $1, you can get an apple* and *You have $1*. In classical logic, you can deduce that you can get an apple, but the original premises would still be true, i.e. you would still have $1, and you could still get an apple. In linear logic, these premises are resources that will be consumed in the process of deduction, and therefore not available for further proof;[6] notationally, the implication above in linear logic is written *$1* $\multimap$ *apple*.

This resource-sensitivity is particularly appropriate when we are concerned with the linguistic expression of semantic content: the contribution of each word and phrase to the meaning of a sentence is unique, and there should be no missing or redundant words in terms of the meaning to be expressed.

We illustrate how this works by showing the more straightforward mapping between our example sentence (1) and its literal meaning representation (5a). The lexical item representing *Bradshaw* is given below in (6). The first line contains the wordform, its part of speech, and an annotation asserting that the f-structure corresponding to the N node immediately dominating the lexical item has an attribute PRED whose value is the semantic form 'Bradshaw'. The second line ($\mathsf{Bradshaw} : \uparrow_\sigma$) contains what is termed the *meaning constructor*, as it gives instructions on how to construct meanings. These are pairs: the lefthand (meaning) side represents the meaning, and the righthand (glue) side represents a logical formula over semantic structures corresponding to those meanings.

(6) *Bradshaw* N ($\uparrow$PRED)='Bradshaw'
$\mathsf{Bradshaw} : \uparrow_\sigma$

The present example is trivial: it should be read as *the semantic projection of the mother node is the meaning* Bradshaw. A σ subscript indicates the semantic projection of a node, so the notation $\uparrow_\sigma$ gives the corresponding element of the semantics via the projection of the mother node to the semantics. The element *goal* is similar:

(7) *goal* N ($\uparrow$PRED)='goal'
$\mathsf{goal} : \uparrow_\sigma$

The verb *kick* is transitive, so it will have the following form.

(8) *kicked* V ($\uparrow$PRED)='kick$\langle$($\uparrow$SUBJ),($\uparrow$OBJ)$\rangle$'
($\uparrow$TENSE)=past
$\lambda X.\lambda Y.\mathsf{kick}(X,Y) :$
$(\uparrow \text{SUBJ})_\sigma \multimap [(\uparrow \text{OBJ})_\sigma \multimap \uparrow_\sigma]$

In the meaning constructor, the semantics of the action of kicking is represented by a lambda term, on the left; the righthand glue side is given in terms of the linear logic implication operator $\multimap$. The first implication says that if $(\uparrow \text{SUBJ})_\sigma$ is available (i.e., if we have already built the semantic projection for the verb's subject—in our example, Bradshaw), it will be consumed and will saturate the first variable of the lambda expression, to produce the new premise that follows the first $\multimap$ symbol, leaving us with $\lambda Y.\mathsf{kick(Bradshaw,}Y) : (\uparrow \text{OBJ})_\sigma \multimap \uparrow_\sigma$. This in turn consumes the semantic projection for the object (in our case, goal) to reduce the lambda term, and produces the semantic resource $\uparrow_\sigma$, i.e., the semantic projection for the verb and its complements, kick(Bradshaw,goal).

[5] It should be noted that the current version of XLE cannot directly handle glue semantics.

[6] Somewhat counterintuitively, even the premise *If you have $1, you can get an apple* is consumed.

For the remaining two elements, we would have the following.

(9) *beautiful* A ($\uparrow$PRED)='beautiful'
$\lambda X.\mathit{beautiful}(X)$:
$(\text{ADJ} \in \uparrow)_\sigma \multimap (\text{ADJ} \in \uparrow)_\sigma$

(10) *a* D ($\uparrow$PRED)='a'
$\lambda X.X : (\text{DET} \uparrow)_\sigma \multimap (\text{DET} \uparrow)_\sigma$

For *beautiful* in (9), the notation $(\text{ADJ} \in \uparrow)_\sigma$ differs in two ways from that introduced earlier. First, it uses an "inside-out" function to refer to the semantic structure of the phrase it modifies; and second, it uses set membership notation, as modifiers are typically represented by sets (as in the f-structure of Figure 2). The expression thus refers to the semantic structure corresponding to the f-structure in which $\uparrow$ appears as a member of the modifier set. In terms of the glue side, all modifiers have this structure: they take and return the same type of element. We treat the determiner in (10) similarly; further, it does not add any meaning element.[7]

All these combined together, then, give the literal semantics of (5a). Such mechanics are more complicated than is necessary for this simple example, which was used only for illustrative purposes here. However, they can equally well provide the more abstract semantics of (5b), as we show in §6.

6 Adding Lexical Functions to LFG

There are a number of changes necessary to incorporate LFs, both in a less straightforward use of glue semantics and in other aspects of the definitions of lexical entries. The lexical entry for the proper noun *Bradshaw* still has the same simple meaning constructor as above in (6). By contrast, *goal* in (11), is a unary predicate: $\lambda X.\mathit{goal}(X)$, i.e., '*X goals*', so to speak. However, in the construction under consideration here, its semantic predicativity is not echoed in syntax, since there is no verb *to goal* in standard English. This is precisely why a support verb is needed in the first place: *kick* ties the noun *goal* to its semantic argument *Bradshaw*. This is rendered in the lexical entry in (11) below with a meaning constructor that checks that there is a meaning available for the subject of the verb of which *goal* is the object.

[7]The determiner could be considered as a quantifier, which would require a much more sophisticated treatment.

(11) *goal* N ($\uparrow$PRED)='goal'
$\lambda X.\mathit{goal}(X)$:
$((\text{OBJ}\uparrow)\ \text{SUBJ})_\sigma \multimap \uparrow_\sigma$

The lexeme *kick* serves only as a support verb to turn *Bradshaw's goal* into a verbal expression, so that it forms a clause. It is a collocation of *goal* that, in the context of football match summaries, does not contribute to the meaning of the sentence in a significant way. Hence, *X kicks a goal* means nothing more than $\lambda X.\mathit{goal}(X)$, that is, the verb *kick* simply recopies its object's meaning, with the constraint that its object is the lexeme *goal* in (12):

(12) *kicked* V ($\uparrow$PRED)='kick$\langle(\uparrow$SUBJ),($\uparrow$OBJ)$\rangle$'
($\uparrow$OBJ PRED)$=_c$'goal'
($\uparrow$TENSE)=past
$\lambda X.X : (\uparrow\text{OBJ})_\sigma \multimap \uparrow_\sigma$

In this example, the second line is a constraining equation, which is LFG's way of handling collocational constraints; it specifies that this rule can only be applied if the predicate of the object of *kick* is *goal*. And just as for the determiner in (10), the meaning side adds nothing to the overall semantics.

We note here that the semantic description provided by glue semantics does not render obsolete the PRED function. It is still needed to encode purely syntactic information: the name of the lexeme and its sub-categorisation. The verb *kick* could control its own collocations, so we need to have access to the name of the lexeme.

Beautiful, in (1), could be replaced with *spectacular* or *brilliant*, for instance. In these kinds of texts, the semantic difference between these expressions is not significant. The adjectives *beautiful*, *brilliant* and *spectacular*, when they modify *goal*, merely denote a positive appreciation: $\lambda X.\mathit{good}(X)$.

(13) *beautiful* A ($\uparrow$PRED)='beautiful'
((ADJ $\in \uparrow$) PRED)$=_c$'goal'
$\lambda X.\mathit{good}(X)$:
$(\text{ADJ} \in \uparrow)_\sigma \multimap (\text{ADJ} \in \uparrow)_\sigma$

The second line is again an LFG constraining equation, which specifies that this rule can only be applied if *beautiful* modifies the lexeme *goal*; the semantic element $\lambda X.\mathit{good}(X)$ will be realised in other ways in different contexts.

The extra lines in the lexical entries are regular, and can be captured using templates, which are the XLE instantiation of LFG's lexical rules. These in fact then correspond very closely to MTT's LFs. For example, for the LF $\texttt{Oper}_1(L)$, which represents the use of support verbs in contexts such as that of *kick* in our examples, the following template could be defined:

(14) @OPER1(L)=
$(\uparrow\text{PRED})=\text{`\%stem}\langle(\uparrow\text{SUBJ}),(\uparrow\text{OBJ})\rangle\text{'}$
$(\uparrow\text{OBJ PRED})=_c\text{`}L\text{'}$
$\lambda X.X : (\uparrow\text{OBJ})_\sigma \multimap \uparrow_\sigma$

The constraining equation on the second line restricts the support verb to the particular lexical element with which it is invoked. The third line constructs the meaning by just passing along the meaning of the existing components with no additions. The template is then invoked in the dictionary:

(15) *kick* V @(OPER1 *goal*)
suffer V @(OPER1 *loss*)
have V @(OPER1 *cold*)

Such templates need only be described once for all languages. For example, the Arrernte dictionary contains the following entry for the expression *goal arrerneme* (literally 'put (a) goal'):

(16) *arrerneme* V (OPER1 *goal*)

One problem with this approach is that collocations must be described in the collocate's entry, which is not very elegant and obfuscates the lexicographer's work. Indeed it is a lot easier, for example, to answer the question "how do you intensify *smoker*?" than "what lexemes can *heavy* intensify?". However, this problem can easily be resolved by writing the dictionary in the format of Figure 5 (similar to the *attention* example in Figure 4), where all collocations are listed under their base headword, and using a compiler to build the corresponding XLE lexical entries.

goal [of X]

`Bon` beautiful/spectacular/brilliant ~
$\texttt{Oper}_1$ X kicks/scores/gets/makes a ~

Figure 5: Dictionary entry for *goal*

In the example we have considered so far, the English expression *kick a goal* and its Arrernte equivalent *goal arrerneme* have the same structure. However, this need not be the case. For example, consider the contrast between the following two sentences:

(17) John abandons the baby.

(18) John-le ampe-Ø ipmentye-Ø
John-ERG baby-NOM abandonment-NOM
iwe-me
leave-N.PST

'John abandons the baby'

Both sentences express the meaning *abandon(John,baby)*, but in English, the predicate is expressed by a single verb, while in Arrernte it is expressed by a noun with a support verb. This construction corresponds to an LF called $\texttt{Labor}_{12}$, which denotes a support verb that takes as its subject the first semantic argument of the base of the collocation (here, *John*), the second argument as its direct object (*baby*), and the base itself as its second object (*ipmentye*).[8] The template for $\texttt{Labor}_{12}$ would look like this:

(19) @LABOR12(L)=
$(\uparrow\text{PRED})=\text{`\%stem}\langle(\uparrow\text{SUBJ}),(\uparrow\text{OBJ}),(\uparrow\text{OBJ2})\rangle\text{'}$
$(\uparrow\text{OBJ2 PRED})=_c\text{`}L\text{'}$
$\lambda X.X : (\uparrow\text{OBJ2})_\sigma \multimap \uparrow_\sigma$

And just as we did for *goal* in (11), we also need a specific entry for *ipmentye* that reflects its behaviour in this collocation, as well as an entry for *iweme* that says it is the $\texttt{Labor}_{12}$ of *ipmentye*:

(20) *ipmentye* N
$(\uparrow\text{PRED})=\text{`ipmentye'}$
$\lambda X\lambda Y.\textit{abandon}(X,Y) :$
$((\text{OBJ2}\uparrow)\ \text{SUBJ})_\sigma \multimap$
$[((\text{OBJ2}\uparrow)\ \text{OBJ})_\sigma \multimap \uparrow_\sigma]$
iweme V @(LABOR12 *ipmentye*)

Hence, given the same meaning as input, the grammar produces different structures, as appropriate for the language being processed.

[8] Since both *ampe* and *ipmentye* are in the nominative form, it is hard to determine which is the first and which is the second object, but this question is largely irrelevant here.

Of course, LFs have their limitations too. In the context of MNLG, there are two problems related to lexicalisation that are worth mentioning here. One is that languages sometimes diverge at the semantic level. For example, there is no direct equivalent to the verb *teach* in Arrernte; one has to say *akaltye antheme*, literally 'give knowledge'. This is a collocation of the noun *akaltye* 'knowledge' that can be captured by an LF; but the problem here lies in the fact that the semantic input in Arrernte should be *cause(X,know(Y,Z))*, while in English it would be *teach(X,Y,Z)*. This is different from the abandonment case discussed above: there, one language uses a straightforward realisation, while the other uses a light verb, but there is no need to decompose the meaning of these expressions to see that they are identical; they both have the same semantic representation. For *teach*~*akaltye antheme*, the two languages do not conceptualise the world in the same way, and these conceptual/semantic differences must be dealt with early in the generation process; the deep realiser must produce different semantic representations depending on the language. At this stage, LFs are irrelevant because we are operating on concepts rather than at the lexical level, where LFs come into play.

Another limitation is that LFs are designed to describe recurrent patterns of collocations. Although most collocations found in languages are instances of a few common patterns, there are many that either express unusual meanings, or that exhibit a very peculiar syntactic or morphological structure. For example, the expression *winning goal* could be described as a collocation. However, the meaning expressed here by *winning* is very specific to this domain, and it cannot be reduced to a recurrent pattern across languages (beyond the equivalent expressions for *winning goal*). *Ad hoc* LFs can still be defined for such collocations, but their use will only be a viable solution in the context of an application within a restricted domain (such as ours).

7 Conclusion

We have proposed a technique for the description of collocations in LFG based on MTT's concept of LFs, in order to solve the problem of complex lexicalisation in NLG. We showed that a direct treatment within LFG's f-structure is not possible because it would require variable values for the attribute PRED, which is not allowed. Also, the semantics of support verbs in particular is tricky and cannot be captured satisfactorily with a PRED attribute. We proposed a treatment using glue semantics, which handles more elegantly the complex correspondence between the semantics and syntax of collocations. The rules that describe collocates use constraining equations so that they apply only in the context of the base of a collocation. We also showed how templates could be used in XLE to define recurrent patterns, effectively defining any given LF once for all languages. The result is an elegant way of describing collocations within the LFG framework. This technique simplifies the task of preparing resources for MNLG by sharing these patterns across languages.

Acknowledgments

We acknowledge the support of ARC grant DP1095443, and thank Mark Johnson for his feedback on the idea.

References

Avery Andrews. 2010. Propositional Glue and the Correspondence Architecture of LFG. *Linguistics and Philosophy*, 33:141–170.

Jury Apresjan, Igor Boguslavsky, Leonid Iomdin, and Leonid Tsinman. 2002. Lexical functions in actual NLP applications. In *Computational Linguistics for the New Millennium: Divergence or Synergy?*, pages 55–72. Peter Lang, Frankfurt.

Peter Austin and Joan Bresnan. 1996. Non-configurationality in Australian aboriginal languages. *Natural Language and Linguistic Theory*, 14(2):215–268.

John Bateman, Christian Matthiessen, Keizo Nanri, and Licheng Zeng. 1991. The re-use of linguistic resources across languages in multilingual generation components. In *Proceedings of the 1991 International Joint Conference on Artificial Intelligence*, volume 2, pages 966–971, Sydney.

John Bateman, Christian Matthiessen, and Licheng Zeng. 1999. Multilingual Natural Language Generation for Multilingual Software: A Functional Linguistic Approach. *Applied Artificial Intelligence*, 13(6):607–639.

Laurent Bourbeau, Denis Carcagno, Eli Goldberg, Richard Kittredge, and Alain Polguère. 1990. Bilingual Generation of Weather Forecasts in an Operations Environment. In *Proceedings of the 13th International Con-*

ference on Computational Linguistics (COLING'90), pages 90–92.

Joan Bresnan. 2001. *Lexical-Functional Syntax*. Blackwell, Oxford, UK.

Miriam Butt, Helge Dyvik, Tracy Holloway King, Hiroshi Masuichi, and Christian Rohrer. 2002. The Parallel Grammar Project. In *Proceedings of COLING-2002 Workshop on Grammar Engineering and Evaluation*, pages 1–7.

Lynn Cahill, Christie Doran, Roger Evans, Rodger Kibble, Chris Mellish, Daniel Paiva, Mike Reape, Donia Scott, and Neil Tipper. 2000. Enabling resource sharing in language generation: an abstract reference architecture. In *Proceedings of the Second International Conference on Language Resources and Evaluation (LREC'00)*, Athens.

Aoife Cahill, Martin Forst, and Christian Rohrer. 2007. Stochastic realisation ranking for a free word order language. In *Proceedings of the Eleventh European Workshop on Natural Language Generation (ENLG'07)*, pages 17–24, Schloss Dagstuhl, Germany.

Charles B. Callaway and James C. Lester. 2002. Narrative prose generation. *Artificial Intelligence*, 139(2):213–252.

Charles Callaway, Elena Not, Alessandra Novello, Cesare Rocchi, Oliviero Stock, and Massimo Zancanaro. 2005. Automatic Cinematography and Multilingual NLG for Generating Video Documentaries. *Artificial Intelligence*, 165(1):57–89.

Mary Dalrymple. 2001. *Lexical Functional Grammar*, volume 42 of *Syntax and Semantics Series*. Academic Press, New York.

Roger Evans, Paul Piwek, Lynne J. Cahill, and Neil Tipper. 2008. Natural language processing in CLIME, a multilingual legal advisory system. *Natural Language Engineering*, 14(1):101–132.

Ulrich Heid and Sybille Raab. 1989. Collocations in multilingual generation. In *Proceedings of the fourth conference of the European chapter of the Association for Computational Linguistics (EACL'89)*, pages 130–136.

Lidja Iordanskaja, Myunghee Kim, Richard Kittredge, Benoît Lavoie, and Alain Polguère. 1992. Generation of Extended Bilingual Statistical Reports. In *Proceedings of the 15th International Conference on Computational Linguistics (COLING'92)*, pages 1019–1023. Nantes, France.

Aravind Joshi and Yves Schabes. 1997. Tree-Adjoining Grammars. In G. Rozenberg and A. Salomaa, editors, *Handbook of Formal Languages*, volume 3, pages 69–124. Springer, Berlin.

Sylvain Kahane and Alain Polguère. 2001. Formal foundation of lexical functions. In *Proceedings of ACL 2001*, Toulouse.

François Lareau and Leo Wanner. 2007. Towards a generic multilingual dependency grammar for text generation. In *Proceedings of Grammar Engineering Across Frameworks (GEAF'07)*, pages 203–223, Palo Alto.

Daniel Marcu, Lynn Carlson, and Maki Watanabe. 2000. An Empirical Study in Multilingual Natural Language Generation: What Should A Text Planner Do? In *Proceedings of the 1st International Conference on Natural language Generation (INLG'00)*, pages 17–23.

John T. Maxwell and Ronald M. Kaplan. 1993. The Interface between Phrasal and Functional Constraints. *Computational Linguistics*, 19(4):571–590.

Igor Mel'čuk. 1995. The future of the lexicon in linguistic description and the explanatory combinatorial dictionary. In I.-H. Lee, editor, *Linguistics in the morning calm*, volume 3. Hanshin, Seoul.

Rachel Nordlinger and Joan Bresnan. 2011. Lexical-Functional Grammar: interactions between morphology and syntax. In R. Borsley and K. Börjars, editors, *Non-Transformational Syntax: Formal and Explicit Models of Grammar*. Wiley-Blackwell, Chichester.

Cécile Paris, Keith Vander Linden, Markus Fischer, Anthony Hartley, Lyn Pemberton, Richard Power, and Donia Scott. 1995. A Support Tool for Writing Multilingual Instructions. In *Proceedings of the 14th International Joint Conference on Artificial Intelligence (IJCAI'95)*, pages 1398–1404, Montreal.

Carl Pollard and Ivan Sag. 1994. *Head-driven phrase structure grammar*. University of Chicago Press, Chicago.

Anne-Marie Rassinoux, Robert H. Baud, Jean-Marie Rodrigues, Christian Lovis, and Antoine Geissbühler. 2007. Coupling Ontology Driven Semantic Representation with Multilingual Natural Language Generation for Tuning International Terminologies. In *Proceedings of the 12th World Congress on Health (Medical) Informatics (MEDINFO'07)*, pages 555–559, Brisbane.

Ehud Reiter and Robert Dale. 2000. *Building Natural Language Generation Systems*. Cambridge University Press.

Mark Steedman. 2000. *The Syntactic Process*. MIT Press.

Leo Wanner, editor. 1996. *Lexical functions in lexicography and natural language processing*, volume 31 of *Studies in Language Companion Series*. John Benjamins, Amsterdam/Philadelphia.

Outcome Polarity Identification of Medical Papers

Abeed Sarker , Diego Mollá-Aliod
Centre for Language Technology
Macquarie University
Sydney, NSW 2109
{abeed.sarker,diego.molla-aliod}@mq.edu.au

Cécile Paris
CSIRO – ICT Centre
Sydney, NSW 2122
cecile.paris@csiro.au

Abstract

A medical publication may or may not present an outcome. When an outcome is present, its polarity may be positive, negative or neutral. Information about the polarity of an outcome is a vital one, particularly for practitioners who use the outcome information for decision making. We model the problem of automatic outcome polarity identification as a three-way document classification problem and attempt to solve it via supervised machine learning. We combine domain knowledge and linguistic features of medical text, and apply natural language processing to extract features for the chosen classifiers. We introduce two novel features — Relative Average Negation Count and Sentence Signature — and show that they are effective in improving classification accuracy. We also include features, such as n-grams and semantic orientation of terms, that have been used for similar text classification problems in other domains. Using these features, we obtain a maximum accuracy of 74.9% for the classification problem. Our experiments suggest that through careful feature selection, machine learning can be used to solve this problem.

1 Introduction

The phenomenal growth of biomedical literature has presented medical practitioners, particularly those practicing Evidence Based Medicine (EBM), with the problem of information overload. The popular practice of EBM requires practitioners to review medical literature before making clinical decisions (Sackett et al., 1996; Greenhalgh, 2006). When reviewing medical publications, EBM practitioners are mostly interested in identifying the outcomes presented and their polarities. The polarity of an outcome can be positive (e.g. *the study shows that drug X is useful for patients suffering from condition Y*), negative (e.g. *the study suggests that drug X is not recommended for patients suffering from condition Y*) or the publication may present a neutral outcome or may not present an outcome at all (e.g. *the study does not produce conclusive results regarding the efficacy of drug X for condition Y*). Manually assessing the outcomes presented by multiple medical papers on a given topic is a time-consuming task and often cannot be efficiently performed at point of care (Ely et al., 1999). Hence, there is a strong need for automatic outcome polarity identification techniques to aid the decision making process of practitioners.

1.1 Motivation

In order to appease the problem of information overload faced by medical domain experts, research has focused on information retrieval, automatic summarisation and question answering of medical documents (Lin and Demner-Fushman, 2007; Fiszman et al., 2009). Intelligent text processing systems that perform automatic summarisation and question answering for this domain can benefit significantly from techniques that can automatically detect the polarity of outcomes presented in documents. Such techniques will be particularly useful for multidocument summarisation, where the detection of contradictory or consistent outcomes presented in separate documents is vital. Furthermore, recent research on quality assessment of evidence presented in multiple medical documents has also acknowledged the importance of automatic polarity detection techniques for measuring consistency of outcomes in medical articles (Sarker et al., 2011). The research presented in this paper is motivated by these factors.

1.2 Contribution

We present a supervised learning approach to solve the problem of outcome polarity identification of medical publications. We focus particularly on medical publication types that are popularly used in EBM practice and model the problem as a three-way classification problem by separating outcomes presented in medical articles into three classes - *Positive*, *Negative* and *No Outcomes*. Despite the strong motivation behind automatic polarity identification of medical documents, there has not been any concrete research work attempting to solve this problem. We therefore approach this problem by building on and combining previously applied approaches for text classification, sentiment analysis, negation detection and polarity identification. One of the intents of this research work is to explore how the above mentioned approaches can be applied to the medical domain. We also present some novel feature selection ideas and show that some of these features increase classification accuracy.

2 Related Work

Research work related to ours has taken place under various umbrella terms (depending on the domain): sentiment analysis (Pang et al., 2002; Pang and Lee, 2004), semantic orientation (Turney, 2002), opinion mining (Pang and Lee, 2008), evidentiality (Chafe and Nichols, 1986), subjectivity (Lyons, 1981; Langacker, 1985) and many more. All these terms refer to the general method of extracting subjectivity or polarity from text (Taboada et al., 2010). A pioneering work in the area of sentiment analysis was performed by Pang et al. (2002), who attempted to automatically classify movie reviews as positive or negative. The authors applied three machine learning algorithms – Naive Bayes, Maximum Entropy and Support Vector Machines (SVMs) – and using features such as unigrams, bigrams, part-of-speech tags and adjectives, obtained a maximum average accuracy of 82.9% (over three-fold cross-validations). In their work, the best average accuracy was produced by the use of unigrams as features only. Turney's (2002) work was similar and involved the use of an unsupervised learning technique based on the mutual information (semantic orientation) between document phrases and the words 'excellent' and 'poor'. The semantic orientation of phrases were automatically computed using a search engine. His approach classified reviews as positive if they had a positive average semantic orientation and negative otherwise, achieving accuracies between 66% and 84% for different data sets. Following on from these works, research in this area has mostly focused on the binary polarity classification problem from opinionated pieces of text. Similar approaches have been applied for classifying the polarities of product reviews, political speeches and news. Pang and Lee (2008) provide an in-depth survey of approaches in this research area. Although similar in nature, the research work described in this paper differs significantly from approaches applied to sentiment analysis approaches for several reasons. The key reason is the complex nature of text in the medical domain with its domain specific terminologies and semantic relationships between terms (Athenikos and Han, 2010).

Research work closely related to ours in the medical domain is that by Niu et al. (2005; 2006). In their work, they perform polarity classification of sentences, obtained from medical article abstracts, using machine learning. The authors collect the abstracts from MEDLINE[1] and manually annotate each sentence into four classes – positive, negative, no outcome and neutral. Besides using unigrams and bigrams, the authors also use negations and semantic categories of medical concepts, and introduce *Change Phrases* – phrases that indicate the increase or decrease of a *good* or *bad* thing – as features. Precision and recall are shown to be approximately 79% over the four classes, using a data set of 1509 sentences and SVMs for learning. *Change Phrases* indicate the polarity of sentences and the concept is similar to *contextual valence shifters* (Polanyi and Zaenen, 2006; Kennedy and Inkpen, 2006) that have been successfully applied to sentiment classification

[1] http://www.nlm.nih.gov/databases/databases_medline.html

research.

We attempt to classify polarities at the document level, rather than at the sentence level. Our survey of literature in this domain did not reveal any work that attempts to address this specific problem despite its possible usefulness. The task itself is particularly challenging because each document may, and usually does, contain multiple sentences with differing polarities. Additionally, unlike the binary classification problem that sentiment analysis is usually modeled as, our work models the problem as a three-way classification (which, we believe, is the minimum number of classes required in the case of medical documents). Machine learning algorithms have been applied to solve various text classification problems, including those in the medical domain — such as identifying high quality medical articles (Kilicoglu et al., 2009). Among machine learning algorithms, SVMs (Vapnik, 1995) have clearly been the most popular for text classification, particularly because of their ability to robustly handle large feature sets and find globally optimum solutions (Uzuner et al., 2009; Taboada et al., 2010). We apply SVMs in our experiments and compare its performance with some other popular classifiers.

Another important aspect of our work is negation detection. Negated terms in medical text usually indicate the presence or absence of specific medical findings. Additionally, they may also indicate the polarity of the outcome presented in a medical article (e.g., drug X shows *no improvement* for patients suffering from condition Y). Recent research work has shown that information on the polarity of phrase-level assertions does not improve performance in a document level classification task (Goldstein and Uzuner, 2010). However, statistics based on the presence/absence of negations have not been incorporated for text classification in this domain. Negation identification has shown to markedly improve performance of medical information retrieval systems. Therefore, there has been a significant amount of work on automatic negation detection techniques in the medical domain, such as the works of Elkin et al. (2005) and Huang et al. (2007) . Rokach et al. (2008) provides a detailed survey of negation detection techniques for the medical domain. A popular and simple negation detection approach is NegEx (Chapman et al., 2001). It is a powerful, regular-expression-based algorithm and uses a list of phrases which, when present in the same sentence as disease names or findings, are indicative of negation. NegEx has been translated to other languages due to its effectiveness. We use a modified version of NegEx for negation detection in our experiments.

3 Data and Annotation

3.1 Data Collection

When collecting data, our focus was on articles that are commonly used for EBM. NLP research in the domain of EBM has shown that despite the presence of a large number of study types (also referred to as publication types) in the domain, only specific study types are commonly used in the practice[2]. These study types include Systematic Reviews, Meta-analyses, Clinical Trials (mostly Randomised Controlled Trials) and Cohort Studies. Although these are the preferred types of studies, Consensus Guidelines, Expert Opinion and Case Studies are also used in EBM practice when higher quality articles are not available on a specific topic. Sarker et al. (2011) provides an analysis of how publication types are distributed in real-life EBM practice.

To collect our data, we initially identified medical publications, which have been used in EBM practice, from the 'Clinical Inquiries' section of the Journal of Family Practice[3] (JFP). This section of JFP contains question-answer type evidence based reviews of specific medical topics that are generated by experts. The reviews also provide references to research articles from which the reviews are generated. We manually obtained a random sample of the abstracts of these references from MEDLINE using the PubMed[4] interface. We wanted to add diversity to our data set by incorporating article abstracts that do not belong to the Family Practice domain but have the potential to be used for EBM. To achieve this, we collected a sample of article abstracts belonging to the study types commonly used in EBM (mentioned above) directly from MEDLINE using the *PublicationType* filter.

[2]A list of publication types used by PubMed can be found at http://www.nlm.nih.gov/mesh/pubtypes.html

[3]http://www.jfponline.com

[4]http://www.ncbi.nlm.nih.gov/pubmed/

3.2 Annotation

We manually classified all the collected abstracts into three classes – *Positive*, *Negative* and *No Outcome*. During annotation, we use the following definitions for the three classes:

Positive: There is a clear indication that a medical process or intervention produces an outcome that is beneficial and/or serves its purpose; or a medical process or intervention is considered to be beneficial overall despite minor adverse effects; or when comparisons are made between two or more interventions or processes and the one that is the focus of the study is mentioned to be better. The following are two examples of positive outcomes:

> *'Depression scores on the Hamilton Rating Scale for Depression and Clinical Global Impressions-Severity scale significantly improved during the bupropion treatment phase.'*

> *'In a group of asymptomatic patients with first episode psychosis and at least one year of previous antipsychotic drug treatment, maintenance treatment with quetiapine compared with placebo resulted in a substantially lower rate of relapse during the following year.'*

Negative: There is a clear indication that an intervention or process produces an outcome that is not beneficial at all and/or is clearly not recommended; or when comparisons are made between two or more interventions or processes, the one that is the focus of the study is not mentioned to be the preferred choice. An example is as follows:

> *'There is a suggestion that routine surgical interference may be harmful by increasing the risk of caesarean section, and this agrees with data from other trials.'*

No Outcome: The outcome is neither positive nor negative or no outcome is specified at all. The latter can happen for systematic reviews or non-systematic reviews that do not present a single polarised answer. Also, when multiple comparisons are made without a final indication that a single process or intervention is preferred. The following is an example:

> *'There is not an important difference in the effects of bed rest compared with exercises in the treatment of acute low back pain, or seven days compared with two to three days of bed rest in patients with low back pain of different duration with and without radiating pain.'*

Our final test data set consists of 520 medical article abstracts, containing 9,221 sentences and 61,579 tokens (6,601 types). Among the 520 documents, 199 are annotated as positive, 161 as negative and 160 as no outcome instances. Approximately one-fourth of our data set consists of articles identified from JFP, while the rest were collected directly from MEDLINE using the approach described above.

The annotation was performed by four annotators (three medical domain experts and one computer scientist). There was about 40% overlap of the data among annotators and we computed Fleiss' Kappa (κ) to measure the extent of agreement among annotators. The formula for this statistic is given by:

$$\kappa = \frac{P_O - P_E}{1 - P_E} \tag{1}$$

where P_O is the observed agreement and P_E is the agreement expected by chance. The κ value we obtained is 70.6%, which falls within the range of values that is usually termed as "good agreement beyond chance".

3.3 Preliminary Analysis

We perform preliminary manual analysis on a small data set (separate from the 520 documents mentioned above) collected and annotated in the same fashion. Our analysis suggests that certain phrases play an important role in polarity determination. For example, *'significantly improves'*, *'no difference'*, *'no result'*, *'side effects'*, *'no improvement'* and similar phrases occur frequently in our data set and provide strong indications regarding the polarity. Similarly, negations also provide cues about the polarity at a document level, e.g., *'not recommended'*. However, a full abstract may, and usually does contain multiple occurrences of such phrases and therefore the presence or absence of these terms in a single sentence may not be indicative of overall polarity. Furthermore, our analysis also suggests that the semantic orientation of words in each abstract may have a correlation with the polarity of the outcome presented. For example, terms such as *'excellent'* tend to occur frequently in positively polarised documents, while terms such as *'unsuccessful'* are more likely to occur in negatively polarised documents. In our experiments, we explore all these possibilities. We attempt to combine various sentence level information to determine overall document polarities. Specific details about our preliminary analysis are provided in the next section, where we provide elaborate details about our feature selection techniques.

4 Methods

We model the problem of document level outcome polarity identification as a three-way classification problem. In this section we describe the features we use for classification, the feature selection techniques and provide justifications behind the choice of the selected features. We also attempt to explain how our feature selection ideas have been influenced by related research work.

4.1 Feature Sets

4.1.1 N-grams.

Word n-grams have been shown to be very important features in text classification problems (Taboada et al., 2010). We therefore use n-grams (n=1,2,3 and 4) from the article abstracts as our first feature set for experimentation. We experiment both with n-gram frequencies and presence. We also experiment with various combinations of n-grams. During preprocessing of the texts, we remove stop words and numbers, stem the individual words using the Porter stemmer and only keep n-grams with frequencies of greater than 4 over the whole data set.

We experiment with two further variations of n-gram feature sets. In the first variation, we only use n-grams from the conclusion sections of the abstracts. Our preliminary analysis suggests that sentences in the conclusion section of documents are most informative regarding the overall outcomes. For abstracts without explicit section headings, we use the last three sentences.

In our last variation, we replace specific medical concepts with a generic *'sem_type'* tag. We use MetaMap[5] to identify domain specific concepts as defined in the UMLS[6] (Unified Medical Language System). The UMLS provides a vast vocabulary of medical concepts and also broad semantic groups into which the concepts can be classified. For example, all disease names fall under the semantic category *Disease or Syndrome (dsyn)*. Replacing each occurrence of a disease or syndrome name with the generic tag ensures that the name does not have an influence on the classifiers used and reduces overfitting. Furthermore, it also enables the identification of specific term patterns in text that can be used for classification (explained later). Generic representations of medical problems have been used in text classification tasks in this domain before, and for our task, we use the same semantic groups as Uzuner et al. (2009): pathological function, disease or syndrome, mental or behavioral disfunction, cell or molecular dysfunction, virus, neoplastic process, anatomic abnormality, acquired abnormality, congenital abnormality and injury or poisoning.

4.1.2 Relative Average Negation Count

As already mentioned, our preliminary analysis suggests that negations provide cues about the overall polarity of an abstract, but the presence of negation in a single sentence may not determine document polarity. Our analysis also suggests that the total number of negations, or the negation count, over the whole document is generally greater for documents presenting a negative outcome than those presenting a positive outcome (the number of negations in documents presenting no outcomes vary significantly). At the same time, the negation count also tends to increase with the length of the abstracts and negations towards the end of the abstracts tend to have greater impact on the final outcome. We therefore use the *Relative Average Negation Count* (RANC) for each document as a feature and define it as follows:

$$RANC_d = \frac{\sum_{i=1}^{l}(n_i \times \frac{i}{l})}{l} \quad (2)$$

where d is a medical abstract containing l sentences in total and n_i is a negation detected in sentence i of the document. The equation shows that each negation is weighted by its relative position and the sum of all the weighted negations is divided by the length

[5] http://metamap.nlm.nih.gov/

[6] http://www.nlm.nih.gov/research/umls/

of the document to give RANC. We experimented with other representations of negations, such as using a vector of negation terms for each document, but found RANC to be the most effective.

To count the number of negations in a document, our algorithm uses a list of negation phrases based on the list used by NegEx (Chapman et al., 2001). In particular, NegEx attempts to identify negations in clinical narratives, and our modifications include adding negation phrases that commonly appear in published papers but are not included in NegEx's original list (e.g. *'not statistically'*). To calculate RANC, our algorithm searches each sentence of an abstract for the presence of any of the terms in our list. All the matches are summed using equation 2 to give the total negation count.

4.1.3 Semantic Orientation

We add a feature set to assess the effect of the semantic orientation of words on overall document polarity. We collect lists of positive and negative words from the General Inquirer dictionary (Stone et al., 1966)[7]. As this list is not specific to the medical domain, we manually modify both lists by removing terms that occur frequently in medical domain texts and whose semantic orientation should not be taken into account when identifying document polarities in this domain. These include terms such as *'disease'*, *'sickness'*, *'intervention'*, *'death'* and *'discharge'*. We have to rely on this time-consuming strategy since there are no such existing lists for the medical domain. For each document, we calculate its average semantic orientation, by counting the number of positive terms and the number of negative terms, subtracting the latter from the former and then dividing by the document length.

4.1.4 Change Phrases and Sentence Signatures

We use an approach similar to Niu et al. (2005; 2006) to identify sentence patterns or *change phrases*. In their work, the authors use a manually created list of *good*, *bad*, *more* and *less* words to identify patterns in sentences. The authors argue that the (sentence level) polarity of an outcome is often determined by how change happens (e.g., a good or bad thing is increased or decreased). For example, consider the following sentence:

> In these three postinfarction trials ACE inhibitor versus placebo significantly *reduced mortality*.

In the sentence, the word *reduce* is a *less* word while the word *mortality* is a *bad* word. Thus the sentence will have the pattern *less-bad* indicating that the sentence has a positive polarity. Similarly a sentence having the pattern *more-good* is likely to have a positive polarity while a sentence with the pattern *more-bad* or *less-good* is likely to have a negative polarity. In our work, we extend the idea of change phrases by including negations and medical semantic types in the patterns. Our intuition is that negations or semantic types can also significantly influence the polarity of sentences. For example, consider the following sentence (modified from the previous one):

> In these three postinfarction trials ACE inhibitor versus placebo *did not reduce mortality*.

The change phrase pattern for this sentence would still be *less-bad* despite the presence of the negation. A more correct pattern for the sentence should be *neg-less-bad* which incorporates the negation. Similarly, the following sentence:

> ... *increased* the probability of *heart failure*.

has a *more-semtype* pattern which may be indicative of negative polarity.

We generate two-term and three-term patterns from each sentence of each abstract and use them as a feature set. We call this feature set *Sentence Signatures* (SS).

4.2 Classification

Using the four feature sets mentioned in this section, we test the accuracy of four machine learning classifiers on our test data set. The four chosen classifiers are — Naive Bayes, Bayes Net, SVMs and C4.5 Decision Tree. Due to the relatively small amount of annotated data available to us, we perform 10-fold cross-validation in our experiments. We use the default implementations of all these classifiers in the software package Weka[8]. For the Bayes Net

[7] Available from http://www.wjh.harvard.edu/~inquirer/.

[8] http://www.cs.waikato.ac.nz/ml/weka/

classifier, we use the K2 search algorithm for local score metrics and the simple estimator for estimating conditional probability tables. For SVMs, we use an RBF kernel and John Platt's sequential minimal optimisation algorithm (Platt, 1999); and solve our multi-class problem using pairwise (1-vs-1) classification. Further details of these classifiers can be found in the documentation provided with the software package.

5 Results and Discussion

Table 1 presents the results of the four classifiers over various combinations of features. The horizontal lines of the table divide the features into groups and the best accuracy obtained for a specific group is shown in bold. The results indicate that the n-grams play an important role in the classification problem, which is consistent with findings in other domains. More specifically, use of uni-, bi- and tri-grams as features show clear improvements in classification but adding longer n-grams does not appear to be beneficial. The results of classification using n-grams only also show that classification accuracies are not significantly different between the use of word frequencies (F) and presence (P). Using n-grams from full abstracts always performs better than using n-grams from conclusion sentences (C) only. Replacing medical terms belonging to specific semantic categories with a generic tag (M) also tends to give better classification accuracies.

Introduction of RANC and SS as features has a positive impact on classification accuracies. The increase in accuracies for our tree-based classifier (C4.5) upon the addition of RANCs as features is particularly significant, which is a clear indication of the importance of this feature set. The highest accuracy we obtain is 74.9% using SVMs for classification and n-grams (n=1,2,3), RANCs and SSs as features. SVMs consistently outperform other classifiers in all the experiments we present, which is what we expected based on the success of SVMs in text classification tasks.

The use of SO as a feature set does not seem to have a positive effect on classification accuracies. This, however, may be due to the absence of a domain-specific dictionary for semantic orientation of terms. Despite our modifications of the list of positive and negative words, this feature set does not play a role in determining polarity. A more in-depth analysis of domain specific terms is required to assess the applicability of this feature set.

Manual analysis of the mis-classified instances reveals a number of key reasons behind the classification errors. Many systematic and non-systematic reviews in our data set present outcomes from multiple trials or studies of both polarities (which is a common feature of this publication type). Manual annotation of these abstracts is easier because the annotators can take the context of the articles into account and identify the overall message represented in the text. When multiple comparisons are presented in a review without a final polarised outcome, we annotated that review as no outcome. However, the n-grams generated by such articles have similarity to articles from the positive and negative classes and are therefore hard to separate automatically.

Furthermore, while RANC plays an important role in identifying negative polarities, introduction of this feature also causes some instances, particularly those with no outcomes, to have large RANCs. This happens when negations occur in multiple places of the abstract text, but none is associated with the final outcome. Negation phrases such as *'no outcome'* and *'no result'* are common in the No Outcome class while various forms of negations are present in articles belonging to the Negative class (e.g, *'not recommend'*). A deeper analysis of negations to see which terms occur more frequently in each of the two classes may reduce this problem.

Finally, the structure and content of the article abstracts vary significantly depending on the type of study. For example, a meta-analysis is considerably different from a randomised controlled trial. A more elaborate approach involving identification of publication types prior to classification and training and testing classifiers on texts belonging to specific study types would perhaps yield better results. Increasing the size of the training set is also likely to result in improved accuracy. However, that will also require significant time contribution for annotation.

6 Conclusion and Future Work

In this work we show that the problem of medical document polarity identification can be treated as a

Features	Naive Bayes	BayesNet	SVM	C4.5
Unigrams (P)	65.2	62.3	67.7	55.0
Unigrams (F)	65.2	62.3	68.3	55.0
Unigrams (P, C)	61.3	60.8	62.5	53.7
Unigrams (F, C)	61.3	60.8	62.5	53.7
Unigrams (M, P)	66.3	62.7	67.9	55.2
Unigrams (M, F)	66.3	62.7	**69.4**	55.2
Unigrams (M, P, C)	62.5	60.8	62.9	53.7
Unigrams (M, F, C)	62.5	60.8	62.9	53.7
Unigrams + bigrams (P)	70.4	63.8	72.7	62.3
Unigrams + bigrams (F)	70.4	63.8	72.9	62.3
Unigrams + bigrams (P, C)	66.0	62.7	69.8	60.5
Unigrams + bigrams (F, C)	65.9	62.7	70.0	60.3
Unigrams + bigrams (M, P)	70.1	63.5	**73.9**	63.7
Unigrams + bigrams (M, F)	66.3	62.7	68.3	60.4
Unigrams + bigrams (M, P, C)	63.1	60.8	65.6	59.0
Unigrams + bigrams (M, F, C)	63.0	61.1	66.3	58.1
N-grams (n=1,2 and 3)(P)	70.6	62.7	74.0	60.6
N-grams (n=1,2 and 3)(F)	70.6	62.7	73.9	60.6
N-grams (n=1,2 and 3)(M, P)	70.8	62.7	**74.2**	61.3
N-grams (n=1,2 and 3)(M, F)	70.8	62.6	74.0	61.3
N-grams (n=1,2,3 and 4)(P)	70.8	62.3	**73.0**	61.5
N-grams (n=1,2,3 and 4)(F)	70.8	62.3	72.6	61.5
N-grams (n=1,2,3 and 4)(M, P)	70.8	62.7	72.9	61.3
N-grams (n=1,2,3 and 4)(M, F)	70.6	61.9	72.3	61.3
Unigrams + bigrams + RANC (M, P)	72.1	68.1+	73.3	70.1+
N-grams (n=1,2 and 3) + RANC (M, P)	71.7	67.3	**74.4**	68.6
Unigrams + bigrams + RANC + SO(M, P)	71.5	66.7	73.3	67.5
N-grams (n=1,2 and 3) + RANC + SO (M, P)	71.6	66.5	**74.4**	67.9
Unigrams + bigrams + RANC + SS(M, P)	72.3+	67.3	73.6	66.5
N-grams (n=1,2 and 3) + RANC +SS (M, P)	72.3+	66.9	**74.9***	68.9
N-grams (n=1,2 and 3) + RANC + SO + SS(M, P)	71.7	67.1	**74.7**	68.0

Table 1: Classifier accuracies for various combinations of features. (P) represents word presence, (F) represents word frequencies, (M) indicates medical terms replaced from the text using the generic tag, (C) indicates only conclusion sentences used. RANC – Relative Average Negation Count, SO – Semantic Orientation, SS – Sentence Signatures. Best result produced by a combination of features shown in bold. Best overall accuracy indicated by *. Best accuracy achieved by a specific classifier indicated by +.

classification problem and machine learning algorithms can be used to solve this problem. Our work is the first of its kind in this domain and therefore we incorporate relevant techniques from related research work. Using carefully extracted linguistic features and domain knowledge, we obtain 74.9% accuracy on a data set that contains a variety of medical publication types. Post-classification analysis of our data reveals a number of possible research tasks that can be performed to further improve classification accuracies. Some classification errors can be attributed to subtle weaknesses in our automatic feature generation techniques and also the similarity in content among documents of differing classes.

Incorporating accurate, automatic outcome polarity detection techniques can considerably benefit automatic summarisation and question answering systems in this domain. This will require improving the accuracy of our classifiers and we will address some possibilities in our future work.

One possibility is to automatically identify the context when extracting features such as words, phrases, negations and signatures. Our analysis showed that in EBM practice, the same article may have different polarities depending on the query posed by the practitioner. The context may also be given by the topic of the article.

Our approach of using conclusion sentences can be improved through the use of classifiers that can identify conclusion/outcome sentences from medical abstracts automatically. Such a classifier has recently been presented by Kim et al. (2011) and it has been shown to be highly accurate at identifying sentences presenting medical outcomes. Future work will therefore involve the use of this method of sentence classification and use only sentences classified as 'outcomes'.

Since the content of publications in this domain vary with the publication types, an approach that automatically detects the publication types followed by the application of customized feature extraction techniques is likely to be more accurate. Careful analysis and ranking of the semantic orientation of words in this domain can also be effective in obtaining higher classification accuracies.

Finally, it is likely that performance can be improved by using a larger data set. This will also make it possible to use separate training and test sets so that the parameters of the classifiers can be optimised based on the training data and then be tested on the test data.

We will attempt to incorporate all the above-mentioned ideas in our future work. Considering the strong motivation behind an approach for automatic polarity detection, improvements in classification accuracy will be extremely beneficial for various automatic text processing applications in this domain.

Acknowledgments

This research work is jointly funded by Macquarie University and CSIRO.

References

Sofia J. Athenikos and Hyoil Han. 2010. Biomedical question answering: A survey. *Computer Methods and Programs in Biomedicine*, 99:1–24, July.

Wallace Chafe and Johanna Nichols. 1986. *Evidentiality: The Linguistic Coding of Epistemology*. Ablex, Norwood, NJ.

Wendy W Chapman, Will Bridewell, Paul Hanbury, Gregory F Cooper, and Bruce G Buchanan. 2001. Evaluation of negation phrases in narrative clinical reports. *Proc AMIA Symp*, pages 105–109.

Peter Elkin, Steven Brown, Brent Bauer, Casey Husser, William Carruth, Larry Bergstrom, and Dietlind W. Roedler. 2005. A controlled trial of automated classification of negation from clinical notes. *BMC medical informatics and decision making*, 5(1):13.

John W. Ely, Jerome A. Osheroff, Mark H. Ebell, George R. Bergus, Barcey T. Levy, M. Lee Chambliss, and Eric R. Evans. 1999. Analysis of questions asked by family doctors regarding patient care. *BMJ*, 319(7206):358–361, August.

Marcelo Fiszman, Dina Demner-Fushman, Halil Kilicoglu, and Thomas C. Rindflesch. 2009. Automatic summarization of medline citations for evidence-based medical treatment: A topic-oriented evaluation. *Journal of Biomedical Informatics*, 42(5):801–813.

Ira Goldstein and Ozlem Uzuner. 2010. Does Negation Really Matter? In *Proceedings of the Workshop on Negation and Speculation in Natural Language Processing*, pages 23–27.

Trisha Greenhalgh. 2006. *How to read a paper: The Basics of Evidence-based Medicine*. Blackwell Publishing, 3 edition.

Yang Huang and Henry J. Lowe. 2007. A novel hybrid approach to automated negation detection in clinical radiology reports. *JAMIA*, 14(3):304–311, May.

Alistair Kennedy and Diana Inkpen. 2006. Sentiment classification of movie and product reviews using contextual valence shifters. *Computational Intelligence*, 33(1):110–125.

Halil Kilicoglu, Dina Demner-Fushman, Thomas C. Rindflesch, Nancy L. Wilczynski, and Brian R. Haynes. 2009. Towards automatic recognition of scientifically rigorous clinical research evidence. *JAMIA*, 16(1):25–31, January.

Su Nam N. Kim, David Martinez, Lawrence Cavedon, and Lars Yencken. 2011. Automatic classification of sentences to support Evidence Based Medicine. *BMC bioinformatics*, 12 Suppl 2.

Ronald W Langacker, 1985. *Iconicity in Syntax*, chapter Observations and speculations on subjectivity, pages 109–150. Amsterdam and Philadelphia.

Jimmy J. Lin and Dina Demner-Fushman. 2007. Answering clinical questions with knowledge-based and statistical techniques. *Computational Linguistics*, 33(1):63–103.

John Lyons. 1981. *Language, Meaning and Context*. Fontana, London.

Yun Niu, Xiaodan Zhu, Jianhua Li, and Graeme Hirst. 2005. Analysis of polarity information in medical text. In *Proceedings of the AMIA Annual Symposium*, pages 570–574.

Yun Niu, Xiaodan Zhu, and Graeme Hirst. 2006. Using outcome polarity in sentence extraction for medical question-answering. In *Proceedings of the AMIA Annual Symposium*, pages 599–603.

Bo Pang and Lillian Lee. 2004. A Sentimental Education: Sentiment Analysis Using Subjectivity Summarization Based on Minimum Cuts. In *Proceedings of the 42nd Annual Meeting of the Association for Computational Linguistics*, pages 271–278.

Bo Pang and Lillian Lee. 2008. Opinion Mining and Sentiment Analysis. *Foundations and Trends in Information Retrieval*, 2(1):1–135.

Bo Pang, Lillian Lee, and Shivakumar Vaithyanathan. 2002. Thumbs up? Sentiment Classification using Machine Learning Techniques. In *Proc EMNLP*.

John C. Platt, 1999. *Fast training of support vector machines using sequential minimal optimization*, pages 185–208. MIT Press, Cambridge, MA, USA.

Livia Polanyi and Annie Zaenen, 2006. *Computing Attitude and Affect in Text: Theory and Applications*, chapter Contextual valence shifters, pages 1–10. Springer, Dordrecht.

Lior Rokach, Roni Romano, and Oded Maimon. 2008. Negation recognition in medical narrative reports. *Information Retrieval*, 11:499–538. 10.1007/s10791-008-9061-0.

David L Sackett, William M C Rosenberg, J A Muir Gray, R Brian Haynes, and W Scott Richardson. 1996. Evidence based medicine: what it is and what it isn't. *BMJ*, 312(7023):71–72.

Abeed Sarker, Diego Mollá-Aliod, and Cecile Paris. 2011. Towards automatic grading of evidence. In *Proceedings of LOUHI 2011 Third International Workshop on Health Document Text Mining and Information Analysis*, pages 51–58.

Philip J Stone, Dexter C Dunphy, Marshall S Smith, and Daniel M Ogilvie. 1966. *The General Inquirer: A Computer Approach to Content Analysis*. MIT Press, Cambridge, MA.

Maite Taboada, Julian Brooke, Milan Tofiloski, Kimberly Voll, and Manfred Stede. 2010. Lexicon-Based Methods for Sentiment Analysis. *Computational Linguistics*, 37(2):267–307.

Peter Turney. 2002. Thumbs up or thumbs down? Semantic orientation applied to unsupervised classification of reviews. In *Proceedings of ACL-02, 40th Annual Meeting of the Association for Computational Linguistics*, pages 417–424, Philadelphia, US. Association for Computational Linguistics.

Ozlem Uzuner, Xiaoran Zhang, and Tawanda Sibanda. 2009. Machine Learning and Rule-based Approaches to Assertion Classification. *JAMIA*, 16:109–115.

Vladimir N. Vapnik. 1995. *The nature of statistical learning theory*. Springer-Verlag New York, Inc., New York, NY, USA.

Topic Modeling for Native Language Identification

Sze-Meng Jojo Wong **Mark Dras** **Mark Johnson**
Centre for Language Technology
Macquarie University
Sydney, NSW, Australia
{sze.wong,mark.dras,mark.johnson}@mq.edu.au

Abstract

Native language identification (NLI) is the task of determining the native language of an author writing in a second language. Several pieces of earlier work have found that features such as function words, part-of-speech n-grams and syntactic structure are helpful in NLI, perhaps representing characteristic errors of different native language speakers. This paper looks at the idea of using Latent Dirichlet Allocation as a feature clustering technique over lexical features to see whether there is any evidence that these smaller-scale features do cluster into more coherent latent factors, and investigates their effect in a classification task. We find that although (not unexpectedly) classification accuracy decreases, there is some evidence of coherent clustering, which could help with much larger syntactic feature spaces.

1 Introduction

Native language identification (NLI), the task of determining the native language of an author writing in a second language, typically English, has gained increased attention in recent years. The problem was first phrased as a text classification task by Koppel et al. (2005), using a machine learner with fundamentally lexical features — function words, character n-grams, and part-of-speech (PoS) n-grams. A number of subsequent pieces of work, such as that of Tsur and Rappoport (2007), Estival et al. (2007), Wong and Dras (2009) and Wong and Dras (2011), have taken that as a starting point, typically along with a wider range of features, such as document structure or syntactic structure.

Wong and Dras (2011) looked particularly at syntactic structure, in the form of production rules and parse reranking templates. They noted that they did not find the expected instances of clearly ungrammatical elements of syntactic structure indicating non-native speaker errors; instead there were just different distributions over regular elements of grammatical structure for different native languages. Our intuition is that it is several elements together that indicate particular kinds of indicative errors, such as incorrect noun-number agreement; and from this, that there might be coherent clusters of correlated features that are indicative of a particular native language. In this preliminary work, we investigate this using the basic lexical features of the original Koppel et al. (2005) model.

Latent Dirichlet Allocation (LDA) — a generative probabilistic model for unsupervised learning — was first introduced by Blei et al. (2003) to discover a set of latent mixture components known as *topics* which are representative of a collection of discrete data. The underlying idea of LDA is that each document from a text corpus is constructed according to a specific distribution of topics, in which words comprising the document are generated based on the word distribution for each selected topic; a topic is typically represented by a set of words such as *species*, *phylogenetic*, *evolution* and so on. Such a model allows multiple topics in one document as well as sharing of topics across documents within the corpus.

LDA can be viewed as a form of dimensionality reduction technique. In this paper, we intend to exploit LDA to discover the extent to which a lower dimension of feature space (i.e. a set of potentially useful clusters of features) in each document affects classification performance. Here we are mapping clusters of features as 'topics' in typical LDA models and the posterior topic distributions inferred are to be used for classifying the native language of the authors against baseline models using the actual features themselves. We are particularly interested in whether the topics appear at all to form coherent clusters, and consequently whether they might potentially be applicable to the much larger class of syntactic features.

The remainder of this paper is structured as follows. In Section 2, we discuss some related work on the two key concepts of this paper: first relevant work in NLI, and then a brief description of LDA with its application to classification. We then describe both the topic models and the classification models used for the corpus to be examined, in Section 3. Section 4 presents classification results, and is followed by discussion in Section 5.

2 Related Work

2.1 Native Language Identification

Most of the existing work on native language identification adopts the supervised machine learning approach to classification. Koppel et al. (2005) is the earliest work in this classification paradigm using as features function words, character n-grams, and PoS bi-grams, together with some spelling mistakes. They used as their corpus the first version of *International Corpus of Learner English* (ICLE), selecting authors writing in English who have as their native language one of Bulgarian, Czech, French, Russian, or Spanish. Koppel et al. (2005) suggested that syntactic features (specifically errors) might be potentially useful, but only explored this idea at a rather shallow level by characterising ungrammatical structures with rare PoS bi-grams. This work of Koppel et al. (2005) was then investigated by Tsur and Rappoport (2007) to test their hypothesis that the choice of words in second language writing is highly influenced by the frequency of native language syllables, through measuring classification accuracy with only character bi-grams as features.

Another work with a similar goal, of developing profiles of authors, is that of Estival et al. (2007). They used a variety of lexical and document structure features over a set of three languages — English, Spanish and Arabic — also looking at predicting other demographic and psychometric author traits in addition to native language.

Wong and Dras (2009) first replicated the work of Koppel et al. (2005) with the three types of lexical feature as mentioned above and then extended the classification model with three syntactic errors commonly observed in non-native English users — subject-verb disagreement, noun-number disagreement and misuse of determiners — which had been identified as being influenced by the native language based on 'constrative analysis' (Lado, 1957). Although the overall classification did not improve over the lexical features alone, an ANOVA analysis showed that there were significant differences amongst different groups of non-native English users in terms of the errors made. In this work the classification task was carried out using the second version of ICLE (Granger et al., 2009), across seven languages (those of Koppel et al. (2005) with the two Asian languages Chinese and Japanese).

The later work of Wong and Dras (2011), on the same data, further explored the usefulness of syntactic features in a broader sense by characterising syntactic errors with cross sections of parse trees obtained from statistical parsing. More specifically, they utilised two types of parse tree substructure to use as classification features — horizontal slices of the trees as sets of CFG production rules and the feature schemas used in discriminative parse reranking (Charniak and Johnson, 2005). It was demonstrated that using these kinds of syntactic features performs significantly better than lexical features alone.

One key phenomenon observed by Wong and Dras (2011) was that there were different proportions of parse production rules indicative of particular native languages. One example is the production rule `NP → NN NN`, which appears to be very common amongst Chinese speakers compared with other native language groups; they claim that this is likely to reflect determiner-noun agreement errors, as that rule is used at the expense of one headed by a plural noun (`NP → NN NNS`). Our intuition here is that there might be coherent clusters of related features, with these clusters characterising typical errors or idiosyncrasies, that are predictive of a particular native language. In this paper we use LDA to cluster features, although in this preliminary work we use only the simpler lexical features of Wong and Dras

(2011).

2.2 Latent Dirichlet Allocation

Latent Dirichlet Allocation is a Bayesian probabilistic model used to represent collections of discrete data such as text corpora, introduced by Blei et al. (2003). It addressed limitations of earlier techniques such as *probabilistic latent semantic indexing*, which is prone to overfitting and unable to generalise to unseen documents. LDA is a relaxation of classical document mixture models in which each document is associated with only a single topic, as it allows documents to be generated based on a mixture of topics with different distributions. We discuss the basic details of LDA, and our particular representation, in Section 3.1.

LDA has been applied to a wide range of tasks, such as building cluster-based models for ad hoc information retrieval (Wei and Croft, 2006) or grounded learning of semantic parsers (Börschinger et al., 2011). Relevant to this paper, it has been applied to a range of text classification tasks.

The original paper of Blei et al. (2003) used LDA as a dimensionality reduction technique over word unigrams for an SVM, for genre-based classification of Reuters news data and classification of collaborative filtering of movie review data, and found that LDA topics actually improved classification accuracy in spite of the dimensionality reduction. This same basic approach has been taken with other data, such as spam filtering of web text (Bíró et al., 2008), where LDA topics improved classification f-measure, or finding scientific topics from article abstracts (Griffiths and Steyvers, 2004), where LDA topics appear to be useful diagnostics for scientific subfields.

It has also been augmented in various ways: supervised LDA, where topic models are integrated with a response variable, was introduced by Blei and McAuliffe (2008) and applied to predicting sentiment scores from movie review data, treating it as a regression problem rather than a classification problem. Work by Wang et al. (2009) followed from that, extending it to classification problems, and applying it to the simultaneous classification and annotation of images. An alternative approach to joint models of text and response variables for sentiment classification of review texts (Titov and McDonald, 2008), with a particular focus on constructing topics related to aspects of reviews (e.g. food, decor, or service for restaurant reviews), found that LDA topics were predictively useful and seemed qualitatively intuitive.

In all of this preceding work, a document to be classified is represented by an exchangeable set of (content) words: function words are generally removed, and are not typically found in topics useful for classification. It is exactly these that are used in NLI, so the above work does guarantee that an LDA-based approach will be helpful here.

Two particularly relevant pieces of work on using LDA in classification are for the related task of authorship attribution, determining which author wrote a particular document. Rajkumar et al. (2009) claim that models with stopwords (function words) alone are sufficient to achieve high accuracy in classification, which seems to peak at 25 topics, and outperform content word-based models; the results presented in Table 2 and the discussion are, however, somewhat contradictory. Seroussi et al. (2011) also include both function words and content words in their models; they find that filtering words by frequency is almost always harmful, suggesting that function words are helping in this task.[1]

In this paper we will explore both function words and PoS n-grams, the latter of which is quite novel to our knowledge in terms of classification using LDA, to investigate whether clustering shows any potential for our task.

3 Experimental Setup

3.1 Mechanics of LDA

3.1.1 General Definition

Formally, each document is formed from a fixed set of vocabulary V and fixed set of topics T ($|T| = t$). Following the characterisation given by Griffiths and Steyvers (2004), the process of generating a corpus of m documents is as follows: first generate a set of multinomial distributions over topics $\boldsymbol{\theta}_j$ for each document D_j according to a T-dimensional Dirichlet distribution with concentration parameter $\boldsymbol{\alpha}$ (i.e. $\boldsymbol{\theta}_j \sim \text{Dir}(\boldsymbol{\alpha})$); then generate a set of multinomial distributions $\boldsymbol{\phi}_i$ over the vocabulary V for each topic i according to a V-dimensional Dirichlet distribution with concentration parameter $\boldsymbol{\beta}$ (i.e. $\boldsymbol{\phi}_i \sim \text{Dir}(\boldsymbol{\beta})$);

[1] They note that for function words the term 'latent factor' is more appropriate than 'topic', with its connotation of semantic content.

and finally generate each of the n_j words for document D_j by selecting a random topic z according $\boldsymbol{\theta}_j$ and then drawing a word $w_{j,k}$ from $\boldsymbol{\phi}_z$ of the selected topic. The overall generative probabilistic model can be summarised as follows:

$$\begin{array}{ll} \boldsymbol{\theta}_j \sim \text{Dir}(\boldsymbol{\alpha}) & j \in 1, ..., m \\ \boldsymbol{\phi}_i \sim \text{Dir}(\boldsymbol{\beta}) & i \in 1, ..., t \\ z_{j,k} \sim \boldsymbol{\theta}_j & j \in 1, ..., m, k \in 1, ..., n_j \\ w_{j,k} \sim \boldsymbol{\phi}_{z_{j,k}} & j \in 1, ..., m, k \in 1, ..., n_j \end{array}$$

From the inference perspective, given a corpus of m documents with n_j words each, the task is to estimate the posterior topic distributions $\boldsymbol{\theta}_j$ for each document D_j as well as the posterior word distributions $\boldsymbol{\phi}_i$ for each topic i that maximise the log likelihood of the corpus. As exact inference of these posterior distributions is generally intractable, there is a wide variety of means of approximate inference for LDA models which include approximation algorithms such as *Variational Bayes* (Blei et al., 2003) and expectation propagation (Minka and Lafferty, 2002) as well as *Markov Chain Monte Carlo* inference algorithm with Gibbs sampling (Griffiths and Steyvers, 2004).

3.1.2 LDA as PCFG

Johnson (2010) showed that LDA topic models can be regarded as a specific type of probabilistic context-free grammar (PCFG), and that Bayesian inference for PCFGs can be used to learn LDA models where the inferred distributions of PCFGs correspond to those distributions of LDA. A general schema used for generating PCFG rule instances for representing m documents with t topics is as follows:[2]

$$\begin{array}{ll} Sentence \rightarrow Doc'_j & j \in 1, ..., m \\ Doc'_j \rightarrow \_j & j \in 1, ..., m \\ Doc'_j \rightarrow Doc'_j\ Doc_j & j \in 1, ..., m \\ Doc_j \rightarrow Topic_i & i \in 1, ..., t; j \in 1, ..., m \\ Topic_i \rightarrow w & i \in 1, ..., t; w \in V \end{array}$$

Each of the rules in the PCFG is associated with a Bayesian inferred probability. The probabilities associated with the rules expanding $Topic_i$ correspond to the word distributions $\boldsymbol{\phi}_i$ of the LDA model, and the probabilities associated with the rules expanding Doc_j correspond to the topic distributions $\boldsymbol{\theta}_j$ of LDA. Similarly, inference on the posterior rule distributions can be approximated with Variational Bayes and Gibbs sampling. We use this PCFG formulation of LDA in this work.

[2]It should be noted that each document is given with a document identifier in which sentences in the document are prefixed with $\_j$.

3.2 Experimental Models

This section describes both the LDA models and the corresponding classification models used for our native language identification task on the ICLE corpus (Version 2) (Granger et al., 2009). Following Wong and Dras (2011), our experimental dataset consists of 490 essays written by non-native English users from seven different groups of language background — namely, Bulgarian, Czech, French, Russian, Spanish, Chinese, and Japanese. There are 70 documents per native language.

Unlike the documents often inferred by LDA topic models which mostly consist of only content words, we represent our documents with function words instead, as this is typical for authorship related tasks, and does not allow unfair clues based on different distribution of domain discourses. In addition, we also experiment with documents represented by another type of lexical features for NLI, PoS bi-grams.

3.2.1 LDA Models for NLI

For each of the models we describe below, we experiment with different numbers of topics, $t = \{5, 10, 15, 20, 25\}$. In terms of the total number of PCFG rules representing each model, there are 490 of the first three rules as shown in the schema (Section 3.1.2), $490 \times t$ of the rule expanding $Doc_j \rightarrow Topic_i$, and $t \times v$ of the rule expanding $Topic_i \rightarrow w$ (see Table 1). All the inferences are performed with the PCFG-based Gibbs sampler implemented by Mark Johnson.[3]

FW-LDA Models The first LDA model is function word based. The vocabulary used for generating documents with this model is therefore a set of function words. We adopt the same set as used in Wong and Dras (2011) which consists of 398 words. An instance of the PCFG rule expanding $Topic_i \rightarrow w$ is $Topic_1 \rightarrow the$; there are 398 such rules for each topic.

[3]Software is available at `http://web.science.mq.edu.au/~mjohnson/Software.htm`.

LDA Models	$t = 5$	$t = 10$	$t = 15$	$t = 20$	$t = 25$
FW-LDA	5,910	10,350	14,790	19,230	23,670
POS-LDA	4,920	8,370	11,820	15,270	18,720
FW+POS-LDA	6,910	12,350	17,790	23,230	28,670

Table 1: Number of PCFG rules for each LDA model with different number of topics t

POS-LDA Models The second model is PoS bi-gram based. We choose bi-grams as it has been shown useful in Tsur and Rappoport (2007), and was used in Wong and Dras (2009). By tagging the 490 documents with Brill tagger (with Brown corpus tags), we extract the 200 most frequent occurring PoS bi-grams to form the vocabulary for this model. An instance of the PCFG rule expanding $Topic_i \rightarrow w$ is $Topic_1 \rightarrow$ *NN_NN*; there are 200 such rules for each topic.

FW-POS-LDA Models The third model combines the first two. We note that this is not typical of topic models: most form topics only over single types, such as content words.[4] The vocabulary then consists of both function words and PoS bi-grams with 598 terms in total. Thus, there are 598 instances of the rule expanding $Topic_i \rightarrow w$ for each topic.

3.2.2 Classification Models for NLI

Here we exploit LDA as a form of feature space dimension reduction to discover clusters of features as represented by 'topics' for classification. Based on each of the LDA models inferred, we take the posterior topic distributions to use as features for classifying into one of the seven native language classes. All the classifications are performed with a maximum entropy learner — MegaM (fifth release) by Hal Daumé III.[5]

Baselines Each LDA classification model (as described in the following) is compared against a corresponding baseline model. These sets of model use the actual features themselves for classification without feature reduction. There are three baselines: function word based with 398 features (FW-BASELINE), PoS bi-gram based with 200 features (POS-BASELINE), and the combination of the first two set of features (FW+POS-BASELINE). For each of these models, we examine two types of feature value — relative frequency and binary.

Function Words Features used in this model (FW-LDA) are the topic distributions inferred from the first LDA model. There are five variants of this based on number of topics (Section 3.2.1). The feature values are the posterior probabilities associated with the PCFG rules expanding $Doc_j \rightarrow Topic_i$ which correspond to the topic distributions $\boldsymbol{\theta}_j$ of the LDA representation.

PoS Bi-grams Similarly, this set of classification models (POS-LDA) uses the topic probabilities inferred from the second LDA model as features. Five variants of this with respect to the different topic numbers are examined as well.

Combined Features The last set of models combine both the function words and PoS bi-grams as classification features. The feature values are then the topic probabilities extracted from the last LDA model (the combined FW+POS-LDA model).

3.3 Evaluation

Often, LDA models are evaluated in terms of goodness of fit of the model to new data, by estimating the *perplexity* or similar of unseen held-out documents given some training documents (Blei et al., 2003; Griffiths and Steyvers, 2004). However, there are issues with all such proposed measures so far, such as importance sampling, harmonic mean, Chib-style estimation, and others; see Wallach et al. (2009) for a discussion. Alternatively, LDA models can be evaluated by measuring performance of some specific applications such as information retrieval and document classification (Titov and McDonald, 2008; Wang et al., 2009; Seroussi et al., 2011). We take this approach here, and adopt the standard measure for classification models — *classification accuracy* — as an indirect evaluation on our LDA models. The evaluation uses 5-fold cross-validation.

4 Classification Results

4.1 Baseline Models

Table 2 presents the classification accuracies achieved by the three baseline models mentioned above (i.e. using the actual features themselves without feature space reduction). These results are aligned with the results presented by Wong and Dras (2009) in their earlier work where binary feature

[4]Those that include multiple types typically treat them in different ways, such as in the separate treatment of content words and movie review ratings of Blei and McAuliffe (2008).

[5]MegaM is available at `http://www.cs.utah.edu/~hal/megam/`.

Baselines	Relative Freq	Binary
FW-BASELINE	33.26	62.45
POS-BASELINE	45.92	53.87
FW+POS-BASELINE	42.65	64.08

Table 2: Classification performance (%) of each baseline model – feature types of relative frequency and binary

values perform much better in general, although the results are lower because the calculation was made under cross-validation rather than on a separate held-out test set (hence with an effectively smaller amount of training data). Combining both the function words and PoS bi-grams yield a higher accuracy as compared to individual features alone. It seems that both features are capturing different useful cues that are predictive of individual native languages.

4.2 LDA Models

The classification performance for each of the LDA models is presented in Tables 3 to 5. Three sets of concentration parameters (Dirichlet priors) were tested on each of the three models to find the best fitted topic model: Table 3 contains results for uniform priors $\alpha = 1$ and $\beta = 1$ (the default); Table 4 is for $\alpha = 50/t$ and $\beta = 0.01$ (as per Steyvers and Griffiths (2007)); and Table 5 is for $\alpha = 5/t$ and $\beta = 0.01$ (since for us, with a small number of topics, the $\alpha = 50/t$ of Steyvers and Griffiths (2007) gives much larger values of α than was the case in Steyvers and Griffiths (2007)). On the whole, weaker priors ($\alpha = 5/t$ and $\beta = 0.01$) lead to a better model as evidenced by the accuracy scores.

As observed in Table 3, the model with 10 topics is the best model under uniform priors for both the individual feature-based models (FW-LDA and POS-LDA) with accuracies of 50.61% and 51.02% respectively, while the combined model (FW+POS-LDA) performs best at 55.51% with 15 topics. It should be noted that these are the outcomes of using the topic probabilities as feature value. (We also investigated the extent to which binary feature values could be useful by setting a probability threshold at 0.1; however, the results are consistently lower.)

By setting a stronger $\alpha = 50/t$ and a much weaker $\beta = 0.01$, the resulting models perform no better than those with uniform priors (see Table 4). The best performing models under this setting are with 25 topics for the individual feature-based models but with 20 topics for the combined

LDA Models	$t = 5$	$t = 10$	$t = 15$	$t = 20$	$t = 25$
FW-LDA	44.89	*50.61*	44.29	47.14	49.59
POS-LDA	47.35	*51.02*	50.00	50.61	49.79
FW+POS-LDA	49.79	54.08	*55.51*	52.86	53.26

Table 3: Classification performance (%) of each LDA-induced model ($\alpha = 1$ and $\beta = 1$); feature values of topic probabilities

LDA Models	$t = 5$	$t = 10$	$t = 15$	$t = 20$	$t = 25$
FW-LDA	32.45	42.45	44.29	45.71	*47.35*
POS-LDA	44.29	46.53	*50.82*	48.76	*50.82*
FW+POS-LDA	47.75	49.39	51.02	*54.49*	50.81

Table 4: Classification performance (%) of each LDA-induced model ($\alpha = 50/t$ and $\beta = 0.01$); feature values of topic probabilities

model. This setting of priors was found to work well for most of the text collections as suggested in Steyvers and Griffiths (2007). However, given that our topic sizes are just within the range of 5 to 25, we also tried $\alpha = 5/t$. The classification results based on $\alpha = 5/t$ and $\beta = 0.01$ are showed in Table 5. This setting leads to the best accuracy (thus far) for each of the models with 25 topics — FW-LDA (52.45%), POS-LDA (53.47%), FW+POS-LDA (56.94%). The overall trajectory suggests that more than 25 topics might be useful.

Overall, the classification performance for each of the LDA-induced models (regardless of the parameter settings) performs worse than the baseline models (Section 4.1) where the actual features were used, contra the experience of Rajkumar et al. (2009) in authorship attribution. The drop is, however, only small in the case of PoS tags; the overall result is dragged down by the drop in function word model accuracies. And comparatively, they are still well above the majority baseline of 14.29% (70/490), so the LDA models are detecting something. On the one hand it is not surprising that reducing a relatively small feature space reduces performance; on the other hand, other work (as discussed in Section 2.2) had found that this had actually helped. While these results are not conclusive — a more systematic search might find better values of α and β — the results of the POS-LDA model suggests some promise for applying the method to a much larger feature space of similar terms: this could either be the unrestricted set of PoS bi-grams, or of syntactic structure features. We investigate this further by looking more deeply in Section 5 at some of the 'topics' (latent factors) found.

LDA Models	$t = 5$	$t = 10$	$t = 15$	$t = 20$	$t = 25$
FW-LDA	41.63	47.14	48.76	45.51	*52.45*
POS-LDA	43.47	49.79	51.22	52.86	*53.47*
FW+POS-LDA	51.84	50.61	53.88	52.62	*56.94*

Table 5: Classification performance (%) of each LDA-induced model ($\alpha = 5/t$ and $\beta = 0.01$); feature values of topic probabilities

5 Discussion

Despite the fact that all the LDA-induced models had lower accuracy scores than the baseline models, the inferred topics (clusters of related features) did demonstrate some useful cues that appear to be indicative of a particular native language. Here we present a discussion of three of these.

Analysis of FW-LDA It is often noted in the literature on second language errors that a typical error of Chinese speakers of English is with articles such as *a*, *an*, and *the*, as Chinese does not have these. Looking at the best performing FW-LDA model (weak priors of $\alpha = 5/t$ and $\beta = 0.01$; 25 topics), we observed that for the three topics — $Topic_8$ (the 8th feature), $Topic_{19}$ (the 19th feature) and $Topic_{20}$ (the 20th feature) — each of these is associated with a much higher feature weight for Chinese as compared to other native language groups (Table 6 shows the analysis on $Topic_8$). As for the function words clustered under these topics, *the* appears to be the most probable one with the highest probabilities of around 0.188, 0.181, and 0.146 for each respectively (i.e. the PCFG rules of $Topic_8 \rightarrow the$, $Topic_{19} \rightarrow the$, and $Topic_{20} \rightarrow the$); this is a higher weighting than for any other word in any topic. To verify that the topic model accurately reflects the data, we found that the relative frequency of *the* in the documents produced by Chinese learners is the highest in comparison with other languages in our corpus. It seems that Chinese learners have a tendency to misuse this kind of word in their English constructions, overusing *the*: this parallels the example given in Wong and Dras (2011), noted in Section 2.1, of the overuse of rules like `NP` $\rightarrow$ `NN NN` (rather than specifically ungrammatical constructions) characterising Chinese texts. However, there is no obvious pattern to the clustering (at least, that is evident to the authors)—if the clusters were to be grouping features in a way representative of errors, one of these topics might reflect misuse of determiners. But, none of these appear to: in $Topic_8$, for example, *a* appears only in 5th place, and no other determiners appear at all in the upper end of the distribution.

Language	Feature Weight	Relative Freq of *the*
Bulgarian	(relative to Bulgarian)	0.0814
Czech	-0.0457	0.0648
French	0.2124	0.0952
Russian	0.0133	0.0764
Spanish	-0.0016	0.0903
Chinese	*3.2409*	*0.1256*
Japanese	0.4485	0.0661

Table 6: Analysis on FW-LDA for $Topic_8$

Language	Feature Weight	Relative Freq of *NN_NN*
Bulgarian	(relative to Bulgarian)	0.0126
Czech	0.7777	0.0157
French	0.2566	0.0148
Russian	0.0015	0.0129
Spanish	0.0015	0.0142
Chinese	*2.4843*	*0.0403*
Japanese	0.4422	0.0202

Table 7: Analysis on POS-LDA for $Topic_1$

Analysis of POS-LDA However, there is a different story for POS-LDA, in terms of Chinese error phenomena. As shown in Table 7, Chinese has the highest feature weight for the first feature, $Topic_1$ (and also for $Topic_4$). To characterise this, we note that the PoS bi-gram `NN_NN` appears as the top bi-gram under $Topic_1$ ($\sim$0.18) (and also occurs most frequently among Chinese learners as compared to other native language groups). Further, the next four bi-grams are `NN_IN`, `AT_IN`, `IN_NN` and `NN_NNS`, the last of which appears to be in complementary distribution in Chinese errors with `NN_NN` (i.e. Chinese speakers tend to use the singular more often in compound nouns, when a plural might be more appropriate). This observation also seems to be consistent with the finding of Wong and Dras (2011) in which the production rule `NP` $\rightarrow$ `NN NN`, reflecting determiner-noun disagreement, appears to be very common amongst Chinese learners. $Topic_1$ thus seems to be somehow connected with noun-related errors.

Our second instance to look at in some detail is

Language	Feature Weight	Relative Freq of *PPSS_VB*
Bulgarian	(relative to Bulgarian)	0.0111
Czech	0.7515	0.0137
French	-0.7080	0.0074
Russian	-0.2097	0.0116
Spanish	-0.3394	0.0117
Chinese	-0.1987	0.0059
Japanese	*2.0707*	*0.0224*

Table 8: Analysis on POS-LDA for $Topic_8$

Native Languages	Absolute Frequency										
	I	They	Thou	We	You	it	she	they	we	you	Total
Bulgarian	229	66	0	52	38	1	0	297	338	219	1240
Czech	483	188	0	166	34	1	0	459	348	202	1881
French	161	55	0	71	4	2	0	282	261	90	926
Russian	355	100	1	76	28	1	0	332	286	110	1289
Spanish	157	52	0	49	6	2	1	361	360	107	1095
Chinese	143	52	0	9	2	2	0	259	66	30	563
Japanese	*1062*	104	0	115	13	4	0	310	473	71	*2152*

Table 9: Pronoun usage across seven native language groups (absolute frequency of words tagged with PPSS)

for Japanese. Our expectation is that there are likely to be errors related to pronouns, as Japanese often omits them. In his comprehensive survey of second language acquisition, Ellis (2008) describes four measures of crosslinguistic influence: error (negative transfer), where differences between the languages lead to errors; facilitation (positive transfer), where similarities between the languages lead to a reduction in errors (relative to learners of other languages); avoidance, where constructions that are absent in the native language are avoided in the second language; and overuse, where constructions are used more frequently in an incorrect way in the second language, because of overgeneralisation.

A priori, it is difficult to predict which of these types of influence might be the case. The classic study of avoidance by Schachter (1974) examines Persian, Arab, Chinese, and Japanese learners of English, and their performance on using relative clauses. It found that even though Persian and Arabic have similar (right-branching) relative clauses to English, and Japanese and Chinese have different (left-branching) ones, the Japanese and Chinese learners made fewer errors; but that that was because they avoided using the construction. On the other hand, for a grammatically less complex phenomenon such as article use, several studies such as those of Liu and Gleason (2002) show that there can be a developmental aspect to crosslinguistic influence, with initial errors or avoidance turning to overuse because of overgeneralisation, which is later corrected; intermediate learners thus show the greatest level of overuse.

Looking at $Topic_8$ and $Topic_{20}$ under the POS-LDA model, relative to other topics inferred, top-ranking PoS bi-grams are mostly related to pronouns (such as *PPSS_VB*, *PPSS_MD*, and *PPSS_VBD*). Much higher feature weights are associated to these two topics for Japanese (as seen in Table 8 the analysis on $Topic_8$). Bi-grams of *PPSS_VB* and *PPSS_MD* occur much more often in Japanese learners' writings, and they are the first and the fifth terms under $Topic_8$, which seems to capture some of these phenomena.

To understand what these were saying about Japanese pronoun usage, we looked at a breakdown of pronoun use (see Table 9). Most apparently, the texts by Japanese speakers use more pronouns than any others. As the texts in the ICLE corpus are written by intermediate speakers, this could indicate a very strong instance of overuse. Looking at the distribution of pronouns, the Japanese speakers make much more use of the pronoun *I* than others: this has been noted elsewhere by Ishikawa (2011) on different corpora, particularly in the use of phrases such as *I think*. (The phrase *I think* is over-represented among Japanese speakers in our data also.)

Overall, then, POS-LDA seems to provide useful clustering of terms, while FW-LDA does not. This accords with the classification accuracies seen.

Analysis of FW+POS-LDA One question about the combined models was whether topics split along feature type — if that were the case, for a rough 2:1 ratio of function words to PoS bi-grams under 15 topics, there might be 10 topics whose upper rankings are dominated by function words, and 5 by PoS bi-grams. However, they are relatively evenly spread: for the top 20 words in each topic (uniform priors; 15 topics), the proportion of function words varied from 0.22 to 0.44, mean 0.339 and standard deviation 0.063. The topics thus appear to be quite mixed.

Looking into the combined model, $Topic_3$ and $Topic_{11}$ inferred by this model are amongst the features that associated with high feature weights for Chinese. Coinciding with our expectation, the two potential terms indicative of Chinese — *NN_NN* and *the* — topped the lists of $Topic_3$ and $Topic_{11}$ respectively (where *the* also appears as the second most probable in $Topic_3$).

6 Conclusion

Although the LDA-induced classification models with feature space reduction somewhat underperformed in relation to the full feature-based models (the baselines), the 'topics' (latent factors) found appear in fact to be capturing useful information for individual native languages. Given the performance of POS-LDA, and the fact that the clustering seems more intuitive here, it seems promising to explore LDAs further with larger class of unrestricted PoS bi-grams, or of syntactic features such as the parse tree substructures used in Wong and Dras (2011). This could be complemented by using the adaptor grammars of Johnson (2010) to capture collocational pairings. Another potential approach that could be combined with this is to deploy the supervised LDA proposed by Blei and McAuliffe (2008), which might produce feature clusters that are more closely aligned to native language identification cues.

Acknowledgments

We acknowledge the support of ARC grant LP0776267. We also thank the anonymous reviewers, particularly for insightful critiques of the analysis of the topic models.

References

István Bíró, Jácint Szabó, and András A. Benczúr. 2008. Latent dirichlet allocation in web spam filtering. In *Proceedings of the 4th International Workshop on Adversarial Information Retrieval on the Web*, pages 29–32, Beijing, China, April.

David Blei and Jon McAuliffe. 2008. Supervised topic models. In J.C. Platt, D. Koller, Y. Singer, and S. Roweis, editors, *Advances in Neural Information Processing Systems 20*, pages 121–128. MIT Press, Cambridge, MA.

David M. Blei, Andrew Ng, and Michael Jordan. 2003. Latent Dirichlet allocation. *Journal of Machine Learning Research*, 3:993–1022.

Benjamin Börschinger, Bevan K. Jones, and Mark Johnson. 2011. Reducing grounded learning tasks to grammatical inference. In *Proceedings of the 2011 Conference on Empirical Methods in Natural Language Processing*, pages 1416–1425, Edinburgh, Scotland, July.

Eugene Charniak and Mark Johnson. 2005. Coarse-to-fine n-best parsing and MaxEnt discriminative reranking. In *Proceedings of the 43rd Annual Meeting on Association for Computational Linguistics*, pages 173–180, Ann Arbor, Michigan, June.

Rod Ellis. 2008. *The Study of Second Language Acquisition, 2nd edition*. Oxford University Press, Oxford, UK.

Dominique Estival, Tanja Gaustad, Son-Bao Pham, Will Radford, and Ben Hutchinson. 2007. Author profiling for English emails. In *Proceedings of the 10th Conference of the Pacific Association for Computational Linguistics (PACLING)*, pages 263–272.

Sylviane Granger, Estelle Dagneaux, Fanny Meunier, and Magali Paquot. 2009. *International Corpus of Learner English (Version 2)*. Presses Universitaires de Louvain, Louvian-la-Neuve.

Thomas L. Griffiths and Mark Steyvers. 2004. Finding scientific topics. *Proceedings of the National Academy of Sciences*, 101(suppl. 1):5228–5235.

Shun'ichiro Ishikawa. 2011. A New Horizon in Learner Corpus Studies: The Aim of the ICNALE Project. In G. Weir, S. Ishikawa, and K. Poonpon, editors, *Corpora and Language Technologies in Teaching, Learning and Research*, pages 3–11. University of Strathclyde Press, Glasgow, UK.

Mark Johnson. 2010. PCFGs, Topic Models, Adaptor Grammars and Learning Topical Collocations and the Structure of Proper Names. In *Proceedings of the 48th Annual Meeting of the Association for Computational Linguistics*, pages 1148–1157, Uppsala, Sweden, July.

Moshe Koppel, Jonathan Schler, and Kfir Zigdon. 2005. Automatically determining an anonymous author's native language. In *Intelligence and Security Informatics*, volume 3495 of *Lecture Notes in Computer Science*, pages 209–217. Springer-Verlag.

Robert Lado. 1957. *Linguistics Across Cultures: Applied Linguistics for Language Teachers*. University of Michigan Press, Ann Arbor, MI, US.

Dilin Liu and Johanna L. Gleason. 2002. Acquisition of the Article *the* by Nonnative Speakers of English: An Analysis of Four Nongeneric Uses. *Studies in Second Language Acquisition*, 24:1–26.

Thomas Minka and John Lafferty. 2002. Expectation-propagation for the generative aspect model. In *Proceedings of the Eighteenth Conference on Uncertainty in Artificial Intelligence*, pages 352–359.

Arun Rajkumar, Saradha Ravi, Venkatasubramanian Suresh, M. Narasimha Murty, and C. E. Veni Madhavan. 2009. Stopwords and stylometry: A latent Dirichlet allocation approach. In *Proceedings of the NIPS 2009 Workshop on Applications for Topic Models: Text and Beyond (Poster Session)*, Whistler, Canada, December.

J. Schachter. 1974. An error in error analysis. *Language Learning*, 27:205–214.

Yanir Seroussi, Ingrid Zukerman, and Fabian Bohnert. 2011. Authorship attribution with latent Dirichlet allocation. In *Proceedings of the Fifteenth Conference on Computational Natural Language Learning*, pages 181–189, Portland, Oregon, June.

Mark Steyvers and Tom Griffiths. 2007. Probabilistic Topic Models. In T. Landauer, D. Mcnamara, S. Dennis, and W. Kintsch, editors, *Handbook of Latent Semantic Analysis*, chapter 21, pages 427–448. Lawrence Erlbaum Associates.

Ivan Titov and Ryan McDonald. 2008. A joint model of text and aspect ratings for sentiment summarization. In *Proceedings of ACL-08: HLT*, pages 308–316, Columbus, Ohio, June.

Oren Tsur and Ari Rappoport. 2007. Using classifier features for studying the effect of native language on the choice of written second language words. In *Proceedings of the Workshop on Cognitive Aspects of Computational Language Acquisition*, pages 9–16.

Hanna Wallach, Iain Murray, Ruslan Salakhutdinov, and David Mimno. 2009. Evaluation Methods for Topic Models. In *Proceedings of the 26 th International Conference on Machine Learning*, Montreal, Canada.

Chong Wang, David Blei, and Fei-Fei Li. 2009. Simultaneous image classification and annotation. In *Proceedings of the IEEE Conference on Computer Vision and Pattern Recognition*, pages 1903–1910, June.

Xing Wei and W. Bruce Croft. 2006. LDA-Based Document Models for Ad-hoc Retrieval. In *Proceedings of the 29th Annual International ACM SIGIR Conference (SIGIR'06)*, pages 178–185.

Sze-Meng Jojo Wong and Mark Dras. 2009. Contrastive analysis and native language identification. In *Proceedings of the Australasian Language Technology Association Workshop 2009*, pages 53–61, Sydney, Australia, December.

Sze-Meng Jojo Wong and Mark Dras. 2011. Exploiting parse structures for native language identification. In *Proceedings of the 2011 Conference on Empirical Methods in Natural Language Processing*, pages 1600–1610, Edinburgh, Scotland, July.

Peer-reviewed papers: Poster presentations

A word-based approach for diacritic restoration in Māori

John Cocks
Department of Computing and Mathematical Sciences
University of Waikato
Waikato, New Zealand
chaopay@hotmail.com

Te Taka Keegan
Department of Computing and Mathematical Sciences
University of Waikato
Waikato, New Zealand
tetaka1@gmail.com

Abstract

This paper describes a supervised algorithm for diacritic restoration based on naive Bayes classifiers that act at word-level. Classifications are based on a rich set of features, extracted automatically from training data in the form of diacritically marked text. The method requires no additional resources, which makes it language independent. The algorithm was evaluated on one language, namely Māori and an accuracy exceeding 99% was observed.

1 Introduction

The Māori language, along with other Polynesian languages, features a written diacritic mark above vowels, signifying a lengthened pronunciation of the vowel. Māori texts without diacritics are quite common in electronic media. The problem arises as most keyboards are designed for English and the process of inserting diacritics becomes laborious. In all but the most ambiguous cases, a native reader can still infer the writer's intended meaning. However, the absence of diacritics can still confuse or slow down a reader and it makes pronunciation and meaning difficult for learners of the language. For other languages using diacritics, such as German or French, this problem can typically be handled by a simple lexicon lookup procedure that translates words without diacritics into the properly marked format (Wagachar and Pauw, 2006). However, this is not the case for languages such as Māori where comprehensive lexicons are not publically available.

This paper proposes a machine learning approach to diacritic restoration that employs a naive Bayes classifier that acts at word-level. The proposed algorithm predicts the placement of diacritics on the basis of local word context. The algorithm is contrasted with a traditional grapheme-based algorithm, originally proposed by Scannell (2010), showing a significant increase in accuracy for diacritic restoration in Māori.

The remainder of the paper is organized as follows: In Section 2, previous work on diacritic restoration is discussed. Section 3 outlines the use of diacritics in Māori. Section 4 describes the dataset used in training and testing each model. Section 5 outlines the baseline models for diacritic restoration used in this paper. Section 6 discusses the Naive Bayes classifier. Section 7 and 8 describe the grapheme-based and word-based models, respectively. Section 9 discusses the results obtained from the baseline, grapheme-based and word-based models. Finally, future work is discussed in Section 10.

2 Previous Work

Until recently, the majority of research on diacritic restoration was directed at major languages such as German and French and less emphasis directed towards minority languages. These methods typically employ the use of large lexicons which are not publically available for resource scarce languages. In recent past, Pauw and Schryver (2009) presented a memory-based approach to diacritic restoration that act at the level of the morpheme for numerous African languages, reporting scores exceeding 90%. Scannell (2010) describes a similar approach, reporting a high degree of accuracy for numerous languages using training data in the form of a web-crawled corpus. Moreover, the diacritic restoration methods presented by Scannell (2010) report a score of 97.5% for Māori. This can be seen as an increase of 1% over the baseline method which chooses the most frequent pattern in the training set. In order to determine the feasibility of the approach proposed in this paper, the experiments outlined by Scannell (2010) are reproduced using a large, high quality corpus and the scores are contrasted with those obtained from the proposed word-level algorithms.

3 Diacritics in Māori

The Māori alphabet consists of 15 characters: 10 consonants and 5 vowels. Vowels in Māori can be pronounced both short and long, so in written form, long vowels carry a diacritical mark. In Māori texts where diacritics have been omitted, long vowels are predominately substituted for short vowels. Table 1 shows the complete set of vowels in Māori.

Short	a	e	i	o	u
Long	ā	ē	ī	ō	ū

Table 1: Short and long vowels in Māori

During substitution, genuine ambiguity arises when two or more distinct words have the same base word-form. To exemplify this ambiguity, consider the Māori word *wāhine* (women). The base word form after diacritics have been removed is *wahine* (woman – singular of wāhine).

4 Dataset

The diacritic restoration algorithms presented in this paper were trained and evaluated on a fully diacritically marked corpus containing approximately 4.2 million words. The corpus was compiled from a comprehensive collection of short stories, bible verses, dictionary definitions and conversational texts. Table 2 displays statistical data extracted from the corpus.

1. Words	4,281,708
2. Words with diacritics	859,083 (20.06%)
3. Words with 0 ambiguity	1,656,051 (38.68%)
4. Words with 1 ambiguity	2,346,874 (54.81%)
5. Words with 2 ambiguities	98,995 (2.31%)
6. Words with 3 or more ambiguities	179,788 (4.20%)

Table 2: Statistical corpus data

The second statistic shows on average, every fifth word in the corpus contains a diacritic. More interestingly, the third statistics shows approximately 39% of the words have no ambiguity and can be correctly restored with a simple lookup procedure; whereas an inflated 61% of the words are ambiguous, and cannot be correctly restored without classification.

5 Baseline Models

In order to determine the significance of the word-based algorithms, two baseline models are defined. The first baseline model assumes no diacritic markings exist. The second baseline model identifies candidate words for diacritic marking, and chooses the most frequent pattern observed in the training set. Candidate words are identified as sharing the same base word-form after diacritics have been removed. For example, the words *āna*, *ānā* and *anā* share the same base word-form *ana*. If two or more candidate words are observed equally, the model randomly chooses a candidate word.

6 Naive Bayes Classifier

In spite of their naive design, naive Bayes classifiers are widely used in various classification tasks in natural language processing. Naive Bayes classifiers are a set of probabilistic learning algorithms based on applying Bayes' theorem with the naive assumption of independence between features. Given a class variable c and a dependent feature vector $x1$ through xn, Bayes' theorem states the following relation:

$$P(c|x1, ..., xn) \propto P(c)\prod_{i=1}^{n} P(xi|c) \quad (1)$$

$P(c)$ is interpreted as the conditional probability of class c occurring, and $P(xi|c)$ is interpreted as the conditional probability of attribute xi occurring given class c.

To find the most likely classification cf, given the attribute values $x1$ through xn, equation (1) can be rewritten as:

$$cf = \arg\max \; P(c)\prod_{i=1}^{n} P(xi \mid c) \quad (2)$$

In practice, equation (2) often results in a floating point underflow as n increases. It is therefore better to perform the computation by adding logarithms of probabilities instead of multiplying probabilities as in (3).

$$cf = \arg\max \left[\log P(c) + \sum_{i=1}^{n} \log P(xi|c) \right] \quad (3)$$

7 Grapheme-Based Model

Scannell (2010) employs a naive Bayes classifier at the grapheme-level, reporting a high degree of accuracy for numerous languages. These classifiers are trained using various feature sets, each consisting of grapheme-based n-grams relative to the target grapheme. Each n-gram is represented by the vector (o, n), where o represents the offset of the n-gram from the target grapheme, and n represents the length of the n-gram. These feature sets are outlined below. Note that this paper proposes a new grapheme-level feature set: FSG5.

- FSG1: Features (-3, 1), (-2, 1), (-1, 1), (1, 1), (2, 1), (3, 1). That is the three monograms on either side of the target grapheme.
- FSG2: Features (-5, 1), (-4, 1), (-3, 1), (-2, 1), (-1, 1), (1, 1), (2, 1), (3, 1), (4, 1), (5, 1). That is the five monograms on either side of the target grapheme.
- FSG3: (-4, 3), (-3, 3), (-2, 3), (-1, 3), (0, 3), (1, 3), (2, 3). That is the two trigrams on either side of the target grapheme and the three trigrams containing the target grapheme.
- FSG4: (-3, 3), (-1, 3), (1, 3). That is the single trigram on either side of the target grapheme and the single trigram containing the target grapheme.
- FSG5: (-2, 5), (-3, 5), (-1, 5). That is the n-grams of length 5 centered on the target grapheme, and the two n-grams of length 5 starting at offsets -3 and -1.

8 Word-Based Model

This paper improves upon previously mentioned approaches to diacritic restoration by applying diacritic classification at the word-level as opposed to the grapheme-level. This approach extracts word-based n-grams relative to the target word. These features are outlined below:

- FSW1: Features (-1, 1). That is the monogram preceding the target word.
- FSW2: Features (-2, 2). That is the bigram preceding the target word.
- FSW3: Features (-3, 3). That is the trigram preceding the target word.
- FSW4: Features (1, 1). That is the monogram following the target word.
- FSW5: Features (1, 2). That is the bigram following the target word.
- FSW6: Features (1, 3). That is the trigram following the target word.
- FSW7: Features (-1, 1), (-2, 2). That is the monogram and bigram preceding the target word.
- FSW8: Features (1, 1), (1, 2). That is the monogram and bigram following the target word.
- FSW9: Features (-1, 1), (1, 1). That is the monogram on either side of the target word.
- FSW10: Features (-2, 2), (-1, 1), (1, 1), (1, 2). That is the monogram and bigram on either side of the target word.

- FSW11: (-1, 3), (-2, 2), (1, 2), (-1, 4), (-2, 4).

8.1 Naive Bayes Estimates

In order to apply a Naive Bayes classifier to the task of diacritic restoration, estimates for the parameters $P(c)$ and $P(xi|c)$ in equation (3) outlined above must be found. Assuming a diacritically marked text T is a sequence of words wi through wn, where n is the number of words in the text, T can be represented as:

$$T = w1, w2, \ldots, wn \qquad (4)$$

Further, assume each word wi in T has an associated base word-form bi, where bi is the result of removing all diacritics from wi. Thus a text T has a base word-form sequence Tb associated with it, which can be written as follows:

$$Tb = b1, b2, \ldots, bn \qquad (5)$$

Let Wd be the set of distinct words in T and let Bd be the set of distinct base word-forms in Tb. Further, let $f: B \rightarrow Ws$ be a function that maps a base word-form bi to a set of words Ws, where Ws is a subset of Wd, and each word in Ws has a corresponding base word-form equal to bi. The goal is to find, for each base word-form bi in Tb, the word w in $f(b)$, such that w maximizes the probability for all words in $f(b)$. Using Bayes theorem in (3), the prior probability for each word w in $f(b)$ can be estimated by:

$$P(w) = \frac{Nw}{N} \qquad (5)$$

Where Nw is the number of occurrences of word w in text T, and N is the total number of occurrences of each word in $f(b)$ in text T. Further, the conditional probability for each word w in $f(b)$ is estimated as:

$$P(w) = \frac{Nwi + 1}{Ni + n} \qquad (6)$$

Where Nwi is the number of occurrences of word w with feature i in text T, and Ni is the total number of occurrences of each word w in $f(b)$ with feature i in text T, and n is the number of words in $f(b)$. To avoid zero estimates, Laplace smoothing is employed.

9 Evaluation

To evaluate the accuracy of the algorithms, a 10-fold cross validation is used. For each experiment, the corpus is partitioned into ten subsets where one subset is used as test data while the remaining nine are used as training data. The experimental results shown in table 3 show that the word-based naive Bayes models significantly outperform the grapheme-based naive Bayes models. Evidently, the FSW11 feature set resulted in the highest accuracy of 99.01%. This can be seen as an increase of 1.9% over the second baseline method which chooses the most frequent pattern in the training data.

Feature Set	Accuracy (%) (proportion of words)
Baseline1	79.94
Baseline2	**97.11**
FSG1	79.94
FSG2	79.94
FSG3	84.45
FSG4	87.02
FSG5	**95.07**
FSW1	98.50
FSW2	98.33
FSW3	97.94
FSW4	98.28
FSW5	98.34
FSW6	98.01
FSW7	98.65
FSW8	98.54
FSW9	98.65
FSW10	98.85
FSW11	**99.01**

Table 3: Accuracy for the baseline, grapheme-based and word-based algorithms

A paired t-test was performed to determine if the increase in accuracy between Baseline2 and FSW11 feature set was significant. The mean increase in accuracy ($M=1.8928$, $SD=0.0234$, $N=10$) was significantly greater than zero, $t(9)=255.68$, two-tail $p=1.08989E\text{-}18$, providing evidence that FSW11 had a significant increase in accuracy over the Baseline2 feature set. A 95% C.I. about mean accuracy increase is (1.8761, 1.9096).

10 Conclusion and Future Work

This paper presented a method for diacritic restoration based on naive Bayes classifiers that act at grapheme and word level. The use of grapheme-based naive Bayes classifiers in the context of diacritic restoration has already been proposed earlier by Scannell (2010). The experiments presented in this paper extend upon the work by Scannell by proposing training naive Bayes classifiers at the word-level opposed to the grapheme-level. The results show that a word-based naive Bayes model can significantly outperform a grapheme-based naive Bayes model for diacritic restoration in Māori. This paper provides a case study for other Polynesian languages which are closely related to Māori. For future work, the algorithms outlined in this paper will be evaluated across several of these languages where appropriate training data exists in the form of diacritically marked text.

Acknowledgments

The research presented in this paper was made possible through the support of the University of Waikato and Ngā Pae o Te Māramatanga. A demonstration system for Māori diacritic restoration can be found at http://www.greenstone.org/macroniser.

References

Paul, G. and Schryver, M. 2009. African Language Technology: The Data-Driven Perspective.

Santic, N. and Snajder, J. 2009. Automatic Diacritics Restoration in Croatian Texts.

Scannell, K. 2010. Statistical Unicodification of African Languages. Department of Mathematics and Computer Science, Saint Louis University, St Louis, Missouri, USA.

Wagachar, P. and Pauw, G. 2006. A Grapheme-Based Approach for Accent Restoration in Gikuyu. School of Computing and Informatics, University of Nairobi, Nairobi, Kenya.

Yarosky, D. 1996. A Comparison of Corpus-Based Techniques for Restoring Accents in Spanish and French Text. Department of Computer Science, John Hopkins University, Baltimore, MD.

The Interpretation of Complement Anaphora: The Case of *The Others*[*]

Nobuaki Akagi
Centre for Cognition and its Disorders
(CCD), Macquarie University
nobuakagi@mq.edu.au

Francesco-Alessio Ursini
Centre for Cognition and its Disorders
(CCD), Macquarie University
francescoalessio.ursini@mq.edu.au

Abstract

This paper presents an experimental study on the interpretation of the complement anaphora *the others* in inter-sentential discourse. It aims to offer an answer to the following two empirical questions. First, how complement anaphora denote the "complement set", a set of referents that includes those referents not denoted by the matching anaphoric antecedent. Second, what are the exact interpretation principles that govern the anaphoric potential of complement anaphora. The answers to these two questions shed light on how complement anaphora fit into a broader theory of anaphora resolution, and what is the most accurate logical and psychological model of this aspect of grammar.

1 Introduction

Complement anaphora can be seen as a particular sub-set of natural language anaphora. Noun phrases (NPs) that act as complement anaphora usually occur in inter-sentential environments (e.g. discourses). These NPs appear to refer not to the relevant set of discourse referents currently under discussion[1], but rather to the set making up the "rest" of discourse referents.

The semantic properties of complement anaphora were first discussed in Moxey and Sanford (1993), who investigated these anaphora from an experimental perspective. They can be illustrated in a simple and pre-theoretical way via the following examples:

(1) Few children ate their ice-cream. *They* chose strawberry flavor

(2) Few children ate their ice-cream. *They* threw it around the room instead

(3) Few children ate their ice-cream. *The others* threw it around the room instead

Consider the mini-discourses in examples (1)-(3) as being uttered in a context in which there are nine children, but only three children ate their ice-cream out of these nine. The first sentence in each mini-discourse denotes the set of three children that ate their ice-cream, and thus focuses on a certain relevant set of children. The anaphoric (pronominal) NPs *they* and *the others*, however, differ with respect to the anaphoric relation they establish. In (1), *they* refers to the three children who ate ice-cream, and combines with the second verb phrase (i.e. *chose strawberry flavor*), which further explains the children's choices. In (2), *they* refers to those children who did *not* eat their ice-cream, but decided to do something else with it, as the second verb phrase clarifies (i.e. *threw it around the room*).

[*]We would like to thank the participants for their involvement in the experiment. We would also like two thank three anonymous reviewers for suggestions and comments, which we think helped in improving the paper. The second author would like to thank his Princess for the constant support and encouragement.

[1]We adopt the standard practice of dynamic semantics approaches and label as "discourse referents" the individuals in the Universe of Discourse denoted by NPs (Kartunnen, 1976; Kamp, 1981; Heim, 1982). We assume that these anaphora denote "sets" of referents, even if our analysis is compatible with theories of Plurality, both "static" (Schwarzschild, 1996; Link, 1998); or dynamic, as in *Discourse Representation Theory* (DRT) (Nouwen, 2003; Kamp, van Genabith and Reyle, 2005; Brasoveanu, 2008).

The discussion in Moxey and Sanford (1993) also indirectly mentions that some pronominal NPs may explicitly refer to this "other" set. This reference to the set of "ice-cream-throwing children" is made explicit by the special type of plural pronominal NP *the others*, in (3). This plural pronominal NP explicitly refers to those children who are involved in a different event than the one described in the first sentence. These children form a different, possibly "complementary" set to the set of (few) ice-cream-eating children. Although Moxey and Sanford (1993) do not offer experimental evidence on *the others*, they suggest that this NP should explicitly refer to this "other" set of referents. These findings motivated Moxey and Sanford (1993) to introduce the term "complement anaphora", a type of anaphora that denotes some other set of referents than the previously introduced one(s).

Even if the ability of these anaphora to refer to this specific set of referents is taken more or less as uncontroversial, the exact status of this set appears to be subject to debate. The two goals of this paper concern some central themes of these debates. A first goal is to offer experimental evidence regarding the interpretation of complement anaphora, focusing on the still poorly studied *the others*[2], by native speakers of English. A second goal is discuss which of the current approaches to complement anaphora found in the literature appears to be supported by the experimental evidence offered in this paper.

So, the general aim of this paper is to shed light on how different mechanisms of anaphora resolution proposed in the literature can model complement anaphora. We will propose that mechanisms of anaphora resolution behind complement anaphora are the same as other anaphora, but also that the set denoted by complement anaphora involves a specific computation of its members. So, we will suggest that a logically and psychologically precise model of anaphora resolution must also incorporate a way to compute complement anaphora, as anaphora denoting "other" sets in discourse.

The paper is organized as follows. The rest of the introduction presents some background assumptions (section 1.1), and three sets of theories on complement anaphora (section 1.2). Section 2 presents an experiment that aims to adjudicate between these competing theories. Section 3 offers some conclusions.

1.1 Background: Generalized Quantifier Theory

In this section we discuss some notions of *Generalized Quantifier Theory* (GQ theory) (Barwise and Cooper, 1981), shared by all approaches to complement anaphora. We follow a simple presentation of these core assumptions, offered in Nouwen (2003).

GQ theory assumes that standard declarative sentences of English can be assigned the syntactic structure $[[DetNP]VP]$. This structure is interpreted as the relation $Det'(A, B)$. Taking the first sentence in examples (1)-(3), if Det is a determiner such as *few*, then A is the set denoted by the NP in *restrictor* position. The label "restrictor" refers to the role of an NP as a constituent that restricts the range of the determiner it combines with. This NP combines with a determiner (e.g. *children*, to form the *generalized quantifier few children*). The set B is the set denoted by a Verb Phrase (VP) in the *nuclear scope* position (e.g. *ate their ice-cream*). The label "nuclear scope" refers to the minimal syntactic unit on which a Generalized Quantifier scopes over. The interpretation of this structure will amount to a relation between two sets, plus a condition on the cardinality of this relation. This is roughly represented by the relation $Few'(A, B)$, which can be informally read as: "there are referents that are children, and are eating ice-cream, and are small in number".

A key property is *conservativity*. The proposition denoted by the first sentence in (1)-(3), which we represent as $Few'(A, B)$, is equivalent to the proposition represented as $Few'(A, A \cap B)$. This is the proposition obtained by "selecting" those elements of the restrictor set which are also part of the nuclear scope set. In words, if few children ate their ice-cream, then few children were children who ate their ice-cream.

As Nouwen (2003) discusses, anaphora select their antecedent among the sets introduced by a previous sentence or discourse. One set that can act as an antecedent is the *maximal* set A, but anaphora can also refer to the set $A \cap B$, known as the *reference*

[2]We leave aside any discussion on whether NPs are anaphoric or referential. We will focus on inter-sentential, and thus anaphoric examples, in this paper Poesio and Vieira (1998); Elbourne (2005); Schwarz (2009).

set. In the previously mentioned scenario, the nine boys under discussion correspond to the maximal set A, which is the denotation of the restrictor NP *children*. The reference set $A \cap B$ corresponds to the set of children who are children having eaten ice-cream. These assumptions are shared by all approaches to complement anaphora. These approaches differ in how they explain that *they* in (2) and *the others* in (2) can denote the so-called *complement set*. We will discuss these differences, and the nature of this set, in the next section.

1.2 Three Approaches

1.2.1 The "Complement Set" Approach

The first type of approach stems from the experimental work of Moxey and Sanford (1993); Sanford et al. (1994), and includes dynamic semantics proposals (Kibble, 1997; Nouwen, 2003). Their shared assumption is that complement anaphora select the complement set as their semantic antecedent. This set is defined below.

Sanford and associates offered this approach because they investigated the difference in anaphoric potential between closely related quantifiers, e.g. *a few* vs. *few*, or vs. *few of the*. The experiments mainly involved a *continuation task*. In this task, participants were offered a paper on which the first sentence of a mini-discourse, followed by the pronoun *they*, was written. Participants were invited to continue the mini-discourse by completing the second sentence, without any specific restrictions on its content.

Participants were asked to complete incomplete mini-discourses such as:

(4) A few children ate their ice-cream. They...

(5) Few of the children ate their ice-cream. They...

(6) Few children ate their ice-cream. They...

Once participants completed this task, they were asked to which set of referents *they* referred to, in their continuation. Using these examples as a guide, the five possible answers to this follow-up question were: *children in general*, *all the children*, *the children who ate ice-cream*, *the children who did not eat ice-cream*, or *none of the above*.

The main finding was that, while mini-discourses such as (4) seldom licensed continuations involving complement anaphora, mini-discourses such as (5) and (6) could license continuations involving complement anaphora, as in e.g. (2). When participants chose a complement anaphora continuation, they defended their choice by claiming that *they* referred to those referents that were not involved in the event described by the previous sentence. The authors suggested that this set of children corresponded to the *complement set*, the set-theoretic difference between maximal set and the set denoted by the VP, represented as $A - B$. So, in the opportune syntactic and discourse-bound context, reference to complement anaphora was possible. Although Sanford and associates did not investigate *the others* and similar "overt" complement anaphora, they suggested that the same considerations would hold for these anaphora.

The proposal in Nouwen (2003) offers a more precise, dynamic treatment of this phenomenon. According to this treatment, anaphoric relations are identity relations between sets of referents. Both *they* and *the others*, as anaphoric expressions, establish an identity between a novel referent set (e.g. the set C) and a previous referent set. Complement anaphora differ from other anaphora because they establish a relation between this novel referent and the complement set, the identity relation $C = (A - B)$[3]. So, speakers should interpret *they* in (2) and (3) as denoting the relation $C = (A - B)$, according to this proposal.

1.2.2 The "Sloppy Reference" Approach

The second type of approach contends that reference to the complement set is a consequence of the possibility that anaphoric elements may have *collective* or *distributive* reference[4]. An anaphoric pronoun may receive either interpretation, depending on whether it combines with a distributive or collective predicate.

[3] This notation for anaphora resolution, borrowed from DRT, is only used in the first two chapters of Nouwen (2003), as a different approach (and notation) is developed in the remainder of Nouwen's work.

[4] This distinction focuses on whether predicates can apply to each referent in the denotation of an NP (distributive reference), or to these referents as "collective" (collective reference) (Nouwen, 2003; Link, 1998; Winter, 2001).

Works such as Corblin (1996); Geurts (1997) observed that, under Sanford et al.'s approach, the pronoun *they* appears to violate a general principle of anaphoric relations. Anaphoric elements must receive their interpretation from an *overt* antecedent, either introduced by a NP in previous discourse, or accessible from the context (Elbourne, 2005; Elbourne, 2008). In cases such as (2) and (3), both *they* and *the others* appear to violate this assumption. Their interpretation seems to depend on a referent not explicitly introduced, but rather "implied" by *few children*, the only NP that can act as an anaphoric antecedent.

As an alternative explanation, Geurts (1997) proposes[5] that complement anaphora interpretations arise when a pronoun refers to the maximal set A. If P is a predicate (e.g. "eating ice-cream") then a combination of pronoun and predicate ($P(A)$) may receive a collective interpretation. In this case, the predicate holds true even if a subset D of A makes it true (we have $D \subseteq A$ (read: "D is a subset of A"). A sentence involving a complement anaphora will thus denote $P(D)$, the contextually salient set of children eating ice-cream, from which "other" children are excluded. This account does not treat overt complement anaphora NPs such as *the others* and, as Geurts (1997) concedes, may license that the contextually salient set may be even empty, given its "sloppy" reference.

1.2.3 The "Lexicalist" Approach

The third type of approach is exemplified by recent works such as Kotek (2008); Dotlačil (2010). These approaches assume that the lexical, compositional semantics of *the others* determines which are the referents that make up the complement set. Three assumptions are relevant.

First, pronouns are considered as semantically equivalent to definite NPs. Definite NPs are then assumed to denote the maximal set. So, *they* and *the others* are respectively considered as semantically equivalent to *the children* and *the other children*[6]. The adjectival element *others* contributes by combining with an NP and restricting the maximal set A to a sub-set O that excludes previously mentioned (sets of) referents. The relation $O \subseteq A$ represents the relation between this set and the maximal set.

Second, the set O is a disjointed set from the set denoted by the previous VP ("contrast set", in Dotlačil's terms), a property represented as $\neg(O \cap B)$. In words, no referent which is part of the *others* set is also a referent that ate his ice-cream. So, *the others* denotes a sub-set of the maximal set that does not include previously referred referents, a property represented as $(O \subseteq A \cap \neg(O \cap B))$[7].

Third, anaphora are combined and interpreted with respect to their clause-mate VP. The second sentence in (3), according to this assumption, denotes the set $P(O \subseteq A \cap \neg(O \cap B))$. In words, the second sentence denotes the set of children that throw their ice-cream against the wall (i.e. $P(O \subseteq A)$), and that also do not eat their ice-cream (i.e. $P(\neg(O \cap B))$. So, this approach includes both the "lexical" content of *the others* and other complement anaphora, but also its ability to establish an anaphoric relation in discourse. It captures the intuition that these anaphora denote the complement set as a *result* of explicitly individuating this referent in discourse.

1.2.4 Three Approaches: Predictions

These three types of approaches appear only to differ with respect to their assumption on the computation of the complement set, and its resulting denotation. In the opportune context, however, each approach makes slightly different predictions with respect to the interpretation of complement anaphora. These predictions are as follows.

The first approach predicts that complement anaphora denote a set of referents which have not been involved in previous discourse, the complement set (i.e. $A - B$). The second approach predicts that complement anaphora may denote any "group" which is part of the maximal set. This group may be distinct from a previously mentioned set of referents (i.e. $P(D) \subseteq P(A)$, D being a contextually relevant sub-set), but holds no "special" status as a comple-

[5]Neither Corblin (1996) nor Geurts (1997) offer a formal analysis of these properties, in their discussion. The proposed formal analysis is ours, not theirs, but should hopefully make their claims precise.

[6]This is a standard assumption in D-type approaches to pronouns Elbourne (2005), Elbourne (2008).

[7]This is a partial mis-representation of Dotlačil's approach, since Dotlačil couches his approach in a lattice-theoretic perspective.

ment set. The third approach proposes an intermediate position. It predicts that the complement set is the result of first finding those involved in a "new" event, and *then* by excluding previously mentioned referents in discourse (i.e. $P(O \subseteq A \cap \neg(O \cap B))$).

The next section offers an experimental study that attempts to adjudicate among these three categories. It does so by studying how speakers interpret the complement anaphora *the others*, on which there is a dearth of empirical evidence (Moxey and Sanford, 1993). However, the results may be extended to other complement anaphora, as we discuss in the conclusions.

2 The study

2.1 Participants

The experiment involved adult participants (N=20). All participants were native speakers of English and undergraduate students of Psychology, and received course credit for their attendance. Between one and three participants attended a session, for a total of fifteen minutes of experiment time.

2.2 Procedure

The experiment involved a variant of the *Truth-Value Judgement Task* (TVJ task) (Crain and Thornton, 1999). Our choice is based on the following reason. The continuation task used by Sanford et al. (1994) allowed participants to choose a continuation of a discourse which, in the opportune conditions, licensed a complement anaphora reading. However, the nature of the task would make the testing of the precise interpretation rather problematic. Since the task is inherently a *production* task, it does not allow an easy testing of possible differences in *comprehension* among speakers, and thus the testing of our experimental predictions.

The TVJ task provides a simple way to test speakers' intuitions and their competence of grammar. One type of a standard TVJ task, the so-called *description mode*, involves two experimenters. One experimenter acts out the scenario and narrates the events. The other experimenter controls a hand-puppet (e.g. Kermit the Frog). At the end of the story, the puppet offers a yes-no question to the participant about the story, which is aimed at testing whether a participant can interpret a sentence as per predictions.

After a participant offers an answer, a follow-up question is usually offered, in order to test whether his answer is based on a correct understanding of the events described by the story. When a TVJ task involves yes-no questions, the story should describe events in such a way that both a "yes" and a "no" answer should be possible answers. However, only one answer correctly matches the outcome of the story. This condition is known as the *Condition of Plausible Dissent* (Crain & Thornton 1999: chapter 5).

We briefly describe an example of the TVJ task used to test speakers' interpretation of the universal quantifier *every*, to elucidate the structure of the task. In a description mode story, a participant and Kermit the frog observe a story in which five horses are involved in a jumping contest. Each of them has to jump over a fence. Four of them are successful, but one of them trips before completing the task, so that he is unsuccessful at it.

At the end of this story, Kermit the frog asks a sentence like the one in (7):

(7) Has every horse jumped over the fence?

If one assumes that the participant has a interpretation of *every* as denoting the universal quantifier, then the participant will offer a "no" as answer, possibly defending his or her choice by observing that one horse did not complete the target task. Although a "yes" answer could have been entertained, at some point (i.e. when the fallen horse almost completed the jump), the end result made only the "no" answer as the correct one.

The TVJ task thus allows to test participants' comprehension of sentences in a simple and experimentally sound way, whether participants are adults or children. For the purposes of testing our experimental hypothesis, the following changes to the task, involving materials and procedure, were made.

First, rather than acting out the task, we prepared a power-point presentation depicting a story in which a number of characters were involved. An introduction preceded this story, in which the main characters and the instructions were presented to the participants.

Second, each slide included a short text that described the events in which one or more tank engines were involved, and which was matched with a picture illustrating the described events. Instead of using a puppet (Kermit the frog) as in the original TVJ task, we displayed a character known as "Mr. Little Bears" on the PPT screen. Mr. Little Bears played the same role as the puppet.

Third, participants received an answer sheet before the start of the experiment. They were invited to choose their answer between two different options: "yes" and "no". After Mr. Little Bears' question at the end of the story, participants were invited to circle their answer of preference, according to their intuitions. After the experiment, a follow-up question was offered, by asking participants why they offered their answer. For each participant, the main experimenter wrote each participant's reason on offering a "yes" or a "no" answer, on a separate sheet. This choice allowed participants to defend their choice by explaining how they "computed" the complement set.

2.3 Materials

The main characters in the story were Thomas the tank engine, and nine other characters from the eponymous toy line. This list of tank engines included Thomas, Duncan, Mighty Mac, Spencer, Arthur, Rosy, Percy, Diesel 10 and Billy. Mr. Little Bears was introduced as an amnesiac bear who would watch the stories with the participants. Because of his bad memory, Mr. Little Bears had to ask a question on the story presented to the experimenters.

The story presented the following set of events. The nine tank engines had to perform two inspections about two alleged ghosts' infestations: one at the Smurfs' castle, one at the Power Puffs' Hotel[8]. Since they had to check two locations, they split in two groups. One group, composed by Thomas, Duncan and Mighty Mac went to the Smurfs' castle. Another group, composed by the remaining six tank engines, went instead to the Power Puffs' Hotel. Thomas was in charge of writing the official report. So, after verifying that there were no ghosts at the Smurfs' castle with Galaxy, he also went to check and sign off the documents with Blossom, the owner of the Power Puffs' Hotel. Thus, Thomas (and Thomas only) visited both locations by the end of the story.

Each slide depicted one tank engine reaching one of the two locations. The tank engines that went to the Smurfs' castle were introduced first, then the remaining six that went to the Power Puffs' Hotel were introduced. The text below each slide closely matched the pictures, and stated that which engine was shown as reaching either location. Thomas was presented as the last tank engine that reached the Power Puffs' Hotel, as he arrived from the Smurfs' castle. A subsequent slide presented Thomas as compiling the documents with Blossom, thus concluding the story.

After the story, Mr. Little Bears appeared in a slide and offered a question to the participants. We chose the quantified NP *few tank engines* as a relevant antecedent, for the following reason. As reported by Moxey and Sanford (1993), NPs such *few tank engines* almost always license complement anaphora interpretation, in the right context. We also chose the pronominal NP *the others* as a target complement anaphora, since it is the only complement anaphora discussed in relevant detail by each of the three types of approach.

The question was:

(8) *Few tank engines* have gone to the Smurfs' castle. Have *the others* gone to the Power Puffs' hotel?

Participants were invited to write down their answer once the question in (8) was presented, as per instructions. Once the experiment was over, the main experimenter asked the follow-up question, on an individual basis. The answers were then collected and analyzed. The predictions of the three approaches discussed in the introduction for this story are as follows.

The Complement Set approach predicts that participants would have answered "no", since the complement anaphora *the others* should denote the complement set. The complement set $A - B$ included the six tank engines that did not go to the Smurfs' castle, disjointed from the reference set $A \cap B$. Its members were: Spencer, Arthur, Rosy, Percy, Diesel 10 and Billy. Since Thomas was part of this set, but also of the reference set of engines that went to the

[8]The choice of "random" fictional locations has a goal: that participants may not be biased by real world knowledge (of cartoons) in their answers, should they have any doubts. See Crain and Thornton (1999) for discussion.

Power Puffs' Hotel, the underlying declarative sentence was false. Participants should have defended their choice by pointing at Thomas as the "offending" tank engine, in the follow-up question.

The Sloppy Reference approach predicts that participants would have answered "yes", by the end of the story. That is, *the others* should denote the set of tank engines that went to the Power Puffs' Hotel, taken as a "group". The complement set is not computed as a difference between two sets, according to this approach. So, participants should have defended their choice by only mentioning the tank engines that went to the Power Puffs' Hotel. The set $P(D)$, with $P(D) \subseteq P(A)$, included Thomas, as well as the other six tank engines.

The Lexicalist approach predicts that participants would have answered "yes", by the end of the story. That is, *the others* in the target question was interpreted by first computing the set of tank engines that went to the Power Puffs' Hotel. Then, this set was restricted to the set of engines who also did not go to the Smurfs' Castle (we have $P(O \subseteq A \cap \neg(O \cap B)))$. So, participants should have defended their choice by pointing out that they excluded Thomas from the denotation of *the others*, and then consider the remaining six engines as the "other" engines.

2.4 Results and Discussion

The answers to the yes-no were as follows: yes=19, no=1 (95%/5%). This result is consistent with the Sloppy Reference and the Lexicalist approach. In the follow-up question, 16 participants observed that Thomas went to both locations, but that "the others" were the six engines that only went to the Power Puffs' Hotel (80% of the total). They explicitly excluded Thomas from the larger set of engines that went to the Power Puffs' Hotel. Three participants observed that some, but not all engines made the story true, although they could not recall their identity (15% of the total). The only participant that answered "no", instead, defended his choice by observing that Thomas had to be included in the relevant "group" of tank engines (5%). So, the underlying declarative sentence was false, according to this participant.

The follow-up answers offer results that are more consistent with the Lexicalist approach, rather than with the Sloppy Reference approach. Most participants explicitly mentioned that they excluded Thomas from a "larger" set, when computing which engines made the sentence true. This is a fact that is not predicted by the Sloppy Reference approach. So, the Lexicalist approach better fits these findings. The Sloppy Reference approach would need a more accurate way to account for this process of "elimination", instead. One further observation on these data is the following. Assume that the Lexicalist approach is a correct model of complement anaphora. In this case, if we expect a 95% rate of follow-up answers that excluded Thomas, then a 80% (16/20) rate is not a statistically significant divergence. The other two approaches appear not to be suited to account the combination of yes-no and follow-up answers, given their low "success" rate. These results invite two important conclusions.

First, complement anaphora appear to be semantically "real", when the opportune syntactic and semantic requirements are met. Participants interpreted *the others* as denoting a certain set of referents. These referents were involved in the event described in the target question, but were not involved in previous events. Participants thus explicitly pointed out that *the others* denoted a distinct (complementary) set of engines from the one previously introduced in discourse.

Second, the results support the Lexicalist approach, and suggest that both the Complement Set and the Sloppy Reference approach may require further revisions. The results suggest that the interpretation of *the others* in discourse is inherently anaphoric, *and* the result of "computing" a certain referent, which is indirectly introduced by the previous context.

The first and second conclusions invite a third "global" conclusion. The interpretation of *the others*, and possibly all complement anaphora, should be part of a general theory of grammar. So, anaphoric elements depend on their lexical content and related predicates for their interpretation, as well as their ability to establish anaphoric relations. In the specific case of the described experimental setup, *the others* selected the set of tank engines which were defined as not involved in an event already introduced in discourse (i.e. going to the Smurfs' castle). They were defined as being involved in another (here, complementary) event (i.e. going to the

Power Puffs' Hotel). So, participants' interpretation of *the others* was based on the context outlined by previous discourse (i.e. the presented story). At the same time, it was also based on the property of this anaphora to select a "complementary" set of referents, because of its specific lexical content.

3 Conclusions

This paper offered experimental evidence about the interpretation of the complement anaphora, and pronominal NP, *the others* in multi-sentential discourse. Three types of approach on the interpretation of this anaphora were discussed. The first approach assumes that *the others* denotes the complement set, a set of referents not previously introduced in discourse, and not introduced by any anaphoric antecedents to *the others*. The second approach assumes that *the others* does not denote the complement set, but denotes a sub-set of the maximal set of referents under discussion (here, tank engines), when defined in discourse. The third approach assumes that *the others* denotes a sub-set of the maximal set of referents, which at the same time is part of the interpretation of the second sentence, and has not been introduced in previous discourse.

We carried out an experiment involving adult speakers of English, in order to adjudicate which approach correctly predicted the interpretation of *the others*. The evidence found suggests that the Lexicalist approach offers a more appropriate analysis of the *the others*, and possibly other complement anaphora. In our experiment, participants interpreted *the others* as denoting the set of tank engines who went to the Power Puffs' Hotel. However, participants also excluded those engines who also took part in previous events (i.e. Thomas, who went to the Smurfs' Castle), as supported by the answers to the follow-up question.

This result also seems to support a view of the semantics of anaphora that could be defined as "truth-conditions plus anaphoric potential". This view has been proposed in some dynamic frameworks (Brasoveanu, 2008), but also in more "static" frameworks which study in detail the properties of anaphoric pronouns (Sanford et al., 1994; Dotlačil, 2010). This view suggests that mechanisms of anaphora resolution have two components. One involves the resolution of an anaphoric relation, and the other involves the computation of the "content" of this relation, and how it is computed from the previous context. So, a logically and psychologically accurate model of anaphora resolution should include at least both components, according to our findings.

This experiment offers an answer to one experimental question, but leaves open several other related questions. One is whether these findings can be extended to the interpretation of *they* as a complement anaphora, as in sentences such as (2). Again, Sanford et al. (1994) found that this seems to be the case, at least indirectly. However, an open question is whether the use of the TVJ task could confirm these results, and offer further insights on the nature of this anaphoric phenomenon. The same reasoning can be extended to other complement anaphora, such as the definite NPs *the other tank engines*, which may also receive a "complement set" interpretation.

Another question is whether the nature of the anaphoric antecedent plays a role in this phenomenon. In this experiment, we only tested one type of determiner, *few*, and left open the question of whether other quantifiers licensed a similar interpretation, when acting as antecedents for *the others*. For instance, Sanford et al. (1994) observed that the minimally different determiner *a few* invariably blocks the emergence of complement anaphora. Similar observations can be extended to both variants of the same quantifier (i.e. *few of the Xs*), as to other quantifiers (e.g. *many*, *no*, and so on). Although interesting and important questions for the topic at hand, both answers will be left for future investigation.

References

Barwise, Jon and Robin Cooper. 1981. Generalized quantiers and natural languages. *Linguistics & Philosophy*, 4(2):159–219.

Brasoveanu, Adrian. 2008. *Structured Nominal and Modal Reference*, Newark, NJ: Rutgers University Ph.D. dissertation.

Corblin, Francis. 1996. Quantification et anaphore discursive: la rfrence aux complémentaires. *Langages* 123(1):51-74.

Crain, Stephen and Rosalind Thornton. 1999. *Investigations in Universal Grammar: A Guide to Experiments in the Acquisition of Syntax and Semantics.* Cambridge, MA: The MIT Press.

Dotlačil, Jacob. 2010. *Anaphora and Distributivity: A study of same, different, reciprocals and others.* Utrecht: Utrecht University Ph.D. dissertation.

Elbourne, Paul. 2005. *Situations and Individuals.* Cambridge, MA: The MIT Press.

Elbourne, Paul. 2008. The interpretation of pronouns. *Language and Linguistics Compass* 2(1): 119-150.

Geurts, Bart. 1997. Book review of Linda M. Moxey and Anthony J. Sanford. Communicating Quantities. 1993. *Journal of semantics* 14(1): 87-94.

Heim, Irene. 1982. *The semantics of definite and indefinite noun phrases.* Amherst, MA: University of Massachussetts Ph.D. Dissertation.

Kamp, Hans. 1981. A theory of truth and semantic representation. In Jeroen A. G. Groenendijk, Theo M. V. Janssen, and Martin J. B. Stokhof (Eds.), *Formal Methods in the Study of Language*, 277–322. Amsterdam: Mathematical Centre.

Kamp, Hans, Josef van Genabith, & Uwe Reyle. 2005. Discourse Representation Theory. In Dov Gabbay & Franz Guenther (eds.), *Handbook of Philosophical Logic*, 125–394. North Holland: North Holland.

Kartunnen, Lauri. 1976. Discourse Referents. In J. D. McCawley (ed.), *Syntax and Semantics 7: Notes from the Linguistic Underground*, 363–385, Academic Press, New York.

Kibble, Rodger. 1997. Complement anaphora and dynamic binding. In Aaron Lawson (Ed.), *Proceedings of SALT VII*, 258–275.

Kotek, Hatas. 2008. Resolving Complement Anaphora. In: Johansson, Christer (ed.). *NEALT Proceedings Series, Vol. 2: Proceedings of the Second Workshop on Anaphora Resolution (WAR II)*, 41–53.

Link, Godehard. 1998. *Algebraic semantics in Language and Philosophy.* Stanford, CA: CSLI publications.

Moxey, Linda and Anthony Sanford 1993. *Communicating quantities. a psychological perspective.* Laurence Erlbaum Associates.

Nouwen, Rick. 2003. *Plural pronominal anaphora in context.* Utrecht: Utrecht University Ph.D. Dissertation.

Poesio, Massimo and Renata Vieira. 1998. A Corpus-based Investigation of Definite Descriptions Use. *Computational Linguistics.* 24(2):183–216.

Sanford Anthony J., Linda M. Moxey and Kevin Patterson. 1994. Psychological studies of quantifiers. *Journal of Semantics* 11(1):153- 170.

Schwarz, Florian. 2009. *Two Types of Definites in Natural Languages.* Ph.D. thesis, University of Massachusetts Amherst.

Schwarzschild, Roger. 1996. *Pluralities.* Dordrecht: Kluwer.

Winter, Yoad. 2001. *Flexibility Principles in Boolean Semantics: coordination, plurality and natural language.* Cambridge, MA: The MIT Press.

The Interpretation of Plural Pronouns in Discourse: The Case of *They**

Francesco-Alessio Ursini
Centre for Cognition and its Disorders
(CCD), Macquarie University
francescoalessio.ursini@mq.edu.au

Nobuaki Akagi
Centre for Cognition and its Disorders
(CCD), Macquarie University
nobuakagi@mq.edu.au

Abstract

This paper presents an experimental study on the interpretation of plural pronoun *they* in discourse, and offers an answer to two questions. The first question is whether the anaphoric interpretation of *they* corresponds to that of its antecedent NP(*maximal* interpretation), or by the "whole" previous sentence (*reference* interpretation). The second question is whether speakers may access only one interpretation or both, although at different "moments" in discourse. The answers to these questions suggest that an accurate logical and psychological model of anaphora resolution includes two principles. A first principle finds a "default" interpretation, a second principle determines when the "alternative" interpretation can (and must) be accessed.

1 Introduction

There is a general consensus that plural pronouns denote plural referents[1]. However, there is little agreement on their *anaphoric potential*: how plural pronouns are interpreted against previous discourse. The following examples illustrate the nature of this debate:

(1) *Some boys* are having dinner. *They* are eating a pizza

(2) *The boys* are having dinner. *They* are eating a pizza

In (1), the indefinite NP *some boys* denotes an unspecified amount of unidentified boys who are having dinner. If we have Mario, Luigi and John as boys in the context, then *some boys* may denote Mario and Luigi as a pair, but not John. In (2), the definite NP *the boys* denotes the "full" group of boys who are having dinner: Mario, John and Luigi. In both cases, NP and determiner combine to denote a referent which includes more "basic" discourse referents as its parts.

The crux of the debate lies on how speakers interpret *they* in these examples. Some approaches assume that only the antecedent NP matters; others, that the rest of a sentence also contributes to this interpretation. A third group assumes that both options are available, but determined by Grammar. Few experimental works offer evidence in favor of one of these approaches. Studies on singular pronouns in intra-sentential contexts abound in the literature on Language Acquisition and Processing (Lukyanenko et al., 2008; Elbourne, 2005b; Koornereef, 2008), and in the NLP literature (Branco, 2005). However, few or no works attempt to study plural pronouns such as *they*, especially in inter-sentential contexts.

The main goal of this paper is to offer experimental data on the interpretation of plural pronouns (e.g. *they*) in inter-sentential, or *anaphoric* con-

*We would like to thank the participants of these experiments for their involvement. We would also like two thank three anonymous reviewers for suggestions and comments, which we think helped in improving the paper. The second author would like to thank his Princess for the constant support and encouragement.

[1]We follow the dynamic semantics literature and label "referents" the singular and plural individuals denoted by Noun Phrases (NPs) (Kartunnen, 1976; Heim, 1982; Kamp, 1981; Kamp and Reyle, 1993).

texts[2]. These data, in turn, are used to outline which models of anaphora resolution, among current approaches, appear to correctly capture how speakers resolve anaphoric relations in discourse. We focus on two sub-goals. First, we investigate whether speakers interpret *they* in discourse as denoting "all" or the "relevant" referents denoted by its anaphoric antecedent. Second, we investigate whether speakers may change their interpretation of *they*, if the extra-linguistic context allows this change.

Overall, we address the following general question: which is a logical and psychological model of anaphora resolution, that can predict how speakers interpret plural pronouns in discourse. Anticipating matters a bit, we suggest that anaphora resolution involves two components. The first component establishes the anaphoric relation between a pronoun and its antecedent, so that a pronoun receives the same interpretation of its antecedent, whether it is a maximal or reference one. The second principle allows to change this relation, when the context of discourse licenses this change. So, we suggest that theories of anaphora resolution that include these components are more accurate than theories that include only one component.

The paper is organized as follows. We define some general assumptions on plural NPs and *Generalized Quantifier* Theory (section 1.1) shared by all theoretical approaches. We discuss three theoretical approaches to plural pronouns (section 1.2). We then present the experiment that tests these three approaches (section 2). We discuss the results, and their theoretical import, in the conclusions (section 3).

1.1 Background: Plural NPs and Generalized Quantifier Theory

We start our discussion from theories of Plural Nouns. Theories of plural NPs assume that these terms denote *mereological structures*, power-sets generated by the set of referents in the denotation of the corresponding singular NP (Schwarzschild, 1996; Chierchia, 1998; Link, 1998; Winter, 2001). If a singular NP such as *boy* denotes Mario, Luigi and John as distinct referents ($\mathbf{boy}' = \{m, l, j\}$), then *boys* denotes its corresponding power-set $^*\mathbf{boy}'$, generated by the * (star) operator[3].

Each of the sub-sets in the denotation of a plural can be treated as a distinct referent, since the two notions are equivalent in a lattice-oriented approach (e.g. Mario, Mario and Luigi as a pair). Plural pronouns, being morpho-syntactically plural, denote a plural referent, in part determined by the interpretation of previous plural NPs, and the determiners they combine with. We turn to GQ to spell out the relevant details on this latter process.

GQ theory assumes that English sentences can be assigned the syntactic structure $[[DetNP]VP]$ (Barwise and Cooper, 1981; Nouwen, 2003; Szabolczi, 2010). The NP is in the *restrictor* position, since it restricts the range of entities quantified over. The VP is the *Nuclear Scope* position, since it introduces the minimal scope of the quantifier. In (1), the first sentence has the structure [[*Some boys*] *are having dinner*]; *boys* is NP in the restrictor, *are having dinner* is VP in the nuclear scope.

The relation $Det'(A, B)$ represents the interpretation of this structure. A Determiner denotes a relation between sets (i.e. Det'), combined with a cardinality condition on this relation. For instance, the relation $Some'(A, B)$ roughly stands for a relation between A and B, which includes at least one referent in its denotation. The relation $The'(A, B)$ roughly stands for a relation in which there is a unique maximal individual in its denotation. While A is the set of boys, B is the set of eating entities in discourse.

An important property of quantifiers is *conservativity*. It states that this relation is equivalent to $Det'(A, A \cap B)$: in words and using (1) as an example, that some boys are boys who are having dinner. The set A is known as the *maximal set*, here the set of all boys under discussion. The $A \cap B$ is known as the *reference set*, in this case the set of all boys who are also having dinner. The three sets of approaches sketched in the introduction differ on which sets acts as the anaphoric interpretation of *they*, as we explain in the next section. A note: we will respectively call A and $A \cap B$ the *maximal referent* and the *reference*

[2] We leave aside *referential* pronouns, pronouns that appear without a previous explicit antecedent (e.g. *they* in *they are eating a pizza*, (Elbourne, 2005a; Elbourne, 2005b; Schwarz, 2009).

[3] In extensional format, this set (a *full join lattice*) is: $^*\mathbf{boy}' = \{\emptyset, m, l, j, \{m, l\}, \{j, l\}, \{m, j\}, \{m, l, j\}\}$. We follow Landman (2004) and include the empty set in the denotation of plural terms.

referent, to keep terminological differences between frameworks at a minimum. Let us now discuss the three sets of approaches to plural pronouns and their anaphoric interpretation.

1.2 Three Sets of Theories

1.2.1 The First Set: Maximal Approaches

The first set includes approaches that treat pronouns as covert definite descriptions. Two variants of this approach are usually known as the *E-type* or *D-type* approach. They vary in syntactic but not semantic assumptions, so they can be "merged" in one approach (Elbourne 2005a, 2008). The basic intuition behind these approaches is that *they* in (1) can be treated as standing for the definite description *the boys*, which then takes a Quantified NP as its anaphoric antecedent in previous discourse (e.g. *some boys*, *the boys*).

Given these assumptions, these approaches predict that *they* denotes the maximal referent. So, in (2) *they* denotes the plural referent $A = \{j, m, l\}$, the referent denoted by *the boys* (Mario, Luigi and John as a trio). In (1), it denotes the plural referent $A = \{m, l\}$, denoted by *some boys* (Mario and Luigi). For this reason, we label these approaches as the "Maximal" approaches.

1.2.2 The Second Set: Reference Approaches

The second set includes approaches that vary in syntactic and semantic details, as they either assume that pronouns denote bound variables (Geurts, 1999; Kamp et al., 2005; Kibble, 1997; Heusinger, 2003) or identity functions (Jacobson, 1999; Jacobson, 2004). They all converge on one assumption, that anaphoric pronouns are interpreted as denoting the reference referent individuated by the previous sentence. We focus on DRT's analysis, for the sake of simplicity.

Let us take (1) as an example. According to these theories, the pronoun *they* in (1) denotes a plural referent. The VP *are having dinner* restricts the interpretation of the antecedent of *they*, the quantified NP *some boys*. The whole sentence denotes the reference referent, the set $A \cap B$: the set of boys who are having dinner. In DRT, this is roughly represented as the Discourse Representation Structure (DRS) $[\{Y, x\} : Y = \Sigma x, B(x)]$, in which a plural referent "Y" is identified with another plural referent, represented as Σx[4]. In words, the pronoun *they* is interpreted as denoting those boys who are having dinner and are also having a pizza. This is represented via the anaphoric relation $Y = A \cap B$, with the plural referent Σx standing for A. Given these assumptions, these approaches predict that *they* denotes the reference referent. For this reason, we label these approaches as the "Reference" approaches.

1.2.3 The Third Set: Flexible Approaches

The third set includes frameworks that propose that both the maximal and reference interpretation are possible, for pronouns (Chierchia, 1995; Nouwen, 2003; Brasoveanu, 2008)[5]. Two assumptions play a role in determining which interpretation speakers choose.

First, formal properties of the antecedent NP determine which referent is anaphorically identified with the interpretation of a plural pronoun. Strong determiners such as *the* select the maximal referent interpretation, weak determiners[6] such as *some* select the reference referent interpretation.

Second, the "alternative" interpretation of a pronoun is accessed when the "default" one cannot be accessed. One example is the following:

(3) The boys went to the pub, the girls went to the pool. *They* took a schooner of Fat Yak

In (3), *they* refers to both (all) boys and girls, by default. However, since this interpretation is contradictory, the alternative one is selected; *they* denotes the "people" that could actually go to the pub and grab a schooner. This is possible only if *they* can be interpreted as either denoting the maximal or reference referent, but not if it has a "fixed" interpretation. For this reason, we use the "Flexible" label for these approaches.

[4]Informally, a DRS is a combination of one or more "conditions" (properties such as $B(x)$, relations such as $x = y$) and a universe of discourse (the set of referents {Y,x}). Conditions are interpreted conjunctively. The symbol Σ represents that x is a mereological sum of referents, i.e. a plural referent. The notation used here is roughly the one used in Geurts (1999).

[5]We leave aside a discussion of *Centering Theory*, which offers little or no treatment of plural pronouns (Nouwen, 2001; Poesio et al., 2004).

[6]Weak determiners are determiners that can occur in *there* sentences, while strong determiners cannot (e.g. *there is some boy waiting* vs. **there is every boy waiting*) (Barwise and Cooper, 1981).

1.2.4 Three Approaches: The Predictions

The predictions of these approaches on the interpretation of *they* in discourse can be summed up as follows. The first set, that of Maximal approaches, predicts that *they* always denotes the maximal referent that is denoted by its antecedent NP. The second set, that of Reference approaches, predicts that *they* always denotes the reference referent, that is denoted by the previous sentence. The third set, that of Flexible approaches, allows both interpretations. One interpretation acts as the "default" interpretation, and may be either a maximal or a reference one. The other is the "alternative" interpretation, and must be properly licensed in context. The experiment described in the next section offers evidence testing which of these three approaches seems to make the correct predictions on the interpretation of *they*.

2 The study

2.1 Participants

The experiment involved adult participants (N=25). All participants were native speakers of English, undergraduate students of Psychology, and received course credit for their attendance. Between one and four participants attended each session, for a total of twenty minutes of experiment time.

2.2 Procedure

The experiment involved a variant of the *Truth-Value Judgement Task* (TVJ task) (Crain and Thornton, 1999). Most experiments involving this test are used to test children. However, given its flexibility, this task can be used to also test adults. A brief presentation of the task will help us in offering a reason for our choice. One type of a standard TVJ task, the so-called *description mode*, involves two experimenters. One experimenter acts out the scenario and narrates the events. The other experimenter controls a hand-puppet (e.g. Kermit the Frog), which is described as observing the events of the story with the participant.

At the end of the story, the puppet asks a question about the story to the participant, to be sure that he has understood the events he has observed, so he offers a yes-no question to the participant regarding the story. After a participant offers an answer, a follow-up question is usually offered, in order to test whether an offered answer is based on a correct understanding of the events described by the story.

When a TVJ task experiment involves yes-no questions, the story should describe events in such a way that both a "yes" and a "no" answer should be possible answers. However, only one of the answers correctly matches the outcome of the story. This condition is known as the *Condition of Plausible Dissent* (Crain & Thornton 1995: chapter 5).

An example is the following. One experimenter narrates a story of five horses involved in a jumping contest. Four horses jump successfully, one trips and fails. Another experimenter, as Kermit, asks (4):

(4) Has every horse jumped over the fence?

Assume that the participant has a correct interpretation of *every* as denoting the universal quantifier. Then, she will likely offer a "no" as answer, since one horse did not complete the target task. Although a "yes" answer could have been entertained, at some point (i.e. the fallen horse almost completed the jump), the end result made only the "no" answer as the correct one. The TVJ task thus allows a simple way to test grammar competence in a relatively simple and effortless way. The specific nature of our empirical questions motivated a few changes to the task. Our changes to the standard task were as follows.

First, our two experimental questions required that participants could choose between either interpretation, possibly *changing* interpretation in the opportune context. So, the experiment included a *sequence* of three stories. The first story tested if participants could access both interpretations. The second story tested if participants could change their initial interpretation, in an opportune licensing context. The third story tested if participants maintained the "new" choice, if the context did not license a further change of interpretation.

Second, we prepared a power-point presentation depicting this sequence, instead of acting out the stories. Each slide depicted a single event involving one or more characters, with the text accurately describing this event. At the end of each story Mr. Little Bears, a character taking the role of Kermit as the puppet, appeared in a slide and offered a question to the participants.

Third, participants received an answer sheet before the start of experiment, on which they were invited to write down their answer by circling either a "yes" or "no" answer, for each story. Participants had to write down an answer after each of Mr. Little Bears' questions, story by story. After the experiment, the answers sheets were collected, and two follow-up questions were offered. A first question asked why they offered their answer in the first story. A second question asked why they offered their answer in the second and third story.

There were two reasons for collecting follow-up answers in this way. A first reason was that, since participants had three distinct but related answers, asking a follow-up question after each story would have likely made the participants aware of their own choices. This awareness could have biased the results in one way or another, so we removed this potential source of confounding. A second was that, via an "open" answer, it was possible to better understand the reasons behind participants' choices. Answers were coded according to the characters that motivated a given answer. Specific details are offered in the next section.

2.3 Materials

The stories involved five characters from the *Thomas and the tank engines* line of toys. This list of tank engines included Thomas, Duncan, Spencer, Diesel 10 and Arthur. The other recurring character, Mr. Little Bears, was introduced as an amnesiac bear that was going to watch the stories with the participants. Because of his bad memory, he had to ask a question after each story. Other characters were temporarily involved in each story. The five tank engines remained the main characters in all three stories.

The structure of the stories was as follows. In the first story, the tank engines had to deliver a jewel to Pikachu the Pokemon, as their first job of the day. Each of tank engines individually went to Pikachu's station but Spencer, during his trip, decided to stop at the local aquarium and ended up not delivering his jewel to Pikachu, unlike Thomas, Duncan, Arthur and Diesel 10.

Mr. Little Bears appeared in the next slide and offered a question. This question followed a sentence that introduced an anaphoric antecedent for *they*. We chose the definite NP *the engines* as an antecedent, for the following reasons. As a strong determiner, *the* should license the maximal referent interpretation as a default (Barwise and Cooper, 1981; Nouwen, 2003). Participants could also have chosen the reference referent interpretation may also be licensed, if they could access the alternative interpretation. Hence, a "yes" or "no" answer easily pointed out which interpretation participants chose.

The first target question was (5):

(5) "It's nice to see that *the engines* are working hard, but I am not sure about one thing: Have *they* gone to the station?"

If participants would have interpreted *they* as denoting the maximal referent, they would have answered "no". One engine, Spencer, did not reach the station. If participants interpreted *they* as denoting the reference referent, they would have answered "yes". The the other four tank engines reached the station.

The second story described a similar complex set of events, although the engine not reaching a given destination became Arthur, not Spencer. At the end of this story, Mr. Little Bears offered the second question, in (6):

(6) *The poor engines*, their memory is not so good too! but I am not sure about one thing: Have *they* gone to the Power Puffs Hotel?"

So, participants could have changed their initial answer (from instance, from "yes" to "no"). This because the group of engines that completed the action changed, and Arthur, not Spencer made the maximal interpretation false. So, the context licensed a change from a possible default (maximal) interpretation to an alternative (reference) one.

The third story presented a different set of events, but the same result. Arthur did not reach the same destination as the other engines. Mr. Little Bears then offered the third question, in (7):

(7) "Things have become pretty hectic for *the engines*! But I am not sure about one thing: Have *they* gone to the engines' house?"

If a change of interpretation is determined by change of salient group, then no change in interpretation should have occurred, since the "offending" engine was still Arthur.

Participants were invited to write down their answer, once each question was presented. After the experiment, they were asked the follow-up questions, on an individual basis. The specific predictions of the three approaches for these stories are as follows.

The Maximal approach predicts that participants interpreted *they* as always denoting the maximal referent, the maximal referent (that is, $\{t, d, d10, s, a\}$[7]). So, participants should have answered "no" in each story. They should have defended this choice because one engine, first Spencer then Arthur, always failed to reach the target destination.

The Reference approach predicts that participants should have interpreted *they* as always denoting the reference referent. This referent changed from the first to the second story (i.e. from $\{t, d, d10, a\}$ to $\{t, d, d10, s\}$), but in each story "some" or perhaps "most" engines reached their goal. So, participants should have always answered "yes", and defended this choice, because of this reason.

The Flexible approach predicts that participants should have interpreted *they* in a flexible way. In the first story, the default interpretation of *they* is the maximal one. So, first question invited a "no" answer. In the second and third story, the context licensed and strongly favoured the alternative, reference interpretation. So, participants should have answered first "no", then "yes" twice, pointing out that the second and third story were about a salient group of engines.

2.4 Results and Discussion

The results were the following:

- First Story: yes=0, no=25, 0%/100%;
- Second Story: yes=23, no=2, 92%/8%;
- Third Story: yes=24, no=1, 96%/4%;

These data suggest that the Flexible approach makes the most accurate predictions on the interpretation of *they*. Again, recall that participants could choose either a "yes" or a "no" answer, after each story. The Maximal and Reference approach do not predict the change from a "no" to a "yes" answer between first and second story. Both approaches predict either all "no" (Maximal approach) or all "yes" answers (Reference approach), so these results are not entirely predicted by these two approaches. The Flexible approach predicts a "no" answer in the first story, and a "yes" answer in the second and third story. So, this approach correctly predicts the data. The follow-up answers offer a more fine-grained perspective.

In the follow-up question time, almost all participants defended their choice by arguing that, when they answered "no" after the first story, they did so because one tank engine made the underlying declarative sentence false (i.e. Arthur). For the second and the third story, the follow-up questions revealed some interesting results. Most participants changed interpretation because they observed that in each story "four", or most (but not all) of the engines made the story true (22/25 participants). One participant noted that for a given trio, the story was always true, although he could not recall their exact identity. The only participant that answered "no" in the third story changed his interpretation twice (i.e. he answered "no-yes-no"), and admitted that he was confused by the stories. Two participants answered from "no" to "yes" in the third story, because they did not notice that the "offending" engine changed beforehand, from first to second story.

Overall, these answers to the follow-up questions, combined with the yes-no answers, offer support in favor of the Flexible approach. They also suggest that the Maximal and the Reference approach may require revision. Since these approaches do not predict that the interpretation of *they* may change in the opportune context, they cannot explain the whole range of findings in our experiment. With these facts in mind, we shall move to the conclusions.

3 Conclusions

This paper offered experimental evidence on the interpretation of the plural pronoun *they* in discourse. Three approaches to its interpretation were discussed and tested. The Maximal approach claims that plural pronouns denote all the referents denoted by their antecedent, in the context of discourse. The Reference approach claims that plural pronouns al-

[7]We represent plural referents in a set-theoretic format, with t for "Thomas", d for "Duncan", $d10$ for "Diesel 10", s for "Spencer", a for "Arthur".

ways denote the reference plural referent denoted by the combination of anaphoric antecedent and clausemate VP. The Flexible approach claims that plural pronouns receive a default interpretation (for instance, the maximal one), but also that the alternative interpretation may be accessed, if licensed (for instance, the reference one).

Two questions were addressed: what is the default interpretation of this *they* in discourse, and whether other interpretations are accessible, once the opportune context licenses them. In order to test these two hypotheses, we devised a variant of the TVJ Task that tested both hypotheses in their order of "accessibility", via the presentation of a sequence of stories. The findings invite the following conclusions.

The findings of the first story suggest that participants interpreted *they* as denoting the maximal referent, as per predictions of the Maximal and Flexible approach. Participants interpreted *they* as denoting the plural referent made of the five tank engines involved in the story (Thomas, Duncan, Diesel 10, Arthur, Spencer), and found that Spencer's actions made the underlying declarative sentence false. Hence, they invariably offered "no" as answer, as they also argued in the follow-up question.

The findings of the second and third story, on the other hand, suggest that participants would change their interpretation of *they*, as denoting a reference referent, in the opportune context. This is in line with the predictions of the Flexible approach. Almost all participants changed their answer from "no" to "yes", from first to second story, since the story made it clear that not all tank engines were salient, only a certain group, which however varied across participants.

Overall, *they* and perhaps plural anaphora in general appear to have an alternative interpretation, because their interpretation may be changed, if the context licenses this change. However, as the data also seem to suggest, this second interpretation is dependent on discourse context. For instance, if *they* has a strong quantifier as its antecedent (e.g. *the boys*), it will be interpreted as denoting a maximal referent (first story). It can be re-interpreted as denoting a reference referent, however, if the context licenses this inference (second, third story). These facts suggest that the Flexible set of approaches is on the right track, while the Maximal and the Reference sets of approaches may need further revisions.

These data also invite the following answer to our general question: what is an accurate logical and psychological model of anaphora resolution. If a model of anaphora resolution must account how speakers access anaphoric relations and resolve them in discourse, then such a model must include two complementary principles. One principle tracks the interpretation of a pronoun's antecedent NP, and assigns it to the pronoun. So, a pronoun receives a maximal or reference interpretation, depending on the formal properties of its antecedent. A second principle tracks whether this interpretation is consistent with rest of the explicit context, the sentence that the antecedent is part of. So, this principle may license the change of interpretation to the "other" type, in the opportune context.

So, a theory of anaphora resolution that correctly describes and predicts the data at hand must be flexible enough, that it allows the re-interpretation of plural pronouns in discourse. This flexibility depends on the ability for the theory to correctly establish which is the default interpretation of the antecedent NP of a pronoun, and which is the alternative interpretation. Further empirical evidence may also elucidate whether these findings can be generalized to other quantifiers (e.g. *some boys*) and anaphora. For the time being, we shall leave such inquiries for future research.

References

Barwise, Jon and Robin Cooper. 1981. Generalized quantiers and natural languages. *Linguistics & Philosophy*, 4(2):159–219.

Branco, António, Tony McEnery, Ruslan Mitkov. 2005. *Anaphora processing: linguistic, cognitive and computational modelling*. Amsterdam, John Benjamins.

Brasoveanu, Adrian. 2008. *Structured Nominal and Modal Reference*, Newark, NJ: Rutgers University Ph.D. dissertation.

Chierchia, Gennaro. 1995. *Dynamics of meaning: Anaphora, Presupposition and the Theory of Grammar*. Chicago, MN: Chicago University Press.

Chierchia, Gennaro. 1998. Reference to Kinds across Language. *Natural Language Semantics* 6(4):339–405.

Crain, Stephen and Rosalind Thornton. 1999. *Investigations in Universal Grammar: A Guide to Experiments*

in the Acquisition of Syntax and Semantics. Cambridge, MA: The MIT Press.
Elbourne, Paul. 2005a. *Situations and Individuals*. Cambridge, Mass.: MIT Press.
Elbourne, Paul. 2005b. On the acquisition of Principle B. *Linguistic Inquiry* 36(3): 333-365.
Elbourne, Paul. 2008. The interpretation of pronouns. *Language and Linguistics Compass* 2(1):119-150.
Geurts, Bart. 1999. *Presuppositions and Pronouns*. Elsevier, Oxford.
Heim, Irene. 1982. *The semantics of definite and indefinite noun phrases*. Amherst, MA: University of Massachussetts Ph.D. Dissertation.
Heusinger, Klaus von. 2003. The Double Dynamics of Definite Descriptions. In: Jaroslav Peregrin (ed.). *Meaning in the Dynamic Turn*, 150–168. Amsterdam: Elsevier.
Jacobson, Pauline. 1999. Towards a variable-free semantics. *Linguistics & Philosophy* 22(1):117–184.
Jacobson, Pauline. 2004. Binding without pronouns (and pronouns without binding). In Geert-Jan Kruiff & Rick Oherle (eds.), *Binding and Resource Sensitivity*, 43–94. Dordrecht: Kluwer Academic Press.
Kamp, Hans. 1981. A theory of truth and semantic representation. In Jeroen A. G. Groenendijk, Theo M. V. Janssen, and Martin J. B. Stokhof (Eds.), *Formal Methods in the Study of Language*, 277–322. Amsterdam: Mathematical Centre.
Kamp, Hans, Josef van Genabith, & Uwe Reyle. 2005. Discourse Representation Theory. In Dov Gabbay & Franz Guenther (eds.), *Handbook of Philosophical Logic*, 125-394. North Holland: North Holland.
Kamp, Hans & Uwe Reyle. 1993. *From Discourse to Logic*. Dordrecht: Kluwer.
Kartunnen, Lauri. 1976. Discourse Referents. In J. D. McCawley (ed.), *Syntax and Semantics 7: Notes from the Linguistic Underground*, 363-85, Academic Press, New York.
Kibble, Rodger. 1997. Complement anaphora and dynamic binding. In Aaron Lawson (Ed.), *Proceedings of SALT VII*, 258–275.
Koornereef, Arnout. 2008. *Eye-catching Anaphora*. Utrecht: LOT International Dissertation Series.
Landman, Fred. 2004. *Indefinites and the type of sets*. London: Blackwell studies in Semantics.
Link, Godehard. 1998. *Algebraic semantics in Language and Philosophy*. Stanford, CA: CSLI publications.
Lukyanenko, Cynthia, Anastasia Conroy and Jeffrey Lidz. 2008. *Infants' Adherence to Principle C: Evidence from 30-month-olds*. Manuscript, University of Maryland.
Nouwen, Rick. 2001. A plural resolution logic. In Kristina Striegnitz (ed.), *Proceedings of the 2001 ESSLLI Student Session*, 227–239. University of Helsinki.
Nouwen, Rick. 2003. *Plural pronominal anaphora in context*. Utrecht: LOT International Dissertation Series.
Poesio, Massimo, Rosemary Stevenson, Barbara di Eugenio & John Hitzeman. 2004. Centering: A Parametric theory and its instantiations. *Computational Linguistics* 30(3):309–363.
Schwarz, Florian. 2009. *Two Types of Definites in Natural Languages*. Ph.D. thesis, University of Massachusetts Amherst.
Schwarzschild, Roger. 1996. *Pluralities*. Dordrecht: Kluwer.
Szabolczi, Anna. 2010. *Quantification*. Cambridge: Cambridge University Press.
Winter, Yoad. 2001. *Flexibility Principles in Boolean Semantics: coordination, plurality and natural language*. Cambridge, MA: The MIT Press.

Learning from student responses: A domain-independent natural language tutor

Jenny McDonald[1], Alistair Knott[2], Richard Zeng[1] and Ayelet Cohen[1]
[1]Higher Education Development Centre, University of Otago
[2]Dept of Computer Science, University of Otago
jenny.mcdonald@otago.ac.nz

Abstract

Providing timely and individualised feedback to students in large undergraduate classes is problematic. In this paper we describe our approach to creating a simple, surface-based, domain-independent natural language tutor which uses simple machine learning techniques as a step towards resolving this issue. The focus of our efforts was on developing a high-quality tutorial dialogue plan, creating well-designed questions, and building a model of student responses derived from real student data. We present some early evaluation results and briefly outline the opportunities that our approach and the new tutorial dialogue system present.

1 Introduction

The study this paper describes arose out of a practical need expressed by one of the coordinators of an undergraduate first year health sciences course:

> For large class sizes of 1500-1800 students, is it possible to use technology to provide timely individualised feedback to students on their understanding of key concepts?

Natural language intelligent tutoring systems (ITS) seemed to offer some promise for supporting and enhancing student understanding of key concepts in this domain. For example, Circsim Tutor (Evens and Michael, 2006) is a natural language tutor designed expressly to develop health sciences student understanding of the baroreceptor reflex in humans (the baroreceptor reflex is one of the mechanisms for maintaining blood pressure in humans). Nevertheless derision and dismisal of ITS as a failed enterprise are common views among many educational researchers and practising teachers, for example, Laurillard (2002) and Ramsden (2003). With a few exceptions, even today, within Higher Education, ITS are hardly in widespread practical use for teaching and learning (Reeves and Hedberg, 2003). There are some good practical reasons for this. Murray (1999), in his review of ITS authoring systems, addresses a key one:

> Building an explicit model of anything is not an easy task, and requires analysis, synthesis, and abstraction skills along with a healthy dose of creativity. ...it is difficult to reduce the entire design task to low level decisions that yield a quality product...some degree of holistic understanding and abstract thinking will eventually have to come into play.

Worse still, in practice it is seldom feasible to adapt a system designed for a specific teaching and learning context to another. So for example, while Circsim Tutor deals with the baroreceptor reflex it deals with it at a level which is too advanced for the broader introductory-level course on cardiovascular homeostasis that we were dealing with. Even if this were not the case, there would likely be differences in emphasis in terms of the curriculum and adapting a deep system like Circsim would be a non-trivial task.

As the authors' primary focus is on teaching and learning development across a tertiary institution, we required a system that would be both responsive and practical in real class settings and which could be readily adapted to a wide range of domains. We decided to build a very simple, surface-based, domain-independent natural language tutor using simple machine learning techniques, and to focus our efforts on developing a high-quality *lesson plan*. The lesson plan should have two components. Firstly, there should be a well-designed set of questions for the tutor to ask, to probe students' knowledge of the domain. Secondly, for each question there should be a good model of the range of common answers which students are likely to provide, so that the tutor can give suitable responses to each of these, and give students the individualised feedback which is the key goal of the system.

This development method hinges firstly on in-depth interactions with the teaching staff of the course, and secondly on the acquisition of high-quality training data from actual students. Consequently, there were two stages in the development of the system. In the first stage, we produced a detailed set of questions, in close liaison with the teaching staff, and devised a detailed script, providing for possible student responses to each question, along with appropriate tutor actions, and then used an existing surface-based dialogue engine to put these questions to students and give responses based on simple pattern-matching techniques. This stage-one system was mainly intended as a means for gathering training data for the full system, though of course we intended it to have some educational merit as well. In the second stage, we refined the script we had developed in the first stage to add new response categories, manually classified student responses to each question, trained a set of classifiers on the revised set of categories and developed a second dialogue manager which deployed these classifiers.

Of the few readily available domain-independent tutorial dialogue systems, TuTalk from the Learning Research and Development Centre at the University of Pittsburgh, is one that provides a relatively easy way to author dialogues using only a text editor and scripts can be authored much like writing a natural one-to-one dialogue. The TuTalk scripting language represents each tutor turn as a finite state machine (FSM) and the author can define multiple classes of student response that lead from the current tutor turn to the next tutor turn or state. A simple chat-style interface is all that is required for a user to interact with the system (Jordan, 2007).

However, TuTalk 'out of the box' includes many features and options that we did not need and added processing overhead to response times especially for longer responses. We were also aware that the basic natural language understanding module that came with it was fairly rudimentary and yielded poor precision and recall when classifying most student responses other than those to simple binary or limited-option questions. Nevertheless, with the addition of a web interface, a large cohort of students could potentially access and use the system, and early feedback from students indicated that even though their responses were often not well 'understood' they found the dialogue useful as a study and revision tool (the default position was always to provide a model answer): for these reasons we felt that TuTalk would allow us to rapidly acquire a large corpus of authentic student responses to questions posed in the dialogue. Once we had captured this data we could then proceed to build a very simple, surface-based natural language dialogue system which retained a FSM model for representing the dialogue. The large corpus acquired via the TuTalk system would be used to both train the new system and to inform revision of the script itself.

In the next section of this paper we describe collecting the dialogue corpus and evaluating performance. The third section outlines the new dialogue system architecture and describes how we have utilised components from the Natural Language Toolkit (Bird, 2006). The fourth section describes the iterative process we are using to both develop the script and build a set of classifiers for student responses based on insights and intuitions from real student data. In the fifth section we present some early classifier test results and in the final section we discuss the educational research opportunities that both our approach and new tutorial dialogue system present.

Dialogue excerpt
TUTOR: Would you like more practice with the ideas we've discussed so far, before we move on? STUDENT: yes please TUTOR: If heart rate drops and stroke volume remains the same, what will happen to cardiac output? STUDENT: decrease TUTOR: Well done. Cardiac Output is determined in part by Stroke Volume. How do you calculate CO? STUDENT: co = heart rate x stroke volume TUTOR: Cool, that's right. If cardiac output increases and TPR remains the same what will happen to mean arterial pressure? STUDENT: increase

Table 1: Tutorial dialogue excerpt

2 Collecting the dialogue corpus

In close consultation with the course lecturers an initial tutorial script covering the curriculum on cardiovascular homeostasis was developed. The script was written by a medical graduate using lecture notes, laboratory manuals and self-directed learning material from the course and required approval from the teaching team before it could be deployed for students. The teaching team wanted to be certain the script contained no errors of fact and that it had some educational merit. Table 1 shows an excerpt from a tutorial dialogue session. The script was refined by incorporating utterances, captured from pilot dialogue interactions between the system and student and staff volunteers (N=34), back into the script. Incorrect behaviour of the script was dealt with through adjustments to tutor turns and improvements to script flow was made following feedback from students and tutors on the course and from examination of the dialogue transcripts. Feedback from students and some of the teaching staff indicated to us that the system even without much in the way of 'understanding' still had some value as a learning and teaching tool because it always provided model answers to questions.

2.1 Student responses

The cardiovascular homeostasis tutorial was released to the first year undergraduate class at the beginning of their module on the human cardiovascular system. Tutorial use was optional. 437 students accessed the system during the course (total class enrolment=1800) and produced a total of 532 dialogues; several students accessed the dialogue more than once. However from the total number of dialogues, only 242 dialogues were completed through to the half-way point and only 127 dialogues were completed to the end. A handful of dialogues were interrupted because of system-related problems but the majority that terminated before completion did so because because the students simply ended their session. Feedback from course tutors and comments from the students themselves supported our inutition that poor system 'understanding' of student dialogue contributions was probably a key reason for the fall-off in use. Nevertheless, it served its purpose in capturing a large quantity of training data which is mainly what it was for.

3 Dialogue system architecture

Clearly we needed to improve the 'understanding' performance of the dialogue system if we were to hope to provide individualised feedback on free text input: two options were considered. Either we could continue to use TuTalk and replace the existing TuTalk natural language understanding (NLU) module along with making adjustments to the script design and dialogue manager (DM) or we could build another dialogue system from scratch. In the end we chose to start from scratch for three main reasons. First, the natural language toolkit (NLTK) already provided many of the functions required in a simple dialogue system such as tokenisers, stemmers and a range of classifiers. Second, for our purposes, we didn't require many of the features built into TuTalk and we had experienced some performance issues with the system. Third, a very simple modular system that could be easily extended or adapted, and which utilised well established libraries would provide a solid base from which to do further work in this area. Fig. 1 provides an overview of our system architecture.

The dialogue system is written in python and

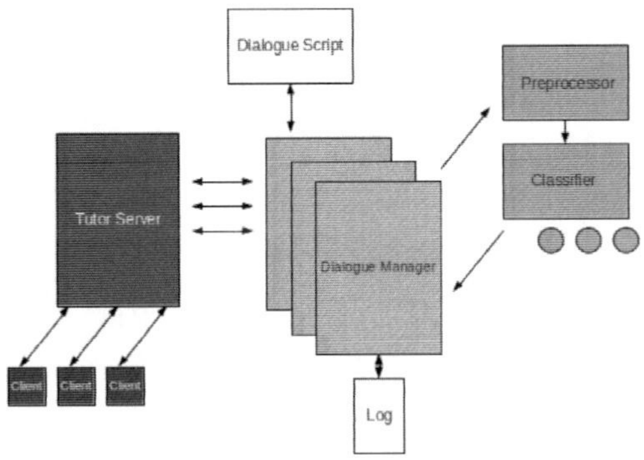

Figure 1: Architecture of Dialogue System.

utilises several NLTK libraries, Peter Norvig's 'toy' spell checker, and the Asyncore and Asynchat libraries to manage multiple simultaneous client connections. The server can readily communicate with any web-application front end using XML-formatted messages. We have also built a java-based web application through which multiple clients can connect to the tutorial server (Fig. 2).

The structure of the tutorial dialogue is determined entirely by the dialogue script. We wanted to use a FSM model for the dialogue since this permits an organic authoring process and there is no theoretical limit to how deep or broad the dialogue becomes.

The script structure itself is based on Core and Allen's (1997) dialogue coding scheme and each dialogue contribution is divided into forward and backward functional layers. Jumping to alternative parts of the script is embedded in the forward function rather than being treated as a separate layer. This seems to work well with the notion of 'action-directive' functions proposed by Core and Allen. In effect the forward functions always advance the dialogue even if some elements are repeated along the way. It also seems like a more intuitive and less confusing approach than incorporating special tags in either the backward layer, or inventing a new layer to handle them. The script is an XML file which is defined in our XML schema for the dialogue system and which essentially comprises a series of dialogue contributions.

An example of a single dialogue contribution, called a contribution node is given in Figure 3. In this example, the unique id of the dialogue contribution is "check-hr". Apart from the start and end nodes of the dialogue, every contribution node has a backward and forward layer. The backward layers contains responses appropriate to the previous dialogue context, for example an utterance to establish grounding (Clark and Schaefer, 1989), and the forward layer sets up the next dialogue context.

```
<contribution-node id="check-hr"
parent-node="start"
default="true">

<backward class="yes">
<acknowledge/>
</backward>

<forward>
<assert>We're going to talk about
what blood pressure is; we'll discuss
why the body needs to regulate blood
pressure, and find out how the body
does this. Let's start by revising
some simple ideas that are central to
understanding what blood pressure is.
You should already be familiar with
some of these.</assert>

<assert>HR or heart rate is the number
of times the heart beats each minute.
A normal adult HR is around
72 beats/min.
</assert>

<info-request value="How would you
check what someone&apos;s HR is?"
define="You could take their
pulse."/>

</forward>
</contribution-node>
```

Figure 3: *check-hr* contribution node

While the tutorial system is primarily designed for single-initiative dialogue, the opportunity for limited mixed-initiative is incorporated through classifying question contributions at any stage of the dialogue and searching for possible answers within the dialogue script. In addition, the script can be designed to accomodate opportunities for eliciting further explanation where the need is apparent from examination of previous student responses. (For an explanation of this see Section 4).

Each client connection to the system creates an

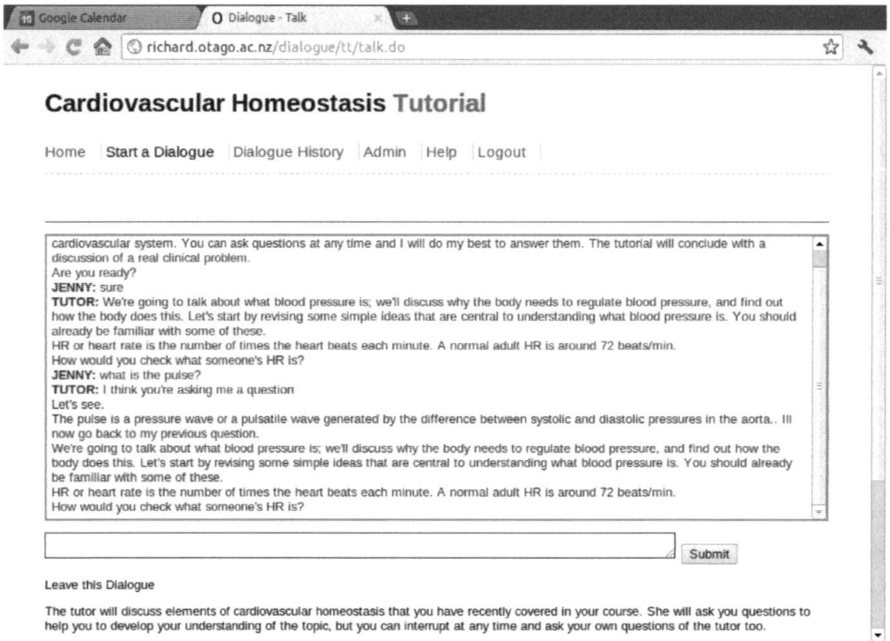

Figure 2: Screenshot of Dialogue System Web Client.

instance of the dialogue manager which sends tutor contributions to the client according to the preloaded script and receives student contributions which are then classified and determine the next tutor contribution. The pseudocode given in Fig. 4 illustrates how the dialogue manager processes each contribution node.

The dialogue system is intended to be domain neutral since the content and structure of the dialogue is determined solely by the dialogue script (note that we have yet to demonstrate this by building scripts outside the domain discussed in this paper). Scripts are designed according to the XML schema specified for the dialogue system. A domain-appropriate dictionary is required for the spell checker: for our cardiovascular homeostasis tutorial we combined the text from pilot student responses, the script itself, the relevant section from an accessible human physiology text (`http://en.wikibooks.org/wiki/Human_Physiology/The_cardiovascular_system`) and the NLTK plain text ABC science corpus.

4 Building classifiers and revising the script

Tutorial dialogue script revision and classifier development are currently underway. The approach we have taken is to do these two tasks hand-in-hand. In this section we describe the rationale for this approach by way of illustrative examples.

In general, a separate classifier is required for each dialogue contribution in the script. So for example, the dialogue contribution *check-hr* has its own classifier. In this case, one of the possible classes for text classified is *correct-simple* and this is specified in the backward class attribute value.

Each backward layer must have a class attribute. When the previous student dialogue contribution matches this class, this contribution node becomes the current node. In the example above, responses to the parent contribution node *check-hr* are processed by a single classifier into one of the classes listed in Table 2. If classification fails then the dialogue contribution which is specified as the default is chosen.

The process of building a classifier for each dialogue contribution requires a number of steps. First, classification by hand of a training set derived

```
If there is user input
=>Normalise and spell-check raw input
=>Select appropriate classifier
for current dialogue contribution
based on dc label
=>Get next dialogue contribution
node from classifier result

If dialogue contribution has a backward
layer
=>send contents to client

If dialogue contribution has a
forward layer
=>send any assertions to client
=>send info requests to client

if action is required (for
example jump to a specific dialogue
contribution or question answering
routine)
=>go to required node
```

Figure 4: Dialogue manager pseudocode

check-hr classifier
correct
correct-simpler
question
incomplete

Table 2: Possible classes for check-hr

from the student corpus. The XML schema of the NPSChat corpus provided with the NLTK was a useful model for us to follow in marking-up the corpus and allowed us to use the appropriate NLTK corpus reader directly. The classes used are created based on inspection of student responses although the class *question* and the class *correct* are used in each classifier. For example, examination of student responses to the question:

> How would you check what someone's HR is?

led to us developing a class *correct-simpler* given that a handful of students suggested using an ecg or blood-pressure cuff and stethoscope. These methods are not the easiest ways to achieve this but they are valid answers and lend themselves to seeking a simpler method in order to check student understanding.

This process in turn may require a new dialogue contribution for the script. For example, the con-

```
<contribution-node id="hr-simpler"
parent-node="check-hr">

<backward class="correct-simpler">
<acknowledge/>
<part-agree/>
</backward>

<forward>
<info-request value="Can you
think of a simpler method?"
action="check-hr"/>
</forward>

</contribution-node>
```

Figure 5: *hr-simpler* contribution node

tribution node *hr-simpler* (Fig. 5.) was only created after the classifier for *check-hr* had been built and then became an addition to the original script. This is why we suggest script revision and building of classifiers should be done together.

For each dialogue context a training set is created. Typically the first 100 student responses for each tutor question are classified by a human marker, although this number may be less where it is clear that there is little variabiliy in student responses (for example, in the case of binary questions) or more where there is a wide range of student responses. Once a suitable training set is marked up the set is divided into 5 folds and a Naive Bayes classifier trained on 4/5 folds initially using simple *bag of words* as the featureset and then tested on the remaining fold. A 5-way cross-validation is carried out and accuracies for each of the 5 test sets calculated. The average accuracy across the 5 test sets and standard deviation is also recorded.

This process is then repeated using different featuresets (for example, bag of words, word length, first word, with/without stemming, with/without stopwords etc) until the highest accuracy and least variability in test set results is achieved. Some features are particularly appropriate in a given context. For example, length of response is a good predictor of an incomplete answer in the *check-hr* context above. A student common response in this context was simply 'pulse' and the human classifier had de-

Question Type	Example
binary	'Are you ready?'
limited-option	'How would you check somone's heart-rate?'
open	'What is the pulse?'

Table 3: Question Types

cided these responses were incomplete and required, 'count' or 'measure' or a similar qualifier before accepting this as a correct answer. Response length helped to distinguish these responses from correct responses.

Once the best features for a given dialogue-contribution classifier have been established the size of the training set is increased in order to expose the classifier to a larger number of samples and improve accuracy. Finally, where uncommon but pedagogically useful student responses are found, the training data may be weighted with these in order to increase the likelyhood that similar responses are correctly classified.

The classifier is evaluated with previously unseen data and scored relative to a human marker. The entropy of the probability distribution (E) is calculated for each unseen response and this is used to determine appropriate thresholds for classification. For example, if E is close to zero the classifier confidence is generally very high. E 1 indicates low confidence and less difference between the class rankings.

Finally the classifier is serialised, along with its associated feaureset parameters and saved for use in the dialogue system itself.

5 Testing classifiers

In general there are three types of tutor question in our cardiovascular homeostasis dialogue: binary, limited-option and open. An example of each is given in Table 3.

Evaluation of classifiers for binary questions has resulted in the highest accuracy with the smallest amount of training data (98-99 percent on training set size of 200). Typically, for this question type, there are only two class options plus a third to cater for a question initiative from the student. In this section we focus on classifying responses for the remaining two question types, limited-option and open, since these tend to be more educationally interesting and relevant, and harder to classify. Data is presented for an example of each type of question.

1. Limited-option. The *check-hr* dialogue contribution is a good example. Even with free text, there is a reasonably limited number of ways to answer the question, 'How would you check someone's heart-rate?'. Indeed the great majority of student responses were of the form *count the pulse, measure the pulse, take the pulse, etc*. Best results were achieved using a combination of the NLTK Porter stemmer on tokenised words, word length, first word, and a custom regular expression feature to pick up reference to ECG or blood pressure. Using these features, accuracy increased from a best of 0.72 to 0.90 when training data increased from a fold size of 19 to a fold size of 204 (Refer Fig. 3). Variability in training set accuracy was reduced when stopwords were removed from less than 0.03 to less than 0.01.

Evaluation on the trained classifier on a previously unseen sample of 20 was surprisingly 100 percent with entropy values between 0.00 for a student response, 'by measuring their pulse rate' to 0.81 for 'by listening to their pulse'.

2. Open. A good example in this case, is the question, 'What is the pulse?'. There is a wide range of ways in which an answer to this question could be reasonably expressed. The model answer given is 'The pulse is a pressure wave or a pulsatile wave generated by the difference between systolic and diastolic pressures in the aorta.' To give an idea of how open this type of question is, the following is an alternate but valid expression of the same idea, 'The pulse is generated by contraction of the heart during systole and is transmitted as a wave to the peripheral arteries.'

Similar to the first case the average accuracy of the classifier we created for this question plateaued at 0.89 with a training data fold size of 194, however it performed far worse on smaller training sets achieving an average accuracy of only 0.41 with a training data fold size of 19. The most useful features in this case were word stems, word length and first word. We had a total of 8 classes as there was a wider range of student responses to the question.

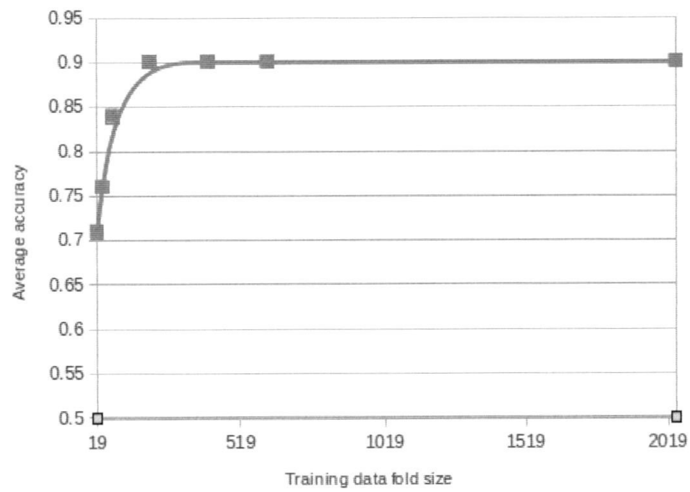

Figure 6: check-hr Training data. Fold size vs Average accuracy

Two of these classes were needed to deal with commonly occuring misconceptions. However one of the classes is redundant. The *incorrect* class regularly failed to correctly identify incorrect answers. The reason for this is likely to be the high degree of variability in incorrect answers unless they demonstrate a commonly held misconception. We expect to achieve better results on our unseen evaluation data after removing the incorrect class from the training set.

6 Discussion

Our goal was to build a very simple, surface-based, domain-independent natural language tutor using simple machine learning techniques, and to focus our efforts on developing a high-quality lesson plan, so that the tutor can ask well-designed questions, and has a good model of the range of possible answers which students will provide for these. Our development method requires in-depth interactions with the teaching staff of the course, plus the acquisition of high-quality training data from actual students.

In this paper we have focussed particularly on describing the system and reporting our approach to building classifiers and script revision in order to achieve this goal. The results of our early classifier evaluations look promising in terms of the ability of the system to 'understand' student responses and take appropriate action. Our next task is to evaluate our system and revised tutorial script with a new cohort of first-year health sciences students. We also plan to compare student learning outcomes against the same script using a multi-choice selection rather than free text responses. Previous investigations in this area have produced equivocal results. For example, Corbett et al. (2006).

We see potential for our approach and the system in a number of areas: supporting the rapid capture of tutorial corpora across a range of subject domains, developing faster and more flexible approaches to authoring tutorial dialogues and of course we hope to make headway with the problem of providing timely and individualised feedback to students which is so keenly sought by our colleagues teaching large undergraduate courses.

References

Steven Bird. 2006. NLTK: the natural language toolkit. In *Proceedings of the COLING/ACL on Interactive presentation sessions*, COLING-ACL '06, pages 69–72, Stroudsburg, PA, USA. Association for Computational Linguistics.

Herbert H. Clark and Edward F. Schaefer. 1989. Contributing to discourse. *Cognitive Science*, 13(2):259–294.

Albert Corbett, Angela Wagner, Sharon Lesgold, Harry Ulrich, and Scott Stevens. 2006. The impact on learning of generating vs. selecting descriptions in analyzing algebra example solutions. In *Proceedings of the 7th international conference on Learning sciences*, ICLS '06, pages 99–105. International Society of the Learning Sciences.

Mark G. Core and James F. Allen. 1997. Coding dialogs with the damsl annotation scheme. In *Working Notes of the AAAI Fall Symposium on Communicative Action in Humans and Machines*, pages 28–35, Cambridge, MA, November.

Martha Evens and Joel Michael. 2006. *One-on-One Tutoring by Humans and Computers*. Lawrence Erlbaum Associates.

Pamela Jordan. 2007. Topic initiative in a simulated peer dialogue agent. In *Artificial Intelligence in Education (AIED 07)*.

Diana Laurillard. 2002. *Rethinking University Teaching*. Routledge Falmer, 2nd edition.

Tom Murray. 1999. Authoring intelligent tutoring systems: An analysis of state of the art. *International Journal of Artificial Intelligence in Education*, 10:98–129.

Paul Ramsden. 2003. *Learning to teach in higher education*. Routledge Falmer, 2nd edition.

Thomas C Reeves and John G Hedberg. 2003. *Interactive learning systems evaluation*. Englewood Cliffs, New Jersey : Educational Technology Publications.

Detection of child exploiting chats from a mixed chat dataset as a text classification task

Md Waliur RahmanMiah
School of Science, Information Technology and Engineering
University of Ballarat
walimiah@students.ballarat.edu.au

John Yearwood
School of Science, Information Technology and Engineering
University of Ballarat
j.yearwood@ballarat.edu.au

Sid Kulkarni
School of Science, Information Technology and Engineering
University of Ballarat
s.kulkarni@ballarat.edu.au

Abstract

Detection of child exploitation in Internet chatting is an important issue for the protection of children from prospective online paedophiles. This paper investigates the effectiveness of text classifiers to identify Child Exploitation (CE) in chatting. As the chatting occurs among two or more users by typing texts, the text of chat-messages can be used as the data to be analysed by text classifiers. Therefore the problem of identification of CE chats can be framed as the problem of text classification by categorizing the chat-logs into predefined CE types. Along with three traditional text categorizing techniques a new approach has been made to accomplish the task. Psychometric and categorical information by LIWC (Linguistic Inquiry and Word Count) has been used and improvement of performance in some classifier has been found. For the experiments of current research the chat logs are collected from various websites open to public. Classification-via-Regression, J-48-Decision-Tree and Naïve-Bayes classifiers are used. Comparison of the performance of the classifiers is shown in the result.

1 Introduction

The online chatting has become a popular tool for personal as well as group communication. It is cheap, convenient, virtual and private in nature. In an online chatting one can hide ones personal information behind the monitor. This makes it a source of fun in one hand but possess threat on the other hand. The privacy and virtual nature of this medium increased the chance of some heinous acts which one may not commit in the real world. O'Connell (2003) informs that the Internet affords greater opportunity for adults with a sexual interest in children to gain access to children. Communication between victim and predator can take place whilst both are in their respective real world homes but sharing a private virtual space. Young (2005) profiles this kind of virtual opportunist as 'situational sex offenders' along with the 'classical sex offenders'. Both these types of offenders are taking the advantages of the Internet to solicit and exploit children. This kind of solicitation or grooming by the use of an online medium for the purpose of exploiting a child may refer to the problem of 'online child exploitation'.

Currently there is no such system that can automatically identify the elements of child exploitation in chat text. It is very difficult for parents or the members of Law and Enforcement Agency (LEA) to watch over the children all the time to protect them from online paedophiles loitering over the vast space of the Internet. An online automatic CE detection system can be useful. Regarding offline, most of the chatting programs have the options of storing the chat-texts in log-archives. According to Krone (2005) and pjfi.org chat-logs can be used as evidence to proof a paedophile attempting to exploit children. Therefore after an online child exploitation occur; a LEA member can retrieve those offline archived chat logs from the hard drive of the accused to produce as evidence in the court of law. However manual identification of the evidence is a tedious and time consuming work, as one may have to read hundreds or thousands of pages of chat-texts from different chat-logs. Thus it is prone to error due to exhaustion. Moreover manual process may lead to a biased decision. Therefore a research to develop such an automatic system will have a significant contribution in both the online and offline situation for the protection of children from exploitation.

This paper introduces the results of the preliminary experiments of an ongoing research aims to develop a novel methodology that can automatically identify the child exploitation in chats through the analysis of the contents of the chat-logs using data-mining and machine learning techniques. For the experiments the chat logs are collected from various websites open to public. Three classifiers, named Classification-via-Regression, J-48-Decision-Tree and Naïve-Bayes classifiers are used from the WEKA data mining tool. Along with term based feature set a new kind of features named psychometric and word categorical information has been used. The LIWC (Linguistic Inquiry and Word Count) is used to get this information of the chat-terms. The result and performances of the classifiers are compared in the experiment and result section.

The contributions of this paper are many fold. First, in the information and language technology field currently it is difficult to find a good number of researches focusing on the issue of detection of internet child exploitation. This paper emphasises on this issue and examines the technical aspects of chat messages that can be used to find a solution. Second, the experiments in the current paper use archived chat logs instead of single chat posts. Single chat posts contain only a few terms, on the other hand a log of chats contain a good number of terms which provides more facility for a machine learning system to learn the prediction function of a class. Third, this research uses psychometric information for the first time to detect CE chats. No other research has been found that is doing the same. This psychometric information seems enriching the feature set that improves the performance of some classifiers.

The remainder of this paper is organized as follows. Section 2 reviews the related works. Section 3 describes the methodology followed in this research. The experimental results are analysed in section 4 while section 5 presents conclusion and future work.

2 Related work

In the recent years, IT research community has paid good attention to the chat-text analysis and chat-mining. Different applications evolved in this area though are not perfect in all situations. Literature review suggests that most of the existing techniques have good performance only for its specific context. The context of the current research is particularly unique; it focuses on detecting CE chats. In addition, it uses archived chat logs instead of single chat posts used by others. Therefore the existing works does not match with the current research problem. As any technique that corresponds to the same context is not found, related works on chat massages is discussed in this section.

Following subsections provide a short description of the analysis of unique properties of chat messages, psychological aspect of child exploitation and a brief overview of the related existing work on chat text.

2.1 Analysis of Chat messages

The texts in the chat possess some unique characteristics that distinguish them from other literary formal texts (Rosa and Ellen 2009; Kucukyilmaz et al. 2008). Chat-users suppose to type spontaneously and instantly. Therefore the individual post is very brief, as short as a word. Frequently it is confined within a couple of words. Generally the chats do not follow any grammar rules. Therefore the chat-text is grammatically informal and unstructured. This made them more difficult to process by traditional sentence parsers. Chat-users are though typing texts, but are actually trying to talk with each other through it. So the text is typed very quickly, frequently unedited, errors and abbreviations are more common. For example, “ASL” is a common chat abbreviation for Age, Sex and Location asked at the introduction stage. “P911” is a chatting code used by teenagers. It stands for “Parent Alert!”(teenchatdecoder.com). These kinds of previously unseen abbreviations and erroneous texts are difficult to be handled by any currently available text processing techniques.

Chatting is a purely textual communication medium. So for transferring emotional feelings like happiness, sadness and angers, emoticons (emotion + icon = emoticon; a chat jargon) are widely used. These are different sequences of punctuation marks that display graphical representation of different emotional feelings. For example, ":-)" means "happy" and ":-(" represents "sad". Another way of emotion transfer is by emphasizing a word with repeating some specific characters. For example, "soryyyyyyyyyyyy". This kind of deliberate misspelling is also frequent in chat text. The emoticons and intentional misspelled words may contain valuable contextual information in a chat text. For example, in the grooming phase the perpetrator may reconstruct relation by an emphasized "soryyyyyyyyy" when the child felt threatening by any obtrusive language. Another example may be the emoticon for "hug (>:d<)" and "kiss (:-*)" for a soft introduction of sexual stage. However, preserving such information makes traditional text processing methods (e.g., stemming and part of speech tagging) unsuitable for processing chat text (Kucukyilmaz et al. 2008).

The concern of the current research is child exploiting (CE) chats. This kind of chats is done between an adult perpetrator and a child victim. The perpetrator types the text targeting to entice the child. Therefore this type of chats can be considered as a special type of chats inheriting the above mentioned general properties as well as having special CE properties. Sexually explicit language, though not found in the beginning, may be introduced gradually in the text as the conversation progresses. Matching those words may show some preliminary detection of exploitation, yet this raises some confusions. If the perpetrator is an experienced groomer he may cleverly avoid sexually exploiting words. Instead he may use other words for gentle and soft pressure on the child's sexual boundaries. On the other hand a chat log between two adults, who have sexual relationship, may also have sexually explicit languages in their intimate private chat sessions. Matching only sexually explicit words does not solve the problem. A robust analysis of the entire chat text is required that may detect the particular child exploiting (CE) profile in the chat log.

2.2 Psychological information and LIWC

Rachel O'Connell (2003) identified psychological progressive stages in online child exploitation. The exploitation does not occur instantly. It starts by making an innocent friendship and gradually advances towards the stage of exploitation through a psychological progression. A perpetrator tends to follow the model of luring communication theory, proposed by Olson et.al. (2007). According to this model a perpetrator builds up a deceptive psychological trust. This indicates that the terms used in the process of exploitation are categorically and psychologically different than the terms used in general chatting. Therefore analysing the psychological and categorical information of the chat terms would be helpful to learn the psychological pattern of the exploitation. To find out the categorical and psychological properties of terms LIWC (Linguistic Inquiry and Word Count) has been used in this current research. According to Pennebaker et al.(2007) LIWC is a text analysis application designed to provide an efficient and effective method for studying the various emotional, cognitive, and structural components present in the terms of a text. The LIWC system counts the number of structural and psychologically significant words in the text. For example it gives the count of the words that contain the following information: social, family, friend, sexual, positive emotion, negative emotion, sad, anger, anxiety etc.

2.3 Existing Work on Chat-text

Wu et al. (2005) applied transformation based learning for tagging the chat post. For this purpose the authors used templates incorporating regular expressions. A tag is the type of the post, for example, a statement, a yes no question or a wh-question. The authors provided a list of 15 predefined tags. However the list of the tags does not include any tag that indicate child exploition.

Adams and Martell (2008) worked on topic detection and topic thread extraction in chat-logs. Each chat post or line is treated as a document. The typical TF-IDF-based vector space model approach along with cosine similarity measure is used. The authors used chat text from the Internet public chat rooms. The focus of the paper was conversation topic thread detection and extraction in a chat session. Attention for the topic of 'child exploitation' is not provided.

Text Classification (TC) techniques are used for decades for content based document processing tasks. Besides these applications in formal literary texts, in recent years TC is also been applied into the informal texts like chats. Using text classifiers

Bengel et al. (2004) developed a system that creates a concept-based profile that represents a summary of the topics discussed in a chat room or by an individual participant. Vector space classifiers are used to categorize the concepts of chat message. Though about luring activities in the online chat room is mentioned in this paper as an example of detection of chat topics but neither specific experimental result nor any guideline provided. Moreover no particular result was provided regarding the accuracy of the system.

Kucukyilmaz et al. (2008) worked on authorship attribution and authorship characterization in chat messages. Different supervised classification techniques are used for extracting information from the chat messages. Both term-based and writing-style-based approach is used to identify the author of the chat message. The chat messages were in Turkish instead of English.

Rosa and Ellen (2009) applied traditional text classifiers to categorize military micro-texts. The micro-text is like a post (a line) in a chat among defence personnel. The posts are categorized into different predefined categories of military interest. Child sex exploitation was neither any context of the categorization nor the authors used any civilian chat ; they used only military chat.

Bifet and Frank (2010) used classifiers to analyse sentiment in twitter messages. The twitter messages are small texts somewhat similar to chat messages. Instead of prequential accuracy the authors used Kappa statistics to measure the predictive accuracy of classifiers.

Focuses of the above mentioned researches are different than the focus of current research. Therefore it is very unlikely that any of these researches would be directly applied to solve the problem of the detection of CE chats. This research used supervised machine learning methods i.e. classifiers to learn the distinctive features of CE chats and then applied for the detection.

3 Methodology

3.1 Formulation of the Problem of Chat Classification

To understand the problem of detection of child exploitation (CE) one need to look on chats from the CE point of view. In this view, chats can be defined into the following three categories:

1. CE chat: These are Child Exploiting (CE) chats. An adult perpetrator is involved in this type of chat with a minor. The purpose of the perpetrator is to solicit the child and achieve sexual gratification. The exploitation may occur either online or a physical meeting is arranged for further abuse.

2. Near to CE chat: These chats are Sex Fantasy (SF) chats between two adults. Sexual gratification is one of the common motives in both the CE and the SF types of chats. Similar sexually explicit terms are present in both of them. They may also have similar progression style. As no minor child is involved, these chats are not CE. However both types have some similarity, so we consider SF chats as near to CE type.

3. Far from CE chat: Other general (GN) type of chats which does not have any similarity with CE type chats and easy to distinguish from them. For example chat between a client and an expert to solve a technical problem.

After defining the categories of chats from the CE point of view, the problem of predicting the type of a chat is similar to the text classification problem with careful consideration of the unique characteristics of chat. Using supervised machine learning methods a solution to this problem is to generate a prediction function (*f*) that maps each chat-log (***D***) onto one of the class type (***C***), given as $f: D \rightarrow C$. In a binary classification the class type (***C***) includes CE type chats and NonCE type chats. In the case of multi-class classification the suspected CE chats are one of the predefined multiple types. The prediction function (*f*) can be learned by training classification algorithms over a representative set of chat-logs whose types are known. In the experiments of current research two different types of feature sets are used in the supervised machine learning process. First type is the traditional term-based feature set where the vocabulary of the message collection in the chat log constitutes the feature set. Each term corresponds to a feature. For the second type of feature set a new approach has been made in this research. The word categorical and psychometric information from LIWC is used as the feature set. Each chat-log file is considered as a document. By this formulation, the problem of chat classification is reduced to a standard text classification problem.

3.2 Procedural Framework

Figure 1 on the next page illustrates the procedural framework followed in the experiments of the current research.

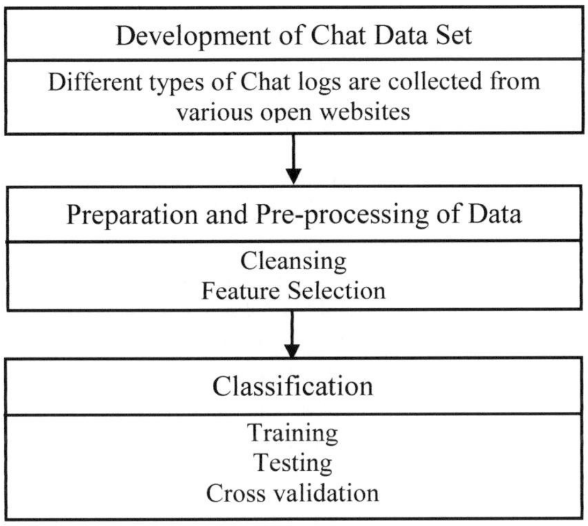

Figure 1: Procedural framework

Development of Chat Dataset: Due to the sexually explicit nature of the child exploiting chats, and the surrounding legal and ethical issues, it is difficult to find such data in an authenticated academically available research databases. However, a number of such chat-logs are found in the Perverted Justice Foundation Incorporated (PJFI) website available at http://pjfi.org. The PJFI worked with Law and Enforcement Agency (LEA) in a covert operation to catch the online paedophiles. The chat logs contain chat-text between users posing as a child and perpetrators trying to procure children over the Internet for exploitation. The perpetrators involved in those chats are prosecuted according to US law. The chat-texts were used as evidence and finally the perpetrators were convicted. In absence of chats between a real child and a paedophile these chat-texts may work as a benchmark because they contain evidence of child exploitation and the evidence are established in the court of Law. The chat-logs are open for all in the World Wide Web. Permission through email from the administrator of the website has been received to use those chat-logs for the purpose of current research.

For the classification experiments different other kinds of chats are also needed which include SF and GN type chats. Websites like http://www.fugly.com and http://chatdump.com have a collection of anonymous chats. The chats were provided by volunteers making fun with people online. Some of the chats can be considered as SF type. This type of chats contains elements of sex fantasy. However as the main purpose was only to make fun, in some part of the chat one of the user behave weirdly to make fun out of the already built sex fantasy. For example, after a considerable time of chatting and starting up a romantic relationship, a user appears to be a different person (though he is not) and turns the conversation into a different direction other than sex fantasy. An example excerpt of a turning point is as bellow:

```
    Man: Hello?
    Man: Who is this?
    Man: What the hell do you think you're
doing?
    Man: cybering with my 10 year old son?
    Woman: OMG
    Woman: I didn't know he was 10. I'm
sooo sorry
    Woman: The Profile said he was 26!
    Man: This is MY account. NOT his.
```

Figure 2: Example of an edited portion of a SF chat

We collected the chats and edited this kind of direction changing parts to keep it as SF. To test the chat-logs are really SF or not, we mixed them with some CE type chat logs and some GN type chat logs to make a collection of 120 chat logs. The collection was sent to an expert researcher of psychology to verify the SF types. The researcher of psychology identified 73 of the collections as SF types. To increase the number of chats in SF type, some of the SF chats are randomly crossed with each other. Finally 85 SF type chats are used in the experiments.

The main objective of this experiment is to observe if the text classifiers are capable of distinguishing CE type chats among different other types of chats. In the experiments the data set consists of text of a number of chat-log files. The logs include child exploiting offensive CE chat-logs, general non offensive (GN) chat-logs and sex fantasy type SF chat-logs. Each log is a member of the data set and is considered as an individual instance. The instances are divided into three classes; CE, SF and

GN. The total number of instances was 392. Among the 392 instances 200 were CE chat-logs, 85 were SF type and 107 were GN type chat-logs.

Preparation and Pre-processing of Data: The chat log files were pre-processed by cleansing and feature selection. In cleansing stage the usernames are removed. Then the text is converted into string vectors.

Two types of features are selected for two sets of experiments. In one set of experiment the term-based features are used. The other set of experiment used psychometric and categorical information from LIWC. The categorical counts are used as features in the classifiers.

Classification: Three classifiers from WEKA datamining tool are used in the classification experiments. These are Naïve Bayes (NB), J48-Decision Tree (J48-DT) and Classification via Regression (CvR) classifiers. Training, testing and 10 fold cross validations are done. An analysis of the results is given in the following section.

4 Experimental Result and Analysis

4.1 Result

A number of experiments have been done with different combination of the available chat data set. The combination of the data set is indicated in the corresponding table. The odd numbered tables show the confusion matrices of experiments with term-based feature set whereas the even numbered tables are for experiments with feature set based on psychometric and categorical information from LIWC. For example, the Table 1 corresponds to the results in the Experiment Set-1. It uses 392 instances of chat logs, where 200 are of CE type, 107 are of GN type and 85 are of SF type. Table 1.1, 1.2 and 1.3 show the confusion matrices of the results from Naïve Bayes (NB), J48-Decision Tree (J48-DT) and Classification via Regression (CvR) classifiers respectively. In the confusion matrices the rows specify true class and columns show the prediction of the classifier. Experiment Set-1 does not use psychometric information. It uses term-based feature set. On the other hand, Experiment Set-2 uses psychometric and categorical information as the feature set with the same chat dataset as of Experiment Set-1. The results of Experiment Set-2 are in Table 2.

4.2 Analysis of Result

From the results it can be seen that psychometric and categorical information improves the performance of some classifiers. Table 1.1 and 2.1 shows the result of for Naïve Bayes (NB) classifier. In these tables the correctly detected chats for the CE types are increased by 11.3% (from 168 to 187). Moreover incorrect classification of the CE type chats are decreased by 59.4% (from 28+4=32 to 7+6=13). Similar improvements are found in all results with NB classifiers using psychometric information. Results of Classification via regression (CvR) classifier is also improved in some cases (Table 2.3, 4.3 and 8.3) when psychometric information feature set is used. In those cases it is detecting more CE chats, however at the same time it is predicting more chats as CE which are actually not CE. For the J48-Decision Tree (J48-DT), psychometric information does not make any improvement.

Comparing the results of multiclass classification with binary classification (Table 2 and 4) it is found that the effectiveness of the classifiers are almost same in regards of correctly predicting CE chats. For example, NB classifier correctly detects CE chats 187 times in multiclass classification and 188 times in binary classification. Regarding the false negative case the figure is also very near, 13 and 12. The other two classifiers are also having nearby results.

The results of Experiment Set-5 and 6 (Table-5 and 6) and Experiment Set-7 and 8 (Table 7 and 8) shows that classifiers find more difficulties to distinguish CE vs. SF chats than to distinguish CE vs. GN chats. For example, the result of NB using LIWC (Table 6.1 and 8.1) shows that, incorrectly classified instances in CE vs. SF is 9.8% ((10+18)/285) which is much higher than 4.5% ((10+4)/307) in CE vs GN. Results of other classifiers also support this idea.

The aim of current research is to detect CE chats. Therefore the classifier should not spare any suspected chat-log. It has to be very strict in catching CE chats even if it makes some incorrect prediction about some other non CE chats. That means the classifier can be flexible in Type-I error

Tables : Confusion Matrices for different Classification Experiments

Experiments with Term-based feature set

Table 1: Confusion Matrices for Experiment Set-1: CE vs. GN vs. SF

Total Number of Instances 392; CE = 200, GN = 107, SF = 85

Naïve Bayes			J48-Decision Tree			Clas. Via Regression			
CE	GN	SF	CE	GN	SF	CE	GN	SF	
168	28	4	181	7	12	188	2	10	CE
4	103	0	10	77	20	5	91	11	GN
2	57	26	13	22	50	5	17	63	SF
Table 1.1			Table 1.2			Table 1.3			

Table 3: Confusion Matrices for Experiment Set-3: CE vs.NonCE

Total Number of Instances 392; CE = 200, NonCE = 192

Naïve Bayes		J48-Decision Tree		Clas. via Regression		
CE	NonCE	CE	Non CE	CE	Non CE	
154	46	183	17	178	22	CE
10	182	19	173	17	175	NonCE
Table 3.1		Table 3.2		Table 3.3		

Table 5: Confusion Matrices for Experiment Set-5: CE vs. SF

Total Number of Instances 285; CE = 200, SF = 85

Naïve Bayes		J48-Decision Tree		Clas. via Regression		
CE	SF	CE	SF	CE	SF	
179	21	179	21	188	12	CE
3	82	18	67	12	73	SF
Table 5.1		Table 5.2		Table 5.3		

Table 7: Confusion Matrices for Experiment Set-7: CE vs. GN

Total Number of Instances 307; CE = 200, GN = 107

Naïve Bayes		J48-Decision Tree		Clas. via Regression		
CE	GN	CE	GN	CE	GN	
171	29	186	14	185	15	CE
4	103	11	96	15	92	GN
Table 7.1		Table 7.2		Table 7.3		

Experiments with feature set of psychometric and word categorical information from LIWC

Table 2: Confusion Matrices for Experiment Set-2: CE vs. GN vs. SF

Total Number of Instances 392; CE = 200, GN = 107, SF = 85

Naïve Bayes			J48-Decision Tree			Clas. via Regression			
CE	GN	SF	CE	GN	SF	CE	GN	SF	
187	7	6	174	12	14	189	10	1	CE
3	95	9	17	77	13	11	86	10	GN
14	13	58	11	12	62	20	13	52	SF
Table 2.1			Table 2.2			Table 2.3			

Table 4: Confusion Matrices for Experiment Set-4: CE vs. NonCE

Total Number of Instances 392; CE = 200, NonCE = 192

Naïve Bayes		J48-Decision Tree		Clas. via Regression		
CE	NonCE	CE	Non CE	CE	Non CE	
188	12	170	30	182	18	CE
22	170	20	172	37	155	NonCE
Table 4.1		Table 4.2		Table 4.3		

Table 6: Confusion Matrices for Experiment Set-6: CE vs. SF

Total Number of Instances 285; CE = 200, SF = 85

Naïve Bayes		J48-Decision Tree		Clas. via Regression		
CE	SF	CE	SF	CE	SF	
190	10	176	24	185	15	CE
18	67	17	68	24	61	SF
Table 6.1		Table 6.2		Table 6.3		

Table 8: Confusion Matrices for Experiment Set-8: CE vs. GN

Total Number of Instances 307; CE = 200, GN = 107

Naïve Bayes		J48-Decision Tree		Clas. via Regression		
CE	GN	CE	GN	CE	GN	
190	10	192	8	188	12	CE
4	103	14	93	21	86	GN
Table 8.1		Table 8.2		Table 8.3		

(False positive) but should minimize Type-II error (False negative) as much as possible. Considering this, we try to find out the classifier which is performing best among the three classifiers. In multiclass classifications, in the case of term-based feature set (Table1) CvR is detecting the highest number of CE chats. It is predicting 188 chats as CE whereas prediction by NB is 168 and prediction by J48-DT is 181. Both NB and CvR are competing with each other when psychometric information are used (Table 2). Both of them are detecting almost the same number of CE chats (187 and 189). The number of false negative is also about the same (13 and 11).

In binary classification in Table 3 and 4, NB with psychometric information (Table 4.1), is performing the best. It is detecting 188 CE chats out of 200 and CvR (Table 4.3) is catching 182, whereas J48-DT (Table3.2) catching 183.

5 Conclusion and Future Work

Psychometric and categorical information can be used by classifiers as a feature set to predict the suspected child exploitation in chats. The new feature set significantly improves the performance of Naïve Bayes (NB) classifiers to predict CE type chats. In some cases it also improves the performance of Classification via Regression (CvR) classifier. It seems that the chat dataset is enriched by the psychometric and categorical information. However it is interesting that while it is improving the performance of two classifier (NB and CvR), the same enriched dataset does not improve the performance of another classifier (J48-DT). It can be a future scope to look at the profile of CE chats and investigate the interesting behavior of different classifiers.

Though the text classifiers are classifying logs of chat text into predefined suspected CE type they do not provide any particular aspect of the chat that can be used as evidence of the chat being an artifact of child exploitation. Therefore, further analysis is required to detect specific evidences inside the suspected CE chat. This is another future scope of this research.

References

Adams, P. H., and Martell, C. H. 2008. Topic Detection and Extraction in Chat. *In Proceedings of the IEEE International Conference on Semantic Computing 2008 (ICSC '08),* Santa Clara, CA, USA, p. 581-588.

Bengel, J., Gauch, S., Mittur, E., and Vijayaraghavan, R. 2004. ChatTrack: Chat Room Topic Detection using Classification. *In Intelligence and Security Informatics. In the series of Lecture Notes in Computer Science,* Vol. 3073, p. 266-277, Springer.

Bifet, A., and Frank, E. 2010. Sentiment Knowledge Discovery in Twitter Streaming Data. *In Proceedings of the 13th International Conference on Discovery Science (DS10),* Canberra, Australia, p. 1-15.

chatdump.com. Available at http://chatdump.com/ (accessed January 2011).

fugly.com. Available at http://www.fugly.com/victims/ (accessed January 2011).

Hall, M., Frank, E., Holmes, G., Pfahringer, B., Reutemann, P., and Witten, I. H. 2009. The WEKA Data Mining Software: An Update. *In ACM SIGKDD Explorations Newsletter,* Vol. 11 (1), p. 10-18, ACM.

Krone, Tony. 2005. Queensland Police Stings in Online Chat Rooms. *In Trends & Issues in Crime and Criminal Justice Series,* Australian Institute Of Criminology. Retrieved from http://www.aic.gov.au/documents/B/C/E/%7BBCEE2309-71E3-4EFA-A533-A39661BD1D29%7Dtandi301.pdf (accessed No vember 2010).

Kucukyilmaz, T., Cambazoglu, B. B., Aykanat, C., and Can, F. 2008. Chat Mining: Predicting User and Message Attributes in Computer-Mediated Communication. *In Information Processing & Management,* Vol. 44 (4), p. 1448-1466, Elsevier.

O'Connell, Rachel. 2003. A Typology of Child Cybersexploitation and Online Grooming Practices. Cyberspace Research Unit, University of Central Lancashire. Retrieved from http://image.guardian.co.uk/sys-files/Society/documents/2003/07/17/ Groomingreport.pdf (accessed August 2010).

Olson, L. N., Daggs, J. L., Ellevold, B. L., and Rogers, T. K. K. 2007. Entrapping the Innocent: Toward a Theory of Child Sexual Predators' Luring Communication. *In Communication Theory,* Vol. 17 (3), p. 231-251, Wiley-Blackwell.

Pennebaker, J. W., Chung, C. K., Ireland, M., Gonzales, A., and Booth, R. J. 2007. *The Development and Psychometric Properties of LIWC2007.* Published in LIWC.Net. Available at http://www.liwc.net/LIWC2007LanguageManual.pdf (accessed November, 2010).

pjfi.org. Perverted Justice Foundation Incorporated. Available at http://pjfi.org/ (accessed January 2011).

Rosa, K. D., and Ellen, J. 2009. Text Classification Methodologies Applied to Micro-Text in Military Chat. *In Proceedings of the Eighth IEEE International Conference on Machine Learning and Applications (ICMLA '09),* Miami Beach, Florida, USA, p. 710-714.

teenchatdecoder.com. Available at http://www.teenchatdecoder.com/ (accessed November 2010).

Wu, T., M. Khan, F., A. Fisher, T., A. Shuler, L., and M. Pottenger, W. 2005. Posting Act Tagging using Transformation-Based Learning. *In Foundations of Data Mining and Knowledge Discovery. In the series of Studies in Computational Intelligence,* Vol. 6, p. 319-331, Springer.

Young, K. 2005. Profiling Online Sex Offenders, Cyber Predators, and Pedophiles. *In Journal of Behavioral Profiling,* Vol. 5 (1), p. 1-18, ABP.

ENGAGE: Automated Gestures for Animated Characters

Marcin Nowina-Krowicki, Andrew Zschorn, Michael Pilling and Steven Wark
Command, Control, Communications and Intelligence Division,
Defence Science and Technology Organisation,
Edinburgh, South Australia
{firstname.lastname}@dsto.defence.gov.au

Abstract

There is a rapidly growing body of work in the use of Embodied Conversational Agents (ECA) to convey complex contextual relationships through verbal and non-verbal communication, in domains ranging from military C2 to e-learning. In these applications the subject matter expert is often naïve to the technical requirements of ECAs. ENGAGE (the Extensible Natural Gesture Animation Generation Engine) is designed to automatically generate appropriate and 'realistic' animation for ECAs based on the content provided to them. It employs syntactic analysis of the surface text and uses predefined behaviour models to generate appropriate behaviours for the ECA. We discuss the design of this system, its current applications and plans for its future development.

1 Introduction

The Defence Science and Technology Organisation has an active research program into the use of multimedia narrative to provide situational awareness for military C2 (Wark and Lambert 2007). In common usage, face-to-face communication is the predominant, and often most effective, way for people to give and obtain complex contextual information. Embodied Conversational Agents (ECA) provide verbal and non-verbal communication modes similar to face-to-face communication. Gestures such as nods and facial expressions are very important in listener engagement with the speaker and their message.

Programming these gestures into an ECA animation is time consuming and requires specialised expertise. The subject matter experts developing content for ECAs are often naïve with respect to these technical requirements. A system to automatically generate appropriate non-verbal behaviour allows the content creator to concentrate on the information and not on how the ECA will animate it.

Figure 1 – Virtual Advisers present photo-realistic models of people

The BEAT system from MIT (Cassell et al. 2001) demonstrated this capability. DSTO has developed ENGAGE (Extensible Natural Gesture Animation Generation Engine) based on the principles demonstrated in BEAT, and extended them to incorporate modifiers such as confidence, importance, and urgency.

1.1 Virtual Adviser

DSTO has been using ECAs dubbed Virtual Advisers (VAs) as a mechanism for augmenting situational awareness in military C2 (Taplin et al. 2001; Wark and Lambert 2007; Wark et al. 2009). Virtual Advisers are computer generated talking heads using photo realistic textures with real-time animation and commercial-off-the-shelf text-to-speech (TTS) generation. Virtual Advisers can also include rolling text captions and multimedia monitors à la television news services. Virtual Advisers have been designed for modularity and can be delivered to users in a number of ways.

VAs are used to present situation briefs incorporating other media such as tables and diagrams, images, video, 3D models and so on. They are being used to provide prepared presentations, or dynamically generated content incorporating a dialog management system with a conversational interface (Estival et al. 2003). When connected to a decision support system they can also alert people to new or changing situations (Lambert 1999; Wark et al. 2003).

Virtual Advisers augment human support staff by providing a capability that can be deployed and accessed simultaneously from multiple geographically distributed locations. They can present the same information numerous times, on demand, without imposing an additional staffing burden. Virtual Advisers can augment existing decision support systems by explaining the information produced, not just showing it.

1.2 Talking Head Markup Language

Content is provided to VAs in the form of Talking Head Markup Language (THML). THML is tagged text that describes what the VA is to say and do. It includes commands to direct the VA: to say text; to adopt degrees of fundamental facial expressions (happy, sad, angry, afraid, surprised, contempt, disgust) (Ekman and Friesen 1977); to make eyebrow and head movements; and to direct gaze. It also includes commands to control the underlying TTS system, the appearance of the VA and its environment, and synchronise with other applications.

THML is designed to be simple for humans to read and write and to support on-the-fly authorship.

2 VA Architecture

Virtual Advisers are implemented using a modular, distributed architecture. All components communicate using a client-server model. The system consists of three core components; a rendering engine, system controller (THConsole), and Text-to-Speech service. Automated behaviour generation can be provided by ENGAGE. The content to be delivered by the VA can either be authored by a user or by a dynamic content generation system that feeds the THConsole the THML to be presented on demand.

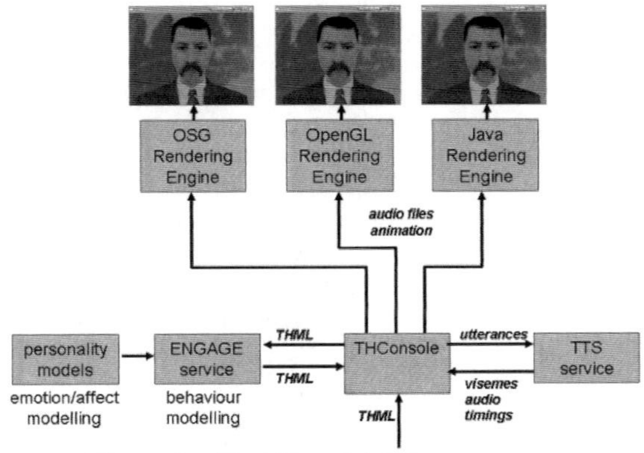

Figure 2 – The Virtual Adviser system

2.1 Rendering Engines

Rendering Engines are used to display the VA. They receive low-bandwidth rendering and timing instructions from the THConsole and output correctly synchronised 3D graphics, video, audio and application control.

C++ and Java toolkits have been developed to provide reusable, cross platform, core components to help facilitate the rapid development of new Rendering Engines for novel delivery mediums. These toolkits provide common underlying functionality such as: character animation; pluggable audio; instruction parsing; event based timeline; and networking support. The character animation system is built on top of the Cal3D library (Cal3D Team 2011). It provides skeletal and morph target character animation and a flexible model loading system. The Java Abstract Gaming Tools library (JAGaToo 2011) provides a port of the Cal3D library from C++ and is used in our Java toolkit.

Rendering Engines are developed by extending the core toolkits and providing environment specific support, such as accelerated 3D graphics and any other capabilities appropriate for the target medium.

Currently, VAs can be delivered in one of three ways: as a Desktop Application that can be controlled via an integrated Desktop service or invoked independently; embedded as an overlay or 3D model inside other applications such as DSTO's Virtual Battlespace II geospatial display (Wark et al. 2009); and as an Applet displayed on web pages and integrated into mainstream wiki systems, such as Atlassian's Confluence and the ubiquitous, open source, MediaWiki.

Desktop and embedded delivery is facilitated by a Rendering Engine built with the high performance OpenSceneGraph 3D library

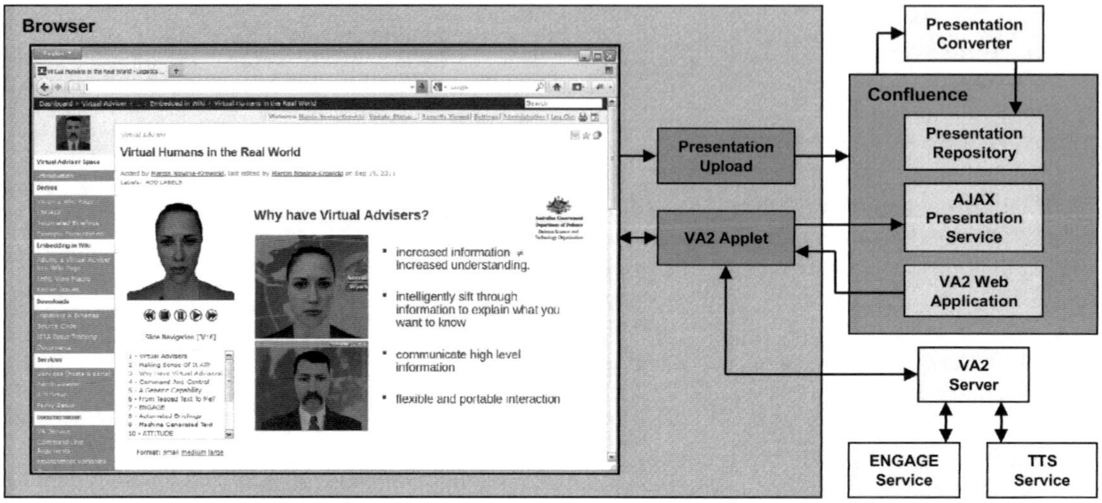

Figure 3 – Virtual Advisers can be embedded on web pages to give dynamic presentations

(OSG Community 2011). Highlights of this solution include: integrated video and multimedia display; tickertape captioning; stereoscopic viewing; and Render-to-Texture support. The Render-to-Texture support allows the Virtual Adviser to be rendered as an overlay or texture in other applications.

Web delivery is via a Java-based Applet using the Java OpenGL (JOGL) bindings. The Applet works on all major platforms and web browsers that support the Java plug-in. Wiki integration for Confluence and MediaWiki allow users to easily embed and control a Virtual Adviser on a wiki page. A system for automatically presenting a converted PowerPoint presentation on a web or wiki page has also been developed and demonstrated.

2.2 THConsole

The Talking Head Console (THConsole) acts as the system controller. It interprets THML provided to it by a content generation system or user and coordinates the use of ENGAGE and the TTS service to produce the necessary animation instructions, synthesised audio and timing information, which is used by Rendering Engines to display VAs. Where ENGAGE is unavailable, the THConsole will process the script as is using only the marked up behaviour in the input THML.

The THConsole provides a flexible deployment capability. It is written as a small Java library that can be run in a number of different ways including: as an interactive CLI application that can have data either typed directly into it or piped from other processes or files; a TCP server that can be controlled via remote clients; or embedded as a component inside other applications and controlled using its public API.

How THML is handled depends on its context. Where commands are not inside an utterance, the THConsole can process them directly and send them to the Rendering Engine for immediate display. In contrast, utterances and the commands nested inside utterances are handled using a three pass process that requires the use of external services. The first pass optimises the input by chunking the say statement at sentence boundaries. The advantage of chunked input is that it greatly improves the throughput of both ENGAGE and the TTS and provides concurrency by allowing the Rendering Engine to begin executing one sentence while subsequent sentences are still being processed by the THConsole. The second pass expands the script using ENGAGE, if the service is available, to automatically generate behaviour. The final pass calls on the TTS service to generate synthesized audio and timing information for all events in utterance. The TTS results are then processed by the THConsole with timing information applied to all behaviour and actions in the utterance. Finally, rendering instructions are sent to the Rendering Engine for display.

2.3 Text-to-Speech Service

The Text-to-Speech service provides synthesized audio and timing information to enable synchronization of audio with animation and other events. In addition the service provides the ability to change the current voice, alter the speech rate and control volume. A TCP client-server architecture is used for service control. Generated files are served using a HTTP server to allowing a pull model where clients retrieve the audio and timing information as they need them.

Currently the TTS service uses Nuance's RealSpeak Solo 4 TTS engine (Nuance 2011). Other systems that have been used include Rhetorical System's rVoice TTS and the open source Festival Speech Synthesis System.

3 ENGAGE System

ENGAGE uses syntactic analysis of THML and behaviour models to generate appropriate synchronised behaviour. Parameters that control the application of these behaviour models can be embedded in the input speech instructions.

There are five main components in the ENGAGE system. Four of these components are arranged in a strict processing chain. The input stream is first sent to the Pre-processor, which prepares the input's speech instructions for syntax analysis. The Language component then adds syntax analysis to the speech parts of the input. The Behaviour component generates appropriate behaviours. Finally the post-processor produces mark-up for the virtual character system consisting of speech and synchronised behaviour. The fifth component of the system, the Behaviour Models, are used in both the language and behaviour components of the system to produce behaviour that is tailored to the current personality profile in use and model parameters provided in the input.

Following Cassell et al. (2001) and Lee and Marsella (2006), we use an XML document to store the processing results of each stage in the pipeline process. Each processing node is implemented as XSL transforms that can modify and augment the XML document. This pipeline approach ensures the separation of gesture generation from gesture realisation. This means that different behaviour models can be easily plugged in to achieve different behaviours in the VAs. The following sections examine each component in detail.

3.1 Pre-processor

The pre-processor prepares the THML input for processing. It takes as input a character stream of speech and other instructions and produces as output an XML tree ready for language syntax analysis. In the current implementation the Pre-processor uses a three stage process where input is first tokenised, then filtered and finally serialised to XML.

3.1.1 Tokeniser

The tokeniser is responsible for separating and extracting the various components of the input ready for filtering and serialisation to XML. It takes the character stream as input and produces an ordered list of "word" and "tag" tokens as output. The "word" tokens represent the dialogue that is to be spoken by the animated character, while the "tag" tokens represent all other instructions in the input stream, usually THML tags or

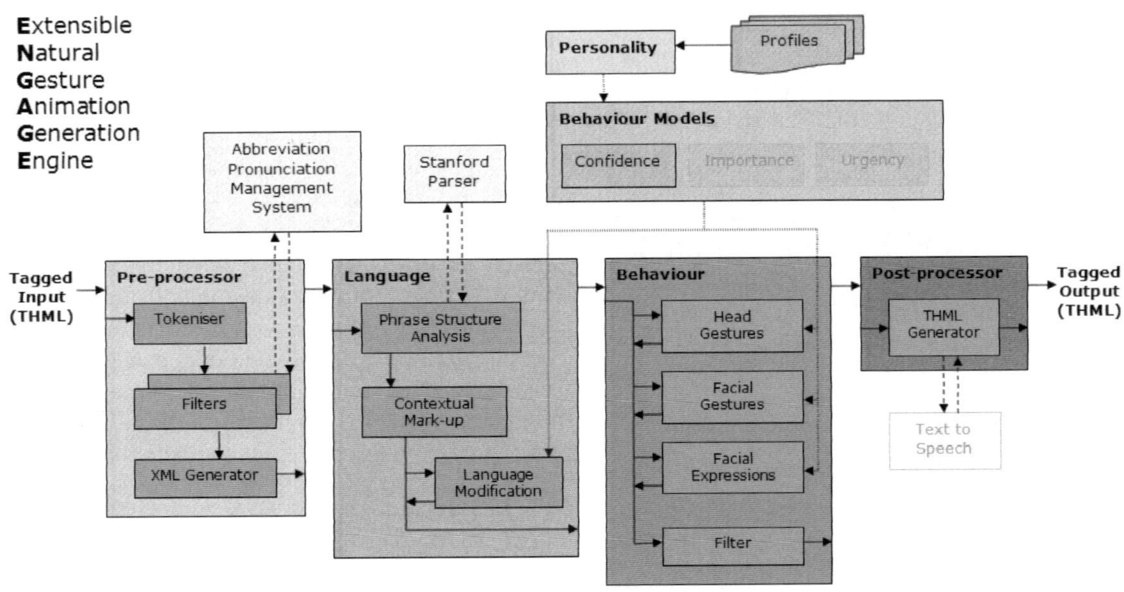

Figure 4 – The ENGAGE system.

ENGAGE processing instructions. The ordered list of tokens is then returned ready for filtering.

3.1.2 Filters

The filtering stage of the Pre-processor examines the input tokens and performs any additional processing on them ready for XML serialisation and processing. The filter set currently consists of an acronym and abbreviation filter and an ENGAGE tag filter for marking specific "tag" tokens as processing instructions for ENGAGE.

The acronym and abbreviation filter uses a context sensitive Abbreviation Pronunciation Management System (APMS) to expand any acronyms and abbreviated words. This allows correct phrase structure analysis in the language module and provides the Text-to-speech system with contextually correct phonetic spellings to facilitate correct pronunciation of the abbreviations.

3.1.3 Abbreviation Pronunciation Management System (APMS)

The correct pronunciation of some words, particularly abbreviations, can be difficult to determine from their written form with pronunciations often varying depending on the context in which they appear. Text-to-speech engines can do a very good job of inferring correct pronunciation of written forms, including initialisms and acronyms, but are not perfect, and don't have mechanisms to distinguish how different contexts can change pronunciations.

Large numbers of abbreviations are used in the defence domain, both in written forms such as reports, and in the spoken language. To always replace written forms with pronunciation forms directly in THML scripts would be tedious, and it would make the script harder for a reader to understand. Also, in the future we expect that THML scripts will be automatically generated from text that was never intended to be spoken by a VA. We want to make the process of authoring THML scripts simple and natural, to aid both authors and future automation. Thus, we want to move the problem of deciding how to pronounce abbreviations to the Virtual Adviser and away from the author.

We have developed the Abbreviation Pronunciation Management System (APMS) to replace written abbreviations with pronunciation spellings in a context-sensitive way in ENGAGE.

Consider the written abbreviation "RAAF", which can be pronounced as "R double-A F", "raff", or "Royal Australian Air Force". The pronunciation chosen can have a significant effect on comprehensibility of the speaker's message. For instance, it could be confusing to use the pronunciation "raff" when talking of a coalition military operation. On the other hand, using the longest form, "Royal Australian Air Force", could distract from the content of the message and socially separate a speaker from their audience if the context were an Australian military operation, where "raff" is the most common pronunciation.

In the APMS we use string tokens to identify contexts of abbreviation pronunciation. We allow contexts to inherit pronunciation replacements from a single parent, forming a branching hierarchy of contexts, or ontology. Child contexts may include different pronunciation replacements than its ancestors. This enables the addition of more specific contexts to handle more specific pronunciation replacements, while inheriting more general pronunciation replacements. For example, the context "general.australia.gov" may include the pronunciation replacement RAAF ⇨ "R double-A F", while the context "general.australia.gov.mil" may include the pronunciation replacement RAAF ⇨ "raff".

Database: The APMS database provides the persistent store of translations between text inputs and more vocally accurate textual or phonetic spellings. Each of these translations is given for a particular context. If no translation can be found in the given most specific context, progressively more general contexts are searched until a translation is found. For instance, the search may progress from "ship" to "Navy" to "military" contexts.

The system is implemented using PostgreSQL because of the richness of its stored procedure language and integral support for recursion for hierarchical data. This allows recursive searches to occur entirely within the database, avoiding returning intermediate results and executing recursion from the client which could be prohibitively expensive. Pronunciation lookup is done entirely server side. In normal operation, the system is further optimised by pre-calculating the best answer between voice, accent and context for any defined word and storing these answers in a cache. This noticeably enhances speed at the acceptable expense of higher disk usage.

As pronunciations necessarily drift and evolve, a script that had been rendered correctly may degrade as the underlying database evolves. The database records the times that pronunciations are added and when a pronunciation is revised the old version is retained. To access prior pronunciations, the caller need only specify a reference time and the database provides the pronunciation as it was then. For efficiency the system allows each caller their own cache which pre-calculates pronunciations for the caller's preferred reference time. It also provides a table in which to record such reference times, along with a short name and comment. This schema has the advantage of archiving all "snapshots" of the database online at very low storage cost, with only the snapshots in current use being instantiated out into the cache.

Usage: To use the APMS, THML scripts are marked-up to identify the context ontology it is to use. Scripts are then marked-up throughout to identify the current context for abbreviation replacement. As scripts are processed by ENGAGE, each space-separated word within '<say>' tags is analysed, given the current abbreviation context, to see if it should be replaced by a pronunciation spelling.

3.1.4 XML Generator

The XML Generator concludes the pre-processing stage by producing an XML tree from the tokenised and filtered input ready for Language and behaviour processing. The filtered "word" and "tag" tokens are marked up as XML elements in the pre-processed XML tree. Any "tag" tokens that have been marked as processing instructions for ENGAGE (such as behaviour models and parameters) are expanded and added as either attributes or elements depending on the scope of their behaviour.

3.2 Behaviour Models

Behaviour models are used to control and tailor the language and behaviour produced by ENGAGE. In this first version of the system, behaviour can be controlled using a Confidence Engine to manage the level of uncertainty displayed by the character. It is envisaged that future incarnations of the system will feature Behaviour Models for controlling the level of importance and urgency in the information being presented.

3.2.1 Personality and Personality Profiles

The Personality component provides the system with a means of varying language and behaviour parameters for the Behaviour model based on different Personality profiles.

Each Personality profile represents a set of language and behaviour parameters that can be used to alter the output of the various Behaviour Models. A Personality profile can inherit parameters from other personality models. This allows common traits to be pushed up to a common ancestor personality profile. In the first cut of the system this is achieved through cascading, where parameters are overridden by each successive include and can be further specialised in the child personality profile. In future a more powerful inheritance model will be implemented that allows groups or individual parameters to be included from specified parent profiles.

A User Interface has been developed to help generate personality profiles and tweak output behaviour. This interface provides the user with a set of parameter sliders that allow the various Behaviour Model parameters to be modified either individually or as grouped sets. The results of these changes can be tested and tweaked in real time allowing the user to see the results immediately.

3.2.2 Confidence

The Confidence Engine allows the system to control the level of uncertainty displayed by the character based on a confidence measure and parametric personality profile that can be assigned to the input utterance. Personality profiles are used to provide the Confidence module its parameters and allow the behaviour to be tailored for different personality types.

Currently the Confidence Behaviour Model is used in the Language Modification and Behaviour Generation phases of ENGAGE processing; how the Confidence Engine is applied will be discussed further in their Langauge Modification and Behaviour sections.

3.3 Language

Our primary intent is to generate natural-looking gestures to accompany the VAs speech. Therefore, and following Cassel (2000), Cassel et al. (2001) and Lee and Marsella (2006), syntactic analysis of the text to be spoken is important for behaviour generation and realisation. The text to be spoken is found within '<say>' tags in the THML scripts that drive the VA.

3.3.1 Phrase Structure Analysis

Each sentence found in THML '<say>' tags are sent to an automatic English parser for a full phrase structure analysis. At present we use the Stanford Parser to perform this function (The Stanford NLP Group 2011). The Stanford Parser uses a statistical method to perform phrase structure analysis. The tag set used is from the Penn treebank.

Syntactic and POS attributes are assigned as attributes to the individual word elements in the XML tree. These attributes can then be used in later processing stages such as contextual markup, language modification and behaviour generation.

3.3.2 Contextual Mark-up

Hiyakumoto et al. (1997) and Cassell et al (2001) use automatic theme/rheme analysis to aid behaviour generation, as it is stated that gestures are more frequently found in the rheme, or comment, part of the sentences (Cassell 2000). In order to perform automatic theme/rheme analysis these systems keep a record of all terms mentioned, and, broadly, determine that re-occurrences of those terms or closely related terms constitute the theme, or topic, of the clause.

At this stage the ENGAGE system does not maintain a history of words previously spoken by virtual characters. It is possible to add such a capability, and once done this will provide the system with a context-based approach for identifying the theme and rheme. Currently, for most suitable parses we simply identify all those words up to and including the head verb of the top-level phrase as forming the theme, and the remainder forms the rheme. Where the parser output is unrecognized, all the words up to and including the first verb in the sentence is labelled as the theme, and the remainder labelled as the rheme.

3.3.3 Language Modification

Language Modification is performed by applying the Behaviour Models to the language tree.

The Confidence Engine can insert disfluencies (as interjections), hesitations and information to alter speech rate into the XML language tree. The Confidence Engine uses the current confidence value assigned to the utterance and personality profile to determine if disfluencies and hesitations are added at various points in the utterance. Currently, disfluencies and hesitations may be added at any of the following locations:

- the start of the utterance
- before prepositions
- before verbs
- before nouns
- before the introduction of new domain words

Speech rate changes are added at both an utterance level and around inserted disfluencies.

3.4 Behaviour

The Behaviour phase of ENGAGE processing seeks to assign contextually appropriate non-verbal behaviours and expressions to the XML processing tree based on the markup added during the Language phase. As ENGAGE development is driven by the needs of the VA system, the current library of behaviours covers head gestures, facial gestures and facial expressions. Other gestures such as arm and body motion are envisioned for future development iterations of the system.

To generate behaviour ENGAGE runs the XML processing tree through a number of Behaviour Generators and the Behaviour Models. The XML tree is then pruned and passed to the Post-processing stage.

3.4.1 Head Gestures

For characters to emphasise objects and actions that they are introducing to the context, head-nods are generated for nouns and verbs in rheme sections of their speech.

The Confidence Behaviour Model can also add head drops and tilts to control the level of uncertainty displayed by the character, depending on the current confidence value and personality model in use.

Head drops are generated at changes in confidence value and influence the amplitude of head nods generated.

Head tilts may be added where there are hesitations with no disfluency in the speech.

3.4.2 Facial Gestures

For characters to emphasise objects and actions that they are introducing to the context, eyebrow movements are generated for nouns and verbs in rheme sections of their speech.

Also, in accordance with the way English and some other language speakers behave, eyebrow movements are added to sentences that end with a question-mark or exclamation-mark.

The Confidence Engine may specify changes in the rate and duration of blinks, as well as insert frowns and cheek puffs into the output tree. Cheek puffs and changes to blink rate and duration may be added to hesitations where there is no disfluency, while frowns may be added during disfluencies.

3.4.3 Facial Expressions

The Confidence Engine may specify changes in the level of anxiety, a combination of both anger and fear, displayed by the character. Anxiety may be changed whenever the confidence value changes.

3.4.4 Filter

The final stage of behaviour processing generates a filtered animation tree representing just the information that should be marked up in the post processing stage. The filtered tree produced consists of just words, tags and behaviours, with all extra language and intermediate processing tags pruned from the XML tree.

3.5 Post-processor

The Post-processor takes the filtered XML tree generated by the Language and Behaviour modules and generates a character stream of processing instructions for the VA. In our current implementation a THML Generator is used to produce the final ENGAGE output.

3.5.1 THML Generator

The THML Generator takes the resulting filtered XML tree generated by the Behaviour module as input and generates a character stream of synchronised THML instructions as output.

The output THML stream includes the speech, behaviour and other tags to be processed by the THConsole to generate appropriate instructions for the Virtual Adviser Rendering Engine.

In the current architecture ENGAGE does not use the TTS system to provide timing information for any of the marked-up behaviour that it produces. Instead, all behaviour is marked relative to the start or end of word, context or utterance boundaries. Appropriate timing information will be applied in the TTS processing pass coordinated by the THConsole. This approach allows ENGAGE to be an optional component of the system and also allows the THConsole to do further processing before generating timing information from the TTS without adding an unnecessary second TTS pass.

3.6 Responsiveness

As one of the usage modes of VAs is as a conversational interface, the speed at which it can produce results is important. ENGAGE is generally quicker to respond than TTS engines, so its impact on the overall system response time is negligible.

4 Future Work

Future work will look at semantic analysis of surface text to provide more targeted, contextually appropriate gestural animation.

The behaviour models currently used with ENGAGE have been developed as a proof of concept only. Further work is needed to refine these behaviour models to effectively communicate aspects such as uncertainty, importance, and urgency.

We also plan on investigating other Text-to-Speech solutions to provide finer control of prosody and expressive delivery of content to complement the animation.

5 Conclusions

The ENGAGE system developed at DSTO can be used to augment the real-time animation of ECAs by automatically inserting gesture animation based on the syntax of the sentences given to the system. This simplifies the task of generating 'realistic' behaviours based on surface text alone, supporting content authoring without requiring expertise in human behavioural modelling. In most cases observed so far, this has improved user engagement with the ECAs.

Acknowledgments

We wish to thank all the people that have contributed to the development of the Virtual Adviser system over the years. We would also like to thank the Research Leader C2 and Chief C3ID for their support and leadership.

References

Cal3D Team. (2011). Cal3D - 3D Character Animation Library, https://gna.org/projects/cal3d/

Cassell, J. (2000). "Nudge nudge wink wink: elements of face-to-face conversation for embodied conversational agents", *Embodied conversational agents*. MIT Press, pp. 1-27.

Cassell, J., Vilhjálmsson, H. H., and Bickmore, T. (2001). "BEAT: the Behavior Expression Animation Toolkit"*SIGGRAPH '01: Proceedings of the 28th annual conference on Computer graphics and interactive techniques*. City: ACM: New York, NY, USA, pp. 477-486.

Ekman, P., and Friesen, W. V. (1977). *Facial Action Coding System*, Pao Alto, U.S.A.: Consulting Psychologists Press Inc.

Estival, D., Broughton, M., Zschorn, A., and Pronger, E. (2003). "Spoken Dialogue for Virtual Advisers in a Semi-Immersive Command and

Control Environment"*4th SIGdial Workshop on Discourse and Dialogue*. City: Sapporo, Japan.

Hiyakumoto, L., Prevost, S., and Cassell, J. (1997). "Semantic and Discourse Information for Text-to-Speech Intonation"*ACL Workshop on Concept-to-Speech Technology*. City, pp. 47-56.

JAGaToo. (2011). JAGaToo - Java Abstract Gaming Tools, http://sourceforge.net/projects/jagatoo/

Lambert, D. A. "Advisers with attitude for situation awareness." *Presented at Proceedings of the 1999 Workshop on Defense Applications of Signal Processing*, LaSalle, Illinois.

Lee, J., and Marsella, S. (2006). "Nonverbal Behavior Generator for Embodied Conversational Agents", J. Gratch, M. Young, R. Aylett, D. Ballin, and P. Olivier, (eds.), *Intelligent Virtual Agents*. City: Springer Berlin Heidelberg, pp. 243-255.

Nuance. (2011). Nuance, http://australia.nuance.com/

OSG Community. (2011). OpenSceneGraph, http://www.openscenegraph.org

Taplin, P., Fox, G., Coleman, M., Wark, S., and Lambert, D. "Situation Awareness Using a Virtual Adviser." *Presented at Talking Head Workshop, OZCHI 2001*, Fremantle, Australia.

The Stanford NLP Group. (2011). The Stanford Parser: A statistical parser, http://nlp.stanford.edu/software/lex-parser.shtml

Wark, S., and Lambert, D. A. (2007). "Presenting The Story Behind The Data: Enhancing Situational Awareness Using Multimedia Narrative"*3rd IEEE Workshop on Situation Management (SIMA 2007)*. City: Orlando, FL.

Wark, S., Lambert, D. A., Nowina-Krowicki, M., Zschorn, A., and Pang, D. (2009). "Situational Awareness: Beyond Dots on Maps to Virtually Anywhere"*SimTecT 2009*. City: Adelaide, Australia.

Wark, S., Zschorn, A., Perugini, D., Tate, A., Beautement, P., Bradshaw, J. M., and Suri, N. (2003). "Dynamic Agent Systems in the CoAX Binni 2002 Experiment"*6th International Conference on Information Fusion (Fusion 2003)*. City: Cairns, Australia.